DIARY OF SAMUEL PEPYS -

BY

Samuel Pepys

DIARY OF SAMUEL PEPYS — COMPLETE 1666 N.S.

Published by Wallachia Publishers

New York City, NY

First published circa 1703

ABOUT WALLACHIA PUBLISHERS

Wallachia Publishers mission is to publish the world's finest European history texts. More information on our recent publications and catalog can be found on our website.

1666

Henry B. Wheatley F.S.A. Edited With Additions By
CAMBRIDGE DEIGHTON BELL & CO. GEORGE BELL & SONS YORK ST. COVENT
GARDENLONDON

January 1st (New-Yeare's Day). Called up by five o'clock, by my order, by Mr. Tooker, who wrote, while I dictated to him, my business of the Pursers; and so, without eating or drinking, till three in the afternoon, and then, to my great content, finished it. So to dinner, Gibson and he and I, and then to copying it over, Mr. Gibson reading and I writing, and went a good way in it till interrupted by Sir W. Warren's coming, of whom I always learne something or other, his discourse being very good and his brains also. He being gone we to our business again, and wrote more of it fair, and then late to bed.

2nd. Up by candlelight again, and wrote the greatest part of my business fair, and then to the office, and so home to dinner, and after dinner up and made an end of my fair writing it, and that being done, set two entering while to my Lord Bruncker's, and there find Sir J. Minnes and all his company, and Mr. Boreman and Mrs. Turner, but, above all, my dear Mrs. Knipp, with whom I sang, and in perfect pleasure I was to hear her sing, and especially her little Scotch song of "Barbary Allen;"

and to make our mirthe the completer, Sir J. Minnes was in the highest pitch of mirthe, and his mimicall tricks, that ever I saw, and most excellent pleasant company he is, and the best mimique that ever I saw, and certainly would have made an excellent actor, and now would be an excellent teacher of actors. Thence, it being post night, against my will took leave, but before I come to my office, longing for more of her company, I returned and met them coming home in coaches, so I got into the coach where Mrs. Knipp was and got her upon my knee (the coach being full) and played with her breasts and sung, and at last set her at her house and so good night. So home to my lodgings and there endeavoured to have finished the examining my papers of Pursers' business to have sent away to-night, but I was so sleepy with my late early risings and late goings to bed that I could not do it, but was forced to go to bed and leave it to send away to-morrow by an Expresse.

3rd. Up, and all the morning till three in the afternoon examining and fitting up my Pursers' paper and sent it away by an Expresse. Then comes my wife, and I set her to get supper ready against I go to the Duke of Albemarle and back again; and at the Duke's with great joy I received the good news of the decrease of the plague this week to 70, and but 253 in all; which is the least Bill hath been known these twenty years in the City. Through the want of people in London is it, that must make it so low below the ordinary number for Bills. So home, and find all my good company I had bespoke, as Coleman and his wife, and Laneare, Knipp and her surly husband; and good musique we had, and, among other things, Mrs. Coleman sang my words I set of "Beauty retire," and I think it is a good song, and they praise it mightily. Then to dancing and supper, and mighty merry till Mr. Rolt come in, whose pain of the tooth-ake made him no company, and spoilt ours; so he away, and then my wife's teeth fell of akeing, and she to bed. So forced to break up all with a good song, and so to bed.

4th. Up, and to the office, where my Lord Bruncker and I, against Sir W. Batten and Sir J. Minnes and the whole table, for Sir W. Warren in the business of his mast contract, and overcome them and got them to do what I had a mind to, for indeed my Lord being unconcerned in what I aimed at. So home to dinner, where Mr. Sheldon come by invitation from Woolwich, and as merry as I could be with all my thoughts about me and my wife still in pain of her tooth. He anon took leave and took Mrs. Barbary his niece home with him, and seems very thankful to me for the L10 I did give him for my wife's rent of his house, and I am sure I am beholding to him, for it was a great convenience to me, and then my wife home to London by water and I to the office till 8 at night, and so to my Lord Bruncker's, thinking to have been merry, having appointed a meeting for Sir J. Minnes and his company and Mrs. Knipp again, but whatever hindered I know not, but no company come, which vexed me because it disappointed me of the glut of mirthe I hoped for. However, good discourse with my Lord and merry, with Mrs. Williams's descants upon Sir J. Minnes's and Mrs. Turner's not coming. So home and to bed.

5th. I with my Lord Bruncker and Mrs. Williams by coach with four horses to London, to my Lord's house in Covent-Guarden. But, Lord! what staring to see a nobleman's coach come to town. And porters every where bow to us; and such begging of beggars! And a delightfull thing it is to see the towne full of people again as now it is; and shops begin to open, though in many places seven or eight together, and more, all shut; but yet the towne is full, compared with what it used to be. I mean the City end; for Covent-Guarden and Westminster are yet very empty of people, no Court nor gentry being there. Set Mrs. Williams down at my Lord's house and he and I to Sir G. Carteret, at his chamber at White Hall, he being come to town last night to stay one day. So my Lord and he and I much talke about the Act, what credit we find upon it, but no private talke between him and I. So I to the 'Change, and there met Mr. Povy, newly come to town, and he and I to Sir George Smith's and there dined nobly. He tells me how my Lord Bellases complains for want of money and of him and me therein, but I value it not, for I know I do all that can be done. We had no time to talk of particulars, but leave it to another day, and I away to Cornhill to expect my Lord Bruncker's coming back again, and I staid at my stationer's house, and by and by comes my Lord, and did take me up and so to Greenwich, and after sitting with them a while at their house, home, thinking to get Mrs. Knipp, but could not, she being busy with company, but sent me a pleasant letter, writing herself "Barbary Allen." I went therefore to Mr. Boreman's for pastime, and there staid an houre or two talking with him, and reading a discourse about the River of Thames, the reason of its being choked up in several places with shelfes; which is plain is, by the encroachments made upon the River, and running out of causeways into the River at every wood-wharfe; which was not heretofore when Westminster Hall and White Hall were built, and Redriffe Church, which now are sometimes overflown with water. I had great satisfaction herein. So home and to my papers for lacke of company, but by and by comes little Mrs. Tooker and sat and supped with me, and I kept her very late talking and making her comb my head, and did what I will with her. So late to bed.

6th. Up betimes and by water to the Cockepitt, there met Sir G. Carteret and, after discourse with the Duke, all together, and there saw a letter wherein Sir W. Coventry did take notice to the Duke with a commendation of my paper about Pursers, I to walke in the Parke with the Vice-Chamberlain, and received his advice about my deportment about the advancing the credit of the

Act; giving me caution to see that we do not misguide the King by making them believe greater matters from it than will be found. But I see that this arises from his great trouble to see the Act succeede, and to hear my name so much used and my letters shown at Court about goods served us in upon the credit of it. But I do make him believe that I do it with all respect to him and on his behalfe too, as indeed I do, as well as my owne, that it may not be said that he or I do not assist therein. He tells me that my Lord Sandwich do proceed on his journey with the greatest kindnesse that can be imagined from the King and Chancellor, which was joyfull newes to me. Thence with Lord Bruncker to Greenwich by water to a great dinner and much company; Mr. Cottle and his lady and others and I went, hoping to get Mrs. Knipp to us, having wrote a letter to her in the morning, calling myself "Dapper Dicky," in answer to hers of "Barbary Allen," but could not, and am told by the boy that carried my letter, that he found her crying; but I fear she lives a sad life with that ill-natured fellow her husband: so we had a great, but I a melancholy dinner, having not her there, as I hoped. After dinner to cards, and then comes notice that my wife is come unexpectedly to me to towne. So I to her. It is only to see what I do, and why I come not home; and she is in the right that I would have a little more of Mrs. Knipp's company before I go away. My wife to fetch away my things from Woolwich, and I back to cards and after cards to choose King and Queene, and a good cake there was, but no marks found; but I privately found the clove, the mark of the knave, and privately put it into Captain Cocke's piece, which made some mirthe, because of his lately being knowne by his buying of clove and mace of the East India prizes. At night home to my lodging, where I find my wife returned with my things, and there also Captain Ferrers is come upon business of my Lord's to this town about getting some goods of his put on board in order to his going to Spain, and Ferrers presumes upon my finding a bed for him, which I did not like to have done without my invitation because I had done [it] several times before, during the plague, that he could not provide himself safely elsewhere. But it being Twelfth Night, they had got the fiddler and mighty merry they were; and I above come not to them, but when I had done my business among my papers went to bed, leaving them dancing, and choosing King and Queene.

7th (Lord's day). Up, and being trimmed I was invited by Captain Cocke, so I left my wife, having a mind to some discourse with him, and dined with him. He tells me of new difficulties about his goods which troubles me and I fear they will be great. He tells me too what I hear everywhere how the towne talks of my Lord Craven being to come into Sir G. Carteret's place; but sure it cannot be true. But I do fear those two families, his and my Lord Sandwich's, are quite broken. And I must now stand upon my own legs. Thence to my lodging, and considering how I am hindered by company there to do any thing among my papers, I did resolve to go away to-day rather than stay to no purpose till to-morrow and so got all my things packed up and spent half an hour with W. Howe about his papers of accounts for contingencies and my Lord's accounts, so took leave of my landlady and daughters, having paid dear for what time I have spent there, but yet having been quiett and my health, I am very well contented therewith. So with my wife and Mercer took boat and away home; but in the evening, before I went, comes Mrs. Knipp, just to speake with me privately, to excuse her not coming to me yesterday, complaining how like a devil her husband treats her, but will be with us in towne a weeke hence, and so I kissed her and parted. Being come home, my wife and I to look over our house and consider of laying out a little money to hang our bedchamber better than it is, and so resolved to go and buy something to-morrow, and so after supper, with great joy in my heart for my coming once again hither, to bed.

8th. Up, and my wife and I by coach to Bennett's, in Paternoster Row, few shops there being yet open, and there bought velvett for a coate, and camelott for a cloake for myself; and thence to a place to look over some fine counterfeit damasks to hang my wife's closett, and pitched upon one, and so by coach home again, I calling at the 'Change, and so home to dinner and all the afternoon look after my papers at home and my office against to-morrow, and so after supper and considering the uselessness of laying out so much money upon my wife's closett, but only the chamber, to bed.

9th. Up, and then to the office, where we met first since the plague, which God preserve us in! At noon home to dinner, where uncle Thomas with me, and in comes Pierce lately come from Oxford, and Ferrers. After dinner Pierce and I up to my chamber, where he tells me how a great difference hath been between the Duke and Duchesse, he suspecting her to be naught with Mr. Sidney.

But some way or other the matter is made up; but he was banished the Court, and the Duke for many days did not speak to the Duchesse at all. He tells me that my Lord Sandwich is lost there at Court, though the King is particularly his friend. But people do speak every where slightly of him; which is a sad story to me, but I hope it may be better again. And that Sir G. Carteret is neglected, and hath great enemies at work against him. That matters must needs go bad, while all the town, and every boy in the streete, openly cries, "The King cannot go away till my Lady Castlemaine be ready to come along with him;" she being lately put to bed And that he visits her and Mrs. Stewart every morning before he eats his breakfast. All this put together makes me very sad, but yet I hope I shall do pretty well among them for all this, by my not meddling with either of their matters. He and Ferrers gone I paid uncle Thomas his last quarter's money, and then comes Mr. Gawden and he and I talked above stairs together a good while about his business, and to my great joy got him to declare that of the L500 he did give me the other day, none of it was for my Treasurershipp for Tangier (I first telling him how matters stand between Povy and I, that he was to have half of whatever was coming to me by that office), and that he will gratify me at 2 per cent. for that when he next receives any money. So there is L80 due to me more than I thought of. He gone I with a glad heart to the office to write, my letters and so home to supper and bed, my wife mighty full of her worke she hath to do in furnishing her bedchamber.

10th. Up, and by coach to Sir G. Downing, where Mr. Gawden met me by agreement to talke upon the Act. I do find Sir G. Downing to be a mighty talker, more than is true, which I now know to be so, and suspected it before, but for all that I have good grounds to think it will succeed for goods and in time for money too, but not presently. Having done with him, I to my Lord Bruncker's house in Covent-Garden, and, among other things, it was to acquaint him with my paper of Pursers, and read it to him, and had his good liking of it. Shewed him Mr.

Coventry's sense of it, which he sent me last post much to my satisfaction. Thence to the 'Change, and there hear to our grief how the plague is encreased this week from seventy to eighty-nine. We have also great fear of our Hambrough fleete, of their meeting the Dutch; as also have certain newes, that by storms Sir Jer. Smith's fleet is scattered, and three of them come without masts back to Plymouth, which is another very exceeding great disappointment, and if the victualling ships are miscarried will tend to the losse of the garrison of Tangier. Thence home, in my way had the opportunity I longed for, of seeing and saluting Mrs. Stokes, my little goldsmith's wife in Paternoster Row, and there bespoke some thing, a silver chafing-dish for warming plates, and so home to dinner, found my wife busy about making her hangings for her chamber with the upholster. So I to the office and anon to the Duke of Albemarle, by coach at night, taking, for saving time, Sir W. Warren with me, talking of our businesses all the way going and coming, and there got his reference of my pursers' paper to the Board to consider of it before he reads it, for he will never understand it I am sure. Here I saw Sir W. Coventry's kind letter to him concerning my paper, and among others of his letters, which I saw all, and that is a strange thing, that whatever is writ to this Duke of Albemarle, all the world may see; for this very night he did give me Mr. Coventry's letter to read, soon as it come to his hand, before he had read it himself, and bid me take out of it what concerned the Navy, and many things there was in it, which I should not have thought fit for him to have let any body so suddenly see; but, among other things, find him profess himself to the Duke a friend into the inquiring further into the business of Prizes, and advises that it may be publique, for the righting the King, and satisfying the people and getting the blame to be rightly laid where it should be, which strikes very hard upon my Lord Sandwich, and troubles me to read it. Besides, which vexes me more, I heard the damned Duchesse again say to twenty gentlemen publiquely in the room, that she would have Montagu sent once more to sea, before he goes his Embassy, that we may see whether he will make amends for his cowardice, and repeated the answer she did give the other day in my hearing to Sir G. Downing, wishing her Lord had been a coward, for then perhaps he might have been made an Embassador, and not been sent now to sea. But one good thing she said, she cried mightily out against the having of gentlemen Captains with feathers and ribbands, and wished the King would send her husband to sea with the old plain sea Captains, that he served with formerly, that would make their ships swim with blood, though they could not make legs

as Captains nowadays can. It grieved me to see how slightly the Duke do every thing in the world, and how the King and every body suffers whatever he will to be done in the Navy, though never so much against reason, as in the business of recalling tickets, which will be done notwithstanding all the arguments against it. So back again to my office, and there to business and so to bed.

11th. Up and to the office. By and by to the Custome House to the Farmers, there with a letter of Sir G. Carteret's for L3000, which they ordered to be paid me. So away back again to the office, and at noon to dinner all of us by invitation to Sir W. Pen's, and much other company. Among others, Lieutenant of the Tower, and Broome, his poet, and Dr. Whistler, and his (Sir W.

Pen's) son-in-law Lowder, servant—[lover]—to Mrs. Margaret Pen, and Sir Edward Spragg, a merry man, that sang a pleasant song pleasantly. Rose from table before half dined, and with Mr. Mountney of the Custome House to the East India House, and there delivered to him tallys for L3000 and received a note for the money on Sir R. Viner. So ended the matter, and back to my company, where staid a little, and thence away with my Lord Bruncker for discourse sake, and he and I to Gresham College to have seen Mr. Hooke and a new invented chariott of Dr. Wilkins, but met with nobody at home! So to Dr. Wilkins's, where I never was before, and very kindly received and met with Dr. Merritt, and fine discourse among them to my great joy, so sober and so ingenious. He is now upon finishing his discourse of a universal character. So away and I home to my office about my letters, and so home to supper and to bed.

12th. By coach to the Duke of Albemarle, where Sir W. Batten and I only met. Troubled at my heart to see how things are ordered there without consideration or understanding. Thence back by coach and called at Wotton's, my shoemaker, lately come to towne, and bespoke shoes, as also got him to find me a taylor to make me some clothes, my owne being not yet in towne, nor Pym, my Lord Sandwich's taylor. So he helped me to a pretty man, one Mr. Penny, against St. Dunstan's Church. Thence to the 'Change and there met Mr. Moore, newly come to towne, and took him home to dinner with me and after dinner to talke, and he and I do conclude my Lord's case to be very bad and may be worse, if he do not get a pardon for his doings about the prizes and his business at Bergen, and other things done by him at sea, before he goes for Spayne. I do use all the art I can to get him to get my Lord to pay my cozen Pepys, for it is a great burden to my mind my being bound for my Lord in L1000 to him. Having done discourse with him and directed him to go with my advice to my Lord expresse to-morrow to get his pardon perfected before his going, because of what I read the other night in Sir W. Coventry's letter, I to the office, and there had an extraordinary meeting of Sir J. Minnes, Sir W. Batten, and Sir W. Pen, and my Lord Bruncker and I to hear my paper read about pursers, which they did all of them with great good will and great approbation of my method and pains in all, only Sir W. Pen, who must except against every thing and remedy nothing, did except against my proposal for some reasons, which I could not understand, I confess, nor my Lord Bruncker neither, but he did detect indeed a failure or two of mine in my report about the ill condition of the present pursers, which I did magnify in one or two little things, to which, I think, he did with reason except, but at last with all respect did declare the best thing he ever heard of this kind, but when Sir W. Batten did say, "Let us that do know the practical part of the Victualling meet Sir J. Minnes, Sir W. Pen and I and see what we can do to mend all," he was so far from offering or furthering it, that he declined it and said, he must be out of towne. So as I ever knew him never did in his life ever attempt to mend any thing, but suffer all things to go on in the way they are, though never so bad, rather than improve his experience to the King's advantage. So we broke up, however, they promising to meet to offer some thing in it of their opinions, and so we rose, and I and my Lord Bruncker by coach a little way for discourse sake, till our coach broke, and tumbled me over him quite down the side of the coach, falling on the ground about the Stockes, but up again, and thinking it fit to have for my honour some thing reported in writing to the Duke in favour of my pains in this, lest it should be thought to be rejected as frivolous, I did move it to my Lord, and he will see it done to-morrow. So we parted, and I to the office and thence home to my poor wife, who works all day at home like a horse, at the making of her hangings for our chamber and the bed. So to supper and to bed.

13th. At the office all the morning, where my Lord Bruncker moved to have something wrote in my matter as I desired him last night, and it was ordered and will be done next sitting. Home with his Lordship to Mrs. Williams's, in Covent-Garden, to dinner (the first time I ever was there), and there met Captain Cocke; and pretty merry, though not perfectly so, because of the fear that there is of a great encrease again of the plague this week. And again my Lord Bruncker do tell us, that he hath it from Sir John Baber; who is related to my Lord Craven, that my Lord Craven do look after Sir G. Carteret's place, and do reckon himself sure of it. After dinner Cocke and I together by coach to the Exchange, in our way talking of our matters, and do conclude that every thing must breake in pieces, while no better counsels govern matters than there seem to do, and that it will become him and I and all men to get their reckonings even, as soon as they can, and expect all to breake. Besides, if the plague continues among us another yeare, the Lord knows what will become of us. I set him down at the 'Change, and I home to my office, where late writing letters and doing business, and thence home to supper and to bed. My head full of cares, but pleased with my wife's minding her worke so well, and busying herself about her house, and I trust in God if I can but clear myself of my Lord Sandwich's bond, wherein I am bound with him for L1000 to T. Pepys, I shall do pretty well, come what will come.

14th (Lord's day). Long in bed, till raised by my new taylor, Mr. Penny, [who comes and brings me my new velvet coat, very handsome, but plain, and a day hence will bring me my camelott cloak.] He gone I close to my papers and to set all in order and to perform my vow to finish my journall and other things before I kiss any woman more or drink any wine, which I must be forced to do to-morrow if I go to Greenwich as I am invited by Mr. Boreman to hear Mrs. Knipp sing, and I would be glad to go, so as we may be merry. At noon eat the second of the two cygnets Mr. Shepley sent us for a new-year's gift, and presently to my chamber again and so to work hard all day about my Tangier accounts, which I am going again to make up, as also upon writing a letter to my father about Pall, whom it is time now I find to think of disposing of while God Almighty hath given me something to give with her, and in my letter to my father I do offer to give her L450 to make her own L50 given her by my uncle up L500. I do also therein propose Mr. Harman the upholster for a husband for her, to whom I have a great love and did heretofore love his former wife, and a civil man he is and careful in his way, beside, I like his trade and place he lives in, being Cornhill. Thus late at work, and so to supper and to bed. This afternoon, after sermon, comes my dear fair beauty of the Exchange, Mrs. Batelier, brought by her sister, an acquaintance of Mercer's, to see my wife. I saluted her with as much pleasure as I had done any a great while. We sat and talked together an houre, with infinite pleasure to me, and so the fair creature went away, and proves one of the modestest women, and pretty, that ever I saw in my life, and my [wife] judges her so too.

15th. Busy all the morning in my chamber in my old cloth suit, while my usuall one is to my taylor's to mend, which I had at noon again, and an answer to a letter I had sent this morning to Mrs. Pierce to go along with my wife and I down to Greenwich to-night upon an invitation to Mr. Boreman's to be merry to dance and sing with Mrs. Knipp. Being dressed, and having dined, I took coach and to Mrs. Pierce, to her new house in Covent-Garden, a very fine place and fine house. Took her thence home to my house, and so by water to Boreman's by night, where the greatest disappointment that ever I saw in my life, much company, a good supper provided, and all come with expectation of excesse of mirthe, but all blank through the waywardnesse of Mrs. Knipp, who, though she had appointed the night, could not be got to come. Not so much as her husband could get her to come; but, which was a pleasant thing in all my anger, I asking him, while we were in expectation what answer one of our many messengers would bring, what he thought, whether she would come or no, he answered that, for his part, he could not so much as thinke. By and by we all to supper, which the silly master of the feast commended, but, what with my being out of humour, and the badnesse of the meate dressed, I did never eat a worse supper in my life. At last, very late, and supper done, she came undressed, but it brought me no mirthe at all; only, after all being done, without singing, or very little, and no dancing, Pierce and I to bed together, and he and I very merry to find how little and thin clothes they give us to cover us, so that we were fain to lie in our stockings and drawers, and lay all our coates and clothes upon the bed. So to sleep.

16th. Up, and leaving the women in bed together (a pretty black and white) I to London to the office, and there forgot, through business, to bespeake any dinner for my wife and Mrs. Pierce. However, by noon they come, and a dinner we had, and Kate Joyce comes to see us, with whom very merry. After dinner she and I up to my chamber, who told me her business was chiefly for my advice about her husband's leaving off his trade, which though I wish enough, yet I did advise against, for he is a man will not know how to live idle, and employment he is fit for none. Thence anon carried her and Mrs. Pierce home, and so to the Duke of Albemarle, and mighty kind he to me still. So home late at my letters, and so to bed, being mightily troubled at the newes of the plague's being encreased, and was much the saddest news that the plague hath brought me from the beginning of it; because of the lateness of the year, and the fear, we may with reason have, of its continuing with us the next summer. The total being now 375, and the plague 158.

17th. Busy all the morning, settling things against my going out of towne this night. After dinner, late took horse, having sent for Lashmore to go with me, and so he and I rode to Dagenhams in the dark. There find the whole family well. It was my Lord Crew's desire that I should come, and chiefly to discourse with me of Lord Sandwich's matters; and therein to persuade, what I had done already, that my Lord should sue out a pardon for his business of the prizes, as also for Bergen, and all he hath done this year past, before he begins his Embassy to Spayne. For it is to be feared that the Parliament will fly out against him and particular men, the next Session. He is glad also that my Lord is clear of his sea-imployment, though sorry as I am, only in the manner of its bringing about. By and by to supper, my Lady Wright very kind. After supper up to wait on my Lady Crew, who is the same weake silly lady as ever, asking such saintly questions. Down to my Lord again and sat talking an houre or two, and anon to prayers the whole family, and then all to bed, I handsomely used, lying in the chamber Mr. Carteret formerly did, but sat up an houre talking sillily with Mr. Carteret and Mr. Marre, and so to bed.

18th. Up before day and thence rode to London before office time, where I met a note at the doore to invite me to supper to Mrs. Pierces because of Mrs. Knipp, who is in towne and at her house: To the office, where, among other things, vexed with Major Norwood's coming, who takes it ill my not paying a bill of Exchange of his, but I have good reason for it, and so the less troubled, but yet troubled, so as at noon being carried by my Lord Bruncker to Captain Cocke's to dinner, where Mrs. Williams was, and Mrs. Knipp, I was not heartily merry, though a glasse of wine did a little cheer me. After dinner to the office. Anon comes to me thither my Lord Bruncker, Mrs. Williams, and Knipp. I brought down my wife in her night-gowne, she not being indeed very well, to the office to them and there by and by they parted all and my wife and I anon and Mercer, by coach, to Pierces; where mighty merry, and sing and dance with great pleasure; and I danced, who never did in company in my life, and Captain Cocke come for a little while and danced, but went away, but we staid and had a pretty supper, and spent till two in the morning, but got home well by coach, though as dark as pitch, and so to bed.

19th. Up and ready, called on by Mr. Moone, my Lord Bellases' secretary, who and I good friends though I have failed him in some payments. Thence with Sir J. Minnes to the Duke of Albemarle's, and carried all well, and met Norwood but prevented him in desiring a meeting of the Commissioners for Tangier. Thence to look for Sir H. [Cholmly], but he not within, he coming to town last night. It is a remarkable thing how infinitely naked all that end of the towne, Covent-Garden, is at this day of people; while the City is almost as full again of people as ever it was. To the 'Change and so home to dinner and the office, whither anon comes Sir H. Cholmley to me, and he and I to my house, there to settle his accounts with me, and so with great pleasure we agreed and great friends become, I think, and he presented me upon the foot of our accounts for this year's service for him L100, whereof Povy must have half. Thence to the office and wrote a letter to Norwood to satisfy him about my nonpayment of his bill, for that do still stick in my mind. So at night home to supper and to bed.

20th. To the office, where upon Mr. Kinaston's coming to me about some business of Colonell Norwood's, I sent my boy home for some papers, where, he staying longer than I would have him, and being vexed at the business and to be kept from my fellows in the office longer than was fit, I become angry, and boxed my boy when he came, that I do hurt my thumb so much, that I was not able to stir all the day after, and in great pain. At noon to dinner, and then to the office again, late, and so to supper and to bed.

21st (Lord's day). Lay almost till noon merrily and with pleasure talking with my wife in bed. Then up looking about my house, and the roome which my wife is dressing up, having new hung our bedchamber with blue, very handsome. After dinner to my Tangier accounts and there stated them against to-morrow very distinctly for the Lords to see who meet tomorrow, and so to supper and to bed.

22nd. Up, and set my people to work in copying Tangier accounts, and I down the river to

Greenwich to the office to fetch away some papers and thence to Deptford, where by agreement my Lord Bruncker was to come, but staid almost till noon, after I had spent an houre with W. Howe talking of my Lord Sandwich's matters and his folly in minding his pleasures too much now-a-days, and permitting himself to be governed by Cuttance to the displeasing of all the Commanders almost of the fleete, and thence we may conceive indeed the rise of all my Lord's misfortunes of late. At noon my Lord Bruncker did come, but left the keys of the chests we should open, at Sir G. Carteret's lodgings, of my Lord Sandwich's, wherein Howe's supposed jewells are; so we could not, according to my Lord Arlington's order, see them today; but we parted, resolving to meet here at night: my Lord Bruncker being going with Dr. Wilkins, Mr. Hooke, and others, to Colonell Blunts, to consider again of the business of charriots, and to try their new invention. Which I saw here my Lord Bruncker ride in; where the coachman sits astride upon a pole over the horse, but do not touch the horse, which is a pretty odde thing; but it seems it is most easy for the horse, and, as they say, for the man also. Thence I with speede by water home and eat a bit, and took my accounts and to the Duke of Albemarle, where for all I feared of Norwood he was very civill, and Sir Thomas Ingram beyond expectation, I giving them all content and I thereby settled mightily in my mind, for I was weary of the employment, and had had thoughts of giving it over. I did also give a good step in a business of Mr. Hubland's, about getting a ship of his to go to Tangier, which during this strict embargo is a great matter, and I shall have a good reward for it, I hope. Thence by water in the darke down to Deptford, and there find my Lord Bruncker come and gone, having staid long for me. I back presently to the Crowne taverne behind the Exchange by appointment, and there met the first meeting of Gresham College since the plague. Dr. Goddard did fill us with talke, in defence of his and his fellow physicians going out of towne in the plague-time; saying that their particular patients were most gone out of towne, and they left at liberty; and a great deal more, &c. But what, among other fine discourse pleased me most, was Sir G. Ent about Respiration; that it is not to this day known, or concluded on among physicians, nor to be done either, how the action is managed by nature, or for what use it is. Here late till poor Dr. Merriot was drunk, and so all home, and I to bed.

23rd. Up and to the office and then to dinner. After dinner to the office again all the afternoon, and much business with me. Good newes beyond all expectation of the decrease of the plague, being now but 79, and the whole but 272. So home with comfort to bed. A most furious storme all night and morning.

24th. By agreement my Lord Bruncker called me up, and though it was a very foule, windy, and rainy morning, yet down to the waterside we went, but no boat could go, the storme continued so. So my Lord to stay till fairer weather carried me into the Tower to Mr. Hore's and there we staid talking an houre, but at last we found no boats yet could go, so we to the office, where we met upon an occasion extraordinary of examining abuses of our clerkes in taking money for examining of tickets, but nothing done in it. Thence my Lord and I, the weather being a little fairer, by water to Deptford to Sir G. Carteret's house, where W. Howe met us, and there we opened the chests, and saw the poor sorry rubys which have caused all this ado to the undoing of W. Howe; though I am not much sorry for it, because of his pride and ill nature. About 200 of these very small stones, and a cod of muske (which it is strange I was not able to smell) is all we could find; so locked them up again, and my Lord and I, the wind being again very furious, so as we durst not go by water, walked to London quite round the bridge, no boat being able to stirre; and, Lord! what a dirty walk we had, and so strong the wind, that in the fields we many times could not carry our bodies against it, but were driven backwards. We went through Horsydowne, where I never was since a little boy, that I went to enquire after my father, whom we did give over for lost coming from Holland. It was dangerous to walk the streets, the bricks and tiles falling from the houses that the whole streets were covered with them; and whole chimneys, nay, whole houses in two or three places, blowed down. But, above all, the pales on London-bridge on both sides were blown away, so that we were fain to stoop very low for fear of blowing off of the bridge. We could see no boats in the Thames afloat, but what were broke loose, and carried through the bridge, it being ebbing water. And the greatest sight of all was, among other parcels of ships driven here and there in clusters together, one was quite overset and lay with her masts all along in the water, and keel above water. So walked home, my Lord away to his house and I to dinner, Mr. Creed being come to towne and to dine with me, though now it was three o'clock. After dinner he and I to our accounts and very troublesome he is and with tricks which I found plainly and was vexed at; while we were together comes Sir G. Downing with Colonell Norwood, Rumball, and Warrupp to visit me. I made them drink good wine and discoursed above alone a good while with Sir G. Downing, who is very troublesome, and then with Colonell Norwood, who hath a great mind to have me concerned with him in everything; which I like, but am shy of adventuring too much, but will thinke of it. They gone, Creed and I to finish the settling his accounts. Thence to the office, where the Houblans and we discoursed upon a rubb which we have for one of the ships I hoped to have got to go out to Tangier for them. They being gone, I to my office-business late, and then home to supper and even sacke for lacke of a little wine, which I was forced to drink against my oathe, but without pleasure.

25th. Up and to the office, at noon home to dinner. So abroad to the Duke of Albemarle and Kate Joyce's and her husband, with whom I talked a great deale about Pall's business, and told them what portion I would give her, and they do mightily like of it and will proceed further in speaking with Harman, who hath already been spoke to about it, as from them only, and he is mighty glad of it, but doubts it may be an offence to me, if I should know of it, so thinks that it do come only from Joyce, which I like the better. So I do believe the business will go on, and I desire it were over. I to the office then, where I did much business, and set my people to work against furnishing me to go to Hampton Court, where the King and Duke will be on Sunday next. It is now certain that the King of France hath publickly declared war against us, and God knows how little fit we are for it. At night comes Sir W. Warren, and he and I into the garden, and talked over all our businesses. He gives me good advice not to embarke into trade (as I have had it in my thoughts about Colonell Norwood) so as to be seen to mind it, for it will do me hurte, and draw my mind off from my business and embroile my estate too soon. So to the office business, and I find him as cunning a man in all points as ever I met with in my life and mighty merry we were in the discourse of our owne trickes. So about to o'clock at night I home and staid with him there settling my Tangier-Boates business and talking and laughing at the folly of some of our neighbours of this office till two in the morning and so to bed.

26th. Up, and pleased mightily with what my poor wife hath been doing these eight or ten days with her owne hands, like a drudge in fitting the new hangings of our bed-chamber of blue, and putting the old red ones into my dressing-room, and so by coach to White Hall, where I had just now notice that Sir G. Carteret is come to towne. He seems pleased, but I perceive he is heartily troubled at this Act, and the report of his losing his place, and more at my not writing to him to the prejudice of the Act. But I carry all fair to him and he to me. He bemoans the Kingdom as in a sad state, and with too much reason I doubt, having so many enemys about us and no friends abroad, nor money nor love at home. Thence to the Duke of Albemarle, and there a meeting with all the officers of the Navy, where, Lord! to see how the Duke of Albemarle flatters himself with false hopes of money and victuals and all without reason. Then comes the Committee of Tangier to sit, and I there carry all before me very well. Thence with Sir J. Bankes and Mr. Gawden to the 'Change, they both very wise men. After 'Change and agreeing with Houblon about our ships, D. Gawden and I to the Pope's Head and there dined and little Chaplin (who a rich man grown). He gone after dinner, D. Gawden and I to talke of the Victualling business of the Navy in what posture it is, which is very sad also for want of money. Thence home to my chamber by oathe to finish my Journall. Here W. Hewer came to me with L320 from Sir W. Warren, whereof L220 is got clearly by a late business of insurance of the Gottenburg ships, and the other L100 which was due and he had promised me before to give me to my very extraordinary joy, for which I ought and do bless God and so to my office, where late providing a letter to send to Mr. Gawden in a manner we concluded on to-day, and so to bed.

27th. Up very betimes to finish my letter and writ it fair to Mr. Gawden, it being to demand several arrears in the present state of the victualling, partly to the King's and partly to give him occasion to say something relating to the want of money on his own behalf. This done I to the office, where all the morning. At noon after a bit of dinner back to the office and there fitting myself in all points to give an account to the Duke and Mr. Coventry in all things, and in my Tangier business, till three o'clock in the morning, and so to bed,

28th. And up again about six (Lord's day), and being dressed in my velvett coate and plain cravatte took a hackney coach provided ready for me by eight o'clock, and so to my Lord Bruncker's with all my papers, and there took his coach with four horses and away toward Hampton Court, having a great deale of good discourse with him, particularly about his coming to lie at the office, when I went further in inviting him to than I intended, having not yet considered whether it will be convenient for me or no to have him here so near us, and then of getting Mr. Evelyn or Sir Robert Murray into the Navy in the room of Sir Thomas Harvey. At Brainford I 'light, having need to shit, and went into an Inne doore that stood open, found the house of office and used it, but saw no people, only after I was in the house, heard a great dogg barke, and so was afeard how I should get safe back again, and therefore drew my sword and scabbard out of my belt to have ready in my hand, but did not need to use it, but got safe into the coach again, but lost my belt by the shift, not missing it till I come to Hampton Court. At the Wicke found Sir J. Minnes and Sir W. Batten at a lodging provided for us by our messenger, and there a good dinner ready. After dinner took coach and to Court, where we find the King, and Duke, and Lords, all in council; so we walked up and down: there being none of the ladies come, and so much the more business I hope will be done. The Council being up, out comes the King, and I kissed his hand, and he grasped me very kindly by the hand. The Duke also, I kissed his, and he mighty kind, and Sir W. Coventry. I found my Lord Sandwich there, poor man! I see with a melancholy face, and suffers his beard to grow on his upper lip more than usual. I took him a little aside to know when I should wait on him, and where: he told me, and that it would be best to meet at his lodgings, without being seen to walk together. Which I liked very well; and, Lord! to see in what difficulty I stand, that I dare not walk with Sir W. Coventry, for fear my Lord or Sir G. Carteret should see me; nor with either of them, for fear Sir W. Coventry should. After changing a few words with Sir W. Coventry, who assures me of his respect and love to me, and his concernment for my health in all this sickness, I went down into one of the Courts, and there met the King and Duke; and the Duke called me to him. And the King come to me of himself, and told me, "Mr. Pepys," says he, "I do give you thanks for your good service all this year, and I assure you I am very sensible of it." And the Duke of Yorke did tell me with pleasure, that he had read over my discourse about pursers, and would have it ordered in my way, and so fell from one discourse to another. I walked with them quite out of the Court into the fields, and then back to my Lord Sandwich's chamber, where I find him very melancholy and not well satisfied, I perceive, with my carriage to Sir G. Carteret, but I did satisfy him and made him confess to me, that I have a very hard game to play; and told me he was sorry to see it, and the inconveniences which likely may fall upon me with him; but, for all that, I am not much afeard, if I can but keepe out of harm's way in not being found too much concerned in my Lord's or Sir G. Carteret's matters, and that I will not be if I can helpe it. He hath got over his business of the prizes, so far as to have a privy seale passed for all that was in his distribution to the officers, which I am heartily glad of; and, for the rest, he must be answerable for what he is proved to have. But for his pardon for anything else, he thinks it not seasonable to aske it, and not usefull to him; because that will not stop a Parliament's mouth, and for the King, he is sure enough of him. I did aske him whether he was sure of the interest and friendship of any great Ministers of State and he told me, yes. As we were going further, in comes my Lord Mandeville, so we were forced to breake off and I away, and to Sir W. Coventry's chamber, where he not come in but I find Sir W. Pen, and he and I to discourse. I find him very much out of humour, so that I do not think matters go very well with him, and I am glad of it. He and I staying till late, and Sir W. Coventry not coming in (being shut up close all the afternoon with the Duke of Albemarle), we took boat, and by water to Kingston, and so to our lodgings, where a good supper and merry, only I sleepy, and therefore after supper I slunk away from the rest to bed, and lay very well and slept soundly, my mind being in a great delirium between joy for what the King and Duke have said to me and Sir W. Coventry, and trouble for my Lord Sandwich's concernments, and how hard it will be for me to preserve myself from feeling thereof.

29th. Up, and to Court by coach, where to Council before the Duke of Yorke, the Duke of Albemarle with us, and after Sir W. Coventry had gone over his notes that he had provided with the Duke of Albemarle, I went over all mine with good successe, only I fear I did once offend the Duke of Albemarle, but I was much joyed to find the Duke of Yorke so much contending for my discourse about the pursers against Sir W. Pen, who opposes it like a foole; my Lord Sandwich come in in the middle of the business, and, poor man, very melancholy, methought, and said little at all, or to the business, and sat at the lower end, just as he ccme, no roome being made for him, only I did give him my stoole, and another was reached me. After council done, I walked to and again up and down the house, discoursing with this and that man. Among others tooke occasion to thanke the Duke of Yorke for his good opinion in general of my service, and particularly his favour in conferring on me the Victualling business. He told me that he knew nobody so fit as I for it, and next, he was very glad to find that to give me for my encouragement, speaking very kindly of me. So to Sir W. Coventry's to dinner with him, whom I took occasion to thanke for his favour and good thoughts of what little service I did, desiring he would do the last act of friendship in telling me of my faults also. He told me he would be sure he would do that also, if there were any occasion for it. So that as much as it is possible under so great a fall of my Lord Sandwich's, and difference between them, I may conclude that I am thoroughly right with Sir W. Coventry. I dined with him with a great deale of company, and much merry discourse. I was called away before dinner ended to go to my company who dined at our lodgings. Thither I went with Mr. Evelyn (whom I met) in his coach going that way, but finding my company gone, but my Lord Bruncker left his coach for me; so Mr. Evelyn and I into my Lord's coach, and rode together with excellent discourse till we come to Clapham, talking of the vanity and vices of the Court, which makes it a most contemptible thing; and indeed in all his discourse I find him a most worthy person. Particularly he entertained me with discourse of an Infirmary, which he hath projected for the sick and wounded seamen against the next year, which I mightily approve of; and will endeavour to promote it, being a worthy thing, and of use, and will save money. He set me down at Mr. Gawden's, where nobody yet come home, I having left him and his sons and Creed at Court, so I took a book and into the gardens, and there walked and read till darke with great pleasure, and then in and in comes Osborne, and he and I to talk of Mr. Jaggard, who comes from London, and great hopes there is of a decrease this week also of the plague. Anon comes in Creed, and after that Mr. Gawden and his sons, and then they bringing in three ladies, who were in the house, but I do not know them, his daughter and two nieces, daughters of Dr. Whistler's, with whom and Creed mighty sport at supper, the ladies very pretty and mirthfull. I perceive they know Creed's gut and stomach as well as I, and made as much mirthe as I with it at supper. After supper I made the ladies sing, and they have been taught, but, Lord! though I was forced to commend them, yet it was the saddest stuff I ever heard. However, we sat up late, and then I, in the best chamber like a prince, to bed, and Creed with me, and being sleepy talked but little.

30th. Lay long till Mr. Gawden was gone out being to take a little journey. Up, and Creed and I some good discourse, but with some trouble for the state of my Lord's matters. After walking a turne or two in the garden, and bid good morrow to Mr. Gawden's sons, and sent my service to the ladies, I took coach after Mr. Gawden's, and home, finding the towne keeping the day solemnly, it being the day of the King's murther, and they being at church, I presently into the church, thinking to see Mrs. Lethulier or Batelier, but did not, and a dull sermon of our young Lecturer, too bad. This is the first time I have been in this church since I left London for the plague, and it frighted me indeed to go through the church more than I thought it could have done, to see so [many] graves lie so high upon the churchyards where people have been buried of the plague. I was much troubled at it, and do not think to go through it again a good while. So home to my wife, whom I find not well, in bed, and it seems hath not been well these two days. She rose and we to dinner, after dinner up to my chamber, where she entertained me with what she hath lately bought of clothes for herself, and Damask linnen, and other things for the house. I did give her a serious account how matters stand with me, of favour with the King and Duke, and of danger in reference to my Lord's and Sir G. Carteret's falls, and the dissatisfaction I have heard the Duke of Albemarle hath acknowledged to somebody, among other things, against my Lord Sandwich, that he did bring me into the Navy against his desire and endeavour for another, which was our doting foole Turner. Thence from one discourse to another, and looking over my house, and other things I spent the day at home, and at night betimes to bed. After dinner this day I went down by water to Deptford, and fetched up what money there was of W. Howe's contingencies in the chest there, being L516 13s. 3d. and brought it home to dispose of.

31st. Lay pretty long in bed, and then up and to the office, where we met on extraordinary occasion about the business of tickets. By and by to the 'Change, and there did several businesses, among others brought home my cozen Pepys, whom I appointed to be here to-day, and Mr. Moore met us upon the business of my Lord's bond. Seeing my neighbour Mr. Knightly walk alone from the 'Change, his family being not yet come to town, I did invite him home with me, and he dined with me, a very sober, pretty man he is. He is mighty solicitous, as I find many about the City that live near the churchyards, to have the churchyards covered with lime, and I think it is needfull, and ours I hope will be done. Good pleasant discourse at dinner of the practices of merchants to cheat the "Customers," occasioned by Mr. Moore's being with much trouble freed of his prize goods, which he bought, which fell into the Customers' hands, and with much ado hath cleared them. Mr. Knightly being gone, my cozen Pepys and Moore and I to our business, being the clearing of my Lord Sandwich's bond wherein I am bound with him to my cozen for L1000 I have at last by my dexterity got my Lord's consent to have it paid out of the money raised by his prizes. So the bond is cancelled, and he paid by having a note upon Sir Robert Viner, in whose hands I had lodged my Lord's money, by which I am to my extraordinary comfort eased of a liablenesse to pay the sum in case of my Lord's death, or troubles in estate, or my Lord's greater fall, which God defend! Having settled this matter at Sir R. Viner's, I took up Mr. Moore (my cozen going home) and to my Lord Chancellor's new house which he is building, only to view it, hearing so much from Mr. Evelyn of it; and, indeed, it is the finest pile I ever did see in my life, and will be a glorious house. Thence to the Duke of Albemarle, who tells me Mr. Coventry is come to town and directs me to go to him about some business in hand, whether out of displeasure or desire of ease I know not; but I asked him not the reason of it but went to White Hall, but could not find him there, though to my great joy people begin to bustle up and down there, the King holding his resolution to be in towne to-morrow, and hath good encouragement, blessed be God! to do so, the plague being decreased this week to 56, and the total to 227. So after going to the Swan in the Palace, and sent for Spicer to discourse about my last Tangier tallys that have some of the words washed out with the rain, to have them new writ, I home, and there did some business and at the office, and so home to supper, and to bed.

February 1st. Up and to the office, where all the morning till late, and Mr. Coventry with us, the first time since before the plague, then hearing my wife was gone abroad to buy things and see her mother and father, whom she hath not seen since before the plague, and no dinner provided for me ready, I walked to Captain Cocke's, knowing my Lord Bruncker dined there, and there very merry, and a good dinner. Thence my Lord and his mistresse, Madam Williams, set me down at the Exchange, and I to Alderman Backewell's to set all my reckonings straight there, which I did, and took up all my notes. So evened to this day, and thence to Sir Robert Viner's, where I did the like, leaving clear in his hands just L2000 of my owne money, to be called for when I pleased. Having done all this I home, and there to the office, did my business there by the post and so home, and spent till one in the morning in my chamber to set right all my money matters, and so to bed.

2nd. Up betimes, and knowing that my Lord Sandwich is come to towne with the King and Duke, I to wait upon him, which I did, and find him in very good humour, which I am glad to see with all my heart. Having received his commands, and discoursed with some of his people about my Lord's going, and with Sir Roger Cuttance, who was there, and finds himself slighted by Sir W. Coventry, I advised him however to look after employment lest it should be said that my Lord's friends do forsake the service after he hath made them rich with the prizes. I to London, and there among other things did look over some pictures at Cade's for my house, and did carry home a silver drudger

for my cupboard of plate, and did call for my silver chafing dishes, but they are sent home, and the man would not be paid for them, saying that he was paid for them already, and with much ado got him to tell me by Mr. Wayth, but I would not accept of that, but will send him his money, not knowing any courtesy I have yet done him to deserve it. So home, and with my wife looked over our plate, and picked out L40 worth, I believe, to change for more usefull plate, to our great content, and then we shall have a very handsome cupboard of plate. So to dinner, and then to the office, where we had a meeting extraordinary, about stating to the Duke the present debts of the Navy, for which ready money must be had, and that being done, I to my business, where late, and then home to supper, and to bed.

3rd. Up, and to the office very busy till 3 o'clock, and then home, all of us, for half an hour to dinner, and to it again till eight at night, stating our wants of money for the Duke, but could not finish it. So broke up, and I to my office, then about letters and other businesses very late, and so home to supper, weary with business, and to bed.

4th. Lord's day; and my wife and I the first time together at church since the plague, and now only because of Mr. Mills his coming home to preach his first sermon; expecting a great excuse for his leaving the parish before any body went, and now staying till all are come home; but he made but a very poor and short excuse, and a bad sermon. It was a frost, and had snowed last night, which covered the graves in the churchyard, so as I was the less afeard for going through. Here I had the content to see my noble Mrs. Lethulier, and so home to dinner, and all the afternoon at my Journall till supper, it being a long while behindhand. At supper my wife tells me that W. Joyce has been with her this evening, the first time since the plague, and tells her my aunt James is lately dead of the stone, and what she had hath given to his and his brother's wife and my cozen Sarah. So after supper to work again, and late to bed.

5th. Up, and with Sir W. Batten (at whose lodgings calling for him, I saw his Lady the first time since her coming to towne since the plague, having absented myself designedly to shew some discontent, and that I am not at all the more suppliant because of my Lord Sandwich's fall), to my Lord Bruncker's, to see whether he goes to the Duke's this morning or no. But it is put off, and so we parted. My Lord invited me to dinner to-day to dine with Sir W. Batten and his Lady there, who were invited before, but lest he should thinke so little an invitation would serve my turne I refused and parted, and to Westminster about business, and so back to the 'Change, and there met Mr. Hill, newly come to town, and with him the Houblands, preparing for their ship's and his going to Tangier, and agreed that I must sup with them to-night. So home and eat a bit, and then to White Hall to a Committee for Tangier, but it did not meet but was put off to to-morrow, so I did some little business and visited my Lord Sandwich, and so, it raining, went directly to the Sun, behind the Exchange, about seven o'clock, where I find all the five brothers Houblons, and mighty fine gentlemen they are all, and used me mighty respectfully. We were mighty civilly merry, and their discourses, having been all abroad, very fine. Here late and at last accompanied home with Mr. J. Houblon and Hill, whom I invited to sup with me on Friday, and so parted and I home to bed.

6th. Up, and to the office, where very busy all the morning. We met upon a report to the Duke of Yorke of the debts of the Navy, which we finished by three o'clock, and having eat one little bit of meate, I by water before the rest to White Hall (and they to come after me) because of a Committee for Tangier, where I did my business of stating my accounts perfectly well, and to good liking, and do not discern, but the Duke of Albemarle is my friend in his intentions notwithstanding my general fears. After that to our Navy business, where my fellow officers were called in, and did that also very well, and then broke up, and I home by coach, Tooker with me, and staid in Lumbard Streete at Viner's, and sent home for the plate which my wife and I had a mind to change, and there changed it, about L50 worth, into things more usefull, whereby we shall now have a very handsome cupboard of plate. So home to the office, wrote my letters by the post, and to bed.

7th. It being fast day I staid at home all day long to set things to rights in my chamber by taking out all my books, and putting my chamber in the same condition it was before the plague. But in the morning doing of it, and knocking up a nail I did bruise my left thumb so as broke a great deal of my flesh off, that it hung by a little. It was a sight frighted my wife, but I put some balsam of Mrs. Turner's to it, and though in great pain, yet went on with my business, and did it to my full content, setting every thing in order, in hopes now that the worst of our fears are over as to the plague for the next year. Interrupted I was by two or three occasions this day to my great vexation, having this the only day I have been able to set apart for this work since my coming to town. At night to supper, weary, and to bed, having had the plasterers and joiners also to do some jobbs.

8th. Up, and all the morning at the office. At noon to the 'Change, expecting to have received from Mr. Houbland, as he promised me, an assignment upon Viner, for my reward for my getting them the going of their two ships to Tangier, but I find myself much disappointed therein, for I spoke with him and he said nothing of it, but looked coldly, through some disturbance he meets with in our business through Colonell Norwood's pressing them to carry more goods than will leave room for some of their own. But I shall ease them. Thence to Captain Cocke's, where Mr. Williamson, Wren, Boldell and Madam Williams, and by and by Lord Bruncker, he having been with the King and Duke upon the water to-day, to see Greenwich house, and the yacht Castle is building of, and much good discourse. So to White Hall to see my Lord Sandwich, and then home to my business till night, and then to bed.

9th. Up, and betimes to Sir Philip Warwicke, who was glad to see me, and very kind. Thence to Colonell Norwood's lodgings, and there set about Houblons' business about their ships. Thence to Westminster, to the Exchequer, about my Tangier business to get orders for tallys, and so to the Hall, where the first day of the Terme, and the Hall very full of people, and much more than was expected, considering the plague that hath been. Thence to the 'Change, and to the Sun behind it to dinner with the Lieutenant of the Tower, Colonell Norwood and others, where strange pleasure they seem to take in their wine and meate, and discourse of it with the curiosity and joy that methinks was below men of worthe. Thence home, and there very much angry with my people till I had put all things in good forwardnesse about my supper for the Houblons, but that being done I was in good humour again, and all things in good order. Anon the five brothers Houblons come and Mr. Hill, and a very good supper we had, and good company and discourse, with great pleasure. My new plate sets off my cupboard very nobly. Here they were till about eleven at night with great pleasure, and a fine sight it is to see these five brothers thus loving one to another, and all industrious merchants. Our subject was principally Mr. Hill's going for them to Portugall, which was the occasion of this entertainment. They gone, we to bed.

10th. Up, and to the office. At noon, full of business, to dinner. This day comes first Sir Thomas Harvy after the plague, having been out of towne all this while. He was coldly received by us, and he went away before we rose also, to make himself appear yet a man less necessary. After dinner, being full of care and multitude of business, I took coach and my wife with me. I set her down at her mother's (having first called at my Lord Treasurer's and there spoke with Sir Ph. Warwicke), and I to the Exchequer about Tangier orders, and so to the Swan and there staid a little, and so by coach took up my wife, and at the old Exchange bought a muffe, and so home and late at my letters, and so to supper and to bed, being now-a-days, for these four or five months, mightily troubled with my snoring in my sleep, and know not how to remedy it.

11th (Lord's day). Up, and put on a new black cloth suit to an old coate that I make to be in mourning at Court, where they are all, for the King of Spayne.—[Philip IV., who died September 17th, 1665.]—To church I, and at noon dined well, and then by water to White Hall, carrying a captain of the Tower (who desired his freight thither); there I to the Parke, and walked two or three turns of the Pell Mell with the company about the King and Duke; the Duke speaking to me a good deal. There met Lord Bruncker and Mr. Coventry, and discoursed about the Navy business; and all of us much at a loss that we yet can hear nothing of Sir Jeremy Smith's fleete, that went away to the Streights the middle of December, through all the storms that we have had since, that have driven back three or four of them with their masts by the board. Yesterday come out the King's Declaration of War against the French, but with such mild invitations of both them and the Dutch to come over hither with promise of their protection, that every body wonders at it. Thence home with my Lord Bruncker for discourse sake, and thence by hackney coach home, and so my wife and I mighty pleasant discourse, supped and to bed. The great wound I had Wednesday last in my thumb having with once dressing by Mrs. Turner's balsam been perfectly cured, whereas I did not hope to save my nail, whatever else ill it did give me. My wife and I are much thoughtfull now-a-days about Pall's coming up in order to a husband.

12th. Up, and very busy to perform an oathe in finishing my Journall this morning for 7 or 8 days past. Then to several people attending upon business, among others Mr. Grant and the executors of Barlow for the L25 due for the quarter before he died, which I scrupled to pay, being obliged but to pay every half year. Then comes Mr. Caesar, my boy's lute-master, whom I have not seen since the plague before, but he hath been in Westminster all this while very well; and tells me in the height of it, how bold people there were, to go in sport to one another's burials; and in spite too, ill people would breathe in the faces (out of their windows) of well people going by. Then to dinner before the 'Change, and so to the 'Change, and then to the taverne to talk with Sir William Warren, and so by coach to several places, among others to my Lord Treasurer's, there to meet my Lord Sandwich, but missed, and met him at [my] Lord Chancellor's, and there talked with him about his accounts, and then about Sir G. Carteret, and I find by him that Sir G. Carteret has a worse game to play than my Lord Sandwich, for people are jeering at him, and he cries out of the business of Sir W. Coventry, who strikes at all and do all. Then to my bookseller's, and then received some books I have new bought, and here late choosing some more to new bind, having resolved to give myself L10 in books, and so home to the office and then home to supper, where Mr. Hill was and supped with us, and good discourse; an excellent person he still appears to me. After supper, and he gone, we to bed.

13th. Up, and all the morning at the office. At noon to the 'Change, and thence after business dined at the Sheriffe's [Hooker], being carried by Mr. Lethulier, where to my heart's content I met with his wife, a most beautifull fat woman. But all the house melancholy upon the sickness of a daughter of the house in childbed, Mr. Vaughan's lady. So all of them undressed, but however this lady a very fine woman. I had a salute of her, and after dinner some discourse the Sheriffe and I about a parcel of tallow I am buying for the office of him. I away home, and there at the office all the afternoon till late at night, and then away home to supper and to bed. Ill newes this night that the plague is encreased this week, and in many places else about the towne, and at Chatham and elsewhere. This day my wife wanting a chambermaid with much ado got our old little Jane to be found out, who come to see her and hath lived all this while in one place, but is so well that we will not desire her removal, but are mighty glad to see the poor wench, who is very well and do well.

14th (St. Valentine's day). This morning called up by Mr. Hill, who, my wife thought, had been come to be her Valentine; she, it seems, having drawne him last night, but it proved not. However, calling him up to our bed-side, my wife challenged him. I up, and made myself ready, and so with him by coach to my Lord Sandwich's by appointment to deliver Mr. Howe's accounts to my Lord. Which done, my Lord did give me hearty and large studied thanks for all my kindnesse to him and care of him and his business. I after profession of all duty to his Lordship took occasion to bemoane myself that I should fall into such a difficulty about Sir G. Carteret, as not to be for him, but I must be against Sir W. Coventry, and therefore desired to be neutrall, which my Lord approved and confessed reasonable, but desired me to befriend him privately. Having done in private with my Lord I brought Mr. Hill to kisse his hands, to whom my Lord professed great respect upon my score. My Lord being gone, I took Mr. Hill to my Lord Chancellor's new house that is building, and went with trouble up to the top of it, and there is there the noblest prospect that ever I saw in my life, Greenwich being nothing to it; and in every thing is a beautiful house, and most strongly built in every respect; and as if, as it hath, it had the Chancellor for its master. Thence with him to his paynter, Mr. Hales, who is drawing his picture, which will be mighty like him, and pleased me so, that I am resolved presently to have my wife's and mine done by him, he having a very masterly hand. So with mighty satisfaction to the 'Change and thence home, and after dinner abroad, taking Mrs. Mary Batelier with us, who was just come to see my wife, and they set me down at my Lord Treasurer's, and themselves went with the coach into the fields to take the ayre. I staid a meeting of the Duke of Yorke's, and the officers of the Navy and Ordnance. My Lord Treasurer lying in bed of the gowte. Our business was discourse of the straits of the Navy for want of money, but after long discourse as much out of order as ordinary people's, we come to no issue, nor any money promised, or like to be had, and yet the worke must be done. Here I perceive Sir G. Carteret had prepared himself to answer a choque of Sir W. Coventry, by offering of himself to shew all he had paid, and what is unpaid, and what moneys and assignments he hath in his hands, which, if he makes good, was the best thing he ever did say in his life, and the best timed, for else it must have fallen very foule on him. The meeting done I away, my wife and they being come back and staying for me at the gate. But, Lord! to see how afeard I was that Sir W. Coventry should have spyed me once whispering with Sir G. Carteret, though not intended by me, but only Sir G. Carteret come to me and I could not avoyde it. So home, they set me down at the 'Change, and I to the Crowne, where my Lord Bruncker was come and several of the Virtuosi, and after a small supper and but little good discourse I with Sir W. Batten (who was brought thither with my Lord Bruncker) home, where I find my wife gone to Mrs. Mercer's to be merry, but presently come in with Mrs. Knipp, who, it seems, is in towne, and was gone thither with my wife and Mercer to dance, and after eating a little supper went thither again to spend the whole night there, being W. Howe there, at whose chamber they are, and Lawd Crisp by chance. I to bed.

15th. Up, and my wife not come home all night. To the office, where sat all the morning. At noon to Starky's, a great cooke in Austin Friars, invited by Colonell Atkins, and a good dinner for Colonell Norwood and his friends, among others Sir Edward Spragg and others, but ill attendance. Before dined, called on by my wife in a coach, and so I took leave, and then with her and Knipp and Mercer (Mr. Hunt newly come out of the country being there also come to see us) to Mr. Hales, the paynter's, having set down Mr. Hunt by the way. Here Mr. Hales' begun my wife in the posture we saw one of my Lady Peters, like a St. Katharine.

While he painted, Knipp, and Mercer, and I, sang; and by and by comes Mrs. Pierce, with my name in her bosom for her Valentine, which will cost me money. But strange how like his very first dead colouring is, that it did me good to see it, and pleases me mightily, and I believe will be a noble picture. Thence with them all as far as Fleete Streete, and there set Mercer and Knipp down, and we home. I to the office, whither the Houblons come telling me of a little new trouble from Norwood about their ship, which troubles me, though without reason. So late home to supper and to bed. We hear this night of Sir Jeremy Smith, that he and his fleete have been seen at Malaga; which is good newes.

16th. Up betimes, and by appointment to the Exchange, where I met Messrs. Houblons, and took them up in my coach and carried them to Charing Crosse, where they to Colonell Norwood to see how they can settle matters with him, I having informed them by the way with advice to be easy with him, for he may hereafter do us service, and they and I are like to understand one another to very good purpose. I to my Lord Sandwich, and there alone with him to talke of his affairs, and particularly of his prize goods, wherein I find he is wearied with being troubled, and gives over the care of it to let it come to what it will, having the King's release for the dividend made, and for the rest he thinks himself safe from being proved to have anything more. Thence to the Exchequer, and so by coach to the 'Change, Mr. Moore with me, who tells me very odde passages of the indiscretion of my Lord in the management of his family, of his carelessnesse, &c., which troubles me, but makes me rejoice with all my heart of my being rid of the bond of L1000, for that would have been a cruel blow to me. With Moore to the Coffee-House, the first time I have been there, where very full, and company it seems hath been there all the plague time. So to the 'Change, and then home to dinner, and after dinner to settle accounts with him for my Lord, and so evened with him to this day. Then to the office, and out with Sir W. Warren for discourse by coach to White Hall, thinking to have spoke with Sir W. Coventry, but did not, and to see the Queene, but she comes but to Hampton Court to-night. Back to my office and there late, and so home to supper and bed. I walked a good while to-night with Mr. Hater in the garden, talking about a husband for my sister, and reckoning up all our clerks about us, none of which he thinks fit for her and her portion. At last I thought of young Gawden, and will thinke of it again.

17th. Up, and to the office, where busy all the morning. Late to dinner, and then to the office again, and there busy till past twelve at night, and so home to supper and to bed. We have newes of Sir Jeremy Smith's being very well with his fleete at Cales.—[Cadiz]

18th (Lord's day). Lay long in bed discoursing with pleasure with my wife, among other things about Pall's coming up, for she must be here a little to be fashioned, and my wife hath a mind to go down for her, which I am not much against, and so I rose and to my chamber to settle several things. At noon comes my uncle Wight to dinner, and brings with him Mrs. Wight, sad company to me, nor was I much pleased with it, only I must shew respect to my uncle. After dinner they gone, and it being a brave day, I walked to White Hall, where the Queene and ladies are all come: I saw some few of them, but not the Queene, nor any of the great beauties. I endeavoured to have seen my Lord Hinchingbrooke, who come to town yesterday, but I could not. Met with Creed and walked with him a turne or two in the Parke, but without much content, having now designs of getting money in my head, which allow me not the leisure I used to have with him, besides an odde story lately told of him for a great truth, of his endeavouring to lie with a woman at Oxford, and her crying out saved her; and this being publickly known, do a little make me hate him. Thence took coach, and calling by the way at my bookseller's for a booke I writ about twenty years ago in prophecy of this year coming on, 1666, explaining it to be the marke of the beast, I home, and there fell to reading, and then to supper, and to bed.

19th. Up, and by coach to my Lord Sandwich's, but he was gone out. So I to White Hall, and there waited on the Duke of Yorke with some of the rest of our brethren, and thence back again to my Lord's, to see my Lord Hinchingbroke, which I did, and I am mightily out of countenance in my great expectation of him by others' report, though he is indeed a pretty gentleman, yet nothing what I took him for, methinks, either as to person or discourse discovered to me, but I must try him more before I go too far in censuring. Hence to the Exchequer from office to office, to set my business of my tallys in doing, and there all the morning. So at noon by coach to St. Paul's Church-yarde to my Bookseller's, and there bespoke a few more books to bring all I have lately bought to L10. Here I am told for certain, what I have heard once or twice already, of a Jew in town, that in the name of the rest do offer to give any man L10 to be paid L100, if a certain person now at Smyrna be within these two years owned by all the Princes of the East, and particularly the grand Signor as the King of the world, in the same manner we do the King of England here, and that this man is the true Messiah. One named a friend of his that had received ten pieces in gold upon this score, and says that the Jew hath disposed of L1100 in this manner, which is very strange; and certainly this year of 1666 will be a year of great action; but what the consequences of it will be, God knows! Thence to the 'Change, and from my stationer's thereabouts carried home by coach two books of Ogilby's, his AEsop and Coronation, which fell to my lot at his lottery. Cost me L4 besides the binding. So home. I find my wife gone out to Hales, her paynter's, and I after a little dinner do follow her, and there do find him at worke, and with great content I do see it will be a very brave picture. Left her there, and I to my Lord Treasurer's, where Sir G. Carteret and Sir J. Minnes met me, and before my Lord Treasurer and Duke of Albemarle the state of our Navy debts were laid open, being very great, and their want of money to answer them openly professed, there being but L1,500,000 to answer a certaine expense and debt of L2,300,000. Thence walked with Fenn down to White Hall, and there saw the Queene at cards with many ladies, but none of our beauties were there. But glad I was to see the Queene so well, who looks prettily; and methinks hath more life than before, since it is confessed of all that she miscarryed lately; Dr. Clerke telling me yesterday at White Hall that he had the membranes and other vessels in his hands which she voided, and were perfect as ever woman's was that bore a child. Thence hoping to find my Lord Sandwich, away by coach to my

Lord Chancellor's, but missed him, and so home and to office, and then to supper and my Journall, and to bed.

20th. Up, and to the office; where, among other businesses, Mr. Evelyn's proposition about publique Infirmarys was read and agreed on, he being there: and at noon I took him home to dinner, being desirous of keeping my acquaintance with him; and a most excellent humoured man I still find him, and mighty knowing. After dinner I took him by coach to White Hall, and there he and I parted, and I to my Lord Sandwich's, where coming and bolting into the dining-room, I there found Captain Ferrers going to christen a child of his born yesterday, and I come just pat to be a godfather, along with my Lord Hinchingbrooke, and Madam Pierce, my Valentine, which for that reason I was pretty well contented with, though a little vexed to see myself so beset with people to spend me money, as she of a Valentine and little Mrs. Tooker, who is come to my house this day from Greenwich, and will cost me 20s., my wife going out with her this afternoon, and now this christening. Well, by and by the child is brought and christened Katharine, and I this day on this occasion drank a glasse of wine, which I have not professedly done these two years, I think, but a little in the time of the sicknesse. After that done, and gone and kissed the mother in bed, I away to Westminster Hall, and there hear that Mrs. Lane is come to town. So I staid loitering up and down till anon she comes and agreed to meet at Swayn's, and there I went anon, and she come, but staid but little, the place not being private. I have not seen her since before the plague. So thence parted and 'rencontrais a' her last 'logis', and in the place did what I 'tenais a mind pour ferais con her'. At last she desired to borrow money of me, L5, and would pawn gold with me for it, which I accepted and promised in a day or two to supply her. So away home to the office, and thence home, where little Mrs. Tooker staid all night with us, and a pretty child she is, and happens to be niece to my beauty that is dead, that lived at the Jackanapes, in Cheapside. So to bed, a little troubled that I have been at two houses this afternoon with Mrs. Lane that were formerly shut up of the plague.

21st. Up, and with Sir J. Minnes to White Hall by his coach, by the way talking of my brother John to get a spiritual promotion for him, which I am now to looke after, for as much as he is shortly to be Master in Arts, and writes me this weeke a Latin letter that he is to go into orders this Lent. There to the Duke's chamber, and find our fellows discoursing there on our business, so I was sorry to come late, but no hurte was done thereby. Here the Duke, among other things, did bring out a book of great antiquity of some of the customs of the Navy, about 100 years since, which he did lend us to read and deliver him back again. Thence I to the Exchequer, and there did strike my tallys for a quarter for Tangier and carried them home with me, and thence to Trinity-house, being invited to an Elder Brother's feast; and there met and sat by Mr. Prin, and had good discourse about the privileges of Parliament, which, he says, are few to the Commons' House, and those not examinable by them, but only by the House of Lords. Thence with my Lord Bruncker to Gresham College, the first time after the sicknesse that I was there, and the second time any met. And here a good lecture of Mr. Hooke's about the trade of felt-making, very pretty. And anon alone with me about the art of drawing pictures by Prince Rupert's rule and machine, and another of Dr. Wren's;

but he says nothing do like squares, or, which is the best in the world, like a darke roome,—[The camera obscura.]—which pleased me mightily. Thence with Povy home to my house, and there late settling accounts with him, which was very troublesome to me, and he gone, found Mr. Hill below, who sat with me till late talking, and so away, and we to bed.

22nd. Up, and to the office, where sat all the morning. At noon home to dinner and thence by coach with my wife for ayre principally for her. I alone stopped at Hales's and there mightily am pleased with my wife's picture that is begun there, and with Mr. Hill's, though I must [owne] I am not more pleased with it now the face is finished than I was when I saw it the second time of sitting. Thence to my Lord Sandwich's, but he not within, but goes to-morrow. My wife to Mrs. Hunt's, who is lately come to towne and grown mighty fat. I called her there, and so home and late at the office, and so home to supper and to bed. We are much troubled that the sicknesse in general (the town being so full of people) should be but three, and yet of the particular disease of the plague there should be ten encrease.

23rd. Up betimes, and out of doors by 6 of the clock, and walked (W. Howe with me) to my Lord Sandwich's, who did lie the last night at his house in Lincoln's Inne Fields. It being fine walking in the morning, and the streets full of people again. There I staid, and the house full of people come to take leave of my Lord, who this day goes out of towne upon his embassy towards Spayne. And I was glad to find Sir W. Coventry to come, though I know it is only a piece of courtshipp. I had much discourse with my Lord, he telling me how fully he leaves the King his friend and the large discourse he had with him the other day, and how he desired to have the business of the prizes examined before he went, and that he yielded to it, and it is done as far as it concerns himself to the full, and the Lords Commissioners for prizes did reprehend all the informers in what related to his Lordship, which I am glad of in many respects. But we could not make an end of discourse, so I promised to waite upon [him] on Sunday at Cranborne, and took leave and away hence to Mr. Hales's with Mr. Hill and two of the Houblons, who come thither to speak with me, and saw my wife's picture, which pleases me well, but Mr. Hill's picture never a whit so well as it did before it was finished, which troubled me, and I begin to doubt the picture of my Lady Peters my wife takes her posture from, and which is an excellent picture, is not of his making, it is so master-like. I set them down at the 'Change and I home to the office, and at noon dined at home and to the office again. Anon comes Mrs. Knipp to see my wife, who is gone out, so I fain to entertain her, and took her out by coach to look my wife at Mrs. Pierce's and Unthanke's, but find her not. So back again, and then my wife comes home, having been buying of things, and at home I spent all the night talking with this baggage, and teaching her my song of "Beauty retire," which she sings and makes go most rarely, and a very fine song it seems to be. She also entertained me with repeating many of her own and others' parts of the play-house, which she do most excellently; and tells me the whole practices of the play-house and players, and is in every respect most excellent company. So I supped, and was merry at home all the evening, and the rather it being my birthday, 33 years, for which God be praised that I am in so good a condition of healthe and estate, and every thing else as I am, beyond expectation, in all. So she to Mrs. Turner's to lie, and we to bed. Mightily pleased to find myself in condition to have these people come about me and to be able to entertain them, and have the pleasure of their qualities, than which no man can have more in the world.

24th. All the morning at the office till past three o'clock. At that houre home and eat a bit alone, my wife being gone out. So abroad by coach with Mr. Hill, who staid for me to speake about business, and he and I to Hales's, where I find my wife and her woman, and Pierce and Knipp, and there sung and was mighty merry, and I joyed myself in it; but vexed at first to find my wife's picture not so like as I expected; but it was only his having finished one part, and not another, of the face; but, before I went, I was satisfied it will be an excellent picture. Here we had ale and cakes and mighty merry, and sung my song, which she [Knipp] now sings bravely, and makes me proud of myself. Thence left my wife to go home with Mrs. Pierce, while I home to the office, and there pretty late, and to bed, after fitting myself for to-morrow's journey.

25th (Lord's day). My wife up between three and four of the clock in the morning to dress herself, and I about five, and were all ready to take coach, she and I and Mercer, a little past five, but, to our trouble, the coach did not come till six. Then with our coach of four horses I hire on purpose, and Leshmore to ride by, we through the City to Branford and so to Windsor, Captain Ferrers overtaking us at Kensington, being to go with us, and here drank, and so through, making no stay, to Cranborne, about eleven o'clock, and found my Lord and the ladies at a sermon in the house; which being ended we to them, and all the company glad to see us, and mighty merry to dinner. Here was my Lord, and Lord Hinchingbroke, and Mr. Sidney, Sir Charles Herbert, and Mr. Carteret, my Lady Carteret, my Lady Jemimah, and Lady Slaning. After dinner to talk to and again, and then to walke in the Parke, my Lord and I alone, talking upon these heads; first, he has left his business of the prizes as well as is possible for him, having cleared himself before the Commissioners by the King's commands, so that nothing or little is to be feared from that point, he goes fully assured, he tells me, of the King's favour. That upon occasion I may know, I desired to know, his friends I may trust to, he tells me, but that he is not yet in England, but continues this summer in Ireland, my Lord Orrery is his father almost in affection. He tells me my Lord of Suffolke, Lord Arlington, Archbishop of Canterbury, Lord Treasurer, Mr. Atturny Montagu, Sir Thomas Clifford in the House of Commons, Sir G. Carteret, and some others I cannot presently remember, are friends that I may rely on for him. He tells me my Lord Chancellor seems his very good friend, but doubts that he may not think him so much a servant of the Duke of Yorke's as he would have him, and indeed my Lord tells me he hath lately made it his business to be seen studious of the King's favour, and not of the Duke's, and by the King will stand or fall, for factions there are, as he tells me, and God knows how high they may come. The Duke of Albemarle's post is so great, having had the name of bringing in the King, that he is like to stand, or, if it were not for him, God knows in what troubles we might be from some private faction, if an army could be got into another hand, which God forbid! It is believed that though Mr. Coventry be in appearance so great against the Chancellor, yet that there is a good understanding between the Duke and him. He dreads the issue of this year, and fears there will be some very great revolutions before his coming back again. He doubts it is needful for him to have a pardon for his last year's actions, all which he did without commission, and at most but the King's private single word for that of Bergen; but he dares not ask it at this time, lest it should make them think that there is something more in it than yet they know; and if it should be denied, it would be of very ill consequence. He says also, if it should in Parliament be enquired into the selling of Dunkirke (though the Chancellor was the man that would have it sold to France, saying the King of Spayne had no money to give for it); yet he will be found to have been the greatest adviser of it; which he is a little apprehensive may be called upon this Parliament. He told me it would not be necessary for him to tell me his debts, because he thinks I know them so well. He tells me, that for the match propounded of Mrs. Mallett for my Lord Hinchingbroke, it hath been lately off, and now her friends bring it on again, and an overture hath been made to him by a servant of hers, to compass the thing without consent of friends, she herself having a respect to my Lord's family, but my Lord will not listen to it but in a way of honour. The Duke hath for this weeke or two been very kind to him, more than lately; and so others, which he thinks is a good sign of faire weather again. He says the Archbishopp of Canterbury hath been very kind to him, and hath plainly said to him that he and all the world knows the difference between his judgment and brains and the Duke of Albemarle's, and then calls my Lady Duchesse the veryest slut and drudge and the foulest worde that can be spoke of a woman almost. My Lord having walked an houre with me talking thus and going in, and my Lady Carteret not suffering me to go back again to-night, my Lord to walke again with me about some of this and other discourse, and then in a-doors and to talke with all and with my Lady Carteret, and I with the young ladies and gentle men, who played on the guittar, and mighty merry, and anon to supper, and then my Lord going away to write, the young gentlemen to flinging of cushions, and other mad sports; at this late till towards twelve at night, and then being sleepy, I and my wife in a passage-room to bed, and slept not very well because of noise.

26th. Called up about five in the morning, and my Lord up, and took leave, a little after six, very kindly of me and the whole company. Then I in, and my wife up and to visit my Lady Slaving in her bed, and there sat three hours, with Lady Jemimah with us, talking and laughing, and by and by my Lady Carteret comes, and she and I to talke, I glad to please her in discourse of Sir G. Carteret, that all will do well with him, and she is much pleased, he having had great annoyance and fears about his well doing, and I fear hath doubted that I have not been a friend to him, but cries out against my Lady Castlemaine, that makes the King neglect his business and seems much to fear that all will go to wracke, and I fear with great reason; exclaims against the Duke of Albemarle, and more the Duchesse for a filthy woman, as indeed she is. Here staid till 9 o'clock almost, and then took coach with so much love and kindnesse from my Lady Carteret, Lady Jemimah, and Lady Slaving, that it joys my heart, and when I consider the manner of my going hither, with a coach and four horses and servants and a woman with us, and coming hither being so much made of, and used with that state, and then going to Windsor and being shewn all that we were there, and had wherewith to give every body something for their pains, and then going home, and all in fine weather and no fears nor cares upon me, I do thinke myself obliged to thinke myself happy, and do look upon myself at this time in the happiest occasion a man can be, and whereas we take pains in expectation of future comfort and ease, I have taught myself to reflect upon myself at present as happy, and enjoy myself in that consideration, and not only please myself with thoughts of future wealth and forget the pleasure we at present enjoy. So took coach and to Windsor, to the Garter, and thither sent for Dr. Childe; who come to us, and carried us to St. George's Chappell; and there placed us among the Knights' stalls (and pretty the observation, that no man, but a woman may sit in a Knight's place, where any brass-plates are set); and hither come cushions to us, and a young singing-boy to bring us a copy of the anthem to be sung. And here, for our sakes, had this anthem and the great service sung extraordinary, only to entertain us. It is a noble place indeed, and a good Quire of voices. Great bowing by all the people, the poor Knights particularly, to the Alter. After prayers, we to see the plate of the chappell, and the robes of Knights, and a man to shew us the banners of the several Knights in being, which hang up over the stalls. And so to other discourse very pretty, about the Order. Was shewn where the late [King] is buried, and King Henry the Eighth, and my Lady [Jane] Seymour. This being done, to the King's house, and to observe the neatness and contrivance of the house and gates: it is the most romantique castle that is in the world. But, Lord! the prospect that is in the balcone in the Queene's lodgings, and the terrace and walk, are strange things to consider, being the best in the world, sure. Infinitely satisfied I and my wife with all this, she being in all points mightily pleased too, which added to my pleasure; and so giving a great deal of money to this and that man and woman, we to our taverne, and there dined, the Doctor with us; and so took coach and away to Eton, the Doctor with me. Before we went to Chappell this morning, Kate Joyce, in a stage-coach going toward London, called to me. I went to her and saluted her, but could not get her to stay with us, having company. At Eton I left my wife in the coach, and he and I to the College, and there find all mighty fine. The school good, and the custom pretty of boys cutting their names in the struts of the window when they go to Cambridge, by which many a one hath lived to see himself Provost and Fellow, that had his name in the window standing. To the Hall, and there find the boys' verses, "De Peste;" it being their custom to make verses at Shrove-tide. I read several, and very good ones they were, and better, I think, than ever I made when I was a boy, and in rolls as long and longer than the whole Hall, by much. Here is a picture of Venice hung up given, and a monument made of Sir H. Wotton's giving it to the College. Thence to the porter's, in the absence of the butler, and did drink of the College beer, which is very good; and went into the back fields to see the scholars play. And so to the chappell, and there saw, among other things, Sir H. Wotton's stone with this Epitaph

But unfortunately the word "Author" was wrong writ, and now so basely altered that it disgraces the stone. Thence took leave of the Doctor, and so took coach, and finely, but sleepy, away home, and got thither about eight at night, and after a little at my office, I to bed; and an houre after, was waked with my wife's quarrelling with Mercer, at which I was angry, and my wife and I fell out. But with much ado to sleep again, I beginning to practise more temper, and to give her her way.

27th. Up, and after a harsh word or two my wife and I good friends, and so up and to the office, where all the morning. At noon late to dinner, my wife gone out to Hales's about her picture, and, after dinner, I after her, and do mightily like her picture, and think it will be as good as my Lady

Peters's. So home mightily pleased, and there late at business and set down my three last days' journalls, and so to bed, overjoyed to thinke of the pleasure of the last Sunday and yesterday, and my ability to bear the charge of these pleasures, and with profit too, by obliging my Lord, and reconciling Sir George Carteret's family.

28th (Ash Wednesday). Up, and after doing a little business at my office I walked, it being a most curious dry and cold morning, to White Hall, and there I went into the Parke, and meeting Sir Ph. Warwicke took a turne with him in the Pell Mall, talking of the melancholy posture of affairs, where every body is snarling one at another, and all things put together looke ominously. This new Act too putting us out of a power of raising money. So that he fears as I do, but is fearfull of enlarging in that discourse of an ill condition in every thing, and the State and all. We appointed another time to meet to talke of the business of the Navy alone seriously, and so parted, and I to White Hall, and there we did our business with the Duke of Yorke, and so parted, and walked to Westminster Hall, where I staid talking with Mrs. Michell and Howlett long and her daughter, which is become a mighty pretty woman, and thence going out of the Hall was called to by Mrs. Martin, so I went to her and bought two bands, and so parted, and by and by met at her chamber, and there did what I would, and so away home and there find Mrs. Knipp, and we dined together, she the pleasantest company in the world. After dinner I did give my wife money to lay out on Knipp, 20s., and I abroad to White Hall to visit Colonell Norwood, and then Sir G. Carteret, with whom I have brought myself right again, and he very open to me; is very melancholy, and matters, I fear, go down with him, but he seems most afeard of a general catastrophe to the whole kingdom, and thinks, as I fear, that all things will come to nothing. Thence to the Palace Yard, to the Swan, and there staid till it was dark, and then to Mrs. Lane's, and there lent her L5 upon L4 01s. in gold. And then did what I would with her, and I perceive she is come to be very bad, and offers any thing, that it is dangerous to have to do with her, nor will I see [her] any more a good while. Thence by coach home and to the office, where a while, and then betimes to bed by ten o'clock, sooner than I have done many a day. And thus ends this month, with my mind full of resolution to apply myself better from this time forward to my business than I have done these six or eight days, visibly to my prejudice both in quiett of mind and setting backward of my business, that I cannot give a good account of it as I ought to do.

MARCH 1665-1666

March 1st. Up, and to the office and there all the morning sitting and at noon to dinner with my Lord Bruncker, Sir W. Batten and Sir W. Pen at the White Horse in Lumbard Streete, where, God forgive us! good sport with Captain Cocke's having his mayde sicke of the plague a day or two ago and sent to the pest house, where she now is, but he will not say anything but that she is well. But blessed be God! a good Bill this week we have; being but 237 in all, and 42 of the plague, and of them but six in the City: though my Lord Bruneker says, that these six are most of them in new parishes where they were not the last week. Here was with us also Mr. Williamson, who the more I know, the more I honour. Hence I slipt after dinner without notice home and there close to my business at my office till twelve at night, having with great comfort returned to my business by some fresh vowes in addition to my former, and-more severe, and a great joy it is to me to see myself in a good disposition to business. So home to supper and to my Journall and to bed.

2nd. Up, as I have of late resolved before 7 in the morning and to the office, where all the morning, among other things setting my wife and Mercer with much pleasure to worke upon the ruling of some paper for the making of books for pursers, which will require a great deale of worke and they will earn a good deale of money by it, the hopes of which makes them worke mighty hard. At noon dined and to the office again, and about 4 o'clock took coach and to my Lord Treasurer's and thence to Sir Philip Warwicke's new house by appointment, there to spend an houre in talking and we were together above an hour, and very good discourse about the state of the King as to money, and particularly in the point of the Navy. He endeavours hard to come to a good understanding of Sir G. Carteret's accounts, and by his discourse I find Sir G. Carteret must be brought to it, and what a madman he is that he do not do it of himself, for the King expects the Parliament will call upon him for his promise of giving an account of the money, and he will be ready for it, which cannot be, I am sure, without Sir G. Carteret's accounts be better understood than they are. He seems to have a great esteem of me and my opinion and thoughts of things. After we had spent an houre thus discoursing and vexed that we do but grope so in the darke as we do, because the people, that should enlighten us, do not helpe us, we resolved fitting some things for another meeting, and so broke up. He shewed me his house, which is yet all unhung, but will be a very noble house indeed. Thence by coach calling at my bookseller's and carried home L10 worth of books, all, I hope, I shall buy a great while. There by appointment find Mr. Hill come to sup and take his last leave of me, and by and by in comes Mr. James Houbland to bear us company, a man I love mightily, and will not lose his acquaintance. He told me in my eare this night what he and his brothers have resolved to give me, which is L200, for helping them out with two or three ships. A good sum and that which I did believe they would give me, and I did expect little less. Here we talked and very good company till late, and then took leave of one another, and indeed I am heartily sorry for Mr. Hill's leaving us, for he is a very worthy gentleman, as most I know. God give him a good voyage and successe in his business. Thus we parted and my wife and I to bed, heavy for the losse of our friend.

3rd. All the morning at the office, at noon to the Old James, being sent for, and there dined with Sir William Rider, Cutler, and others, to make an end with two Scots Maisters about the freight of two ships of my Lord Rutherford's. After a small dinner and a little discourse I away to the Crowne behind the Exchange to Sir W. Pen, Captain Cocke and Fen, about getting a bill of Cocke's paid to Pen, in part for the East India goods he sold us. Here Sir W. Pen did give me the reason in my eare of his importunity for money, for that he is now to marry his daughter. God send her better fortune than her father deserves I should wish him for a false rogue. Thence by coach to Hales's, and there saw my wife sit; and I do like her picture mightily, and very like it will be, and a brave piece of work. But he do complain that her nose hath cost him as much work as another's face, and he hath done it finely indeed. Thence home and late at the office, and then to bed.

4th (Lord's day). And all day at my Tangier and private accounts, having neglected them since Christmas, which I hope I shall never do again; for I find the inconvenience of it, it being ten times the labour to remember and settle things. But I thank God I did it at last, and brought them all fine and right; and I am, I thinke, by all appears to me (and I am sure I cannot be L10 wrong), worth above L4600, for which the Lord be praised! being the biggest sum I ever was worth yet.

5th. I was at it till past two o'clock on Monday morning, and then read my vowes, and to bed with great joy and content that I have brought my things to so good a settlement, and now having my mind fixed to follow my business again and sensible of Sir W. Coventry's jealousies, I doubt, concerning me, partly my siding with Sir G. Carteret, and partly that indeed I have been silent in my business of the office a great while, and given but little account of myself and least of all to him, having not made him one visitt since he came to towne from Oxford, I am resolved to fall hard to it again, and fetch up the time and interest I have lost or am in a fair way of doing it. Up about eight o'clock, being called up by several people, among others by Mr. Moone, with whom I went to Lumbard Streete to Colvill, and so back again and in my chamber he and I did end all our businesses together of accounts for money upon bills of Exchange, and am pleased to find myself reputed a man of business and method, as he do give me out to be. To the 'Change at noon and so home to dinner. Newes for certain of the King of Denmarke's declaring for the Dutch, and resolution to assist them. To the office, and there all the afternoon. In the evening come Mr. James and brother Houblons to agree upon share parties for their ships, and did acquaint me that they had paid my messenger, whom I sent this afternoon for it, L200 for my friendship in the business, which pleases me mightily. They being gone I forth late to Sir H. Viner's to take a receipt of them for the L200 lodged for me there with them, and so back home, and after supper to bed.

6th. Up betimes and did much business before office time. Then to the office and there till noon and so home to dinner and to the office again till night. In the evening being at Sir W. Batten's, stepped in (for I have not used to go thither a good while), I find my Lord Bruncker and Mrs. Williams, and they would of their own accord, though I had never obliged them (nor my wife neither) with one visit for many of theirs, go see my house and my wife; which I showed them and made them welcome with wine and China oranges (now a great rarity since the war, none to be had). There being also Captain Cocke and Mrs. Turner, who had never been in my house since I come to the office before, and Mrs. Carcasse, wife of Mr. Carcasses. My house happened to be mighty clean, and did me great honour, and they mightily pleased with it. They gone I to the office and did some business, and then home to supper and to bed. My mind troubled through a doubtfulness of my having incurred Sir W. Coventry's displeasure by not having waited on him since his coming to towne, which is a mighty faulte and that I can bear the fear of the bad effects of till I have been with him, which shall be to-morrow, God willing. So to bed.

7th. Up betimes, and to St. James's, thinking Mr. Coventry had lain there; but he do not, but at White Hall; so thither I went and had as good a time as heart could wish, and after an houre in his chamber about publique business he and I walked up, and the Duke being gone abroad we walked an houre in the Matted Gallery: he of himself begun to discourse of the unhappy differences between him and my Lord of Sandwich, and from the beginning to the end did run through all passages wherein my Lord hath, at any time, gathered any dissatisfaction, and cleared himself to me most honourably; and in truth, I do believe he do as he says. I did afterwards purge myself of all partiality in the business of Sir G. Carteret, (whose story Sir W. Coventry did also run over,) that I do mind the King's interest, notwithstanding my relation to him; all which he declares he firmly believes, and assures me he hath the same kindnesse and opinion of me as ever. And when I said I was jealous of myself, that having now come to such an income as I am, by his favour, I should not be found to do as much service as might deserve it; he did assure me, he thinks it not too much for me, but thinks I deserve it as much as any man in England. All this discourse did cheer my heart, and sets me right again, after a good deal of melancholy, out of fears of his disinclination to me, upon the differences with my Lord Sandwich and Sir G. Carteret; but I am satisfied throughly, and so went away quite another man, and by the grace of God will never lose it again by my folly in not visiting and writing to him, as I used heretofore to do. Thence by coach to the Temple, and it being a holyday, a fast-day, there 'light, and took water, being invited, and down to Greenwich, to Captain Cocke's, where dined, he and Lord Bruncker, and Matt. Wren, Boltele, and Major Cooper, who is also a very pretty companion; but they all drink hard, and, after dinner, to gaming at cards. So I provoked my Lord to be gone, and he and I to Mr. Cottle's and met Mrs. Williams (without whom he cannot stir out of doors) and there took coach and away home. They carry me to London and set me down at the Temple, where my mind changed and I home, and to writing and heare my boy play on the lute, and a turne with my wife pleasantly in the garden by moonshine, my heart being in great peace, and so home to supper and to bed. The King and Duke are to go to-morrow to Audly End, in order to the seeing and buying of it of my Lord Suffolke.

8th. Up betimes and to the office, where all the morning sitting and did discover three or four fresh instances of Sir W. Pen's old cheating dissembling tricks, he being as false a fellow as ever was born. Thence with Sir. W. Batten and Lord Bruncker to the White Horse in Lumbard Streete to dine with Captain Cocke, upon particular business of canvas to buy for the King, and here by chance I saw the mistresse of the house I have heard much of, and a very pretty woman she is indeed and her husband the simplest looked fellow and old that ever I saw. After dinner I took coach and away to Hales's, where my wife is sitting; and, indeed, her face and necke, which are now finished, do so please me that I am not myself almost, nor was not all the night after in writing of my letters, in consideration of the fine picture that I shall be master of. Thence home and to the office, where very late, and so home to supper and to bed.

9th. Up, and being ready, to the Cockpitt to make a visit to the Duke of Albemarle, and to my great joy find him the same man to me that [he has been] heretofore, which I was in great doubt of, through my negligence in not visiting of him a great while; and having now set all to rights there, I am in mighty ease in my mind and I think shall never suffer matters to run so far backward again as I have done of late, with reference to my neglecting him and Sir W. Coventry. Thence by water down to Deptford, where I met my Lord Bruncker and Sir W. Batten by agreement, and to measuring Mr. Castle's new third-rate ship, which is to be called the Defyance.

And here I had my end in saving the King some money and getting myself some experience in knowing how they do measure ships. Thence I left them and walked to Redriffe, and there taking water was overtaken by them in their boat, and so they would have me in with them to Castle's house, where my Lady Batten and Madam Williams were, and there dined and a deale of doings. I had a good dinner and counterfeit mirthe and pleasure with them, but had but little, thinking how I neglected my business. Anon, all home to Sir W. Batten's and there Mrs. Knipp coming we did spend the evening together very merry. She and I singing, and, God forgive me! I do still see that my nature is not to be quite conquered, but will esteem pleasure above all things, though yet in the middle of it, it has reluctances after my business, which is neglected by my following my pleasure. However musique and women I cannot but give way to, whatever my business is. They being gone I to the office a while and so home to supper and to bed.

10th. Up, and to the office, and there busy sitting till noon. I find at home Mrs. Pierce and Knipp come to dine with me. We were mighty merry; and, after dinner, I carried them and my wife out by coach to the New Exchange, and there I did give my valentine, Mrs. Pierce, a dozen payre of gloves, and a payre of silke stockings, and Knipp for company's sake, though my wife had, by my consent, laid out 20s. upon her the other day, six payre of gloves. Thence to Hales's to have seen our pictures, but could not get in, he being abroad, and so to the Cakehouse hard by, and there sat in the coach with great pleasure, and eat some fine cakes and so carried them to Pierces and away home. It is a mighty fine witty boy, Mrs. Pierces little boy. Thence home and to the office, where late writing letters and leaving a great deale to do on Monday, I home to supper and to bed. The truth is, I do indulge myself a little the more in pleasure, knowing that this is the proper age of my life to do it; and out of my observation that most men that do thrive in the world, do forget to take pleasure during the time that they are getting their estate, but reserve that till they have got one, and then it is too late for them to enjoy it with any pleasure.

11th (Lord's day). Up, and by water to White Hall, there met Mr. Coventry coming out, going along with the Commissioners of the Ordnance to the water side to take barge, they being to go down to the Hope. I returned with them as far as the Tower in their barge speaking with Sir W. Coventry and so home and to church, and at noon dined and then to my chamber, where with great pleasure about one business or other till late, and so to supper and to bed.

12th. Up betimes, and called on by abundance of people about business, and then away by water to Westminster, and there to the Exchequer about some business, and thence by coach calling at several places, to the Old Exchange, and there did much business, and so homeward and bought a silver salt for my ordinary table to use, and so home to dinner, and after dinner comes my uncle and aunt Wight, the latter I have not seen since the plague; a silly, froward, ugly woman she is. We made mighty much of them, and she talks mightily of her fear of the sicknesse, and so a deale of tittle tattle and I left them and to my office where late, and so home to supper and to bed. This day I hear my Uncle Talbot Pepys died the last week, and was buried. All the news now is, that Sir Jeremy Smith is at Cales—[Cadiz]—with his fleete, and Mings in the Elve.—[Elbe]—The King is come this noon to towne from Audly End, with the Duke of Yorke and a fine train of gentlemen.

13th. Up betimes, and to the office, where busy sitting all the morning, and I begin to find a little convenience by holding up my head to Sir W. Pen, for he is come to be more supple. At noon to dinner, and then to the office again, where mighty business, doing a great deale till midnight and then home to supper and to bed. The plague encreased this week 29 from 28, though the total fallen from 238 to 207, which do never a whit please me.

14th. Up, and met by 6 o'clock in my chamber Mr. Povy (from White Hall) about evening reckonings between him and me, on our Tangier business, and at it hard till toward eight o'clock, and he then carried me in his chariot to White Hall, where by and by my fellow officers met me, and we had a meeting before the Duke. Thence with my Lord Bruncker towards London, and in our way called in Covent Garden, and took in Sir John (formerly Dr.) Baber; who hath this humour that he will not enter into discourse while any stranger is in company, till he be told who he is that seems a stranger to him. This he did declare openly to me, and asked my Lord who I was, giving this reason, that he has been inconvenienced by being too free in discourse till he knew who all the company were. Thence to Guildhall (in our way taking in Dr. Wilkins), and there my Lord and I had full and large discourse with Sir Thomas Player, the Chamberlain of the City (a man I have much heard of for his credit and punctuality in the City, and on that score I had a desire to be made known to him), about the credit of our tallys, which are lodged there for security to such as should lend money thereon to the use of the Navy. And I had great satisfaction therein: and the truth is, I find all our matters of credit to be in an ill condition. Thence, I being in a little haste walked before and to the 'Change a little and then home, and presently to Trinity house to dinner, where Captain Cox made his Elder Brother's dinner. But it seemed to me a very poor sorry dinner. I having many things in my head rose, when my belly was full, though the dinner not half done, and home and there to do some business, and by and by out of doors and met Mr. Povy coming to me by appointment, but it being a little too late, I took a little pride in the streete not to go back with him, but prayed him to come another time, and I away to Kate Joyce's, thinking to have spoke to her husband about Pall's business, but a stranger, the Welsh Dr. Powell, being there I forebore and went away and so to Hales's, to see my wife's picture, which I like mighty well, and there had the pleasure to see how suddenly he draws the Heavens, laying a darke ground and then lightening it when and where he will. Thence to walk all alone in the fields behind Grayes Inne, making an end of reading over my dear "Faber fortunae," of my Lord Bacon's, and thence, it growing dark, took two or three wanton turns about the idle places and lanes about Drury Lane, but to no satisfaction, but a great fear of the plague among them, and so anon I walked by invitation to Mrs. Pierces, where I find much good company, that is to say, Mrs. Pierce, my wife, Mrs. Worshipp and her daughter, and Harris the player, and Knipp, and Mercer, and Mrs. Barbary Sheldon, who is come this day to spend a weeke with my wife; and here with musique we danced, and sung and supped, and then to sing and dance till past one in the morning; and much mirthe with Sir Anthony Apsley and one Colonell Sidney, who lodge in the house; and above all, they are mightily taken with Mrs. Knipp. Hence weary and sleepy we broke up, and I and my company homeward by coach and to bed.

15th. Lay till it was full time to rise, it being eight o'clock, and so to the office and there sat till almost three o'clock and then to dinner, and after dinner (my wife and Mercer and Mrs. Barbary being gone to Hales's before), I and my cozen Anthony Joyce, who come on purpose to dinner with me, and he and I to discourse of our proposition of marriage between Pall and Harman, and upon discourse he and I to Harman's house and took him to a taverne hard by, and we to discourse of our business, and I offered L500, and he declares most ingenuously that his trade is not to be trusted on, that he however needs no money, but would have her money bestowed on her, which I like well, he saying that he would adventure 2 or L300 with her. I like him as a most good-natured, and discreet man, and, I believe, very cunning. We come to this conclusion for us to meete one another the next weeke, and then we hope to come to some end, for I did declare myself well satisfied with the match. Thence to Hales's, where I met my wife and people; and do find the picture, above all things, a most pretty picture, and mighty like my wife; and I asked him his price: he says L14, and the truth is, I think he do deserve it. Thence toward London and home, and I to the office, where I did much, and betimes to bed, having had of late so little sleep, and there slept

16th. Till 7 this morning. Up and all the morning about the Victualler's business, passing his account. At noon to the 'Change, and did several businesses, and thence to the Crowne behind the 'Change and dined with my Lord Bruncker and Captain Cocke and Fenn, and Madam Williams, who without question must be my Lord's wife, and else she could not follow him wherever he goes and kisse and use him publiquely as she do. Thence to the office, where Sir W. Pen and I made an end of the Victualler's business, and thence abroad about several businesses, and so in the evening back again, and anon called on by Mr. Povy, and he and I staid together in my chamber till 12 at night ending our reckonings and giving him tallys for all I was to pay him and so parted, and I to make good my Journall for two or three days, and begun it till I come to the other side, where I have scratched so much, for, for want of sleep, I begun to write idle and from the purpose. So forced to breake off, and to bed.—[There are several erasures in the original MS.]

17th. Up, and to finish my Journall, which I had not sense enough the last night to make an end of, and thence to the office, where very busy all the morning. At noon home to dinner and presently with my wife out to Hales's, where I am still infinitely pleased with my wife's picture. I paid him L14 for it, and 25s. for the frame, and I think it is not a whit too deare for so good a picture. It is not yet quite finished and dry, so as to be fit to bring home yet. This day I begun to sit, and he will make me, I think, a very fine picture. He promises it shall be as good as my wife's, and I sit to have it full of shadows, and do almost break my neck looking over my shoulder to make the posture for him to work by. Thence home and to the office, and so home having a great cold, and so my wife and Mrs. Barbary have very great ones, we are at a loss how we all come by it together, so to bed, drinking butter-ale. This day my W. Hewer comes from Portsmouth and gives me an instance of another piece of knavery of Sir W. Pen, who wrote to Commissioner Middleton, that it was my negligence the other day he was not acquainted, as the board directed, with our clerks coming down to the pay. But I need no new arguments to teach me that he is a false rogue to me and all the world besides.

18th (Lord's day). Up and my cold better, so to church, and then home to dinner, and so walked out to St. James's Church, thinking to have seen faire Mrs. Butler, but could not, she not being there, nor, I believe, lives thereabouts now. So walked to Westminster, very fine fair dry weather, but all cry out for lack of rain. To Herbert's and drank, and thence to Mrs. Martin's, and did what I would with her; her husband going for some wine for us. The poor man I do think would take pains if I can get him a purser's place, which I will endeavour. She tells me as a secret that Betty Howlet of the Hall, my little sweetheart, that I used to call my second wife, is married to a younger son of Mr. Michell's (his elder brother, who should have had her, being dead this plague), at which I am glad, and that they are to live nearer me in Thames Streete, by the Old Swan. Thence by coach home and to my chamber about some accounts, and so to bed. Sir Christopher Mings is come home from Hambro without anything done, saving bringing home some pipestaves for us.

19th. Up betimes and upon a meeting extraordinary at the office most of the morning with Lord Bruncker, Sir W. Coventry, and Sir W. Pen, upon the business of the accounts. Where now we have got almost as much as we would have we begin to lay all on the Controller, and I fear he will be run down with it, for he is every day less and less capable of doing business. Thence with my Lord Bruncker, Sir W. Coventry to the ticket office, to see in what little order things are there, and there it is a shame to see how the King is served. Thence to the Chamberlain of London, and satisfy ourselves more particularly how much credit we have there, which proves very little. Thence to Sir Robert Long's, absent. About much the same business, but have not the satisfaction we would have there neither. So Sir W. Coventry parted, and my Lord and I to Mrs. Williams's, and there I saw her closett, where indeed a great many fine things there are, but the woman I hate. Here we dined, and Sir J. Minnes come to us, and after dinner we walked to the King's play-house, all in dirt, they being altering of the stage to make it wider. But God knows when they will begin to act again; but my business here was to see the inside of the stage and all the tiring-rooms and machines; and, indeed, it was a sight worthy seeing. But to see their clothes, and the various sorts, and what a mixture of things there was; here a wooden-leg, there a ruff, here a hobbyhorse, there a crown, would make a man split himself to see with laughing; and particularly Lacy's wardrobe, and Shotrell's. But then again, to think how fine they show on the stage by candle-light, and how poor things they are to look now too near hand, is not pleasant at all. The machines are fine, and the paintings very pretty. Thence mightily satisfied in my curiosity I away with my Lord to see him at her house again, and so take leave and by coach home and to the office, and thence sent for to Sir G. Carteret by and by to the Broad Streete, where he and I walked two or three hours till it was quite darke in his gallery talking of his affairs, wherein I assure him all will do well, and did give him (with great liberty, which he accepted kindly) my advice to deny the Board nothing they would aske about his accounts, but rather call upon them to know whether there was anything more they desired, or was wanting. But our great discourse and serious reflections was upon the bad state of the kingdom in general, through want of money and good conduct, which we fear will undo all. Thence mightily satisfied with this good fortune of this discourse with him I home, and there walked in the darke till 10 o'clock at night in the garden with Sir W. Warren, talking of many things belonging to us particularly, and I hope to get something considerably by him before the year be over. He gives me good advice of circumspection in my place, which I am now in great mind to improve; for I think our office stands on very ticklish terms, the Parliament likely to sit shortly and likely to be asked more money, and we able to give a very bad account of the expence of what we have done with what they did give before. Besides, the turning out the prize officers may be an example for the King giving us up to the Parliament's pleasure as easily, for we deserve it as much. Besides, Sir G. Carteret did tell me tonight how my Lord Bruncker himself, whose good-will I could have depended as much on as any, did himself to him take notice of the many places I have; and though I was a painful man, yet the Navy was enough for any man to go through with in his owne single place there, which much troubles me, and shall yet provoke me to more and more care and diligence than ever. Thence home to supper, where I find my wife and Mrs. Barbary with great colds, as I also at this time have. This day by letter from my father he propounds a match in the country for Pall, which pleased me well, of one that hath seven score and odd pounds land per annum in possession, and expects L1000 in money by the death of an old aunt. He hath neither father, mother, sister, nor brother, but demands L600 down, and L100 on the birth of first child, which I had some inclination to stretch to. He is kinsman to, and lives with, Mr. Phillips, but my wife tells me he is a drunken, ill-favoured, ill-bred country fellow, which sets me off of it again, and I will go on with Harman. So after supper to bed.

20th. Up and to the office, where busy all the morning. At noon dined in haste, and so my wife, Mrs. Barbary, Mercer, and I by coach to Hales's, where I find my wife's picture now perfectly finished in all respects, and a beautiful picture it is, as almost I ever saw. I sat again, and had a great deale done, but, whatever the matter is, I do not fancy that it has the ayre of my face, though it will be a very fine picture. Thence home and to my business, being post night, and so home to supper and to, bed.

21st. Up betimes, and first by coach to my Lord Generall to visitt him, and then to the Duke of Yorke, where we all met and did our usual business with him; but, Lord! how everything is yielded to presently, even by Sir W. Coventry, that is propounded by the Duke, as now to have

Troutbecke, his old surgeon, and intended to go Surgeon-General of the fleete, to go Physician-General of the fleete, of which there never was any precedent in the world, and he for that to have L20 per month. Thence with Lord Bruncker to Sir Robert Long, whom we found in his closett, and after some discourse of business he fell to discourse at large and pleasant, and among other things told us of the plenty of partridges in France, where he says the King of France and his company killed with their guns, in the plain de Versailles, 300 and odd partridges at one bout. Thence I to the Excise Office behind the 'Change, and there find our business of our tallys in great disorder as to payment, and thereupon do take a resolution of thinking how to remedy it, as soon as I can. Thence home, and there met Sir W. Warren, and after I had eat a bit of victuals (he staying in the office) he and I to White Hall. He to look after the business of the prize ships which we are endeavouring to buy, and hope to get money by them. So I to London by coach and to Gresham College, where I staid half an houre, and so away home to my office, and there walking late alone in the darke in the garden with Sir W. Warren, who tells me that at the Committee of the Lords for the prizes to-day, there passed very high words between my Lord Ashly and Sir W. Coventry, about our business of the prize ships. And that my Lord Ashly did snuff and talk as high to him, as he used to do to any ordinary seaman. And that Sir W. Coventry did take it very quietly, but yet for all did speak his mind soberly and with reason, and went away, saying, he had done his duty therein, and so left it to them, whether they would let so many ships go for masts or not: Here he and I talked of 1,000 businesses, all profitable discourse, and late parted, and I home to supper and to bed, troubled a little at a letter from my father, telling me how [he] is like to be sued for a debt of Tom's, by Smith, the mercer.

22nd. Up, and to the office all the morning. At noon my wife being gone to her father's I dined with Sir W. Batten, he inviting me. After dinner to my office close, and did very much business, and so late home to supper and to bed. The plague increased four this week, which troubles me, though but one in the whole.

23rd. Up, and going out of my dressing-room, when ready to go down stairs, I spied little Mrs. Tooker, my pretty little girle, which, it seems, did come yesterday to our house to stay a little while with us, but I did not know of it till now. I was glad of her coming, she being a very pretty child, and now grown almost a woman. I out by six o'clock by appointment to Hales's, where we fell to my picture presently very hard, and it comes on a very fine picture, and very merry, pleasant discourse we had all the morning while he was painting. Anon comes my wife and Mercer and little Tooker, and having done with me we all to a picture drawer's hard by, Hales carrying me to see some landskipps of a man's doing. But I do not [like] any of them, save only a piece of fruit, which indeed was very fine. Thence I to Westminster, to the Chequer, about a little business, and then to the Swan, and there sent for a bit of meat and dined; and after dinner had opportunity of being pleased with Sarah; and so away to Westminster Hall, and there Mrs. Michell tells me with great joy how little Betty Howlett is married to her young son Michell, which is a pretty odd thing, that he should so soon succeed in the match to his elder brother that died of the plague, and to the house and trade intended for him, and more they say that the girle has heretofore said that she did love this little one more than the other brother that was intended her all along. I am mighty glad of this match, and more that they are likely to live near me in Thames Streete, where I may see Betty now and then, whom I from a girle did use to call my second wife, and mighty pretty she is. Thence by coach to Anthony Joyce to receive Harman's answer, which did trouble me to receive, for he now demands L800, whereas he never made exception at the portion, but accepted of L500. This I do not like; but, however, I cannot much blame the man, if he thinks he can get more of another than of me. So home and hard to my business at the office, where much business, and so home to supper and to bed.

24th. Up and to the office, where all the morning. At noon home to dinner, where Anthony Joyce, and I did give my final answer, I would give but L500 with my sister, and did show him the good offer made us in the country, to which I did now more and more incline, and intend to pursue that. After dinner I to White Hall to a Committee for Tangier, where the Duke of Yorke was, and I acquitted myself well in what I had to do. After the Committee up, I had occasion to follow the Duke into his lodgings, into a chamber where the Duchesse was sitting to have her picture drawn by Lilly, who was there at work. But I was well pleased to see that there was nothing near so much resemblance of her face in his work, which is now the second, if not the third time, as there was of my wife's at the very first time. Nor do I think at last it can be like, the lines not being in proportion to those of her face. So home, and to the office, where late, and so to bed.

25th (Lady day and Sunday). Up, and to my chamber in my gowne all the morning about settling my papers there. At noon to dinner, where my wife's brother, whom I sent for to offer making him a Muster-Master and send to sea, which the poore man likes well of and will go, and it will be a good preferment to him, only hazardous. I hope he will prove a good discreet man. After dinner to my papers and Tangier accounts again till supper, and after supper again to them, but by my mixing them, I know not how, my private and publique accounts, it makes me mad to see how hard it is to bring them to be understood, and my head is confounded, that though I did sweare to sit up till one o'clock upon them, yet, I fear, it will be to no purpose, for I cannot understand what I do or have been doing of them to-day.

26th. Up, and a meeting extraordinary there was of Sir W. Coventry, Lord Bruncker, and myself, about the business of settling the ticket office, where infinite room is left for abusing the King in the wages of seamen. Our [meeting] being done, my Lord Bruncker and I to the Tower, to see the famous engraver, to get him to grave a seale for the office. And did see some of the finest pieces of work in embossed work, that ever I did see in my life, for fineness and smallness of the images thereon, and I will carry my wife thither to shew them her. Here I also did see bars of gold melting, which was a fine sight. So with my Lord to the Pope's Head Taverne in Lumbard Streete to dine by appointment with Captain Taylor, whither Sir W. Coventry come to us, and were mighty merry, and I find reason to honour him every day more and more. Thence alone to Broade Street to Sir G. Carteret by his desire to confer with him, who is I find in great pain about the business of the office, and not a little, I believe, in fear of falling there, Sir W. Coventry having so great a pique against him, and herein I first learn an eminent instance how great a man this day, that nobody would think could be shaken, is the next overthrown, dashed out of countenance, and every small thing of irregularity in his business taken notice of, where nobody the other day durst cast an eye upon them, and next I see that he that the other day nobody durst come near is now as supple as a spaniel, and sends and speaks to me with great submission, and readily hears to advice. Thence home to the office, where busy late, and so home a little to my accounts publique and private, but could not get myself rightly to know how to dispose of them in order to passing.

27th. All the morning at the office busy. At noon dined at home, Mr. Cooke, our old acquaintance at my Lord Sandwich's, come to see and dine with me, but I quite out of humour, having many other and better things to thinke of. Thence to the office to settle my people's worke and then home to my publique accounts of Tangier, which it is strange by meddling with evening reckonings with Mr. Povy lately how I myself am become intangled therein, so that after all I could do, ready to breake my head and brains, I thought of another way, though not so perfect, yet the only one which this account is capable of. Upon this latter I sat up till past two in the morning and then to bed.

28th. Up, and with Creed, who come hither betimes to speake with me about his accounts, to White Hall by water, mighty merry in discourse, though I had been very little troubled with him, or did countenance it, having now, blessed be God! a great deale of good business to mind to better purpose than chatting with him. Waited on the Duke, after that walked with Sir W. Clerke into St. James's Parke, and by and by met with Mr. Hayes, Prince Rupert's Secretary, who are mighty, both, briske blades, but I fear they promise themselves more than they expect. Thence to the Cockpitt, and dined with a great deal of company at the Duke of Albemarle's, and a bad and dirty, nasty dinner. So by coach to Hales's, and there sat again, and it is become mighty like. Hither come my wife and Mercer brought by Mrs. Pierce and Knipp, we were mighty merry and the picture goes on the better for it. Thence set them down at Pierces, and we home, where busy and at my chamber till 12 at night, and so to bed. This night, I am told, the Queene of Portugall, the mother to our Queene, is lately dead, and newes brought of it hither this day.

29th. All the morning hard at the office. At noon dined and then out to Lumbard Streete, to look after the getting of some money that is lodged there of mine in Viner's hands, I having no mind to have it lie there longer. So back again and to the office, where and at home about publique and private business and accounts till past 12 at night, and so to bed. This day, poor Jane, my old, little Jane, came to us again, to my wife's and my great content, and we hope to take mighty pleasure in her, she having all the marks and qualities of a good and loving and honest servant, she coming by force away from the other place, where she hath lived ever since she went from us, and at our desire, her late mistresse having used all the stratagems she could to keepe her.

30th. My wife and I mighty pleased with Jane's coming to us again. Up, and away goes Alce, our cooke-mayde, a good servant, whom we loved and did well by her, and she an excellent servant, but would not bear being told of any faulte in the fewest and kindest words and would go away of her owne accord, after having given her mistresse warning fickly for a quarter of a yeare together. So we shall take another girle and make little Jane our cook, at least, make a trial of it. Up, and after much business I out to Lumbard Streete, and there received L2200 and brought it home; and, contrary to expectation, received L35 for the use of L2000 of it [for] a quarter of a year, where it hath produced me this profit, and hath been a convenience to me as to care and security of my house, and demandable at two days' warning, as this hath been. This morning Sir W. Warren come to me a second time about having L2000 of me upon his bills on the Act to enable him to pay for the ships he is buying, wherein I shall have considerable profit. I am loth to do it, but yet speaking with Colvill I do not see but I shall be able to do it and get money by it too. Thence home and eat one mouthful, and so to Hales's, and there sat till almost quite darke upon working my gowne, which I hired to be drawn in; an Indian gowne, and I do see all the reason to expect a most excellent picture of it. So home and to my private accounts in my chamber till past one in the morning, and so to bed, with my head full of thoughts for my evening of all my accounts tomorrow, the latter end of the month, in which God give me good issue, for I never was in such a confusion in my life and that in great sums.

31st All the morning at the office busy. At noon to dinner, and thence to the office and did my business there as soon as I could, and then home and to my accounts, where very late at them, but, Lord! what a deale of do I have to understand any part of them, and in short do what I could, I could not come to any understanding of them, but after I had throughly wearied myself, I was forced to go to bed and leave them much against my will and vowe too, but I hope God will forgive me, for I have sat up these four nights till past twelve at night to master them, but cannot. Thus ends this month, with my head and mind mighty full and disquiett because of my accounts, which I have let go too long, and confounded my publique with my private that I cannot come to any liquidating of them. However, I do see that I must be grown richer than I was by a good deale last month. Busy also I am in thoughts for a husband for my sister, and to that end my wife and I have determined that she shall presently go into the country to my father and mother, and consider of a proffer made them for her in the country, which, if she likes, shall go forward.

APRIL 1666

April 1st (Lord's day). Up and abroad, and by coach to Charing Cross, to wait on Sir Philip Howard; whom I found in bed: and he do receive me very civilly. My request was about suffering my wife's brother to go to sea, and to save his pay in the Duke's guards; which after a little difficulty he did with great respect agree to. I find him a very fine-spoken gentleman, and one of great parts, and very courteous. Much pleased with this visit I to White Hall, where I met Sir G. Downing, and to discourse with him an houre about the Exchequer payments upon the late Act, and informed myself of him thoroughly in my safety in lending L2000 to Sir W. Warren, upon an order of his upon the Exchequer for L2602 and I do purpose to do it. Thence meeting Dr. Allen, the physician, he and I and another walked in the Parke, a most pleasant warm day, and to the Queene's chappell; where I do not so dislike the musique. Here I saw on a post an invitation to all good Catholiques to pray for the soul of such a one departed this life. The Queene, I hear, do not yet hear of the death of her mother, she being in a course of physique, that they dare not tell it her. At noon by coach home, and there by invitation met my uncle and aunt Wight and their cozen Mary, and dined with me and very merry. After dinner my uncle and I abroad by coach to White Hall, up and down the house, and I did some business and thence with him and a gentleman he met with to my Lord Chancellor's new house, and there viewed it again and again and up to the top and I like it as well as ever and think it a most noble house. So all up and down my Lord St. Albans his new building and market-house, and the taverne under the market-house, looking to and again into every place of building, and so away and took coach and home, where to my accounts, and was at them till I could not hold open my eyes, and so to bed. I this afternoon made a visit to my Lady Carteret, whom I understood newly come to towne; and she took it mighty kindly, but I see her face and heart are dejected from the condition her husband's matters stand in. But I hope they will do all well enough. And I do comfort her as much as I can, for she is a noble lady.

2nd. Up, and to the office and thence with Mr. Gawden to Guildhall to see the bills and tallys there in the chamber (and by the way in the streete his new coach broke and we fain to take an old hackney). Thence to the Exchequer again to inform myself of some other points in the new Act in order to my lending Sir W. Warren L2000 upon an order of his upon the Act, which they all encourage me to. There walking with Mr. Gawden in Westminster Hall, he and I to talke from one business to another and at last to the marriage of his daughter. He told me the story of Creed's pretences to his daughter, and how he would not believe but she loved him, while his daughter was in great passion on the other hand against him. Thence to talke of his son Benjamin; and I propounded a match for him, and at last named my sister, which he embraces heartily, and speaking of the lowness of her portion, that it would be less than L1000, he tells me if every thing else agrees, he will out of what he means to give me yearly, make a portion for her shall cost me nothing more than I intend freely. This did mightily rejoice me and full of it did go with him to London to the 'Change; and there did much business and at the Coffee-house with Sir W. Warren, who very wisely did shew me that my matching my sister with Mr. Gawden would undo me in all my places, everybody suspecting me in all I do; and I shall neither be able to serve him, nor free myself from imputation of being of his faction, while I am placed for his severest check. I was convinced that it would be for neither of our interests to make this alliance, and so am quite off of it again, but with great satisfaction in the motion. Thence to the Crowne tavern behind the Exchange to meet with Cocke and Fenn and did so, and dined with them, and after dinner had the intent of our meeting, which was some private discourse with Fenn, telling him what I hear and think of his business, which he takes very kindly and says he will look about him. It was about his giving of ill language and answers to people that come to him about money and some other particulars. This morning Mrs. Barbary and little Mrs. Tooker went away homeward. Thence my wife by coach calling me at White Hall to visit my Lady Carteret, and she was not within. So to Westminster Hall, where I purposely tooke my wife well dressed into the Hall to see and be seen; and, among others, [met] Howlet's daughter, who is newly married, and is she I call wife, and one I love mightily. So to Broad Streete and there met my Lady and Sir G. Carteret, and sat and talked with them a good while and so home, and to my accounts which I cannot get through with. But at it till I grew drowsy, and so to bed mightily vexed that I can come to no better issue in my accounts.

3rd. Up, and Sir W. Warren with me betimes and signed a bond, and assigned his order on the Exchequer to a blank for me to fill and I did deliver him L1900. The truth is, it is a great venture to venture so much on the Act, but thereby I hedge in L300 gift for my service about some ships that he hath bought, prizes, and good interest besides, and his bond to repay me the money at six weeks' warning. So to the office, where busy all the morning. At noon home to dinner, and there my brother Balty dined with me and my wife, who is become a good serious man, and I hope to do him good being sending him a Muster-Master on one of the squadrons of the fleete. After dinner and he gone I to my accounts hard all the afternoon till it was quite darke, and I thank God I do come to bring them very fairly to make me worth L5,000 stocke in the world, which is a great mercy to me. Though I am a little troubled to find L50 difference between the particular account I make to myself of my profits and loss in each month and the account which I raise from my acquittances and money which I have at the end of every month in my chest and other men's hands. However I do well believe that I am effectually L5,000, the greatest sum I ever was in my life yet, and this day I have as I have said before agreed with Sir W. Warren and got of him L300 gift. At night a while to the office and then home and supped and to my accounts again till I was ready to sleepe, there being no pleasure to handle them, if they are not kept in good order. So to bed.

4th. Up, and with Sir W. Pen in his coach to White Hall, in his way talking simply and fondly as he used to do, but I find myself to slight him and his simple talke, I thank God, and that my condition will enable me to do it. Thence, after doing our business with the Duke of Yorke, with Captain Cocke home to the 'Change in his coach. He promises me presently a dozen of silver salts, and proposes a business for which he hath promised Mrs. Williams for my Lord Bruncker a set of plate shall cost him L500 and me the like, which will be a good business indeed. After done several businesses at the 'Change I home, and being washing day dined upon cold meate, and so abroad by coach to Hales's, and there sat till night, mightily pleased with my picture, which is now almost finished. So by coach home, it being the fast day and to my chamber and so after supper to bed, consulting how to send my wife into the country to advise about Pall's marriage, which I much desire, and my father too, and two or three offers are now in hand.

5th. Up, and before office time to Lumbard Streete, and there at Viner's was shewn the silver plates, made for Captain Cocke to present my Lord Bruncker; and I chose a dozen of the same weight to be bespoke for myself, which he told me yesterday he would give me on the same occasion. To the office, where the falsenesse and impertinencies of Sir W. Pen would make a man mad to think of. At noon would have avoided, but could not, dining with my Lord Bruncker and his mistresse with Captain Cocke at the Sun Taverne in Fish Streete, where a good dinner, but the woman do tire me, and indeed how simply my Lord Bruncker, who is otherwise a wise man, do proceed at the table in serving of Cocke, without any means of understanding in his proposal, or defence when proposed, would make a man think him a foole. After dinner home, where I find my wife hath on a sudden, upon notice of a coach going away to-morrow, taken a resolution of going in it to Brampton, we having lately thought it fit for her to go to satisfy herself and me in the nature of the fellow that is there proposed to my sister. So she to fit herself for her journey and I to the office all the afternoon till late, and so home and late putting notes to "It is decreed, nor shall thy fate, &c." and then to bed. The plague is, to our great grief, encreased nine this week, though decreased a few in the total. And this encrease runs through many parishes, which makes us much fear the next year.

6th. Up mighty betimes upon my wife's going this day toward Brampton. I could not go to the coach with her, but W. Hewer did and hath leave from me to go the whole day's journey with her. All the morning upon business at the office, and at noon dined, and Mrs. Hunt coming lent her L5 on her occasions and so carried her to Axe Yard end at Westminster and there left her, a good and understanding woman, and her husband I perceive thrives mightily in his business of the Excise. Thence to Mr. Hales and there sat, and my picture almost finished, which by the word of Mr. and Mrs. Pierce (who come in accidently) is mighty like, and I am sure I am mightily pleased both in the thing and the posture. Thence with them home a little, and so to White Hall and there met by agreement with Sir Stephen Fox and Mr. Ashburnham, and discoursed the business of our Excise tallys; the former being Treasurer of the guards, and the other Cofferer of the King's household. I benefitted much by their discourse. We come to no great conclusion upon our discourse, but parted, and I home, where all things, methinks, melancholy in the absence of my wife. This day great newes of the Swedes declaring for us against the Dutch, and, so far as that, I believe it. After a little supper to bed.

7th. Lay pretty long to-day, lying alone and thinking of several businesses. So up to the office and there till noon. Thence with my Lord Bruncker home by coach to Mrs. Williams's, where Bab. Allen and Dr. Charleton dined. Bab and I sang and were mighty merry as we could be there, where the rest of the company did not overplease. Thence took her by coach to Hales's, and there find Mrs. Pierce and her boy and Mary. She had done sitting the first time, and indeed her face is mighty like at first dash. Thence took them to the cakehouse, and there called in the coach for cakes and drank, and thence I carried them to my Lord Chancellor's new house to shew them that, and all mightily pleased, thence set each down at home, and so I home to the office, where about ten of the clock W. Hewer comes to me to tell me that he has left my wife well this morning at Bugden, which was great riding, and brings me a letter from her. She is very well got thither, of which I am heartily glad. After writing several letters, I home to supper and to bed. The Parliament of which I was afraid of their calling us of the Navy to an account of the expense of money and stores and wherein we were so little ready to give them a good answer [will soon meet]. The Bishop of Munster, every body says, is coming to peace with the Dutch, we having not supplied him with the money promised him.

8th (Lord's day). Up, and was in great trouble how to get a passage to White Hall, it raining, and no coach to be had. So I walked to the Old Swan, and there got a scull. To the Duke of Yorke, where we all met to hear the debate between Sir Thomas Allen and Mr. Wayth; the former complaining of the latter's ill usage of him at the late pay of his ship. But a very sorry poor occasion he had for it. The Duke did determine it with great judgement, chiding both, but encouraging Wayth to continue to be a check to all captains in any thing to the King's right. And, indeed, I never did see the Duke do any thing more in order, nor with more judgement than he did pass the verdict in this business. The Court full this morning of the newes of Tom Cheffin's death, the King's closett-keeper. He was well last night as ever, flaying at tables in the house, and not very ill this morning at six o'clock, yet dead before seven: they think, of an imposthume in his breast. But it looks fearfully among people nowadays, the plague, as we hear, encreasing every where again. To the Chappell, but could not get in to hear well. But I had the pleasure once in my life to see an Archbishop (this was of Yorke) in a pulpit. Then at a loss how to get home to dinner, having promised to carry Mrs. Hunt thither. At last got my Lord Hinchingbroke's coach, he staying at Court; and so took her up in Axe-yard, and home and dined. And good discourse of the old matters of the Protector and his family, she having a relation to them. The Protector

lives in France: spends about L500 per annum. Thence carried her home again and then to Court and walked over to St. James's Chappell, thinking to have heard a Jesuite preach, but come too late. So got a hackney and home, and there to business. At night had Mercer comb my head and so to supper, sing a psalm, and to bed.

9th. Up betimes, and with my Joyner begun the making of the window in my boy's chamber bigger, purposing it shall be a roome to eat and for having musique in. To the office, where a meeting upon extraordinary business, at noon to the 'Change about more, and then home with Creed and dined, and then with him to the Committee of Tangier, where I got two or three things done I had a mind to of convenience to me. Thence by coach to Mrs. Pierce's, and with her and Knipp and Mrs. Pierce's boy and girle abroad, thinking to have been merry at Chelsey; but being come almost to the house by coach near the waterside, a house alone, I think the Swan, a gentleman walking by called to us to tell us that the house was shut up of the sicknesse. So we with great affright turned back, being holden to the gentleman; and went away (I for my part in great disorder) for Kensington, and there I spent about 30s. upon the jades with great pleasure, and we sang finely and staid till about eight at night, the night coming on apace and so set them down at Pierce's, and so away home, where awhile with Sir W. Warren about business, and then to bed,

10th. Up betimes, and many people to me about business. To the office and there sat till noon, and then home and dined, and to the office again all the afternoon, where we sat all, the first time of our resolution to sit both forenoons and afternoons. Much business at night and then home, and though late did see some work done by the plasterer to my new window in the boy's chamber plastered. Then to supper, and after having my head combed by the little girle to bed. Bad news that the plague is decreased in the general again and two increased in the sickness.

11th. To White Hall, having first set my people to worke about setting me rails upon the leads of my wife's closett, a thing I have long designed, but never had a fit opportunity till now. After having done with the Duke of Yorke, I to Hales's, where there was nothing found to be done more to my picture, but the musique, which now pleases me mightily, it being painted true. Thence home, and after dinner to Gresham College, where a great deal of do and formality in choosing of the Council and Officers. I had three votes to be of the Council, who am but a stranger, nor expected any. So my Lord Bruncker being confirmed President I home, where I find to my great content my rails up upon my leads. To the office and did a little business, and then home and did a great jobb at my Tangier accounts, which I find are mighty apt to run into confusion, my head also being too full of other businesses and pleasures. This noon Bagwell's wife come to me to the office, after her being long at Portsmouth. After supper, and past 12 at night to bed.

12th. Up and to the office, where all the morning. At noon dined at home and so to my office again, and taking a turne in the garden my Lady Pen comes to me and takes me into her house, where I find her daughter and a pretty lady of her acquaintance, one Mrs. Lowder, sister, I suppose, of her servant Lowder's, with whom I, notwithstanding all my resolution to follow business close this afternoon, did stay talking and playing the foole almost all the afternoon, and there saw two or three foolish sorry pictures of her doing, but very ridiculous compared to what my wife do. She grows mighty homely and looks old. Thence ashamed at myself for this losse of time, yet not able to leave it, I to the office, where my Lord Bruncker come; and he and I had a little fray, he being, I find, a very peevish man, if he be denied what he expects, and very simple in his argument in this business (about signing a warrant for paying Sir Thos. Allen L1000 out of the groats); but we were pretty good friends before we parted, and so we broke up and I to the writing my letters by the post, and so home to supper and to bed.

13th. Up, being called up by my wife's brother, for whom I have got a commission from the Duke of Yorke for Muster-Master of one of the divisions, of which Harman is Rere-Admirall, of which I am glad as well as he. After I had acquainted him with it, and discoursed a little of it, I went forth and took him with me by coach to the Duke of Albemarle, who being not up, I took a walk with Balty into the Parke, and to the Queene's Chappell, it being Good Friday, where people were all upon their knees very silent; but, it seems, no masse this day. So back and waited on the Duke and received some commands of his, and so by coach to Mr. Hales's, where it is pretty strange to see that his second doing, I mean the second time of her sitting, is less like Mrs.

Pierce than the first, and yet I am confident will be most like her, for he is so curious that I do not see how it is possible for him to mistake. Here he and I presently resolved of going to White Hall, to spend an houre in the galleries there among the pictures, and we did so to my great satisfaction, he shewing me the difference in the payntings, and when I come more and more to distinguish and observe the workmanship, I do not find so many good things as I thought there was, but yet great difference between the works of some and others; and, while my head and judgment was full of these, I would go back again to his house to see his pictures, and indeed, though, I think, at first sight some difference do open, yet very inconsiderably but that I may judge his to be very good pictures. Here we fell into discourse of my picture, and I am for his putting out the Landskipp, though he says it is very well done, yet I do judge it will be best without it, and so it shall be put out, and be made a plain sky like my wife's picture, which will be very noble. Thence called upon an old woman in Pannier Ally to agree for ruling of some paper for me and she will do it pretty cheap. Here I found her have a very comely black mayde to her servant, which I liked very well. So home to dinner and to see my joiner do the bench upon my leads to my great content. After dinner I abroad to carry paper to my old woman, and so to Westminster Hall, and there beyond my intention or design did see and speak with Betty Howlett, at her father's still, and it seems they carry her to her own house to begin the world with her young husband on Monday next, Easter Monday. I please myself with the thoughts of her neighbourhood, for I love the girl mightily. Thence home, and thither comes Mr. Houblon and a brother, with whom I evened for the charter parties of their ships for Tangier, and paid them the third advance on their freight to full satisfaction, and so, they being gone, comes Creed and with him till past one in the morning, evening his accounts till my head aked and I was fit for nothing, however, coming at last luckily to see through and settle all to my mind, it did please me mightily, and so with my mind at rest to bed, and he with me and hard to sleep.

14th. Up about seven and finished our papers, he and I, and I delivered him tallys and some money and so away I to the office, where we sat all the morning. At noon dined at home and Creed with me, then parted, and I to the office, and anon called thence by Sir H. Cholmley and he and I to my chamber, and there settled our matters of accounts, and did give him tallys and money to clear him, and so he being gone and all these accounts cleared I shall be even with the King, so as to make a very clear and short account in a very few days, which pleases me very well. Here he and I discoursed a great while about Tangier, and he do convince me, as things are now ordered by my Lord Bellasses and will be by Norwood (men that do only mind themselves), the garrison will never come to any thing, and he proposes his owne being governor, which in truth I do think will do very well, and that he will bring it to something. He gone I to my office, where to write letters late, and then home and looked over a little more my papers of accounts lately passed, and so to bed.

15th (Easter Day). Up and by water to Westminster to the Swan to lay down my cloak, and there found Sarah alone, with whom after I had staid awhile I to White Hall Chapel, and there coming late could hear nothing of the Bishop of London's sermon. So walked into the Park to the Queene's chappell, and there heard a good deal of their mass, and some of their musique, which is not so contemptible, I think, as our people would make it, it pleasing me very well; and, indeed, better than the anthem I heard afterwards at White Hall, at my coming back. I staid till the King went down to receive the Sacrament, and stood in his closett with a great many others, and there saw him receive it, which I did never see the manner of before. But I do see very little difference between the degree of the ceremonies used by our people in the administration thereof, and that in the Roman church, saving that methought our Chappell was not so fine, nor the manner of doing it so glorious, as it was in the Queene's chappell. Thence walked to Mr. Pierces, and there dined, I alone with him and her and their children: very good company and good discourse, they being able to tell me all the businesses of the Court; the amours and the mad doings that are there; how for certain Mrs. Stewart do do everything with the King that a mistress should do; and that the King hath many bastard children that are known and owned, besides the Duke of Monmouth. After a great deale of this discourse I walked thence into the Parke with her little boy James with me, who is the wittiest boy and the best company in the world, and so back again through White Hall both coming and going, and people did generally take him to be my boy and some would aske me. Thence home to Mr. Pierce again; and he being gone forth, she and I and the children out by coach to Kensington, to where we were the other day, and with great pleasure stayed till night; and were mighty late getting home, the horses tiring and stopping at every twenty steps. By the way we discoursed of Mrs. Clerke, who, she says, is grown mighty high, fine, and proud, but tells me an odd story how Captain Rolt did see her the other day accost a gentleman in Westminster Hall and went with him, and he dogged them to Moorefields to a little blind bawdy house, and there staid watching three hours and they come not out, so could stay no longer but left them there, and he is sure it was she, he knowing her well and describing her very clothes to Mrs. Pierce, which she knows are what she wears. Seeing them well at home I homeward, but the horses at Ludgate Hill made a final stop; so there I 'lighted, and with a linke, it being about 10 o'clock, walked home, and after singing a Psalm or two and supped to bed.

16th. Up, and set my people, Mercer, W. Hewer, Tom and the girle at work at ruling and stitching my ruled book for the Muster-Masters, and I hard toward the settling of my Tangier accounts. At noon dined alone, the girl Mercer taking physique can eat nothing, and W. Hewer went forth to dinner. So up to my accounts again, and then comes Mrs. Mercer and fair Mrs. Turner, a neighbour of hers that my wife knows by their means, to visit me. I staid a great while with them, being taken with this pretty woman, though a mighty silly, affected citizen woman she is. Then I left them to come to me at supper anon, and myself out by coach to the old woman in Pannyer Alley for my ruled papers, and they are done, and I am much more taken with her black maid Nan. Thence further to Westminster, thinking to have met Mrs. Martin, but could not find her, so back and called at Kirton's to borrow 10s. to pay for my ruled papers, I having not money in my pocket enough to pay for them. But it was a pretty consideration that on this occasion I was considering where I could with most confidence in a time of need borrow 10s., and I protest I could not tell where to do it and with some trouble and fear did aske it here. So that God keepe me from want, for I shall be in a very bad condition to helpe myself if ever I should come to want or borrow. Thence called for my papers and so home, and there comes Mrs. Turner and Mercer and supped with me, and well pleased I was with their company, but especially Mrs. Turner's, she being a very pretty woman of person and her face pretty good, the colour of her haire very fine and light. They staid with me talking till about eleven o'clock and so home, W. Hewer, who supped with me, leading them home. So I to bed.

17th. Up, and to the office, where all the morning. At noon dined at home, my brother Balty with me, who is fitting himself to go to sea. So after dinner to my accounts and did proceed a good way in settling them, and thence to the office, where all the afternoon late, writing my letters and doing business, but, Lord! what a conflict I had with myself, my heart tempting me 1000 times to go abroad about some pleasure or other, notwithstanding the weather foule. However I reproached myself with my weaknesse in yielding so much my judgment to my sense, and prevailed with difficulty and did not budge, but stayed within, and, to my great content, did a great deale of business, and so home to supper and to bed. This day I am told that Moll Davis, the pretty girle, that sang and danced so well at the Duke's house, is dead.

18th. [Up] and by coach with Sir W. Batten and Sir Thos. Allen to White Hall, and there after attending the Duke as usual and there concluding of many things preparatory to the Prince and Generall's going to sea on Monday next, Sir W. Batten and Sir T. Allen and I to Mr. Lilly's, the painter's; and there saw the heads, some finished, and all begun, of the Flaggmen in the late great fight with the Duke of Yorke against the Dutch. The Duke of Yorke hath them done to hang in his chamber, and very finely they are done indeed. Here is the Prince's, Sir G. Askue's, Sir Thomas Teddiman's, Sir Christopher Mings, Sir Joseph Jordan, Sir William Barkeley, Sir Thomas Allen, and Captain Harman's, as also the Duke of Albemarle's; and will be my Lord Sandwich's, Sir W. Pen's, and Sir Jeremy Smith's. Being very well satisfied with this sight, and other good pictures hanging in the house, we parted, and I left them, and [to] pass away a little time went to the printed picture seller's in the way thence to the Exchange, and there did see great plenty of fine prints; but did not buy any, only a print of an old pillar in Rome made for a Navall Triumph,

which for the antiquity of the shape of ships, I buy and keepe. Thence to the Exchange, that is, the New Exchange, and looked over some play books and intend to get all the late new plays. So to Westminster, and there at the Swan got a bit of meat and dined alone; and so away toward King's Street, and spying out of my coach Jane that lived heretofore at Jevons, my barber's, I went a little further and stopped, and went on foot back, and overtook her, taking water at Westminster Bridge, and spoke to her, and she telling me whither she was going I over the water and met her at Lambeth, and there drank with her; she telling me how he that was so long her servant, did prove to be a married man, though her master told me (which she denies) that he had lain with her several times in his house. There left her 'sans essayer alcune cose con elle', and so away by boat to the 'Change, and took coach and to Mr. Hales, where he would have persuaded me to have had the landskipp stand in my picture, but I like it not and will have it otherwise, which I perceive he do not like so well, however is so civil as to say it shall be altered. Thence away to Mrs. Pierces, who was not at home, but gone to my house to visit me with Mrs. Knipp. I therefore took up the little girle Betty and my mayde Mary that now lives there and to my house, where they had been but were gone, so in our way back again met them coming back again to my house in Cornehill, and there stopped laughing at our pretty misfortunes, and so I carried them to Fish Streete, and there treated them with prawns and lobsters, and it beginning to grow darke we away, but the jest is our horses would not draw us up the Hill, but we were fain to 'light and stay till the coachman had made them draw down to the bottom of the Hill, thereby warming their legs, and then they came up cheerfully enough, and we got up and I carried them home, and coming home called at my paper ruler's and there found black Nan, which pleases me mightily, and having saluted her again and again away home and to bed..... In all my ridings in the coach and intervals my mind hath been full these three weeks of setting in musique "It is decreed, &c."

19th. Lay long in bed, so to the office, where all the morning. At noon dined with Sir W. Warren at the Pope's Head. So back to the office, and there met with the Commissioners of the Ordnance, where Sir W. Pen being almost drunk vexed me, and the more because Mr. Chichly observed it with me, and it was a disparagement to the office. They gone I to my office. Anon comes home my wife from Brampton, not looked for till Saturday, which will hinder me of a little pleasure, but I am glad of her coming. She tells me Pall's business with Ensum is like to go on, but I must give, and she consents to it, another 100. She says she doubts my father is in want of money, for rents come in mighty slowly. My mother grows very unpleasant and troublesome and my father mighty infirm through his old distemper, which altogether makes me mighty thoughtfull. Having heard all this and bid her welcome I to the office, where late, and so home, and after a little more talk with my wife, she to bed and I after her.

20th. Up, and after an houre or two's talke with my poor wife, who gives me more and more content every day than other, I abroad by coach to Westminster, and there met with Mrs. Martin, and she and I over the water to Stangold, and after a walke in the fields to the King's Head, and there spent an houre or two with pleasure with her, and eat a tansy and so parted, and I to the New Exchange, there to get a list of all the modern plays which I intend to collect and to have them bound up together. Thence to Mr. Hales's, and there, though against his particular mind, I had my landskipp done out, and only a heaven made in the roome of it, which though it do not please me thoroughly now it is done, yet it will do better than as it was before. Thence to Paul's Churchyarde, and there bespoke some new books, and so to my ruling woman's and there did see my work a doing, and so home and to my office a little, but was hindered of business I intended by being sent for to Mrs. Turner, who desired some discourse with me and lay her condition before me, which is bad and poor. Sir Thomas Harvey intends again to have lodgings in her house, which she prays me to prevent if I can, which I promised. Thence to talke generally of our neighbours. I find she tells me the faults of all of them, and their bad words of me and my wife, and indeed do discover more than I thought. So I told her, and so will practise that I will have nothing to do with any of them. She ended all with a promise of shells to my wife, very fine ones indeed, and seems to have great respect and honour for my wife. So home and to bed.

21st. Up betimes and to the office, there to prepare some things against the afternoon for discourse about the business of the pursers and settling the pursers' matters of the fleete according to my proposition. By and by the office sat, and they being up I continued at the office to finish my matters against the meeting before the Duke this afternoon, so home about three to clap a bit of meate in my mouth, and so away with Sir W. Batten to White Hall, and there to the Duke, but he being to go abroad to take the ayre, he dismissed us presently without doing any thing till to-morrow morning. So my Lord Bruncker and I down to walk in the garden [at White Hall], it being a mighty hot and pleasant day; and there was the King, who, among others, talked to us a little; and among other pretty things, he swore merrily that he believed the ketch that Sir W. Batten bought the last year at Colchester was of his own getting, it was so thick to its length. Another pleasant thing he said of Christopher Pett, commending him that he will not alter his moulds of his ships upon any man's advice; "as," says he, "Commissioner Taylor I fear do of his New London, that he makes it differ, in hopes of mending the Old London, built by him." "For," says he, "he finds that God hath put him into the right, and so will keep in it while he is in." "And," says the King, "I am sure it must be God put him in, for no art of his owne ever could have done it;" for it seems he cannot give a good account of what he do as an artist. Thence with my Lord Bruncker in his coach to Hide Parke, the first time I have been there this year. There the King was; but I was sorry to see my Lady Castlemaine, for the mourning forceing all the ladies to go in black, with their hair plain and without any spots, I find her to be a much more ordinary woman than ever I durst have thought she was; and, indeed, is not so pretty as Mrs. Stewart, whom I saw there also. Having done at the Park he set me down at the Exchange, and I by coach home and there to my letters, and they being done, to writing a large letter about the business of the pursers to Sir W. Batten against to-morrow's discourse, and so home and to bed.

22nd (Lord's day). Up, and put on my new black coate, long down to my knees, and with Sir W. Batten to White Hall, where all in deep mourning for the Queene's mother. There had great discourse, before the Duke and Sir W. Coventry begun the discourse of the day about the purser's business, which I seconded, and with great liking to the Duke, whom however afterward my Lord Bruncker and Sir W. Pen did stop by some thing they said, though not much to the purpose, yet because our proposition had some appearance of certain charge to the King it was ruled that for this year we should try another the same in every respect with ours, leaving out one circumstance of allowing the pursers the victuals of all men short of the complement. I was very well satisfied with it and am contented to try it, wishing it may prove effectual. Thence away with Sir W. Batten in his coach home, in our way he telling me the certaine newes, which was afterward confirmed to me this day by several, that the Bishopp of Munster has made a league [with] the Hollanders, and that our King and Court are displeased much at it: moreover we are not sure of Sweden. I home to my house, and there dined mighty well, my poor wife and Mercer and I. So back again walked to White Hall, and there to and again in the Parke, till being in the shoemaker's stockes.—[A cant expression for tight shoes.]—I was heartily weary, yet walked however to the Queene's Chappell at St. James's, and there saw a little mayde baptized; many parts and words whereof are the same with that of our Liturgy, and little that is more ceremonious than ours. Thence walked to Westminster and eat a bit of bread and drank, and so to Worster House, and there staid, and saw the Council up, and then back, walked to the Cockepitt, and there took my leave of the Duke of Albemarle, who is going to-morrow to sea. He seems mightily pleased with me, which I am glad of; but I do find infinitely my concernment in being careful to appear to the King and Duke to continue my care of his business, and to be found diligent as I used to be. Thence walked wearily as far as Fleet Streete and so there met a coach and home to supper and to bed, having sat a great while with Will Joyce, who come to see me, and it is the first time I have seen him at my house since the plague, and find him the same impertinent, prating coxcombe that ever he was.

23rd. Being mighty weary last night, lay long this morning, then up and to the office, where Sir W. Batten, Lord Bruncker and I met, and toward noon took coach and to White Hall, where I had the opportunity to take leave of the Prince, and again of the Duke of Albemarle; and saw them kiss the King's hands and the Duke's; and much content, indeed, there seems to be in all people at their going to sea, and [they] promise themselves much good from them. This morning the House of Parliament do meet, only to adjourne again till winter. The plague, I hear, encreases in the towne much, and exceedingly in the country everywhere. Thence walked to Westminster Hall, and after a little stay, there being nothing now left to keep me there, Betty Howlett being gone, I took coach and away home, in my way asking in two or three places the worth of pearles, I being now come to the time that I have long ago promised my wife a necklace. Dined at home and took Balty with me to Hales's to show him his sister's picture, and thence to Westminster, and there I to the Swan and drank, and so back again alone to Hales's and there met my wife and Mercer, Mrs. Pierce being sitting, and two or three idle people of her acquaintance more standing by. Her picture do come on well. So staid until she had done and then set her down at home, and my wife and I and the girle by coach to Islington, and there eat and drank in the coach and so home, and there find a girle sent at my desire by Mrs. Michell of Westminster Hall, to be my girle under the cooke-mayde, Susan. But I am a little dissatisfied that the girle, though young, is taller and bigger than Su, and will not, I fear, be under her command, which will trouble me, and the more because she is recommended by a friend that I would not have any unkindness with, but my wife do like very well of her. So to my accounts and journall at my chamber, there being bonfires in the streete, for being St. George's day, and the King's Coronation, and the day of the Prince and Duke's going to sea. So having done my business, to bed.

24th. Up, and presently am told that the girle that came yesterday hath packed up her things to be gone home again to Enfield, whence she come, which I was glad of, that we might be at first rid of her altogether rather than be liable to her going away hereafter. The reason was that London do not agree with her. So I did give her something, and away she went. By and by comes Mr. Bland to me, the first time since his coming from Tangier, and tells me, in short, how all things are out of order there, and like to be; and the place never likely to come to anything while the soldiers govern all, and do not encourage trade. He gone I to the office, where all the morning, and so to dinner, and there in the afternoon very busy all day till late, and so home to supper and to bed.

25th. Up, and to White Hall to the Duke as usual, and did our business there. So I away to Westminster (Batty with me, whom I had presented to Sir W. Coventry) and there told Mrs.

Michell of her kinswoman's running away, which troubled her. So home, and there find another little girle come from my wife's mother, likely to do well. After dinner I to the office, where Mr. Prin come to meet about the Chest business; and till company come, did discourse with me a good while alone in the garden about the laws of England, telling me the many faults in them; and among others, their obscurity through multitude of long statutes, which he is about to abstract out of all of a sort; and as he lives, and Parliaments come, get them put into laws, and the other statutes repealed, and then it will be a short work to know the law, which appears a very noble good thing. By and by Sir W. Batten and Sir W. Rider met with us, and we did something to purpose about the Chest, and hope we shall go on to do so. They up, I to present Batty to Sir W. Pen, who at my entreaty did write a most obliging letter to Harman to use him civilly, but the dissembling of the rogue is such, that it do not oblige me at all. So abroad to my ruler's of my books, having, God forgive me! a mind to see Nan there, which I did, and so back again, and then out again to see Mrs. Bettons, who were looking out of the window as I come through Fenchurch Streete. So that indeed I am not, as I ought to be, able to command myself in the pleasures of my eye. So home, and with my wife and Mercer spent our evening upon our new leads by our bedchamber singing, while Mrs. Mary Batelier looked out of the window to us, and we talked together, and at last bid good night. However, my wife and I staid there talking of several things with great pleasure till eleven o'clock at night, and it is a convenience I would not want for any thing in the world, it being, methinks, better than almost any roome in my house. So having, supped upon the leads, to bed. The plague, blessed be God! is decreased sixteen this week.

26th. To the office, where all the morning. At noon home to dinner, and in the afternoon to my office again, where very busy all the afternoon and particularly about fitting of Mr. Yeabsly's accounts for the view of the Lords Commissioners for Tangier. At night home to supper and to bed.

27th. Up (taking Balty with me, who lay at my house last [night] in order to his going away to-day to sea with the pursers of the Henery, whom I appointed to call him), abroad to many several places about several businesses, to my Lord Treasurer's, Westminster, and I know not where. At noon to the 'Change a little, and there bespoke some maps to hang in my new roome (my boy's roome) which will be very-pretty. Home to dinner, and after dinner to the hanging up of maps, and other things for the fitting of the roome, and now it will certainly be one of the handsomest and most usefull roomes in my house. So that what with this room and the room on my leads my house is half as good again as it was. All this afternoon about this till I was so weary and it was late I could do no more but finished the room. So I did not get out to the office all the day long. At night spent a good deale of time with my wife and Mercer teaching them a song, and so after supper to bed.

28th. Up and to the office. At noon dined at home. After dinner abroad with my wife to Hales's to see only our pictures and Mrs. Pierce's, which I do not think so fine as I might have expected it. My wife to her father's, to carry him some ruling work, which I have advised her to let him do. It will get him some money. She also is to look out again for another little girle, the last we had being also gone home the very same day she came. She was also to look after a necklace of pearle, which she is mighty busy about, I being contented to lay out L80 in one for her. I home to my business. By and by comes my wife and presently after, the tide serving, Balty took leave of us, going to sea, and upon very good terms, to be Muster-Master of a squadron, which will be worth L100 this yeare to him, besides keeping him the benefit of his pay in the Guards. He gone, I very busy all the afternoon till night, among other things, writing a letter to my brother John, the first I have done since my being angry with him, and that so sharpe a one too that I was sorry almost to send it when I had wrote it, but it is preparatory to my being kind to him, and sending for him up hither when he hath passed his degree of Master of Arts. So home to supper and to bed.

29th (Lord's day). Up, and to church, where Mr. Mills, a lazy, simple sermon upon the Devil's having no right to any thing in this world. So home to dinner, and after dinner I and my boy down by water to Redriffe and thence walked to Mr. Evelyn's, where I walked in his garden till he come from Church, with great pleasure reading Ridly's discourse, all my way going and coming, upon the Civill and Ecclesiastical Law. He being come home, he and I walked together in the garden with mighty pleasure, he being a very ingenious man; and the more I know him, the more I love him. His chief business with me was to propose having my cozen Thomas Pepys in Commission of the Peace, which I do not know what to say to till I speake with him, but should be glad of it and will put him upon it. Thence walked back again reading and so took water and home, where I find my uncle and aunt Wight, and supped with them upon my leads with mighty pleasure and mirthe, and they being gone I mighty weary to bed, after having my haire of my head cut shorter, even close to my skull, for coolnesse, it being mighty hot weather.

30th. Up and, being ready, to finish my journall for four days past. To the office, where busy all the morning. At noon dined alone, my wife gone abroad to conclude about her necklace of pearle. I after dinner to even all my accounts of this month; and, bless God! I find myself, notwithstanding great expences of late; viz. L80 now to pay for a necklace; near L40 for a set of chairs and couch; near L40 for my three pictures: yet I do gather, and am now worth L5200. My wife comes home by and by, and hath pitched upon a necklace with three rows, which is a very good one, and L80 is the price. In the evening, having finished my accounts to my full content and joyed that I have evened them so plainly, remembering the trouble my last accounts did give me by being let alone a little longer than ordinary, by which I am to this day at a loss for L50, I hope I shall never commit such an error again, for I cannot devise where the L50 should be, but it is plain I ought to be worth L50 more than I am, and blessed be God the error was no greater. In the evening with my [wife] and Mercer by coach to take the ayre as far as Bow, and eat and drank in the coach by the way and with much pleasure and pleased with my company. At night home and up to the leads, but were contrary to expectation driven down again with a stinke by Sir W. Pen's shying of a shitten pot in their house of office close by, which do trouble me for fear it do hereafter annoy me. So down to sing a little and then to bed. So ends this month with great layings-out. Good health and gettings, and advanced well in the whole of my estate, for which God make me thankful.

May 1st. Up, and all the morning at the office. At noon, my cozen Thomas Pepys did come to me, to consult about the business of his being a justice of the Peace, which he is much against; and among other reasons, tells me, as a confidant, that he is not free to exercise punishment according to the Act against Quakers and other people, for religion. Nor do he understand Latin, and so is not capable of the place as formerly, now all warrants do run in Latin. Nor is he in Kent, though he be of Deptford parish, his house standing in Surry. However, I did bring him to incline towards it, if he be pressed to take it. I do think it may be some repute to me to have my kinsman in Commission there, specially if he behave himself to content in the country. He gone and my wife gone abroad, I out also to and fro, to see and be seen, among others to find out in Thames Streete where Betty Howlett is come to live, being married to Mrs. Michell's son; which I did about the Old Swan, but did not think fit to go thither or see them. Thence by water to Redriffe, reading a new French book my Lord Bruncker did give me to-day, "L'Histoire Amoureuse des Gaules,"

being a pretty libel against the amours of the Court of France. I walked up and down Deptford yarde, where I had not been since I come from living at Greenwich, which is some months. There I met with Mr. Castle, and was forced against my will to have his company back with me. So we walked and drank at Halfway house and so to his house, where I drank a cupp of syder, and so home, where I find Mr. Norbury newly come to town to see us. After he gone my wife tells me the ill newes that our Susan is sicke and gone to bed, with great pain in her head and back, which troubles us all. However we to bed expecting what to-morrow would produce. She hath we conceive wrought a little too much, having neither maid nor girle to help her.

2nd. Up and find the girle better, which we are glad of, and with Sir W. Batten to White Hall by coach. There attended the Duke as usual. Thence with Captain Cocke, whom I met there, to London, to my office, to consult about serving him in getting him some money, he being already tired of his slavery to my Lord Bruncker, and the charge it costs him, and gets no manner of courtesy from him for it. He gone I home to dinner, find the girle yet better, so no fear of being forced to send her out of doors as we intended. After dinner. I by water to White Hall to a Committee for Tangier upon Mr. Yeabsly's business, which I got referred to a Committee to examine. Thence among other stops went to my ruler's house, and there staid a great while with Nan idling away the afternoon with pleasure. By and by home, so to my office a little, and then home to supper with my wife, the girle being pretty well again, and then to bed.

3rd. Up, and all the morning at the office. At noon home, and contrary to my expectation find my little girle Su worse than she was, which troubled me, and the more to see my wife minding her paynting and not thinking of her house business, this being the first day of her beginning the second time to paynt. This together made me froward that I was angry with my wife, and would not have Browne to think to dine at my table with me always, being desirous to have my house to myself without a stranger and a mechanique to be privy to all my concernments. Upon this my wife and I had a little disagreement, but it ended by and by, and then to send up and down for a nurse to take the girle home and would have given anything. I offered to the only one that we could get 20s. per weeke, and we to find clothes, and bedding and physique, and would have given 30s., as demanded, but desired an houre or two's time. So I away by water to Westminster, and there sent for the girle's mother to Westminster Hall to me; she came and undertakes to get her daughter a lodging and nurse at next doore to her, though she dare not, for the parish's sake, whose sexton her husband is, to [have] her into her owne house. Thence home, calling at my bookseller's and other trifling places, and in the evening the mother come and with a nurse she has got, who demanded and I did agree at 10s. per weeke to take her, and so she away, and my house mighty uncouth, having so few in it, and we shall want a servant or two by it, and the truth is my heart was a little sad all the afternoon and jealous of myself. But she went, and we all glad of it, and so a little to the office, and so home to supper and to bed.

4th. Up and by water to Westminster to Charing Cross (Mr. Gregory for company with me) to Sir Ph. Warwicke's, who was not within. So I took Gregory to White Hall, and there spoke with Joseph Williamson to have leave in the next Gazette to have a general pay for the Chest at Chatham declared upon such a day in June. Here I left Gregory, and I by coach back again to Sir Philip Warwicke's, and in the Park met him walking, so discoursed about the business of striking a quarter's tallys for Tangier, due this day, which he hath promised to get my Lord Treasurer's warrant for, and so away hence, and to Mr. Hales, to see what he had done to Mrs. Pierces picture, and whatever he pretends, I do not think it will ever be so good a picture as my wife's. Thence home to the office a little and then to dinner, and had a great fray with my wife again about Browne's coming to teach her to paynt, and sitting with me at table, which I will not yield to. I do thoroughly believe she means no hurte in it; but very angry we were, and I resolved all into my having my will done, without disputing, be the reason what it will; and so I will have it. After dinner abroad again and to the New Exchange about play books, and to White Hall, thinking to have met Sir G. Carteret, but failed. So to the Swan at Westminster, and there spent a quarter of an hour with Jane, and thence away home, and my wife coming home by and by (having been at her mother's to pray her to look out for a mayde for her) by coach into the fields to Bow, and so home back in the evening, late home, and after supper to bed, being much out of order for lack of somebody in the room of Su. This evening, being weary of my late idle courses, and the little good I shall do the King or myself in the office, I bound myself to very strict rules till Whitsunday next.

5th. At the office all the morning. After dinner upon a letter from the fleete from Sir W. Coventry I did do a great deale of worke for the sending away of the victuallers that are in the river, &c., too much to remember. Till 10 at night busy about letters and other necessary matter of the office. About 11 home, it being a fine moonshine and so my wife and Mercer come into the garden, and, my business being done, we sang till about twelve at night, with mighty pleasure to ourselves and neighbours, by their casements opening, and so home to supper and to bed.

6th (Lord's day). To church. Home, and after dinner walked to White Hall, thinking to have seen Mr. Coventry, but failed, and therefore walked clear on foot back again. Busy till night in fitting my Victualling papers in order, which I through my multitude of business and pleasure have not examined these several months. Walked back again home, and so to the Victualling Office, where I met Mr. Gawden, and have received some satisfaction, though it be short of what I expected, and what might be expected from me. So after evened I have gone, and so to supper and to bed.

7th. Up betimes to set my Victualling papers in order against Sir W. Coventry comes, which indeed makes me very melancholy, being conscious that I am much to seeke in giving a good answer to his queries about the Victualling business. At the office mighty busy, and brought myself into a pretty plausible condition before Sir W. Coventry come, and did give him a pretty tolerable account of every thing and went with him into the Victualling office, where we sat and examined his businesses and state of the victualling of the fleete, which made me in my heart blushe that I could say no more to it than I did or could. But I trust in God I shall never be in that condition again. We parted, and I with pretty good grace, and so home to dinner, where my wife troubled more and more with her swollen cheek. So to dinner, my sister-in-law with us, who I find more and more a witty woman; and then I to my Lord Treasurer's and the Exchequer about my Tangier businesses, and with my content passed by all things and persons without so much as desiring any stay or loss of time with them, being by strong vowe obliged on no occasion to stay abroad but my publique offices. So home again, where I find Mrs. Pierce and Mrs. Ferrers come to see my wife. I staid a little with them, being full of business, and so to the office, where busy till late at night and so weary and a little conscious of my failures to-day, yet proud that the day is over without more observation on Sir W. Coventry's part, and so to bed and to sleepe soundly.

8th. Up, and to the office all the morning. At noon dined at home, my wife's cheek bad still. After dinner to the office again and thither comes Mr. Downing, the anchor-smith, who had given me 50 pieces in gold the last month to speake for him to Sir W. Coventry, for his being smith at Deptford; but after I had got it granted to him, he finds himself not fit to go on with it, so lets it fall. So has no benefit of my motion. I therefore in honour and conscience took him home the money, and, though much to my grief, did yet willingly and forcibly force him to take it again, the poor man having no mind to have it. However, I made him take it, and away he went, and I glad to have given him so much cause to speake well of me. So to my office again late, and then home to supper to a good lobster with my wife, and then a little to my office again, and so to bed.

9th. Up by five o'clock, which I have not a long time done, and down the river by water to Deptford, among other things to examine the state of Ironworke, in order to the doing something with reference to Downing that may induce him to returne me the 50 pieces. Walked back again reading of my Civill Law Book, and so home and by coach to White Hall, where we did our usual business before the Duke, and heard the Duke commend Deane's ship "The Rupert" before "The Defyance," built lately by Castle, in hearing of Sir W. Batten, which pleased me mightily. Thence by water to Westminster, and there looked after my Tangier order, and so by coach to Mrs. Pierces, thinking to have gone to Hales's, but she was not ready, so away home and to dinner, and after dinner out by coach to Lovett's to have forwarded what I have doing there, but find him and his pretty wife gone to my house to show me something. So away to my Lord

Treasurer's, and thence to Pierces, where I find Knipp, and I took them to Hales's to see our pictures finished, which are very pretty, but I like not hers half so well as I thought at first, it being not so like, nor so well painted as I expected, or as mine and my wife's are. Thence with them to Cornhill to call and choose a chimney-piece for Pierces closett, and so home, where my wife in mighty pain and mightily vexed at my being abroad with these women; and when they were gone called them whores and I know not what, which vexed me, having been so innocent with them. So I with them to Mrs. Turner's and there sat with them a while, anon my wife sends for me, I come, and what was it but to scold at me and she would go abroad to take the ayre presently, that she would. So I left my company and went with her to Bow, but was vexed and spoke not one word to her all the way going nor coming, or being come home, but went up straight to bed. Half an hour after (she in the coach leaning on me as being desirous to be friends) she comes up mighty sicke with a fit of the cholique and in mighty pain and calls for me out of the bed; I rose and held her, she prays me to forgive her, and in mighty pain we put her to bed, where the pain ceased by and by, and so had some asparagus to our bed side for supper and very kindly afterward to sleepe and good friends in the morning.

10th. So up, and to the office, where all the morning. At noon home to dinner and there busy all the afternoon till past six o'clock, and then abroad with my wife by coach, who is now at great ease, her cheeke being broke inward. We took with us Mrs. Turner, who was come to visit my wife just as we were going out. A great deale of tittle tattle discourse to little purpose, I finding her, though in other things a very discreete woman, as very a gossip speaking of her neighbours as any body. Going out towards Hackney by coach for the ayre, the silly coachman carries us to Shoreditch, which was so pleasant a piece of simplicity in him and us, that made us mighty merry. So back again late, it being wondrous hot all the day and night and it lightning exceeding all the way we went and came, but without thunder. Coming home we called at a little ale-house, and had an eele pye, of which my wife eat part and brought home the rest. So being come home we to supper and to bed. This day come our new cook maid Mary, commended by Mrs. Batters.

11th. Up betimes, and then away with Mr. Yeabsly to my Lord Ashly's, whither by and by comes Sir H. Cholmly and Creed, and then to my Lord, and there entered into examination of Mr. Yeabsly's accounts, wherein as in all other things I find him one of the most distinct men that ever I did see in my life. He raised many scruples which were to be answered another day and so parted, giving me an alarme how to provide myself against the day of my passing my accounts. Thence I to Westminster to look after the striking of my tallys, but nothing done or to be done therein. So to the 'Change, to speake with Captain Cocke, among other things about getting of the silver plates of him, which he promises to do; but in discourse he tells me that I should beware of my fellow-officers; and by name told me that my Lord Bruncker should say in his hearing, before Sir W. Batten, of me, that he could undo the man, if he would; wherein I think he is a foole; but, however, it is requisite I be prepared against the man's friendship. Thence home to dinner alone, my wife being abroad. After dinner to the setting some things in order in my dining-room; and by and by comes my wife home and Mrs. Pierce with her, so I lost most of this afternoon with them, and in the evening abroad with them, our long tour by coach, to

Hackney, so to Kingsland, and then to Islington, there entertaining them by candlelight very well, and so home with her, set her down, and so home and to bed.

12th. Up to the office very betimes to draw up a letter for the Duke of Yorke relating to him the badness of our condition in this office for want of money. That being in good time done we met at the office and there sat all the morning. At noon home, where I find my wife troubled still at my checking her last night in the coach in her long stories out of Grand Cyrus, which she would tell, though nothing to the purpose, nor in any good manner.

This she took unkindly, and I think I was to blame indeed; but she do find with reason, that in the company of Pierce, Knipp, or other women that I love, I do not value her, or mind her as I ought. However very good friends by and by, and to dinner, and after dinner up to the putting our dining room in order, which will be clean again anon, but not as it is to be because of the pictures which are not come home. To the office and did much business, in the evening to Westminster and White Hall about business and among other things met Sir G. Downing on White Hall bridge, and there walked half an hour, talking of the success of the late new Act; and indeed it is very much, that that hath stood really in the room of L800,000 now since Christmas, being itself but L1,250,000. And so I do really take it to be a very considerable thing done by him; for the beginning, end, and every part of it, is to be imputed to him. So home by water, and there hard till 12 at night at work finishing the great letter to the Duke of Yorke against to-morrow morning, and so home to bed. This day come home again my little girle Susan, her sicknesse proving an ague, and she had a fit soon almost as she come home. The fleete is not yet gone from the Nore. The plague encreases in many places, and is 53 this week with us.

13th (Lord's day). Up, and walked to White Hall, where we all met to present a letter to the Duke of Yorke, complaining solemnly of the want of money, and that being done, I to and again up and down Westminster, thinking to have spent a little time with Sarah at the Swan, or Mrs. Martin, but was disappointed in both, so walked the greatest part of the way home, where comes Mr. Symons, my old acquaintance, to dine with me, and I made myself as good company as I could to him, but he was mighty impertinent methought too yet, and thereby I see the difference between myself now and what it was heretofore, when I reckoned him a very brave fellow. After dinner he and I walked together as far as Cheapside, and I quite through to Westminster again, and fell by chance into St. Margett's' Church, where I heard a young man play the foole upon the doctrine of purgatory. At this church I spied Betty Howlett, who indeed is mighty pretty, and struck me mightily. After church time, standing in the Church yarde, she spied me, so I went to her, her father and mother and husband being with her. They desired and I agreed to go home with Mr. Michell, and there had the opportunity to have saluted two or three times Betty and make an acquaintance which they are pleased with, though not so much as I am or they think I am. I staid here an houre or more chatting with them in a little sorry garden of theirs by the Bowling Alley, and so left them and I by water home, and there was in great pain in mind lest Sir W. Pen, who is going down to the Fleete, should come to me or send for me to be informed in the state of things, and particularly the Victualling, that by my pains he might seem wise. So after spending an houre with my wife pleasantly in her closett, I to bed even by daylight.

14th. Comes betimes a letter from Sir W. Coventry, that he and Sir G. Carteret are ordered presently down to the Fleete. I up and saw Sir W. Pen gone also after them, and so I finding it a leisure day fell to making cleane my closett in my office, which I did to my content and set up my Platts again, being much taken also with Griffin's mayde, that did cleane it, being a pretty mayde. I left her at it, and toward Westminster myself with my wife by coach and meeting took up Mr. Lovett the varnisher with us, who is a pleasant speaking and humoured man, so my wife much taken with him, and a good deale of worke I believe I shall procure him. I left my wife at the New Exchange and myself to the Exchequer, to looke after my Tangier tallys, and there met Sir G. Downing, who shewed me his present practise now begun this day to paste up upon the Exchequer door a note of what orders upon the new Act are paid and now in paying, and my Lord of Oxford coming by, also took him, and shewed him his whole method of keeping his books, and everything of it, which indeed is very pretty, and at this day there is assigned upon the Act L804,000. Thence at the New Exchange took up my wife again, and so home to dinner, and after dinner to my office again to set things in order. In the evening out with my wife and my aunt Wight, to take the ayre, and happened to have a pleasant race between our hackney-coach and a gentleman's. At Bow we eat and drank and so back again, it being very cool in the evening. Having set home my aunt and come home, I fell to examine my wife's kitchen book, and find 20s. mistake, which made me mighty angry and great difference between us, and so in the difference to bed.

15th. Up and to the office, where we met and sat all the morning. At noon home to dinner, and after dinner by coach to Sir Philip Warwicke's, he having sent for me, but was not within, so I to my Lord Crew's, who is very lately come to towne, and with him talking half an houre of the business of the warr, wherein he is very doubtful, from our want of money, that we shall fail. And I do concur with him therein. After some little discourse of ordinary matters, I away to Sir Philip Warwicke's again, and was come in, and gone out to my Lord Treasurer's; whither I followed him, and there my business was, to be told that my Lord Treasurer hath got L10,000 for us in the Navy, to answer our great necessities, which I did thank him for; but the sum is not considerable. So home, and there busy all the afternoon till night, and then home to supper and to bed.

16th. Up very betimes, and so down the river to Deptford to look after some business, being by and by to attend the Duke and Mr. Coventry, and so I was wiling to carry something fresh that I may look as a man minding business, which I have done too much for a great while to forfeit, and is now so great a burden upon my mind night and day that I do not enjoy myself in the world almost. I walked thither, and come back again by water, and so to White Hall, and did our usual business before the Duke, and so to the Exchequer, where the lazy rogues have not yet done my tallys, which vexes me. Thence to Mr. Hales, and paid him for my picture, and Mr. Hill's, for the first L14 for the picture, and 25s. for the frame, and for the other L7 for the picture, it being a copy of his only, and 5s. for the frame; in all, L22 10s. I am very well satisfied in my pictures, and so took them in another coach home along with me, and there with great pleasure my wife and I hung them up, and, that being done, to dinner, where Mrs. Barbara Sheldon come to see us and dined with us, and we kept her all the day with us, I going down to Deptford, and, Lord! to see with what itching desire I did endeavour to see Bagwell's wife, but failed, for which I am glad, only I observe the folly of my mind that cannot refrain from pleasure at a season above all others in my life requisite for me to shew my utmost care in. I walked both going and coming, spending my time reading of my Civill and Ecclesiastical Law book. Being returned home, I took my wife and Mrs. Barbary and Mercer out by coach and went our Grand Tour, and baited at Islington, and so late home about 11 at night, and so with much pleasure to bed.

17th. Up, lying long, being wearied yesterday with long walking. So to the office, where all the morning with fresh occasion of vexing at myself for my late neglect of business, by which I cannot appear half so usefull as I used to do. Home at noon to dinner, and then to my office again, where I could not hold my eyes open for an houre, but I drowsed (so little sensible I apprehend my soul is of the necessity of minding business), but I anon wakened and minded my business, and did a great deale with very great pleasure, and so home at night to supper and to bed, mightily pleased with myself for the business that I have done, and convinced that if I would but keepe constantly to do the same I might have leisure enough and yet do all my business, and by the grace of God so I will. So to bed.

18th. Up by 5 o'clock, and so down by water to Deptford and Blackewall to dispatch some business. So walked to Dickeshoare, and there took boat again and home, and thence to Westminster, and attended all the morning on the Exchequer for a quarter's tallys for Tangier. But, Lord! to see what a dull, heavy sort of people they are there would make a man mad. At noon had them and carried them home, and there dined with great content with my people, and within and at the office all the afternoon and night, and so home to settle some papers there, and so to bed, being not very well, having eaten too much lobster at noon at dinner with Mr. Hollyard, he coming in and commending it so much.

19th. Up, and to the office all the morning. At noon took Mr. Deane (lately come to towne) home with me to dinner, and there after giving him some reprimands and good advice about his deportment in the place where by my interest he is at Harwich, and then declaring my resolution of being his friend still, we did then fall to discourse about his ship "Rupert," built by him there, which succeeds so well as he hath got great honour by it, and I some by recommending him; the King, Duke, and every body saying it is the best ship that was ever built. And then he fell to explain to me his manner of casting the draught of water which a ship will draw before-hand: which is a secret the King and all admire in him; and he is the first that hath come to any certainty before-hand, of foretelling the draught of water of a ship before she be launched. I must confess I am much pleased in his successe in this business, and do admire at the confidence of Castle who did undervalue the draught Deane sent up to me, that I was ashamed to owne it or him, Castle asking of me upon the first sight of it whether he that laid it down had ever built a ship or no, which made me the more doubtfull of him. He being gone, I to the office, where much business and many persons to speake with me. Late home and to bed, glad to be at a little quiett.

20th (Lord's day). With my wife to church in the morning. At noon dined mighty nobly, ourselves alone. After dinner my wife and Mercer by coach to Greenwich, to be gossip to Mrs. Daniel's child. I out to Westminster, and straight to Mrs. Martin's, and there did what I would with her, she staying at home all the day for me; and not being well pleased with her over free and loose company, I away to Westminster Abbey, and there fell in discourse with Mr. Blagrave, whom I find a sober politique man, that gets money and increase of places, and thence by coach home, and thence by water after I had discoursed awhile with Mr. Yeabsly, whom I met and took up in my coach with me, and who hath this day presented my Lord Ashly with L100 to bespeak his friendship to him in his accounts now before us; and my Lord hath received it, and so I believe is as bad, as to bribes, as what the world says of him. Calling on all the Victualling ships to know what they had of their complements, and so to Deptford, to enquire after a little business there, and thence by water back again, all the way coming and going reading my Lord Bacon's "Faber Fortunae," which I can never read too often, and so back home, and there find my wife come home, much pleased with the reception she had there, and she was godmother, and did hold the child at the Font, and it is called John. So back again home, and after setting my papers in order and supping, to bed, desirous to rise betimes in the morning.

21st. Up between 4 and 5 o'clock and to set several papers to rights, and so to the office, where we had an extraordinary meeting. But, Lord! how it torments me to find myself so unable to give an account of my Victualling business, which puts me out of heart in every thing else, so that I never had a greater shame upon me in my owne mind, nor more trouble as to publique business than I have now, but I will get out of it as soon as possibly I can. At noon dined at home, and after dinner comes in my wife's brother Balty and his wife, he being stepped ashore from the fleete for a day or two. I away in some haste to my Lord Ashly, where it is stupendous to see how favourably, and yet closely, my Lord Ashly carries himself to Mr. Yeabsly, in his business, so as I think we shall do his business for him in very good manner. But it is a most extraordinary thing to observe, and that which I would not but have had the observation of for a great deal of money. Being done there, and much forwarded Yeabsly's business, I with Sir H. Cholmly to my Lord Bellassis, who is lately come from Tangier to visit him, but is not within. So to Westminster Hall a little about business and so home by water, and then out with my wife, her brother, sister, and Mercer to Islington, our grand tour, and there eat and drank. But in discourse I am infinitely pleased with Balty, his deportment in his business of Muster-Master, and hope mighty well from him, and am glad with all my heart I put him into this business. Late home and to bed, they also lying at my house, he intending to go away to-morrow back again to sea.

22nd. Up betimes and to my business of entering some Tangier payments in my book in order, and then to the office, where very busy all the morning. At noon home to dinner, Balty being gone back to sea and his wife dining with us, whom afterward my wife carried home. I after dinner to the office, and anon out on several occasions, among others to Lovett's, and there staid by him and her and saw them (in their poor conditioned manner) lay on their varnish, which however pleased me mightily to see. Thence home to my business writing letters, and so at night home to supper and to bed.

23rd. Up by 5 o'clock and to my chamber settling several matters in order. So out toward

White Hall, calling in my way on my Lord Bellassis, where I come to his bedside, and did give me a full and long account of his matters, how he left them at Tangier. Declares himself fully satisfied with my care: seems cunningly to argue for encreasing the number of men there. Told me the whole story of his gains by the Turky prizes, which he owns he hath got about L5000 by. Promised me the same profits Povy was to have had; and in fine, I find him a pretty subtle man; and so I left him, and to White Hall before the Duke and did our usual business, and eased my mind of two or three things of weight that lay upon me about Lanyon's salary, which I have got to be L150 per annum. Thence to Westminster to look after getting some little for some great tallys, but shall find trouble in it. Thence homeward and met with Sir Philip Warwicke, and spoke about this, in which he is scrupulous. After that to talk of the wants of the Navy. He lays all the fault now upon the new Act, and owns his owne folly in thinking once so well of it as to give way to others' endeavours about it, and is grieved at heart to see what passe things are like to come to. Thence to the Excise Office to the Commissioners to get a meeting between them and myself and others about our concernments in the Excise for Tangier, and so to the 'Change awhile, and thence home with Creed, and find my wife at dinner with Mr. Cooke, who is going down to Hinchinbrooke. After dinner Creed and I and wife and Mercer out by coach, leaving them at the New Exchange, while I to White Hall, and there staid at Sir G. Carteret's chamber till the Council rose, and then he and I, by agreement this morning, went forth in his coach by Tiburne, to the Parke; discoursing of the state of the Navy as to money, and the state of the Kingdom too, how ill able to raise more: and of our office as to the condition of the officers; he giving me caution as to myself, that there are those that are my enemies as well as his, and by name my Lord Bruncker, who hath said some odd speeches against me. So that he advises me to stand on my guard; which I shall do, and unless my too-much addiction to pleasure undo me, will be acute enough for any of them. We rode to and again in the Parke a good while, and at last home and set me down at Charing Crosse, and thence I to Mrs. Pierces to take up my wife and Mercer, where I find her new picture by Hales do not please her, nor me indeed, it making no show, nor is very like, nor no good painting. Home to supper and to bed, having my right eye sore and full of humour of late, I think, by my late change of my brewer, and having of 8s. beer.

24th. Up very betimes, and did much business in my chamber. Then to the office, where busy all the morning. At noon rose in the pleasantest humour I have seen Sir W. Coventry and the whole board in this twelvemonth from a pleasant crossing humour Sir W. Batten was in, he being hungry, and desirous to be gone. Home, and Mr. Hunt come to dine with me, but I was prevented dining till 4 o'clock by Sir H. Cholmly and Sir J. Bankes's coming in about some Tangier business. They gone I to dinner, the others having dined. Mr. Sheply is also newly come out of the country and come to see us, whom I am glad to see. He left all well there; but I perceive under some discontent in my Lord's behalfe, thinking that he is under disgrace with the King; but he is not so at all, as Sir G. Carteret assures me. They gone I to the office and did business, and so in the evening abroad alone with my wife to Kingsland, and so back again and to bed, my right eye continuing very ill of the rheum, which hath troubled it four or five days.

25th. Up betimes and to my chamber to do business, where the greatest part of the morning.

Then out to the 'Change to speake with Captain [Cocke], who tells me my silver plates are ready for me, and shall be sent me speedily; and proposes another proposition of serving us with a thousand tons of hempe, and tells me it shall bring me 6500, if the bargain go forward, which is a good word. Thence to Sir G. Carteret, who is at the pay of the tickets with Sir J. Minnes this day, and here I sat with them a while, the first time I ever was there, and thence to dinner with him, a good dinner. Here come a gentleman over from France arrived here this day, Mr. Browne of St. Mellos, who, among other things, tells me the meaning of the setting out of doggs every night out of the towne walls, which are said to secure the city; but it is not so, but only to secure the anchors, cables, and ships that lie dry, which might otherwise in the night be liable to be robbed. And these doggs are set out every night, and called together in every morning by a man with a home, and they go in very orderly. Thence home, and there find Knipp at dinner with my wife, now very big, and within a fortnight of lying down. But my head was full of business and so could have no sport. So I left them, promising to return and take them out at night, and so to the Excise Office, where a meeting was appointed of Sir Stephen Fox, the Cofferer, and myself, to settle the business of our tallys, and it was so pretty well against another meeting. Thence away home to the office and out again to Captain Cocke (Mr. Moore for company walking with me and discoursing and admiring of the learning of Dr. Spencer), and there he and I discoursed a little more of our matters, and so home, and (Knipp being gone) took out my wife and Mercer to take the ayre a little, and so as far as Hackney and back again, and then to bed.

26th. Up betimes and to the office, where all the morning. At noon dined at home. So to the office again, and a while at the Victualling Office to understand matters there a little, and thence to the office and despatched much business, to my great content, and so home to supper and to bed.

27th (Lord's day). Rose betimes, and to my office till church time to write two copies of my Will fair, bearing date this day, wherein I have given my sister Pall L500, my father for his owne and my mother's support L2,000, to my wife the rest of my estate, but to have L2500 secured to her, though by deducting out of what I have given my father and my sister. I dispatched all before church time and then to church, my wife with me. Thence home to dinner, whither come my uncle Wight, and aunt and uncle Norbury, and Mr. Shepley. A good dinner and very merry. After dinner we broke up and I by water to Westminster to Mrs. Martin's, and there sat with her and her husband and Mrs. Burrows, the pretty, an hour or two, then to the Swan a while, and so home by water, and with my wife by and by by water as low as Greenwich, for ayre only, and so back again home to supper and to bed with great pleasure.

28th. Up and to my chamber to do some business there, and then to the office, where a while, and then by agreement to the Excise Office, where I waited all the morning for the Cofferer and Sir St. Foxe's coming, but they did not, so I and the Commissioners lost their labour and expectation of doing the business we intended. Thence home, where I find Mr. Lovett and his wife came to see us. They are a pretty couple, and she a fine bred woman. They dined with us, and Browne, the paynter, and she plays finely on the lute. My wife and I were well pleased with her company. After dinner broke up, I to the office and they abroad. All the afternoon I busy at the office, and down by water to Deptford. Walked back to Redriffe, and so home to the office again, being thoughtfull how to answer Sir W. Coventry against to-morrow in the business of the Victualling, but that I do trust to Tom Wilson, that he will be ready with a book for me to-morrow morning. So to bed, my wife telling me where she hath been to-day with my aunt Wight, and seen Mrs. Margaret Wight, and says that she is one of the beautifullest women that ever she saw in her life, the most excellent nose and mouth. They have been also to see pretty Mrs. Batelier, and conclude her to be a prettier woman than Mrs. Pierce, whom my wife led my aunt to see also this day.

29th (King's birth-day and Restauration day). Waked with the ringing of the bells all over the towne; so up before five o'clock, and to the office, where we met, and I all the morning with great trouble upon my spirit to think how I should come off in the afternoon when Sir W. Coventry did go to the Victualling office to see the state of matters there, and methinks by his doing of it without speaking to me, and only with Sir W. Pen, it must be of design to find my negligence. However, at noon I did, upon a small invitation of Sir W. Pen's, go and dine with Sir W. Coventry at his office, where great good cheer and many pleasant stories of Sir W. Coventry; but I had no pleasure in them. However, I had last night and this morning made myself a little able to report how matters were, and did readily go with them after dinner to the Victualling office; and there, beyond belief, did acquit myself very well to full content; so that, beyond expectation, I got over this second rub in this business; and if ever I fall on it again, I deserve to be undone. Being broke up there, I with a merry heart home to my office, and thither my wife comes to me, to tell me, that if I would see the handsomest woman in England, I shall come home presently; and who should it be but the pretty lady of our parish, that did heretofore sit on the other side of our church, over against our gallery, that is since married; she with Mrs. Anne Jones, one of this parish, that dances finely, and Mrs. sister did come to see her this afternoon, and so I home and there find Creed also come to me. So there I spent most of the afternoon with them, and indeed she is a pretty black woman, her name Mrs. Horsely. But, Lord! to see how my nature could not refrain from the temptation; but I must invite them to Foxhall, to Spring Gardens, though I had freshly received minutes of a great deale of extraordinary business. However I could not helpe it, but sent them before with Creed, and I did some of my business; and so after them, and find them there, in an arbour, and had met with Mrs. Pierce, and some company with her. So here I spent 20s. upon them, and were pretty merry. Among other things, had a fellow that imitated all manner of birds, and doggs, and hogs, with his voice, which was mighty pleasant. Staid here till night: then set Mrs. Pierce in at the New Exchange; and ourselves took coach, and so set Mrs. Horsely home, and then home ourselves, but with great trouble in the streets by bonefires, it being the King's birth-day and day of Restauration; but, Lord! to see the difference how many there were on the other side, and so few ours, the City side of the Temple, would make one wonder the difference between the temper of one sort of people and the other: and the difference among all between what they do now, and what it was the night when Monk come into the City. Such a night as that I never think to see again, nor think it can be. After I come home I was till one in the morning with Captain Cocke drawing up a contract with him intended to be offered to the Duke to-morrow, which, if it proceeds, he promises me L500.

30th. Up and to my office, there to settle some business in order.to our waiting on the Duke to-day. That done to White Hall to Sir W. Coventry's chamber, where I find the Duke gone out with the King to-day on hunting. So after some discourse with him, I by water to Westminster, and there drew a draught of an order for my Lord Treasurer to sign for my having some little tallys made me in lieu of two great ones, of L2000 each, to enable me to pay small sums therewith. I shewed it to Sir R. Long and had his approbation, and so to Sir Ph. Warwicke's, and did give it him to get signed. So home to my office, and there did business. By and by toward noon word is brought me that my father and my sister are come. I expected them to-day, but not so soon. I to them, and am heartily glad to see them, especially my father, who, poor man, looks very well, and hath rode up this journey on horseback very well, only his eyesight and hearing is very bad. I staid and dined with them, my wife being gone by coach to Barnet, with W. Hewer and Mercer, to meet them, and they did come Ware way. After dinner I left them to dress themselves and I abroad by appointment to my Lord Ashly, who, it is strange to see, how prettily he dissembles his favour to Yeabsly's business, which none in the world could mistrust only I, that am privy to his being bribed. Thence to White Hall, and there staid till the Council was up, with Creed expecting a meeting of Tangier to end Yeabsly's business, but we could not procure it. So I to my Lord Treasurer's and got my warrant, and then to Lovett's, but find nothing done there. So home and did a little business at the office, and so down by water to Deptford and back again home late, and having signed some papers and given order in business, home, where my wife is come home, and so to supper with my father, and mighty pleasant we were, and my wife mighty kind to him and Pall, and so after supper to bed, myself being sleepy, and my right eye still very sore, as it has been now about five days or six, which puts me out of tune. To-night my wife tells me newes has been brought her that Balty's wife is brought to bed, by some fall or fit, before her time, of a great child but dead. If the woman do well we have no reason to be sorry, because his staying a little longer without a child will be better for him and her.

31st. Waked very betimes in the morning by extraordinary thunder and rain, which did keep me sleeping and waking till very late, and it being a holiday and my eye very sore, and myself having had very little sleep for a good while till nine o'clock, and so up, and so saw all my family up, and my father and sister, who is a pretty good-bodied woman, and not over thicke, as I thought she would have been, but full of freckles, and not handsome in face. And so I out by water among the ships, and to Deptford and Blackewall about business, and so home and to dinner with my father and sister and family, mighty pleasant all of us; and, among other things, with a sparrow that our Mercer hath brought up now for three weeks, which is so tame that it flies up and down, and upon the table, and eats and pecks, and do everything so pleasantly, that we are mightily pleased with it. After dinner I to my papers and accounts of this month to sett all straight, it being a publique Fast-day appointed to pray for the good successe of the fleete. But it is a pretty thing to consider how little a matter they make of this keeping of a Fast, that it was not so much as declared time enough to be read in the churches the last Sunday; but ordered by proclamation since: I suppose upon some sudden newes of the Dutch being come out. To my accounts and settled them clear; but to my grief find myself poorer than I was the last by near L20, by reason of my being forced to return L50 to Downing, the smith, which he had presented me with. However, I am well contented, finding myself yet to be worth L5,200. Having done, to supper with my wife, and then to finish the writing fair of my accounts, and so to bed. This day come to town Mr. Homewood, and I took him home in the evening to my chamber, and discoursed with him about my business of the Victualling, which I have a mind to employ him in, and he is desirous of also, but do very ingenuously declare he understands it not so well as other things, and desires to be informed in the nature of it before he attempts it, which I like well, and so I carried him to Mr. Gibson to discourse with him about it, and so home again to my accounts. Thus ends this month, with my mind oppressed by my defect in my duty of the Victualling, which lies upon me as a burden, till I get myself into a better posture therein, and hinders me and casts down my courage in every thing else that belongs to me, and the jealousy I have of Sir W. Coventry's being displeased with me about it; but I hope in a little time to remedy all. As to publique business; by late tidings of the French fleete being come to Rochelle (how true, though, I know not) our fleete is divided; Prince Rupert being gone with about thirty ships to the Westward as is conceived to meet the French, to hinder their coming to join with the Dutch. My Lord Duke of Albemarle lies in the Downes with the rest, and intends presently to sail to the Gunfleete.

June 1st. Being prevented yesterday in meeting by reason of the fast day, we met to-day all the morning. At noon I and my father, wife and sister, dined at Aunt Wight's here hard by at Mr. Woolly's, upon sudden warning, they being to go out of town to-morrow. Here dined the faire Mrs. Margaret Wight, who is a very fine lady, but the cast of her eye, got only by an ill habit, do her much wrong and her hands are bad; but she hath the face of a noble Roman lady. After dinner my uncle and Woolly and I out into their yarde, to talke about what may be done hereafter to all our profits by prizegoods, which did give us reason to lament the losse of the opportunity of the last yeare, which, if we were as wise as we are now, and at the peaceable end of all those troubles that we met with, all might have been such a hit as will never come again in this age, and so I do really believe it. Thence home to my office and there did much business, and at night home to my father to supper and to bed.

2nd. Up, and to the office, where certain newes is brought us of a letter come to the King this morning from the Duke of Albemarle, dated yesterday at eleven o'clock, as they were sailing to the Gunfleete, that they were in sight of the Dutch fleete, and were fitting themselves to fight them; so that they are, ere this, certainly engaged; besides, several do averr they heard the guns all yesterday in the afternoon. This put us at the Board into a tosse. Presently come orders for our sending away to the fleete a recruite of 200 soldiers. So I rose from the table, and to the Victualling office, and thence upon the River among several vessels, to consider of the sending them away; and lastly, down to Greenwich, and there appointed two yachts to be ready for them; and did order the soldiers to march to Blackewall. Having set all things in order against the next flood, I went on shore with Captain Erwin at Greenwich, and into the Parke, and there we could hear the guns from the fleete most plainly. Thence he and I to the King's Head and there bespoke a dish of steaks for our dinner about four o'clock. While that was doing, we walked to the water-side, and there seeing the King and Duke come down in their barge to Greenwich-house, I to them, and did give them an account [of] what I was doing. They went up to the Parke to hear the guns of the fleete go off. All our hopes now are that Prince Rupert with his fleete is coming back and will be with the fleete this even: a message being sent to him to that purpose on Wednesday last; and a return is come from him this morning, that he did intend to sail from St. Ellen's point about four in the afternoon on Wednesday [Friday], which was yesterday; which gives us great hopes, the wind being very fair, that he is with them this even, and the fresh going off of the guns makes us believe the same. After dinner, having nothing else to do till flood, I went and saw Mrs. Daniel, to whom I did not tell that the fleets were engaged, because of her husband, who is in the R. Charles. Very pleasant with her half an hour, and so away and down to Blackewall, and there saw the soldiers (who were by this time gotten most of them drunk) shipped off. But, Lord! to see how the poor fellows kissed their wives and sweethearts in that simple manner at their going off, and shouted, and let off their guns, was strange sport. In the evening come up the River the Katharine yacht, Captain Fazeby, who hath brought over my Lord of Alesbury and Sir Thomas Liddall (with a very pretty daughter, and in a pretty travelling-dress) from Flanders, who saw the

Dutch fleete on Thursday, and ran from them; but from that houre to this hath not heard one gun, nor any newes of any fight. Having put the soldiers on board, I home and wrote what I had to write by the post, and so home to supper and to bed, it being late.

3rd (Lord's-day; Whit-sunday). Up, and by water to White Hall, and there met with Mr. Coventry, who tells me the only news from the fleete is brought by Captain Elliott, of The Portland, which, by being run on board by The Guernsey, was disabled from staying abroad; so is come in to Aldbrough. That he saw one of the Dutch great ships blown up, and three on fire. That they begun to fight on Friday; and at his coming into port, he could make another ship of the King's coming in, which he judged to be the Rupert: that he knows of no other hurt to our ships. With this good newes I home by water again, and to church in the sermon-time, and with great joy told it my fellows in the pew. So home after church time to dinner, and after dinner my father, wife, sister, and Mercer by water to Woolwich, while I walked by land, and saw the Exchange as full of people, and hath been all this noon as of any other day, only for newes. I to St. Margaret's, Westminster, and there saw at church my pretty Betty Michell, and thence to the Abbey, and so to Mrs. Martin, and there did what 'je voudrais avec her.... So by and by he come in, and after some discourse with him I away to White Hall, and there met with this bad newes farther, that the Prince come to Dover but at ten o'clock last night, and there heard nothing of a fight; so that we are defeated of all our hopes of his helpe to the fleete. It is also reported by some Victuallers that the Duke of Albemarle and Holmes their flags were shot down, and both fain to come to anchor to renew their rigging and sails. A letter is also come this afternoon, from Harman in the Henery; which is she [that] was taken by Elliott for the Rupert; that being fallen into the body of the Dutch fleete, he made his way through them, was set on by three fire-ships one after another, got two of them off, and disabled the third; was set on fire himself; upon which many of his men leapt into the sea and perished; among others, the parson first. Have lost above 100 men, and a good many women (God knows what is become of Balty), and at last quenched his own fire and got to Aldbrough; being, as all say, the greatest hazard that ever any ship escaped, and as bravely managed by him. The mast of the third fire-ship fell into their ship on fire, and hurt Harman's leg, which makes him lame now, but not dangerous. I to Sir G. Carteret, who told me there hath been great bad management in all this; that the King's orders that went on Friday for calling back the Prince, were sent but by the ordinary post on Wednesday; and come to the Prince his hands but on Friday; and then, instead of sailing presently, he stays till four in the evening. And that which is worst of all, the Hampshire, laden with merchants' money, come from the Straights, set out with or but just before the fleete, and was in the Downes by five in the clock yesterday morning; and the Prince with his fleete come to Dover but at ten of the clock at night. This is hard to answer, if it be true. This puts great astonishment into the King, and Duke, and Court, every body being out of countenance. So meeting Creed, he and I by coach to Hide Parke alone to talke of these things, and do blesse God that my Lord Sandwich was not here at this time to be concerned in a business like to be so misfortunate. It was a pleasant thing to consider how fearfull I was of being seen with Creed all this afternoon, for fear of people's thinking that by our relation to my Lord Sandwich we should be making ill construction of the

Prince's failure. But, God knows, I am heartily sorry for the sake of the whole nation, though, if it were not for that, it would not be amisse to have these high blades find some checke to their presumption and their disparaging of as good men. Thence set him down in Covent Guarden and so home by the 'Change, which is full of people still, and all talk highly of the failure of the Prince in not making more haste after his instructions did come, and of our managements here in not giving it sooner and with more care and oftener. Thence. After supper to bed.

4th. Up, and with Sir J. Minnes and Sir W. Pen to White Hall in the latter's coach, where, when we come, we find the Duke at St. James's, whither he is lately gone to lodge. So walking through the Parke we saw hundreds of people listening at the Gravel-pits,—[Kensington]—and to and again in the Parke to hear the guns, and I saw a letter, dated last night, from Strowd, Governor of Dover Castle, which says that the Prince come thither the night before with his fleete, but that for the guns which we writ that we heard, it is only a mistake for thunder;

and so far as to yesterday it is a miraculous thing that we all Friday, and Saturday and yesterday, did hear every where most plainly the guns go off, and yet at Deale and Dover to last night they did not hear one word of a fight, nor think they heard one gun. This, added to what I have set down before the other day about the Katharine, makes room for a great dispute in philosophy, how we should hear it and they not, the same wind that brought it to us being the same that should bring it to them: but so it is. Major Halsey, however (he was sent down on purpose to hear newes), did bring newes this morning that he did see the Prince and his fleete at nine of the clock yesterday morning, four or five leagues to sea behind the Goodwin, so that by the hearing of the guns this morning we conclude he is come to the fleete. After wayting upon the Duke, Sir W. Pen (who was commanded to go to-night by water down to Harwich, to dispatch away all the ships he can) and I home, drinking two bottles of Cocke ale in the streete in his new fine coach, where no sooner come, but newes is brought me of a couple of men come to speak with me from the fleete; so I down, and who should it be but Mr. Daniel, all muffled up, and his face as black as the chimney, and covered with dirt, pitch, and tarr, and powder, and muffled with dirty clouts, and his right eye stopped with okum. He is come last night at five o'clock from the fleete, with a comrade of his that hath endangered another eye. They were set on shore at Harwich this morning, and at two o'clock, in a catch with about twenty more wounded men from the Royall Charles. They being able to ride, took post about three this morning, and were here between eleven and twelve. I went presently into the coach with them, and carried them to Somerset-House-stairs, and there took water (all the world gazing upon us, and concluding it to be newes from the fleete, and every body's face appeared expecting of newes) to the Privy-stairs, and left them at Mr. Coventry's lodging (he, though, not being there); and so I into the Parke to the King, and told him my Lord Generall was well the last night at five o'clock, and the Prince come with his fleete and joyned with his about seven. The King was mightily pleased with this newes, and so took me by the hand and talked a little of it. Giving him the best account I could; and then he bid me to fetch the two seamen to him, he walking into the house. So I went and fetched the seamen into the Vane room to him, and there he heard the whole account.

How we found the Dutch fleete at anchor on Friday half seas over, between Dunkirke and Ostend, and made them let slip their anchors. They about ninety, and we less than sixty. We fought them, and put them to the run, till they met with about sixteen sail of fresh ships, and so bore up again. The fight continued till night, and then again the next morning from five till seven at night. And so, too, yesterday morning they begun again, and continued till about four o'clock, they chasing us for the most part of Saturday and yesterday, we flying from them. The Duke himself, then those people were put into the catch, and by and by spied the Prince's fleete coming, upon which De Ruyter called a little council (being in chase at this time of us), and thereupon their fleete divided into two squadrons; forty in one, and about thirty in the other (the fleete being at first about ninety, but by one accident or other, supposed to be lessened to about seventy); the bigger to follow the Duke, the less to meet the Prince. But the Prince come up with the Generall's fleete, and the Dutch come together again and bore towards their own coast, and we with them; and now what the consequence of this day will be, at that time fighting, we know not. The Duke was forced to come to anchor on Friday, having lost his sails and rigging. No particular person spoken of to be hurt but Sir W. Clerke, who hath lost his leg, and bore it bravely. The Duke himself had a little hurt in his thigh, but signified little. The King did pull out of his pocket about twenty pieces in gold, and did give it Daniel for himself and his companion; and so parted, mightily pleased with the account he did give him of the fight, and the successe it ended with, of the Prince's coming, though it seems the Duke did give way again and again. The King did give order for care to be had of Mr. Daniel and his companion; and so we parted from him, and then met the Duke [of York], and gave him the same account: and so broke up, and I left them going to the surgeon's and I myself by water to the 'Change, and to several people did give account of the business. So home about four o'clock to dinner, and was followed by several people to be told the newes, and good newes it is. God send we may hear a good issue of this day's business! After I had eat something I walked to Gresham College, where I heard my Lord Bruncker was, and there got a promise of the receipt of the fine varnish, which I shall be glad to have. Thence back with Mr. Hooke to my house and there lent some of my tables of naval matters, the names of rigging and the timbers about a ship, in order to Dr. Wilkins' book coming out about the Universal Language. Thence, he being gone, to the Crown, behind the 'Change, and there supped at the club with my Lord Bruncker, Sir G. Ent, and others of Gresham College; and all our discourse is of this fight at sea, and all are doubtful of the successe, and conclude all had been lost if the Prince had not come in, they having chased us the greatest part of Saturday and Sunday. Thence with my Lord Bruncker and Creed by coach to White Hall, where fresh letters are come from Harwich, where the Gloucester, Captain Clerke, is come in, and says that on Sunday night upon coming in of the Prince, the Duke did fly; but all this day they have been fighting; therefore they did face again, to be sure. Captain Bacon of The Bristoll is killed. They cry up Jenings of The Ruby, and Saunders of The Sweepstakes. They condemn mightily Sir Thomas Teddiman for a coward, but with what reason time must shew. Having heard all this Creed and I walked into the Parke till 9 or 10 at night, it being fine moonshine, discoursing of the unhappinesse of our fleete, what it would have been if the Prince had not come in, how much the

Duke hath failed of what he was so presumptuous of, how little we deserve of God Almighty to give us better fortune, how much this excuses all that was imputed to my Lord Sandwich, and how much more he is a man fit to be trusted with all those matters than those that now command, who act by nor with any advice, but rashly and without any order. How bad we are at intelligence that should give the Prince no sooner notice of any thing but let him come to Dover without notice of any fight, or where the fleete were, or any thing else, nor give the Duke any notice that he might depend upon the Prince's reserve; and lastly, of how good use all may be to checke our pride and presumption in adventuring upon hazards upon unequal force against a people that can fight, it seems now, as well as we, and that will not be discouraged by any losses, but that they will rise again. Thence by water home, and to supper (my father, wife, and sister having been at Islington today at Pitt's) and to bed.

5th. Up, and to the office, where all the morning, expecting every houre more newes of the fleete and the issue of yesterday's fight, but nothing come. At noon, though I should have dined with my Lord Mayor and Aldermen at an entertainment of Commissioner Taylor's, yet it being a time of expectation of the successe of the fleete, I did not go, but dined at home, and after dinner by water down to Deptford (and Woolwich, where I had not been since I lodged there, and methinks the place has grown natural to me), and thence down to Longreach, calling on all the ships in the way, seeing their condition for sayling, and what they want. Home about 11 of the clock, and so eat a bit and to bed, having received no manner of newes this day, but of The Rainbow's being put in from the fleete, maimed as the other ships are, and some say that Sir W. Clerke is dead of his leg being cut off.

6th. Up betimes, and vexed with my people for having a key taken out of the chamber doors and nobody knew where it was, as also with my boy for not being ready as soon as I, though I called him, whereupon I boxed him soundly, and then to my business at the office and on the Victualling Office, and thence by water to St. James's, whither he [the Duke of York] is now gone, it being a monthly fast-day for the plague. There we all met, and did our business as usual with the Duke, and among other things had Captain Cocke's proposal of East country goods read, brought by my Lord Bruncker, which I make use of as a monkey do the cat's foot. Sir W. Coventry did much oppose it, and it's likely it will not do; so away goes my hopes of L500. Thence after the Duke into the Parke, walking through to White Hall, and there every body listening for guns, but none heard, and every creature is now overjoyed and concludes upon very good grounds that the Dutch are beaten because we have heard no guns nor no newes of our fleete. By and by walking a little further, Sir Philip Frowde did meet the Duke with an expresse to Sir W. Coventry (who was by) from Captain Taylor, the Storekeeper at Harwich, being the narration of Captain Hayward of The Dunkirke; who gives a very serious account, how upon Monday the two fleetes fought all day till seven at night, and then the whole fleete of Dutch did betake themselves to a very plain flight, and never looked back again. That Sir Christopher Mings is wounded in the leg; that the Generall is well. That it is conceived reasonably, that of all the Dutch fleete, which, with what recruits they had, come to one hundred sayle, there is not above fifty got home; and of them, few if any of their flags. And that little Captain Bell, in one of the fire-ships, did at the end of the day fire a ship of 70 guns. We were all so overtaken with this good newes, that the Duke ran with it to the King, who was gone to chappell, and there all the Court was in a hubbub, being rejoiced over head and ears in this good newes. Away go I by coach to the New Exchange, and there did spread this good newes a little, though I find it had broke out before. And so home to our own church, it being the common Fast-day, and it was just before sermon; but, Lord! how all the people in the church stared upon me to see me whisper to Sir John Minnes and my Lady Pen. Anon I saw people stirring and whispering below, and by and by comes up the sexton from my Lady Ford to tell me the newes (which I had brought), being now sent into the church by Sir W. Batten in writing, and handed from pew to pew. But that which pleased me as much as the newes, was, to have the fair Mrs. Middleton at our church, who indeed is a very beautiful lady. Here after sermon comes to our office 40 people almost of all sorts and qualities to hear the newes, which I took great delight to tell them. Then home and found my wife at dinner, not knowing of my being at church, and after dinner my father and she out to Hales's, where my father is to begin to sit to-day for his picture, which I have a desire to have. I all the afternoon at home doing some business, drawing up my vowes for the rest of the yeare to Christmas; but, Lord! to see in what a condition of happiness I am, if I would but keepe myself so; but my love of pleasure is such, that my very soul is angry with itself for my vanity in so doing. Anon took coach and to Hales's, but he was gone out, and my father and wife gone. So I to Lovett's, and there to my trouble saw plainly that my project of varnished books will not take, it not keeping colour, not being able to take polishing upon a single paper. Thence home, and my father and wife not coming in, I proceeded with my coach to take a little ayre as far as Bow all alone, and there turned back and home; but before I got home, the bonefires were lighted all the towne over, and I going through Crouched Friars, seeing Mercer at her mother's gate, stopped, and 'light, and into her mother's, the first time I ever was there, and find all my people, father and all, at a very fine supper at W. Hewer's lodging, very neatly, and to my great pleasure. After supper, into his chamber, which is mighty fine with pictures and every thing else, very curious, which pleased me exceedingly. Thence to the gate, with the women all about me, and Mrs. Mercer's son had provided a great many serpents, and so I made the women all fire some serpents. By and by comes in our faire neighbour, Mrs. Turner, and two neighbour's daughters, Mrs. Tite, the elder of whom, a long red-nosed silly jade; the younger, a pretty black girle, and the merriest sprightly jade that ever I saw. With them idled away the whole night till twelve at night at the bonefire in the streets. Some of the people thereabouts going about with musquets, and did give me two or three vollies of their musquets, I giving them a crowne to drink; and so home. Mightily pleased with this happy day's newes, and the more, because confirmed by Sir Daniel Harvy, who was in the whole fight with the Generall, and tells me that there appear but thirty-six in all of the Dutch fleete left at the end of the voyage when they run home. The joy of the City was this night exceeding great.

7th. Up betimes, and to my office about business (Sir W. Coventry having sent me word that he is gone down to the fleete to see how matters stand, and to be back again speedily); and with the same expectation of congratulating ourselves with the victory that I had yesterday. But my

Lord Bruncker and Sir T. H. that come from Court, tell me quite contrary newes, which astonishes me: that is to say, that we are beaten, lost many ships and good commanders; have not taken one ship of the enemy's; and so can only report ourselves a victory; nor is it certain that we were left masters of the field. But, above all, that The Prince run on shore upon the Galloper, and there stuck; was endeavoured to be fetched off by the Dutch, but could not; and so they burned her; and Sir G. Ascue is taken prisoner, and carried into Holland. This newes do much trouble me, and the thoughts of the ill consequences of it, and the pride and presumption that brought us to it. At noon to the 'Change, and there find the discourse of towne, and their countenances much changed; but yet not very plain. So home to dinner all alone, my father and people being gone all to Woolwich to see the launching of the new ship The Greenwich, built by Chr. Pett. I left alone with little Mrs. Tooker, whom I kept with me in my chamber all the afternoon, and did what I would with her. By and by comes Mr. Wayth to me; and discoursing of our ill successe, he tells me plainly from Captain Page's own mouth (who hath lost his arm in the fight), that the Dutch did pursue us two hours before they left us, and then they suffered us to go on homewards, and they retreated towards their coast: which is very sad newes. Then to my office and anon to White Hall, late, to the Duke of York to see what commands he hath and to pray a meeting to-morrow for Tangier in behalf of Mr. Yeabsly, which I did do and do find the Duke much damped in his discourse, touching the late fight, and all the Court talk sadly of it. The Duke did give me several letters he had received from the fleete, and Sir W. Coventry and Sir W. Pen, who are gone down thither, for me to pick out some works to be done for the setting out the fleete again; and so I took them home with me, and was drawing out an abstract of them till midnight. And as to newes, I do find great reason to think that we are beaten in every respect, and that we are the losers. The Prince upon the Galloper, where both the Royall Charles and Royall Katharine had come twice aground, but got off. The Essex carried into Holland; the Swiftsure missing (Sir William Barkeley) ever since the beginning of the fight. Captains Bacon, Tearne, Wood, Mootham, Whitty, and Coppin, slayne. The Duke of Albemarle writes, that he never fought with worse officers in his life, not above twenty of them behaving themselves like men. Sir William Clerke lost his leg; and in two days died. The Loyall George, Seven Oakes, and Swiftsure, are still missing, having never, as the Generall writes himself, engaged with them. It was as great an alteration to find myself required to write a sad letter instead of a triumphant one to my Lady Sandwich this night, as ever on any occasion I had in my life. So late home and to bed.

8th. Up very betimes and to attend the Duke of York by order, all of us to report to him what the works are that are required of us and to divide among us, wherein I have taken a very good share, and more than I can perform, I doubt. Thence to the Exchequer about some Tangier businesses, and then home, where to my very great joy I find Balty come home without any hurt, after the utmost imaginable danger he hath gone through in the Henery, being upon the quarterdeck with Harman all the time; and for which service Harman I heard this day commended most seriously and most eminently by the Duke of Yorke. As also the Duke did do most utmost right to Sir Thomas Teddiman, of whom a scandal was raised, but without cause, he having behaved himself most eminently brave all the whole fight, and to extraordinary great service and purpose, having given Trump himself such a broadside as was hardly ever given to any ship. Mings is shot through the face, and into the shoulder, where the bullet is lodged. Young Holmes' is also ill wounded, and Ather in The Rupert. Balty tells me the case of The Henery; and it was, indeed, most extraordinary sad and desperate. After dinner Balty and I to my office, and there talked a great deal of this fight; and I am mightily pleased in him and have great content in, and hopes of his doing well. Thence out to White Hall to a Committee for Tangier, but it met not. But, Lord! to see how melancholy the Court is, under the thoughts of this last overthrow (for so it is), instead of a victory, so much and so unreasonably expected. Thence, the Committee not meeting, Creed and I down the river as low as Sir W. Warren's, with whom I did motion a business that may be of profit to me, about buying some lighters to send down to the fleete, wherein he will assist me. So back again, he and I talking of the late ill management of this fight, and of the ill management of fighting at all against so great a force bigger than ours, and so to the office, where we parted, but with this satisfaction that we hear the Swiftsure, Sir W. Barkeley, is come in safe to the Nore, after her being absent ever since the beginning of the fight, wherein she did not appear at all from beginning to end. But wherever she has been, they say she is arrived there well, which I pray God however may be true. At the office late, doing business, and so home to supper and to bed.

9th. Up, and to St. James's, there to wait on the Duke of Yorke, and had discourse with him about several businesses of the fleete. But, Lord! to see how the Court is divided about The Swiftsure and The Essex's being safe. And wagers and odds laid on both sides. I did tell the Duke how Sir W. Batten did tell me this morning that he was sure the Swiftsure is safe. This put them all in a great joy and certainty of it, but this I doubt will prove nothing. Thence to White Ball in expectation of a meeting of Tangier, and we did industriously labour to have it this morning; but we could not get a fifth person there, so after much pains and thoughts on my side on behalfe of Yeabsly, we were fain to breake up. But, Lord! to see with what patience Lord Ashly did stay all the morning to get a Committee, little thinking that I know the reason of his willingnesse. So I home to dinner and back again to White Hall, and, being come thither a little too soon, went to Westminster Hall, and bought a payre of gloves, and to see how people do take this late fight at sea, and I find all give over the thoughts of it as a victory and to reckon it a great overthrow. So to White Hall, and there when we were come all together in certain expectation of doing our business to Yeabsly's full content, and us that were his friends, my Lord Peterborough (whether through some difference between him and my Lord Ashly, or him and me or Povy, or through the falsenesse of Creed, I know not) do bring word that the Duke of Yorke (who did expressly bid me wait at the Committee for the dispatch of the business) would not have us go forward in this business of allowing the losse of the ships till Sir G. Carteret and Sir W. Coventry were come to towne, which was the very thing indeed which we would have avoided. This being told us, we broke up doing nothing, to my great discontent, though I said nothing, and afterwards I find by my Lord Ashly's discourse to me that he is troubled mightily at it, and indeed it is a great abuse of him and of the whole Commissioners that nothing of that nature can be done without Sir G. Carteret or Sir W. Coventry. No sooner was the Committee up, and I going [through] the Court homeward, but I am told Sir W. Coventry is come to town; so I to his chamber, and there did give him an account how matters go in our office, and with some content I parted from him, after we had discoursed several things of the haste requisite to be made in getting the fleete out again and the manner of doing it. But I do not hear that he is at all pleased or satisfied with the late fight; but he tells me more newes of our suffering, by the death of one or two captains more than I knew before. But he do give over the thoughts of the safety of The Swiftsure or Essex. Thence homewards, landed at the Old Swan, and there find my pretty Betty Michell and her husband at their doore in Thames Streete, which I was glad to find, and went into their shop, and they made me drink some of their strong water, the first time I was ever with them there. I do exceedingly love her. After sitting a little and talking with them about several things at great distance I parted and home to my business late. But I am to observe how the drinking of some strong water did immediately put my eyes into a fit of sorenesse again as they were the other day. I mean my right eye only. Late at night I had an account brought me by Sir W. Warren that he has gone through four lighters for me, which pleases me very well. So home to bed, much troubled with our disappointment at the Tangier Committee.

10th (Lord's day). Up very betimes, and down the river to Deptford, and did a good deale of business in sending away and directing several things to the Fleete. That being done, back to London to my office, and there at my office till after Church time fitting some notes to carry to Sir W. Coventry in the afternoon. At noon home to dinner, where my cozen Joyces, both of them, they and their wives and little Will, come by invitation to dinner to me, and I had a good dinner for them; but, Lord! how sicke was I of W. Joyce's company, both the impertinencies of it and his ill manners before me at my table to his wife, which I could hardly forbear taking notice of; but being at my table and for his wife's sake, I did, though I will prevent his giving me the like occasion again at my house I will warrant him. After dinner I took leave and by water to White Hall, and there spent all the afternoon in the Gallery, till the Council was up, to speake with Sir W. Coventry. Walking here I met with Pierce the surgeon, who is lately come from the fleete, and tells me that all the commanders, officers, and even the common seamen do condemn every part of the late conduct of the Duke of Albemarle: both in his fighting at all, in his manner of fighting, running among them in his retreat, and running the ships on ground; so as nothing can be worse spoken of. That Holmes, Spragg, and Smith do all the business, and the old and wiser commanders nothing. So as Sir Thomas Teddiman (whom the King and all the world speak well of) is mightily discontented, as being wholly slighted. He says we lost more after the Prince come, than before too. The Prince was so maimed, as to be forced to be towed home. He says all the fleete confess their being chased home by the Dutch; and yet the body of the Dutch that did it, was not above forty sayle at most. And yet this put us into the fright, as to bring all our ships on ground. He says, however, that the Duke of Albemarle is as high almost as ever, and pleases himself to think that he hath given the Dutch their bellies full, without sense of what he hath lost us; and talks how he knows now the way to beat them. But he says, that even Smith himself, one of his creatures, did himself condemn the late conduct from the beginning to the end. He tells me further, how the Duke of Yorke is wholly given up to his new mistresse, my Lady Denham, going at noon-day with all his gentlemen with him to visit her in Scotland Yard; she declaring she will not be his mistresse, as Mrs. Price, to go up and down the Privy-stairs, but will be owned publicly; and so she is. Mr. Bruncker, it seems, was the pimp to bring it about, and my Lady Castlemaine, who designs thereby to fortify herself by the Duke; there being a falling-out the other day between the King and her: on this occasion, the Queene, in ordinary talke before the ladies in her drawing-room, did say to my Lady Castlemaine that she feared the King did take cold, by staying so late abroad at her house. She answered before them all, that he did not stay so late abroad with her, for he went betimes thence (though he do not before one, two, or three in the morning), but must stay somewhere else. The King then coming in and overhearing, did whisper in the eare aside, and told her she was a bold impertinent woman, and bid her to be gone out of the Court, and not come again till he sent for, her; which she did presently, and went to a lodging in the Pell Mell, and kept there two or three days, and then sent to the King to know whether she might send for her things away out of her house. The King sent to her, she must first come and view them: and so she come, and the King went to her, and all friends again. He tells me she did, in her anger, say she would be even with the King, and print his letters to her. So putting all together, we are and are like to be in a sad condition. We are endeavouring to raise money by borrowing it of the City; but I do not think the City will lend a farthing. By and by the Council broke up, and I spoke with Sir W. Coventry about business, with whom I doubt not in a little time to be mighty well, when I shall appear to mind my business again as I used to do, which by the grace of God I will do. Gone from him I endeavoured to find out Sir G. Carteret, and at last did at Mr. Ashburnham's, in the Old Palace Yarde, and thence he and I stepped out and walked an houre in the church-yarde, under Henry the Seventh's Chappell, he being lately come from the fleete; and tells me, as I hear from every body else, that the management in the late fight was bad from top to bottom. That several said this would not have been if my Lord Sandwich had had the ordering of it. Nay, he tells me that certainly had my Lord Sandwich had the misfortune to have done as they have done, the King could not have saved him. There is, too, nothing but discontent among the officers; and all the old experienced men are slighted. He tells me to my question (but as a great secret), that the dividing of the fleete did proceed first from a proposition from the fleete, though agreed to hence. But he confesses it arose from want of due intelligence, which he confesses we do want. He do, however, call the fleete's retreat on Sunday a very honourable retreat, and that the Duke of Albemarle did do well in it, and would have been well if he had done it sooner, rather than venture the loss of the fleete and crown, as he must have done if the Prince had not come. He was surprised when I told him I heard that the King did intend to borrow some money of the City, and would know who had spoke of it to me; I told him Sir Ellis Layton this afternoon. He says it is a dangerous discourse; for that the City certainly will not be invited to do it, and then for the King to ask it and be denied, will be the beginning of our sorrow. He seems to fear we shall all fall to pieces among ourselves. This evening we hear that Sir Christopher Mings is dead of his late wounds; and Sir W. Coventry did commend him to me in a most extraordinary manner. But this day, after three days' trial in vain, and the hazard of the spoiling of the ship in lying till next spring, besides the disgrace of it, newes is brought that the

Loyall London is launched at Deptford. Having talked thus much with Sir G. Carteret we parted there, and I home by water, taking in my boat with me young Michell and my Betty his wife, meeting them accidentally going to look a boat. I set them down at the Old Swan and myself, went through bridge to the Tower, and so home, and after supper to bed.

11th. Up, and down by water to Sir W. Warren's (the first time I was in his new house on the other side the water since he enlarged it) to discourse about our lighters that he hath bought for me, and I hope to get L100 by this jobb. Having done with him I took boat again (being mightily struck with a woman in a hat, a seaman's mother,—[Mother or mauther, a wench.]—that stood on the key) and home, where at the office all the morning with Sir W. Coventry and some others of our board hiring of fireships, and Sir W. Coventry begins to see my pains again, which I do begin to take, and I am proud of it, and I hope shall continue it. He gone, at noon I home to dinner, and after dinner my father and wife out to the painter's to sit again, and I, with my Lady Pen and her daughter, to see Harman; whom we find lame in bed. His bones of his anckle are broke, but he hopes to do well soon; and a fine person by his discourse he seems to be and my hearty [friend]; and he did plainly tell me that at the Council of War before the fight, it was against his reason to begin the fight then, and the reasons of most sober men there, the wind being such, and we to windward, that they could not use their lower tier of guns, which was a very sad thing for us to have the honour and weal of the nation ventured so foolishly. I left them there, and walked to Deptford, reading in Walsingham's Manual, a very good book, and there met with Sir W. Batten and my Lady at Uthwayt's. Here I did much business and yet had some little mirthe with my Lady, and anon we all come up together to our office, where I was very late doing much business. Late comes Sir J. Bankes to see me, and tells me that coming up from Rochester he overtook three or four hundred seamen, and he believes every day they come flocking from the fleete in like numbers; which is a sad neglect there, when it will be impossible to get others, and we have little reason to think that these will return presently again. He gone, I to end my letters to-night, and then home to supper and to bed.

12th. Up, and to the office, where we sat all the morning. At noon to dinner, and then to White Hall in hopes of a meeting of Tangier about Yeabsly's business, but it could not be obtained, Sir G. Carteret nor Sir W. Coventry being able to be there, which still vexes [me] to see the poor man forced still to attend, as also being desirous to see what my profit is, and get it. Walking here in the galleries I find the Ladies of Honour dressed in their riding garbs, with coats and doublets with deep skirts, just for all the world like mine, and buttoned their doublets up the breast, with perriwigs and with hats; so that, only for a long petticoat dragging under their men's coats, nobody could take them for women in any point whatever; which was an odde sight, and a sight did not please me. It was Mrs. Wells and another fine lady that I saw thus. Thence down by water to Deptford, and there late seeing some things dispatched down to the fleete, and so home (thinking indeed to have met with Bagwell, but I did not) to write my letters very late, and so to supper and to bed.

13th. Up, and by coach to St. James's, and there did our business before the Duke as usual, having, before the Duke come out of his bed, walked in an ante-chamber with Sir H. Cholmly, who tells me there are great jarrs between the Duke of Yorke and the Duke of Albemarle, about the later's turning out one or two of the commanders put in by the Duke of Yorke. Among others, Captain Du Tell, a Frenchman, put in by the Duke of Yorke, and mightily defended by him; and is therein led by Monsieur Blancford, that it seems hath the same command over the Duke of Yorke as Sir W. Coventry hath; which raises ill blood between them. And I do in several little things observe that Sir W. Coventry hath of late, by the by, reflected on the Duke of Albemarle and his captains, particularly in that of old Teddiman, who did deserve to be turned out this fight, and was so; but I heard Sir W. Coventry say that the Duke of Albemarle put in one as bad as he is in his room, and one that did as little. After we had done with the Duke of Yorke, I with others to White Hall, there to attend again a Committee of Tangier, but there was none, which vexed me to the heart, and makes me mighty doubtfull that when we have one, it will be prejudiced against poor Yeabsly and to my great disadvantage thereby, my Lord Peterborough making it his business, I perceive (whether in spite to me, whom he cannot but smell to be a friend to it, or to my Lord Ashly, I know not), to obstruct it, and seems to take delight in disappointing of us; but I shall be revenged of him. Here I staid a very great while, almost till noon, and then meeting Balty I took him with me, and to Westminster to the Exchequer about breaking of two tallys of L2000 each into smaller tallys, which I have been endeavouring a good while, but to my trouble it will not, I fear, be done, though there be no reason against it, but only a little trouble to the clerks; but it is nothing to me of real profit at all. Thence with Balty to Hales's by coach, it being the seventh day from my making my late oathes, and by them I am at liberty to dispense with any of my oathes every seventh day after I had for the six days before going performed all my vowes. Here I find my father's picture begun, and so much to my content, that it joys my very heart to thinke that I should have his picture so well done; who, besides that he is my father, and a man that loves me, and hath ever done so, is also, at this day, one of the most carefull and innocent men, in the world. Thence with mighty content homeward, and in my way at the Stockes did buy a couple of lobsters, and so home to dinner, where I find my wife and father had dined, and were going out to Hales's to sit there, so Balty and I alone to dinner, and in the middle of my grace, praying for a blessing upon (these his good creatures), my mind fell upon my lobsters: upon which I cried, Odd zooks! and Balty looked upon me like a man at a losse what I meant, thinking at first that I meant only that I had said the grace after meat instead of that before meat. But then I cried, what is become of my lobsters? Whereupon he run out of doors to overtake the coach, but could not, so came back again, and mighty merry at dinner to thinke of my surprize. After dinner to the Excise Office by appointment, and there find my Lord Bellasses and the Commissioners, and by and by the whole company come to dispute the business of our running so far behindhand there, and did come to a good issue in it, that is to say, to resolve upon having the debt due to us, and the Household and the Guards from the Excise stated, and so we shall come to know the worst of our condition and endeavour for some helpe from my Lord Treasurer. Thence home, and put off Balty, and so, being invited, to Sir Christopher Mings's funeral, but find them gone to church. However I into the church (which is a fair, large church, and a great chappell) and there heard the service, and staid till they buried him, and then out. And there met with Sir W. Coventry (who was there out of great generosity, and no person of quality there but he) and went with him into his coach, and being in it with him there happened this extraordinary case, one of the most romantique that ever I heard of in my life, and could not have believed, but that I did see it; which was this:—About a dozen able, lusty, proper men come to the coach-side with tears in their eyes, and one of them that spoke for the rest begun and says to Sir W. Coventry, "We are here a dozen of us that have long known and loved, and served our dead commander, Sir Christopher Mings, and have now done the last office of laying him in the ground. We would be glad we had any other to offer after him, and in revenge of him. All we have is our lives; if you will please to get His Royal Highness to give us a fireship among us all, here is a dozen of us, out of all which choose you one to be commander, and the rest of us, whoever he is, will serve him; and, if possible, do that that shall show our memory of our dead commander, and our revenge." Sir W. Coventry was herewith much moved (as well as I, who could hardly abstain from weeping), and took their names, and so parted; telling me that he would move His Royal Highness as in a thing very extraordinary, which was done. Thereon see the next day in this book. So we parted. The truth is, Sir Christopher Mings was a very stout man, and a man of great parts, and most excellent tongue among ordinary men; and as Sir W. Coventry says, could have been the most useful man at such a pinch of time as this. He was come into great renowne here at home, and more abroad in the West Indys. He had brought his family into a way of being great; but dying at this time, his memory and name (his father being always and at this day a shoemaker, and his mother a Hoyman's daughter; of which he was used frequently to boast) will be quite forgot in a few months as if he had never been, nor any of his name be the better by it; he having not had time to will any estate, but is dead poor rather than rich. So we left the church and crowd, and I home (being set down on Tower Hill), and there did a little business and then in the evening went down by water to Deptford, it being very late, and there I staid out as much time as I could, and then took boat again homeward, but the officers being gone in, returned and walked to Mrs. Bagwell's house, and there (it being by this time pretty dark and past ten o'clock) went into her house and did what I would. But I was not a little fearfull of what she told me but now, which is, that her servant was dead of the plague, that her coming to me yesterday was the first day of her coming forth, and that she had new whitened the house all below stairs, but that above stairs they are not so fit for me to go up to, they being not so. So I parted thence, with a very good will, but very civil, and away to the waterside, and sent for a pint of sacke and so home, drank what I would and gave the waterman the rest; and so adieu. Home about twelve at night, and so to bed, finding most of my people gone to bed. In my way home I called on a fisherman and bought three eeles, which cost me three shillings.

14th. Up, and to the office, and there sat all the morning. At noon dined at home, and thence with my wife and father to Hales's, and there looked only on my father's picture (which is mighty like); and so away to White Hall to a committee for Tangier, where the Duke of York was, and Sir W. Coventry, and a very full committee; and instead of having a very prejudiced meeting, they did, though indeed inclined against Yeabsly, yield to the greatest part of his account, so as to allow of his demands to the value of L7,000 and more, and only give time for him to make good his pretence to the rest; which was mighty joy to me: and so we rose up. But I must observe the force of money, which did make my Lord Ashly to argue and behave himself in the business with the greatest friendship, and yet with all the discretion imaginable; and [it] will be a business of admonition and instruction to me concerning him (and other men, too, for aught I know) as long as I live. Thence took Creed with some kind of violence and some hard words between us to St. James's, to have found out Sir W. Coventry to have signed the order for his payment among others that did stay on purpose to do it (and which is strange among the rest my Lord Ashly, who did cause Creed to write it presently and kept two or three of them with him by cunning to stay and sign it), but Creed's ill nature (though never so well bribed, as it hath lately in this case by twenty pieces) will not be overcome from his usual delays. Thence failing of meeting Sir W. Coventry I took leave of Creed (very good friends) and away home, and there took out my father, wife, sister, and Mercer our grand Tour in the evening, and made it ten at night before we got home, only drink at the doore at Islington at the Katherine Wheel, and so home and to the office a little, and then to bed.

15th. Up betimes, and to my Journall entries, but disturbed by many businesses, among others by Mr. Houblon's coming to me about evening their freight for Tangier, which I did, and then Mr. Bland, who presented me yesterday with a very fine African mat, to lay upon the ground under a bed of state, being the first fruits of our peace with Guyland. So to the office, and thither come my pretty widow Mrs. Burrows, poor woman, to get her ticket paid for her husband's service, which I did her myself, and did 'baisser her moucher', and I do hope may thereafter have some day 'sa' company. Thence to Westminster to the Exchequer, but could not persuade the blockheaded fellows to do what I desire, of breaking my great tallys into less, notwithstanding my Lord Treasurer's order, which vexed [me] so much that I would not bestow more time and trouble among a company of dunces, and so back again home, and to dinner, whither Creed come and dined with me and after dinner Mr. Moore, and he and I abroad, thinking to go down the river together, but the tide being against me would not, but returned and walked an houre in the garden, but, Lord! to hear how he pleases himself in behalf of my Lord Sandwich, in the miscarriage of the Duke of Albemarle, and do inveigh against Sir W. Coventry as a cunning knave, but I thinke that without any manner of reason at all, but only his passion. He being gone I to my chamber at home to set my Journall right and so to settle my Tangier accounts, which I did in very good order, and then in the evening comes Mr. Yeabsly to reckon with me, which I did also, and have above L200 profit therein to myself, which is a great blessing, the God of heaven make me thankfull for it. That being done, and my eyes beginning to be sore with overmuch writing, I to supper and to bed.

16th. Up betimes and to my office, and there we sat all the morning and dispatched much business, the King, Duke of Yorke, and Sir W. Coventry being gone down to the fleete. At noon home to dinner and then down to Woolwich and Deptford to look after things, my head akeing from the multitude of businesses I had in my head yesterday in settling my accounts. All the way down and up, reading of "The Mayor of Quinborough," a simple play. At Deptford, while I am there, comes Mr. Williamson, Sir Arthur Ingram and Jacke Fen, to see the new ships, which they had done, and then I with them home in their boat, and a very fine gentleman Mr. Williamson is. It seems the Dutch do mightily insult of their victory, and they have great reason.

Sir William Barkeley was killed before his ship taken; and there he lies dead in a sugar-chest, for every body to see, with his flag standing up by him. And Sir George Ascue is carried up and down the Hague for people to see. Home to my office, where late, and then to bed.

17th (Lord's day). Being invited to Anthony Joyce's to dinner, my wife and sister and Mercer and I walked out in the morning, it being fine weather, to Christ Church, and there heard a silly sermon, but sat where we saw one of the prettiest little boys with the prettiest mouth that ever I saw in [my] life. Thence to Joyce's, where William Joyce and his wife were, and had a good dinner; but, Lord! how sicke was I of the company, only hope I shall have no more of it a good while; but am invited to Will's this week; and his wife, poor unhappy woman, cried to hear me say that I could not be there, she thinking that I slight her: so they got me to promise to come. Thence my father and I walked to Gray's Inne Fields, and there spent an houre or two walking and talking of several businesses; first, as to his estate, he told me it produced about L80 per ann., but then there goes L30 per. ann. taxes and other things, certain charge, which I do promise to make good as far as this L30, at which the poor man was overjoyed and wept. As to Pall he tells me he is mightily satisfied with Ensum, and so I promised to give her L500 presently, and to oblige myself to 100 more on the birth of her first child, he insuring her in L10 per ann. for every L100, and in the meantime till she do marry I promise to allow her L10 per ann. Then as to John I tell him I will promise him nothing, but will supply him as so much lent him, I declaring that I am not pleased with him yet, and that when his degree is over I will send for him up hither, and if he be good for any thing doubt not to get him preferment. This discourse ended to the joy of my father and no less to me to see that I am able to do this, we return to Joyce's and there wanting a coach to carry us home I walked out as far as the New Exchange to find one, but could not. So down to the Milke-house, and drank three glasses of whay, and then up into the Strand again, and there met with a coach, and so to Joyce's and took up my father, wife, sister, and Mercer, and to Islington, where we drank, and then our tour by Hackney home, where, after a little, business at my office and then talke with my Lady and Pegg Pen in the garden, I home and to bed, being very weary.

18th. Up betimes and in my chamber most of the morning setting things to rights there, my Journall and accounts with my father and brother, then to the office a little, and so to Lumbard Streete, to borrow a little money upon a tally, but cannot. Thence to the Exchequer, and there after much wrangling got consent that I should have a great tally broken into little ones. Thence to Hales's to see how my father's picture goes on, which pleases me mighty well, though I find again, as I did in Mrs. Pierce's, that a picture may have more of a likeness in the first or second working than it shall have when finished, though this is very well and to my full content, but so it is, and certainly mine was not so like at the first, second, or third sitting as it was afterward. Thence to my Lord Bellasses, by invitation, and there dined with him, and his lady and daughter; and at dinner there played to us a young boy, lately come from France, where he had been learning a yeare or two on the viallin, and plays finely. But impartially I do not find any goodnesse in their ayres (though very good) beyond ours when played by the same hand, I observed in several of Baptiste's'

(the present great composer) and our Bannister's. But it was pretty to see how passionately my Lord's daughter loves musique, the most that ever I saw creature in my life. Thence after dinner home and to the office and anon to Lumbard Streete again, where much talke at Colvill's, he censuring the times, and how matters are ordered, and with reason enough; but, above all, the thinking to borrow money of the City, which will not be done, but be denied, they being little pleased with the King's affairs, and that must breed differences between the King and the City. Thence down by water to Deptford, to order things away to the fleete and back again, and after some business at my office late home to supper and to bed. Sir W. Coventry is returned this night from the fleete, he being the activest man in the world, and we all (myself particularly) more afeard of him than of the King or his service, for aught I see; God forgive us! This day the great newes is come of the French, their taking the island of St. Christopher's' from us; and it is to be feared they have done the like of all those islands thereabouts this makes the city mad.

19th. Up, and to my office, there to fit business against the rest meet, which they did by and by, and sat late. After the office rose (with Creed with me) to Wm. Joyce's to dinner, being invited, and there find my father and sister, my wife and Mercer, with them, almost dined. I made myself as complaisant as I could till I had dined, but yet much against my will, and so away after dinner with Creed to Penny's, my Tailor, where I bespoke a thin stuff suit, and did spend a little time evening some little accounts with Creed and so parted, and I to Sir. G. Carteret's by appointment; where I perceive by him the King is going to borrow some money of the City; but I fear it will do no good, but hurt. He tells me how the Generall—[The Duke of Albemarle.]—is displeased, and there have been some high words between the Generall and Sir W. Coventry. And it may be so; for I do not find Sir W. Coventry so highly commending the Duke as he used to be, but letting fall now and then some little jerkes: as this day, speaking of newes from Holland, he says, "I find their victory begins to shrinke there, as well as ours here." Here I met with Captain Cocke, and he tells me that the first thing the Prince said to the King upon his coming, was complaining of the Commissioners of the Navy; that they could have been abroad in three or four days but for us; that we do not take care of them which I am troubled at, and do fear may in violence break out upon this office some time or other; for we shall not be able to carry on the business. Thence home, and at my business till late at night, then with my wife into the garden and there sang with Mercer, whom I feel myself begin to love too much by handling of her breasts in a' morning when she dresses me, they being the finest that ever I saw in my life, that is the truth of it. So home and to supper with beans and bacon and to bed.

20th. Up, but in some pain of the collique. I have of late taken too much cold by washing my feet and going in a thin silke waistcoate, without any other coate over it, and open-breasted, but I hope it will go over. I did this morning (my father being to go away to-morrow) give my father some money to buy him a horse, and for other things to himself and my mother and sister, among them L20, besides undertaking to pay for other things for them to about L3, which the poor man takes with infinite kindnesse, and I do not thinke I can bestow it better. Thence by coach to St.

James's as usual to wait on the Duke of York, after having discoursed with Collonell Fitzgerald, whom I met in my way and he returned with me to Westminster, about paying him a sum of 700 and odd pounds, and he bids me defalk L25 for myself,—[Abate from an amount.]—which is a very good thing; having done with the Duke I to the Exchequer and there after much ado do get my business quite over of the difficulty of breaking a great tally into little ones and so shall have it done tomorrow. Thence to the Hall and with Mrs. Martin home and staid with her a while, and then away to the Swan and sent for a bit of meat and dined there, and thence to Faythorne, the picture-seller's, and there chose two or three good Cutts to try to vernish, and so to Hales's to see my father's picture, which is now near finished and is very good, and here I staid and took a nap of an hour, thinking my father and wife would have come, but they did not; so I away home as fast as I could, fearing lest my father this day going abroad to see Mr. Honiwood at Major Russell's might meet with any trouble, and so in great pain home; but to spite me, in Cheapside I met Mrs. Williams in a coach, and she called me, so I must needs 'light and go along with her and poor Knipp (who is so big as she can tumble and looks-every day to lie down) as far as Paternoster Row, which I did do and there staid in Bennett's shop with them, and was fearfull lest the people of the shop, knowing me, should aske after my father and give Mrs. Williams any knowledge of me to my disgrace. Having seen them done there and accompanied them to Ludgate I 'light and into my owne coach and home, where I find my father and wife had had no intent of coming at all to Hales's. So I at home all the evening doing business, and at night in the garden (it having been these three or four days mighty hot weather) singing in the evening, and then home to supper and to bed.

21st. Up, and at the office all the morning; whereby several circumstances I find Sir W. Coventry and the Duke of Albemarle do not agree as they used to do; Sir W. Coventry commending Aylett (in some reproach to the Duke), whom the Duke hath put out for want of courage; and found fault with Steward, whom the Duke keeps in, though as much in fault as any commander in the fleete. At noon home to dinner, my father, sister, and wife dining at Sarah Giles's, poor woman, where I should have been, but my pride would not suffer me. After dinner to Mr. Debasty's to speake with Sir Robert Viner, a fine house and a great many fine ladies. He used me mighty civilly. My business was to set the matter right about the letter of credit he did give my Lord Belassis, that I may take up the tallys lodged with Viner for his security in the answering of my Lord's bills, which we did set right very well, and Sir Robert Viner went home with me and did give me the L5000 tallys presently. Here at Mr. Debasty's I saw, in a gold frame, a picture of a Outer playing on his flute which, for a good while, I took for paynting, but at last observed it a piece of tapestry, and is the finest that ever I saw in my life for figures, and good natural colours, and a very fine thing it is indeed. So home and met Sir George Smith by the way, who tells me that this day my Lord Chancellor and some of the Court have been with the City, and the City have voted to lend the King L100,000; which, if soon paid (as he says he believes it will), will be a greater service than I did ever expect at this time from the City. So home to my letters and then with my wife in the garden, and then upon our leades singing in the evening and so to supper (while at supper comes young Michell, whose wife I love, little Betty

Howlet, to get my favour about a ticket, and I am glad of this occasion of obliging him and give occasion of his coming to me, for I must be better acquainted with him and her), and after supper to bed.

22nd. Up, and before I went out Mr. Peter Barr sent me a tierce of claret, which is very welcome. And so abroad down the river to Deptford and there did some business, and then to Westminster, and there did with much ado get my tallys (my small ones instead of one great one of L2,000), and so away home and there all day upon my Tangier accounts with Creed, and, he being gone, with myself, in settling other accounts till past twelve at night, and then every body being in bed, I to bed, my father, wife, and sister late abroad upon the water, and Mercer being gone to her mother's and staid so long she could not get into the office, which vexed me.

23rd. My father and sister very betimes took their leave; and my wife, with all possible kindnesse, went with them to the coach, I being mightily pleased with their company thus long, and my father with his being here, and it rejoices my heart that I am in condition to do any thing to comfort him, and could, were it not for my mother, have been contented he should have stayed alwayes here with me, he is such innocent company. They being gone, I to my papers, but vexed at what I heard but a little of this morning, before my wife went out, that Mercer and she fell out last night, and that the girle is gone home to her mother's for all-together: This troubles me, though perhaps it may be an ease to me of so much charge. But I love the girle, and another we must be forced to keepe I do foresee and then shall be sorry to part with her. At the office all the morning, much disquiett in my mind in the middle of my business about this girle. Home at noon to dinner, and what with the going away of my father today and the losse of Mercer, I after dinner went up to my chamber and there could have cried to myself, had not people come to me about business. In the evening down to Tower Wharfe thinking to go by water, but could not get watermen; they being now so scarce, by reason of the great presse; so to the Custome House, and there, with great threats, got a couple to carry me down to Deptford, all the way reading Pompey the Great (a play translated from the French by several noble persons; among others, my Lord Buckhurst), that to me is but a mean play, and the words and sense not very extraordinary. From Deptford I walked to Redriffe, and in my way was overtaken by Bagwell, lately come from sea in the Providence, who did give me an account of several particulars in the late fight, and how his ship was deserted basely by the York, Captain Swanly, commander. So I home and there after writing my letters home to supper and to bed, fully resolved to rise betimes, and go down the river to-morrow morning, being vexed this night to find none of the officers in the yarde at 7 at night, nor any body concerned as if it were a Dutch warr. It seems Mercer's mother was here in the morning to speak with my wife, but my wife would not. In the afternoon I and my wife in writing did instruct W. Hewer in some discourse to her, and she in the evening did come and satisfy my wife, and by and by Mercer did come, which I was mighty glad of and eased of much pain about her.

24th. Sunday. Midsummer Day. Up, but, being weary the last night, not so soon as I intended. Then being dressed, down by water to Deptford, and there did a great deale of business, being in a mighty hurry, Sir W. Coventry writing to me that there was some thoughts that the Dutch fleete were out or coming out. Business being done in providing for the carrying down of some provisions to the fleete, I away back home and after dinner by water to White Hall, and there waited till the councill rose, in the boarded gallery, and there among other things I hear that Sir Francis Prujean is dead, after being married to a widow about a yeare or thereabouts. He died very rich, and had, for the last yeare, lived very handsomely, his lady bringing him to it. He was no great painstaker in person, yet died very rich; and, as Dr. Clerke says, was of a very great judgment, but hath writ nothing to leave his name to posterity. In the gallery among others met with Major Halsey, a great creature of the Duke of Albemarle's; who tells me that the Duke, by name, hath said that he expected to have the worke here up in the River done, having left Sir W. Batten and Mr. Phipps there. He says that the Duke of Albemarle do say that this is a victory we have had, having, as he was sure, killed them 8000 men, and sunk about fourteen of their ships; but nothing like this appears true. He lays much of the little success we had, however, upon the fleete's being divided by order from above, and the want of spirit in the commanders; and that he was commanded by order to go out of the Downes to the Gun-fleete, and in the way meeting the Dutch fleete, what should he do? should he not fight them? especially having beat them heretofore at as great disadvantage. He tells me further, that having been downe with the Duke of Albemarle, he finds that Holmes and Spragge do govern most business of the Navy; and by others I understand that Sir Thomas Allen is offended thereat; that he is not so much advised with as he ought to be. He tells me also, as he says, of his own knowledge, that several people before the Duke went out did offer to supply the King with L100,000 provided he would be treasurer of it, to see it laid out for the Navy; which he refused, and so it died. But I believe none of this. This day I saw my Lady Falmouth, with whom I remember now I have dined at my Lord Barkeley's heretofore, a pretty woman: she was now in her second or third mourning, and pretty pleasant in her looks. By and by the Council rises, and Sir W. Coventry comes out; and he and I went aside, and discoursed of much business of the Navy; and afterwards took his coach, and to Hide-Parke, he and I alone: there we had much talke. First, he started a discourse of a talke he hears about the towne, which, says he, is a very bad one, and fit to be suppressed, if we knew how which is, the comparing of the successe of the last year with that of this; saying that that was good, and that bad. I was as sparing in speaking as I could, being jealous of him and myself also, but wished it could be stopped; but said I doubted it could not otherwise than by the fleete's being abroad again, and so finding other worke for men's minds and discourse. Then to discourse of himself, saying, that he heard that he was under the lash of people's discourse about the Prince's not having notice of the Dutch being out, and for him to comeback again, nor the Duke of Albemarle notice that the Prince was sent for back again: to which he told me very particularly how careful he was the very same night that it was resolved to send for the Prince back, to cause orders to be writ, and waked the Duke, who was then in bed, to sign them; and that they went by expresse that very night, being the Wednesday night before the fight, which begun on the Friday; and that for sending them by the post expresse, and not by gentlemen on purpose, he made a sport of it, and said, I knew of none to send it with, but would at least have lost more time in fitting themselves out, than any diligence of theirs beyond that of the ordinary post would have recovered. I told him that this was not so much the towne talke as the reason of dividing the fleete. To this he told me he ought not to say much; but did assure me in general that the proposition did first come from the fleete, and the resolution not being prosecuted with orders so soon as the Generall thought fit, the Generall did send Sir Edward Spragge up on purpose for them; and that there was nothing in the whole business which was not done with the full consent and advice of the Duke of Albemarle.

But he did adde (as the Catholiques call 'le secret de la Masse'), that Sir Edward Spragge—who had even in Sir Christopher Mings's time put in to be the great favourite of the Prince, but much more now had a mind to be the great man with him, and to that end had a mind to have the Prince at a distance from the Duke of Albemarle, that they might be doing something alone—did, as he believed, put on this business of dividing the fleete, and that thence it came.

He tells me as to the business of intelligence, the want whereof the world did complain much of, that for that it was not his business, and as he was therefore to have no share in the blame, so he would not meddle to lay it any where else. That de Ruyter was ordered by the States not to make it his business to come into much danger, but to preserve himself as much as was fit out of harm's way, to be able to direct the fleete. He do, I perceive, with some violence, forbear saying any thing to the reproach of the Duke of Albemarle; but, contrarily, speaks much of his courage; but I do as plainly see that he do not like the Duke of Albemarle's proceedings, but, contrarily, is displeased therewith. And he do plainly diminish the commanders put in by the Duke, and do lessen the miscarriages of any that have been removed by him. He concurs with me, that the next bout will be a fatal one to one side or other, because, if we be beaten, we shall not be able to set out our fleete again. He do confess with me that the hearts of our seamen are much saddened; and for that reason, among others, wishes Sir Christopher Mings was alive, who might inspire courage and spirit into them. Speaking of Holmes, how great a man he is, and that he do for the present, and hath done all the voyage, kept himself in good order and within bounds; but, says he, a cat will be a cat still, and some time or other out his humour must break again. He do not disowne but that the dividing of the fleete upon the presumptions that were then had (which, I suppose, was the French fleete being come this way), was a good resolution. Having had all this discourse, he and I back to White Hall; and there I left him, being [in] a little doubt whether I had behaved myself in my discourse with the policy and circumspection which ought to be used to so great a courtier as he is, and so wise and factious a man, and by water home, and so, after supper, to bed.

25th. Up, and all the morning at my Tangier accounts, which the chopping and changing of my tallys make mighty troublesome; but, however, I did end them with great satisfaction to myself. At noon, without staying to eat my dinner, I down by water to Deptford, and there coming find Sir W. Batten and Sir Jeremy Smith (whom the dispatch of the Loyall London detained) at dinner at Greenwich at the Beare Taverne, and thither I to them and there dined with them. Very good company of strangers there was, but I took no great pleasure among them, being desirous to be back again. So got them to rise as soon as I could, having told them the newes Sir W. Coventry just now wrote me to tell them, which is, that the Dutch are certainly come out. I did much business at Deptford, and so home, by an old poor man, a sculler, having no oares to be got, and all this day on the water entertained myself with the play of Commenius, and being come home did go out to Aldgate, there to be overtaken by Mrs. Margot Pen in her father's coach, and my wife and Mercer with her, and Mrs. Pen carried us to two gardens at Hackny, (which I every day grow more and more in love with,) Mr. Drake's one, where the garden is good, and house and the prospect admirable; the other my Lord Brooke's, where the gardens are much better, but the house not so good, nor the prospect good at all. But the gardens are excellent; and here I first saw oranges grow: some green, some half, some a quarter, and some full ripe, on the same tree, and one fruit of the same tree do come a year or two after the other. I pulled off a little one by stealth (the man being mighty curious of them) and eat it, and it was just as other little green small oranges are; as big as half the end of my little finger. Here were also great variety of other exotique plants, and several labarinths, and a pretty aviary. Having done there with very great pleasure we away back again, and called at the Taverne in Hackny by the church, and there drank and eate, and so in the Goole of the evening home. This being the first day of my putting on my black stuff bombazin suit, and I hope to feel no inconvenience by it, the weather being extremely hot. So home and to bed, and this night the first night of my lying without a waistcoat, which I hope I shall very well endure. So to bed. This morning I did with great pleasure hear Mr. Caesar play some good things on his lute, while he come to teach my boy Tom, and I did give him 40s. for his encouragement.

26th. Up and to my office betimes, and there all the morning, very busy to get out the fleete, the Dutch being now for certain out, and we shall not, we thinke, be much behindhand with them. At noon to the 'Change about business, and so home to dinner, and after dinner to the setting my Journall to rights, and so to the office again, where all the afternoon full of business, and there till night, that my eyes were sore, that I could not write no longer. Then into the garden, then my wife and Mercer and my Lady Yen and her daughter with us, and here we sung in the darke very finely half an houre, and so home to supper and to bed. This afternoon, after a long drowth, we had a good shower of rain, but it will not signify much if no more come. This day in the morning come Mr. Chichly to Sir W. Coventry, to tell him the ill successe of the guns made for the Loyall London; which is, that in the trial every one of the great guns, the whole cannon of seven (as I take it), broke in pieces, which is a strange mishap, and that which will give more occasion to people's discourse of the King's business being done ill. This night Mary my cookemayde, that hath been with us about three months, but find herself not able to do my worke, so is gone with great kindnesse away, and another (Luce) come, very ugly and plaine, but may be a good servant for all that.

27th. Up, and to my office awhile, and then down the river a little way to see vessels ready for the carrying down of 400 land soldiers to the fleete. Then back to the office for my papers, and so to St. James's, where we did our usual attendance on the Duke. Having done with him, we all of us down to Sir W. Coventry's chamber (where I saw his father my Lord Coventry's picture hung up, done by Stone, who then brought it home. It is a good picture, drawn in his judge's robes, and the great seale by him. And while it was hanging up, "This," says Sir W. Coventry, merrily, "is the use we make of our fathers,") to discourse about the proposition of serving us with hempe, delivered in by my Lord Brouncker as from an unknown person, though I know it to be Captain Cocke's. My Lord and Sir William Coventry had some earnest words about it, the one promoting it for his private ends, being, as Cocke tells me himself, to have L500 if the bargain goes on, and I am to have as much, and the other opposing it for the unseasonableness of it, not knowing at all whose the proposition is, which seems the more ingenious of the two. I sat by and said nothing, being no great friend to the proposition, though Cocke intends me a convenience by it. But what I observed most from the discourse was this of Sir W. Coventry, that he do look upon ourselves in a desperate condition. The issue of all standing upon this one point, that by the next fight, if we beat, the Dutch will certainly be content to take eggs for their money (that was his expression); or if we be beaten, we must be contented to make peace, and glad if we can have it without paying too dear for it. And withall we do rely wholly upon the Parliament's giving us more money the next sitting, or else we are undone. Being gone hence, I took coach to the Old Exchange, but did not go into it, but to Mr. Cade's, the stationer, stood till the shower was over, it being a great and welcome one after so much dry weather. Here I understand that Ogleby is putting out some new fables of his owne, which will be very fine and very satyricall. Thence home to dinner, and after dinner carried my wife to her sister's and I to Mr. Hales's, to pay for my father's picture, which cost me L10 the head and 25s. the frame. Thence to Lovett's, who has now done something towards the varnishing of single paper for the making of books, which will do, I think, very well. He did also carry me to a Knight's chamber in Graye's Inne, where there is a frame of his making, of counterfeite tortoise shell, which indeed is most excellently done. Then I took him with me to a picture shop to choose a print for him to vernish, but did not agree for one then. Thence to my wife to take her up and so carried her home, and I at the office till late, and so to supper with my wife and to bed. I did this afternoon visit my Lord Bellasses, who professes all imaginable satisfaction in me. He spoke dissatisfiedly with Creed, which I was pleased well enough with. My Lord is going down to his garrison to Hull, by the King's command, to put it in order for fear of an invasion which course I perceive is taken upon the sea-coasts round; for we have a real apprehension of the King of France's invading us.

28th. Up, and at the office all the morning. At noon home to dinner, and after dinner abroad to Lumbard Streete, there to reckon with Sir Robert Viner for some money, and did sett all straight to my great content, and so home, and all the afternoon and evening at the office, my mind full at this time of getting my accounts over, and as much money in my hands as I can, for a great turne is to be feared in the times, the French having some great design (whatever it is) in hand, and our necessities on every side very great. The Dutch are now known to be out, and we may expect them every houre upon our coast. But our fleete is in pretty good readinesse for them.

29th. Up, and within doors most of the morning, sending a porter (Sanders) up and down to several people to pay them money to clear my month's debts every where, being mighty desirous to have all clear so soon as I can, and to that end did so much in settling my Tangier accounts clear. At noon dined, having first been down at Deptford and did a little business there and back again. After dinner to White Hall to a Committee of Tangier, but I come a little too late, they were up, so I to several places about business, among others to Westminster Hall, and there did meet with Betty Michell at her own mother's shop. I would fain have carried her home by water, but she was to sup at that end of the town. So I away to White Hall, and thence, the Council being up, walked to St. James's, and there had much discourse with Sir W. Coventry at his chamber, who I find quite weary of the warr, decries our having any warr at all, or himself to have been any occasion of it, that he hopes this will make us shy of any warr hereafter, or to prepare better for it, believes that one overthrow on the Dutch side would make them desire peace, and that one on ours will make us willing to accept of one: tells me that Commissioner Pett is fallen infinitely under the displeasure of the Prince and Duke of Albemarle, not giving them satisfaction in the getting out of the fleete, and that the complaint he believes is come to the King, and by Sir W. Coventry's discourse I find he do concur in it, and speaks of his having of no authority in the place where he is, and I do believe at least it will end in his being removed to some other yarde, and I am not sorry for it, but do fear that though he deserves as bad, yet at this time the blame may not be so well deserved. Thence home and to the office; where I met with a letter from Dover, which tells me (and it did come by expresse) that newes is brought over by a gentleman from Callice that the Dutch fleete, 130 sail, are come upon the French coast; and that the country is bringing in picke-axes, and shovells, and wheel-barrows into Callice; that there are 6,000 men armed with head, back, and breast (Frenchmen) ready to go on board the Dutch fleete, and will be followed by 12,000 more. That they pretend they are to come to Dover; and that thereupon the Governor of Dover Castle is getting the victuallers' provision out of the towne into the Castle to secure it. But I do think this is a ridiculous conceit; but a little time will show. At night home to supper and to bed,

30th. Up, and to the office, and mightily troubled all this morning with going to my Lord Mayor (Sir Thomas Bludworth,

a silly man, I think), and other places, about getting shipped some men that they have these two last nights pressed in the City out of houses: the persons wholly unfit for sea, and many of them people of very good fashion, which is a shame to think of, and carried to Bridewell they are, yet without being impressed with money legally as they ought to be. But to see how the King's business is done; my Lord Mayor himself did scruple at this time of extremity to do this thing, because he had not money to pay the pressed-money to the men, he told me so himself; nor to take up boats to carry them down through bridge to the ships I had prepared to carry them down in; insomuch that I was forced to promise to be his paymaster, and he did send his City Remembrancer afterwards to the office, and at the table, in the face of the officers, I did there out of my owne purse disburse L15 to pay for their pressing and diet last night and this morning; which is a thing worth record of my Lord Mayor. Busy about this all the morning, at noon dined and then to the office again, and all the afternoon till twelve at night full of this business and others, and among these others about the getting off men pressed by our officers of the fleete into the service; even our owne men that are at the office, and the boats that carry us. So that it is now become impossible to have so much as a letter carried from place to place, or any message done for us: nay, out of Victualling ships full loaden to go down to the fleete, and out of the vessels of the officers of the Ordnance, they press men, so that for want of discipline in this respect I do fear all will be undone. Vexed with these things, but eased in mind by my ridding of a great deale of business from the office, I late home to supper and to bed. But before I was in bed, while I was undressing myself, our new ugly mayde, Luce, had like to have broke her necke in the darke, going down our upper stairs; but, which I was glad of, the poor girle did only bruise her head, but at first did lie on the ground groaning and drawing her breath, like one a-dying. This month I end in much hurry of business, but in much more trouble in mind to thinke what will become of publique businesses, having so many enemys abroad, and neither force nor money at all, and but little courage for ourselves, it being really true that the spirits of our seamen and commanders too are really broke by the last defeate with the Dutch, and this is not my conjecture only, but the real and serious thoughts of Sir G. Carteret and Sir W. Coventry, whom I have at distinct times heard the same thing come from with a great deale of grief and trouble. But, lastly, I am providing against a foule day to get as much money into my hands as I can, at least out of the publique hands, that so, if a turne, which I fear, do come, I may have a little to trust to. I pray God give me good successe in my choice how to dispose of what little I have, that I may not take it out of publique hands, and put it into worse.

JULY 1666

July 1st (Sunday). Up betimes, and to the office receiving letters, two or three one after another from Sir W. Coventry, and sent as many to him, being full of variety of business and hurry, but among the chiefest is the getting of these pressed men out of the City down the river to the fleete. While I was hard at it comes Sir W. Pen to towne, which I little expected, having invited my Lady and her daughter Pegg to dine with me to-day; which at noon they did, and Sir W. Pen with them: and pretty merry we were. And though I do not love him, yet I find it necessary to keep in with him; his good service at Shearnesse in getting out the fleete being much taken notice of, and reported to the King and Duke [of York], even from the Prince and Duke of Albemarle themselves, and made the most of to me and them by Sir W. Coventry: therefore I think it discretion, great and necessary discretion, to keep in with him. After dinner to the office again, where busy, and then down to Deptford to the yard, thinking to have seen Bagwell's wife, whose husband is gone yesterday back to the fleete, but I did not see her, so missed what I went for, and so back to the Tower several times, about the business of the pressed men, and late at it till twelve at night, shipping of them. But, Lord! how some poor women did cry; and in my life I never did see such natural expression of passion as I did here in some women's bewailing themselves, and running to every parcel of men that were brought, one after another, to look for their husbands, and wept over every vessel that went off, thinking they might be there, and looking after the ship as far as ever they could by moone-light, that it grieved me to the heart to hear them. Besides, to see poor patient labouring men and housekeepers, leaving poor wives and families, taking up on a sudden by strangers, was very hard, and that without press-money, but forced against all law to be gone. It is a great tyranny. Having done this I to the Lieutenant of the Tower and bade him good night, and so away home and to bed.

2nd. Up betimes, and forced to go to my Lord Mayor's, about the business of the pressed men; and indeed I find him a mean man of understanding and dispatch of any publique business. Thence out of curiosity to Bridewell to see the pressed men, where there are about 300; but so unruly that I durst not go among them: and they have reason to be so, having been kept these three days prisoners, with little or no victuals, and pressed out, and, contrary to all course of law, without press-money, and men that are not liable to it. Here I met with prating Colonel Cox, one of the City collonells heretofore a great presbyter: but to hear how the fellow did commend himself, and the service he do the King; and, like an asse, at Paul's did take me out of my way on purpose to show me the gate (the little north gate) where he had two men shot close by him on each hand, and his own hair burnt by a bullet-shot in the insurrection of Venner, and himself escaped. Thence home and to the Tower to see the men from Bridewell shipped. Being rid of him I home to dinner, and thence to the Excise office by appointment to meet my Lord Bellasses and the Commissioners, which we did and soon dispatched, and so I home, and there was called by Pegg Pen to her house, where her father and mother, and Mrs. Norton, the second Roxalana, a fine woman, indifferent handsome, good body and hand, and good mine, and pretends to sing, but do it not excellently. However I took pleasure there, and my wife was sent for, and Creed come in to us, and so there we spent the most of the afternoon. Thence weary of losing so much time I to the office, and thence presently down to Deptford; but to see what a consternation there is upon the water by reason of this great press, that nothing is able to get a waterman to appear almost. Here I meant to have spoke with Bagwell's mother, but her face was sore, and so I did not, but returned and upon the water found one of the vessels loaden with the Bridewell birds in a great mutiny, and they would not sail, not they; but with good words, and cajoling the ringleader into the Tower (where, when he was come, he was clapped up in the hole), they were got very quietly; but I think it is much if they do not run the vessel on ground. But away they went, and I to the Lieutenant of the Tower, and having talked with him a little, then home to supper very late and to bed weary.

3rd. Being very weary, lay long in bed, then to the office and there sat all the day. At noon dined at home, Balty's wife with us, and in very good humour I was and merry at dinner, and after dinner a song or two, and so I abroad to my Lord Treasurer's (sending my sister home by the coach), while I staid there by appointment to have met my Lord Bellasses and Commissioners of Excise, but they did not meet me, he being abroad. However Mr. Finch, one of the Commissioners, I met there, and he and I walked two houres together in the garden, talking of many things; sometimes of Mr. Povy, whose vanity, prodigality, neglect of his business, and committing it to unfit hands hath undone him and outed him of all his publique employments, and the thing set on foot by an accidental revivall of a business, wherein he had three or fours years ago, by surprize, got the Duke of Yorke to sign to the having a sum of money paid out of the Excise, before some that was due to him, and now the money is fallen short, and the Duke never likely to be paid. This being revived hath undone Povy. Then we fell to discourse of the Parliament, and the great men there: and among others, Mr. Vaughan, whom he reports as a man of excellent judgement and learning, but most passionate and 'opiniastre'. He had done himself the most wrong (though he values it not), that is, the displeasure of the King in his standing so long against the breaking of the Act for a trienniall parliament; but yet do believe him to be a most loyall gentleman. He told me Mr. Prin's character; that he is a man of mighty labour and reading and memory, but the worst judge of matters, or layer together of what he hath read, in the world; which I do not, however, believe him in; that he believes him very true to the King in his heart, but can never be reconciled to episcopacy; that the House do not lay much weight upon him, or any thing he says. He told me many fine things, and so we parted, and I home and hard to work a while at the office and then home and till midnight about settling my last month's accounts wherein I have been interrupted by public business, that I did not state them two or three days ago, but I do now to my great joy find myself worth above L5600, for which the Lord's name be praised! So with my heart full of content to bed. Newes come yesterday from Harwich, that the Dutch had appeared upon our coast with their fleete, and we believe did go to the Gun-fleete, and they are supposed to be there now; but I have heard nothing of them to-day. Yesterday Dr. Whistler, at Sir W. Pen's, told me that Alexander Broome, a the great song-maker, is lately dead.

4th. Up, and visited very betimes by Mr. Sheply, who is come to town upon business from

Hinchingbrooke, where he left all well. I out and walked along with him as far as Fleet Streete, it being a fast day, the usual fast day for the plague, and few coaches to be had. Thanks be to God, the plague is, as I hear, encreased but two this week; but in the country in several places it rages mightily, and particularly in Colchester, where it hath long been, and is believed will quite depopulate the place. To St. James's, and there did our usual business with the Duke, all of us, among other things, discoursing about the places where to build ten great ships; the King and Council have resolved on none to be under third-rates; but it is impossible to do it, unless we have more money towards the doing it than yet we have in any view. But, however, the shew must be made to the world. Thence to my Lord Bellasses to take my leave of him, he being going down to the North to look after the Militia there, for fear of an invasion. Thence home and dined, and then to the office, where busy all day, and in the evening Sir W. Pen come to me, and we walked together, and talked of the late fight. I find him very plain, that the whole conduct of the late fight was ill, and that that of truth's all, and he tells me that it is not he, but two-thirds of the commanders of the whole fleete have told him so: they all saying, that they durst not oppose it at the Council of War, for fear of being called cowards, though it was wholly against their judgement to fight that day with the disproportion of force, and then we not being able to use one gun of our lower tier, which was a greater disproportion than the other. Besides, we might very well have staid in the Downs without fighting, or any where else, till the Prince could have come up to them; or at least till the weather was fair, that we might have the benefit of our whole force in the ships that we had. He says three things must [be] remedied, or else we shall be undone by this fleete. 1. That we must fight in a line, whereas we fight promiscuously, to our utter and demonstrable ruine; the Dutch fighting otherwise; and we, whenever we beat them. 2. We must not desert ships of our own in distress, as we did, for that makes a captain desperate, and he will fling away his ship, when there is no hopes left him of succour. 3. That ships, when they are a little shattered, must not take the liberty to come in of themselves, but refit themselves the best they can, and stay out—many of our ships coming in with very small disablenesses. He told me that our very commanders, nay, our very flag-officers, do stand in need of exercising among themselves, and discoursing the business of commanding a fleete; he telling me that even one of our flag-men in the fleete did not know which tacke lost the wind, or which kept it, in the last engagement. He says it was pure dismaying and fear that made them all run upon the Galloper, not having their wits about them; and that it was a miracle they were not all lost. He much inveighs upon my discoursing of Sir John Lawson's saying heretofore, that sixty sail would do as much as one hundred; and says that he was a man of no counsel at all, but had got the confidence to say as the gallants did, and did propose to himself to make himself great by them, and saying as they did; but was no man of judgement in his business, but hath been out in the greatest points that have come before them. And then in the business of fore-castles, which he did oppose, all the world sees now the use of them for shelter of men. He did talk very rationally to me, insomuch that I took more pleasure this night in hearing him discourse, than I ever did in my life in any thing that he said. He gone I to the office again, and so after some business home to supper and to bed.

5th. Up and to the office, where we sat all the morning busy, then at noon dined and Mr. Sheply with me, who come to towne the other day. I lent him 630 in silver upon 30 pieces in gold. But to see how apt every body is to neglect old kindnesses! I must charge myself with the ingratitude of being unwilling to lend him so much money without some pawne, if he should have asked it, but he did not aske it, poor man, and so no harm done. After dinner, he gone, I to my office and Lumbard Streete about money, and then to my office again, very busy, and so till late, and then a song with my wife and Mercer in the garden, and so with great content to bed.

6th. Up, and after doing some business at my office abroad to Lumbard Street, about the getting of a good sum of money, thence home, in preparation for my having some good sum in my hands, for fear of a trouble in the State, that I may not have all I have in the world out of my hands and so be left a beggar. Having put that in a way, I home to the office, and so to the Tower; about shipping of some more pressed men, and that done, away to Broad Streete, to Sir G. Carteret, who is at a pay of tickets all alone, and I believe not less than one thousand people in the streets. But it is a pretty thing to observe that both there and every where else, a man shall see many women now-a-days of mean sort in the streets, but no men; men being so afeard of the press. I dined with Sir G. Carteret, and after dinner had much discourse about our publique business; and he do seem to fear every day more and more what I do; which is, a general confusion in the State; plainly answering me to the question, who is it that the weight of the warr depends [upon]? that it is only Sir W. Coventry. He tells me, too, the Duke of Albemarle is dissatisfied, and that the Duchesse do curse Coventry as the man that betrayed her husband to the sea: though I believe that it is not so. Thence to Lumbard Streete, and received L2000, and carried it home: whereof L1000 in gold. The greatest quantity not only that I ever had of gold, but that ever I saw together, and is not much above half a 100 lb. bag full, but is much weightier. This I do for security sake, and convenience of carriage; though it costs me above L70 the change of it, at 18 1/2d. per piece. Being at home, I there met with a letter from Bab Allen,— [Mrs. Knipp]—to invite me to be god-father to her boy, with Mrs. Williams, which I consented to, but know not the time when it is to be. Thence down to the Old Swan, calling at Michell's, he not being within, and there I did steal a kiss or two of her, and staying a little longer, he come in, and her father, whom I carried to Westminster, my business being thither, and so back again home, and very busy all the evening. At night a song in the garden and to bed.

7th. At the office all the morning, at noon dined at home and Creed with me, and after dinner he and I two or three hours in my chamber discoursing of the fittest way for a man to do that hath money, and find all he offers of turning some into gold and leaving some in a friend's hand is nothing more than what I thought of myself, but is doubtful, as well as I, what is best to be done of all these or other ways to be thought on. He tells me he finds all things mighty dull at Court; and that they now begin to lie long in bed; it being, as we suppose, not seemly for them to be found playing and gaming as they used to be; nor that their minds are at ease enough to follow those sports, and yet not knowing how to employ themselves (though there be work enough for their thoughts and councils and pains), they keep long in bed. But he thinks with me, that there is nothing in the world can helpe us but the King's personal looking after his business and his officers, and that with that we may yet do well; but otherwise must be undone: nobody at this day taking care of any thing, nor hath any body to call him to account for it. Thence left him and to my office all the afternoon busy, and in some pain in my back by some bruise or other I have given myself in my right testicle this morning, and the pain lies there and hath done, and in my back thereupon all this day. At night into the garden to my wife and Lady Pen and Pegg, and Creed, who staid with them till to at night. My Lady Pen did give us a tarte and other things, and so broke up late and I to bed. It proved the hottest night that ever I was in in my life, and thundered and lightened all night long and rained hard. But, Lord! to see in what fears I lay a good while, hearing of a little noise of somebody walking in the house: so rung the bell, and it was my mayds going to bed about one o'clock in the morning. But the fear of being robbed, having so much money in the house, was very great, and is still so, and do much disquiet me.

8th (Lord's day). Up, and pretty well of my pain, so that it did not trouble me at all, and I do clearly find that my pain in my back was nothing but only accompanied my bruise in my stones. To church, wife and Mercer and I, in expectation of hearing some mighty preacher to-day, Mrs. Mary Batelier sending us word so; but it proved our ordinary silly lecturer, which made me merry, and she laughed upon us to see her mistake. At noon W. Hewer dined with us, and a good dinner, and I expected to have had newes sent me of Knipp's christening to-day; but, hearing nothing of it, I did not go, though I fear it is but their forgetfulness and so I may disappoint them. To church, after dinner, again, a thing I have not done a good while before, go twice in one day. After church with my wife and Mercer and Tom by water through bridge to the Spring Garden at Fox Hall, and thence down to Deptford and there did a little business, and so back home and to bed.

9th. Up betimes, and with Sir W. Pen in his coach to Westminster to Sir G. Downing's, but missed of him, and so we parted, I by water home, where busy all the morning, at noon dined at home, and after dinner to my office, where busy till come to by Lovett and his wife, who have brought me some sheets of paper varnished on one side, which lies very white and smooth and, I think, will do our business most exactly, and will come up to the use that I intended them for, and I am apt to believe will be an invention that will take in the world. I have made up a little book of it to give Sir W. Coventry to-morrow, and am very well pleased with it. Home with them, and there find my aunt Wight with my wife come to take her leave of her, being going for the summer into the country; and there was also Mrs. Mary Batelier and her sister, newly come out of France, a black, very black woman, but mighty good-natured people both, as ever I saw. Here I made the black one sing a French song, which she did mighty innocently; and then Mrs. Lovett play on the lute, which she do very well; and then Mercer and I sang; and so, with great pleasure, I left them, having shewed them my chamber, and L1000 in gold, which they wondered at, and given them sweetmeats, and shewn my aunt Wight my father's picture, which she admires. So I left them and to the office, where Mr. Moore come to me and talking of my Lord's family business tells me that Mr. Sheply is ignorantly, we all believe, mistaken in his accounts above L700 more than he can discharge himself of, which is a mighty misfortune, poor man, and may undo him, and yet every body believes that he do it most honestly. I am troubled for him very much. He gone, I hard at the office till night, then home to supper and to bed.

10th. Up, and to the office, where busy all the morning, sitting, and there presented Sir W. Coventry with my little book made up of Lovett's varnished paper, which he and the whole board liked very well. At noon home to dinner and then to the office; the yarde being very full of women (I believe above three hundred) coming to get money for their husbands and friends that are prisoners in Holland; and they lay clamouring and swearing and cursing us, that my wife and I were afeard to send a venison-pasty that we have for supper to-night to the cook's to be baked, for fear of their offering violence to it: but it went, and no hurt done. Then I took an opportunity, when they were all gone into the foreyarde, and slipt into the office and there busy all the afternoon, but by and by the women got into the garden, and come all to my closett window, and there tormented me, and I confess their cries were so sad for money, and laying down the condition of their families and their husbands, and what they have done and suffered for the King, and how ill they are used by us, and how well the Dutch are used here by the allowance of their masters, and what their husbands are offered to serve the Dutch abroad, that I do most heartily pity them, and was ready to cry to hear them, but cannot helpe them. However, when the rest were gone, I did call one to me that I heard complaine only and pity her husband and did give her some money, and she blessed me and went away. Anon my business at the office being done I to the Tower to speak with Sir John Robinson about business, principally the bad condition of the pressed men for want of clothes, so it is represented from the fleete, and so to provide them shirts and stockings and drawers. Having done with him about that, I home and there find my wife and the two Mrs. Bateliers walking in the garden. I with them till almost 9 at night, and then they and we and Mrs. Mercer, the mother, and her daughter Anne, and our Mercer, to supper to a good venison-pasty and other good things, and had a good supper, and very merry, Mistresses Bateliers being both very good-humoured. We sang and talked, and then led them home, and there they made us drink; and, among other things, did show us, in cages, some birds brought from about Bourdeaux, that are all fat, and, examining one of them, they are so, almost all fat. Their name is [Ortolans], which are brought over to the King for him to eat, and indeed are excellent things. We parted from them and so home to bed, it being very late, and to bed.

11th. Up, and by water to Sir G. Downing's, there to discourse with him about the reliefe of the prisoners in Holland; which I did, and we do resolve of the manner of sending them some. So I away by coach to St. James's, and there hear that the Duchesse is lately brought to bed of a boy. By and by called to wait on the Duke, the King being present; and there agreed, among other things, of the places to build the ten new great ships ordered to be built, and as to the relief of prisoners in Holland. And then about several stories of the basenesse of the King of Spayne's being served with officers: they in Flanders having as good common men as any Prince in the world, but the veriest cowards for the officers, nay for the generall officers, as the Generall and Lieutenant-generall, in the whole world. But, above all things, the King did speake most in contempt of the ceremoniousnesse of the King of Spayne, that he do nothing but under some ridiculous form or other, and will not piss but another must hold the chamber-pot. Thence to

Westminster Hall and there staid a while, and then to the Swan and kissed Sarah, and so home to dinner, and after dinner out again to Sir Robert Viner, and there did agree with him to accommodate some business of tallys so as I shall get in near L2000 into my own hands, which is in the King's, upon tallys; which will be a pleasure to me, and satisfaction to have a good sum in my own hands, whatever evil disturbances should be in the State; though it troubles me to lose so great a profit as the King's interest of ten per cent. for that money. Thence to Westminster, doing several things by the way, and there failed of meeting Mrs. Lane, and so by coach took up my wife at her sister's, and so away to Islington, she and I alone, and so through Hackney, and home late, our discourse being about laying up of some money safe in prevention to the troubles I am afeard we may have in the state, and so sleepy (for want of sleep the last night, going to bed late and rising betimes in the morning) home, but when I come to the office, I there met with a command from my Lord Arlington, to go down to a galliott at Greenwich, by the King's particular command, that is going to carry the Savoy Envoye over, and we fear there may be many Frenchmen there on board; and so I have a power and command to search for and seize all that have not passes from one of the Secretarys of State, and to bring them and their papers and everything else in custody some whither. So I to the Tower, and got a couple of musquetiers with me, and Griffen and my boy Tom and so down; and, being come, found none on board but two or three servants, looking to horses and doggs, there on board, and, seeing no more, I staid not long there, but away and on shore at Greenwich, the night being late and the tide against us; so, having sent before, to Mrs. Clerke's and there I had a good bed, and well received, the whole people rising to see me, and among the rest young Mrs. Daniel, whom I kissed again and again alone, and so by and by to bed and slept pretty well,

12th. But was up again by five o'clock, and was forced to rise, having much business, and so up and dressed myself (enquiring, was told that Mrs. Tooker was gone hence to live at London) and away with Poundy to the Tower, and thence, having shifted myself, but being mighty drowsy for want of sleep, I by coach to St. James's, to Goring House, there to wait on my Lord Arlington to give him an account of my night's worke, but he was not up, being not long since married: so, after walking up and down the house below,—being the house I was once at Hartlib's sister's wedding, and is a very fine house and finely furnished,—and then thinking it too much for me to lose time to wait my Lord's rising, I away to St. James's, and there to Sir W. Coventry, and wrote a letter to my Lord Arlington giving him an account of what I have done, and so with Sir W. Coventry into London, to the office. And all the way I observed him mightily to make mirth of the Duke of Albemarle and his people about him, saying, that he was the happiest man in the world for doing of great things by sorry instruments. And so particularized in Sir W. Clerke, and Riggs, and Halsey, and others. And then again said that the only quality eminent in him was, that he did persevere; and indeed he is a very drudge, and stands by the King's business. And this he said, that one thing he was good at, that he never would receive an excuse if the thing was not done; listening to no reasoning for it, be it good or bad. But then I told him, what he confessed, that he would however give the man, that he employs, orders for removing of any obstruction that he thinks he shall meet with in the world, and instanced in several warrants that he issued for breaking open of houses and other outrages about the business of prizes, which people bore with either for affection or fear, which he believes would not have been borne with from the King, nor Duke, nor any man else in England, and I thinke he is in the right, but it is not from their love of him, but from something else I cannot presently say. Sir W. Coventry did further say concerning Warcupp, his kinsman, that had the simplicity to tell Sir W. Coventry, that the Duke did intend to go to sea and to leave him his agent on shore for all things that related to the sea. But, says Sir W. Coventry, I did believe but the Duke of Yorke would expect to be his agent on shore for all sea matters. And then he begun to say what a great man Warcupp was, and something else, and what was that but a great lyer; and told me a story, how at table he did, they speaking about antipathys, say, that a rose touching his skin any where, would make it rise and pimple; and, by and by, the dessert coming, with roses upon it, the Duchesse bid him try, and they did; but they rubbed and rubbed, but nothing would do in the world, by which his lie was found at then. He spoke contemptibly of Holmes and his mermidons, that come to take down the ships from hence, and have carried them without any necessaries, or any thing almost, that they will certainly be longer getting ready than if they had staid here. In fine, I do observe, he hath no esteem nor kindnesse for the Duke's matters, but, contrarily, do slight him and them; and I pray God the Kingdom do not pay too dear by this jarring; though this blockheaded Duke I did never expect better from. At the office all the morning, at noon home and thought to have slept, my head all day being full of business and yet sleepy and out of order, and so I lay down on my bed in my gowne to sleep, but I could not, therefore about three o'clock up and to dinner and thence to the office, where. Mrs. Burroughs, my pretty widow, was and so I did her business and sent her away by agreement, and presently I by coach after and took her up in Fenchurch Streete and away through the City, hiding my face as much as I could, but she being mighty pretty and well enough clad, I was not afeard, but only lest somebody should see me and think me idle. I quite through with her, and so into the fields Uxbridge way, a mile or two beyond Tyburne, and then back and then to Paddington, and then back to Lyssen green, a place the coachman led me to (I never knew in my life) and there we eat and drank and so back to Chasing Crosse, and there I set her down. All the way most excellent pretty company. I had her lips as much as I would, and a mighty pretty woman she is and very modest and yet kinde in all fair ways. All this time I passed with mighty pleasure, it being what I have for a long time wished for, and did pay this day 5s. forfeite for her company. She being gone, I to White Hall and there to Lord Arlington's, and met Mr. Williamson, and find there is no more need of my trouble about the Galliott, so with content departed, and went straight home, where at the office did the most at the office in that wearied and sleepy state I could, and so home to supper, and after supper falling to singing with Mercer did however sit up with her, she pleasing me with her singing of "Helpe, helpe," 'till past midnight and I not a whit drowsy, and so to bed.

13th. Lay sleepy in bed till 8 in the morning, then up and to the office, where till about noon, then out to the 'Change and several places, and so home to dinner. Then out again to Sir R. Vines, and there to my content settled the business of two tallys, so as I shall have L2000 almost more of my owne money in my hand, which pleases me mightily, and so home and there to the office, where mighty busy, and then home to supper and to even my Journall and to bed. Our fleete being now in all points ready to sayle, but for the carrying of the two or three new ships, which will keepe them a day or two or three more. It is said the Dutch is gone off our coast, but I have no good reason to believe it, Sir W. Coventry not thinking any such thing.

14th. Up betimes to the office, to write fair a laborious letter I wrote as from the Board to the Duke of Yorke, laying out our want of money again; and particularly the business of Captain Cocke's tenders of hemp, which my Lord Bruncker brought in under an unknown hand without name. Wherein his Lordship will have no great successe, I doubt. That being done, I down to Thames-streete, and there agreed for four or five tons of corke, to send this day to the fleete, being a new device to make barricados with, instead of junke. By this means I come to see and kiss Mr. Hill's young wife, and a blithe young woman she is. So to the office and at noon home to dinner, and then sent for young Michell and employed him all the afternoon about weighing and shipping off of the corke, having by this means an opportunity of getting him 30 or 40s. Having set him a doing, I home and to the office very late, very busy, and did indeed dispatch much business, and so to supper and to bed. After a song in the garden, which, and after dinner, is now the greatest pleasure I take, and indeed do please me mightily, to bed, after washing my legs and feet with warm water in my kitchen. This evening I had Davila

brought home to me, and find it a most excellent history as ever I read.

15th (Lord's day). Up, and to church, where our lecturer made a sorry silly sermon, upon the great point of proving the truth of the Christian religion. Home and had a good dinner, expecting Mr. Hunt, but there comes only young Michell and his wife, whom my wife concurs with me to be a pretty woman, and with her husband is a pretty innocent couple. Mightily pleasant we were, and I mightily pleased in her company and to find my wife so well pleased with them also. After dinner he and I walked to White Hall, not being able to get a coach. He to the Abbey, and I to White Hall, but met with nobody to discourse with, having no great mind to be found idling there, and be asked questions of the fleete, so walked only through to the Parke, and there, it being mighty hot and I weary, lay down by the canaille, upon the grasse, and slept awhile, and was thinking of a lampoone which hath run in my head this weeke, to make upon the late fight at sea, and the miscarriages there; but other businesses put it out of my head. Having lain there a while, I then to the Abbey and there called Michell, and so walked in great pain, having new shoes on, as far as Fleete Streete and there got a coach, and so in some little ease home and there drank a great deale of small beer; and so took up my wife and Betty Michell and her husband, and away into the fields, to take the ayre, as far as beyond Hackny, and so back again, in our way drinking a great deale of milke, which I drank to take away, my heartburne, wherewith I have of late been mightily troubled, but all the way home I did break abundance of wind behind, which did presage no good but a great deal of cold gotten. So home and supped and away went Michell and his wife, of whom I stole two or three salutes, and so to bed in some pain and in fear of more, which accordingly I met with, for I was in mighty pain all night long of the winde griping of my belly and making of me shit often and vomit too, which is a thing not usual with me, but this I impute to the milke that I drank after so much beer, but the cold, to my washing my feet the night before.

16th. Lay in great pain in bed all the morning and most of the afternoon, being in much pain, making little or no water, and indeed having little within to make any with. And had great twinges with the wind all the day in my belly with wind. And a looseness with it, which however made it not so great as I have heretofore had it. A wonderful dark sky, and shower of rain this morning, which at Harwich proved so too with a shower of hail as big as walnuts. I had some broth made me to drink, which I love, only to fill up room. Up in the afternoon, and passed the day with Balty, who is come from sea for a day or two before the fight, and I perceive could be willing fairly to be out of the next fight, and I cannot much blame him, he having no reason by his place to be there; however, would not have him to be absent, manifestly to avoid being there. At night grew a little better and took a glyster of sacke, but taking it by halves it did me not much good, I taking but a little of it. However, to bed, and had a pretty good night of it,

17th. So as to be able to rise to go to the office and there sat, but now and then in pain, and without making much water, or freely. However, it grew better and better, so as after dinner believing the jogging in a coach would do me good, I did take my wife out to the New Exchange to buy things. She there while I with Balty went and bought a common riding-cloake for myself, to save my best. It cost me but 30s., and will do my turne mighty well. Thence home and walked in the garden with Sir W. Pen a while, and saying how the riding in the coach do me good (though I do not yet much find it), he ordered his to be got ready while I did some little business at the office, and so abroad he and I after 8 o'clock at night, as far almost as Bow, and so back again, and so home to supper and to bed. This day I did bid Balty to agree with the Dutch paynter, which he once led me to, to see landskipps, for a winter piece of snow, which indeed is a good piece, and costs me but 40s., which I would not take the money again for, it being, I think, very good. After a little supper to bed, being in less pain still, and had very good rest.

18th. Up in good case, and so by coach to St. James's after my fellows, and there did our business, which is mostly every day to complain of want of money, and that only will undo us in a little time. Here, among other things, before us all, the Duke of Yorke did say, that now at length he is come to a sure knowledge that the Dutch did lose in the late engagements twenty-nine captains and thirteen ships. Upon which Sir W. Coventry did publickly move, that if his Royal Highness had this of a certainty, it would be of use to send this down to the fleete, and to cause it to be spread about the fleete, for the recovering of the spirits of the officers and seamen; who are under great dejectedness for want of knowing that they did do any thing against the enemy, notwithstanding all that they did to us. Which, though it be true, yet methought was one of the most dishonourable motions to our countrymen that ever was made; and is worth remembering. Thence with Sir W. Pen home, calling at Lilly's, to have a time appointed when to be drawn among the other Commanders of Flags the last year's fight. And so full of work Lilly is, that he was faro to take his table-book out to see how his time is appointed, and appointed six days hence for him to come between seven and eight in the morning. Thence with him home; and there by appointment I find Dr. Fuller, now Bishop of Limericke, in Ireland; whom I knew in his low condition at Twittenham. I had also by his desire Sir W. Pen, and with him his lady and daughter, and had a good dinner, and find the Bishop the same good man as ever; and in a word, kind to us, and, methinks, one of the comeliest and most becoming prelates in all respects that ever I saw in my life. During dinner comes an acquaintance of his, Sir Thomas Littleton; whom I knew not while he was in my house, but liked his discourse; and afterwards, by Sir W. Pen, do come to know that he is one of the greatest speakers in the House of Commons, and the usual second to the great Vaughan. So was sorry I did observe him no more, and gain more of his acquaintance. After dinner, they being gone, and I mightily pleased with my guests, I down the river to Greenwich, about business, and thence walked to Woolwich, reading "The Rivall Ladys" all the way, and find it a most pleasant and fine writ play. At Woolwich saw Mr. Shelden, it being late, and there eat and drank, being kindly used by him and Bab, and so by water to Deptford, it being 10 o'clock before I got to Deptford, and dark, and there to Bagwell's, and, having staid there a while, away home, and after supper to bed. The Duke of Yorke said this day that by the letters from the Generals they would sail with the Fleete this day or to-morrow.

19th. Up in very good health in every respect, only my late fever got by my pain do break out about my mouth. So to the office, where all the morning sitting. Full of wants of money, and much stores to buy, for to replenish the stores, and no money to do it with, nor anybody to trust us without it. So at noon home to dinner, Balty and his wife with us. By and by Balty takes his leave of us, he going away just now towards the fleete, where he will pass through one great engagement more before he be two days older, I believe. I to the office, where busy all the afternoon, late, and then home, and, after some pleasant discourse to my wife, to bed. After I was in bed I had a letter from Sir W. Coventry that tells me that the fleete is sailed this morning; God send us good newes of them!

20th. Up, and finding by a letter late last night that the fleete is gone, and that Sir W. Pen is ordered to go down to Sheernesse, and finding him ready to go to St. James's this morning, I was willing to go with him to see how things go,

and so with him thither (but no discourse with the Duke), but to White Hall, and there the Duke of York did bid Sir W. Pen to stay to discourse with him and the King about business of the fleete, which troubled me a little, but it was only out of envy, for which I blame myself, having no reason to expect to be called to advise in a matter I understand not. So I away to Lovett's, there to see how my picture goes on to be varnished (a fine Crucifix),

which will be very fine; and here I saw some fine prints, brought from France by Sir Thomas Crew, who is lately returned. So home, calling at the stationer's for some paper fit to varnish, and in my way home met with Lovett, to whom I gave it, and he did present me with a varnished staffe, very fine and light to walk with. So home and to dinner, there coming young Mrs. Daniel and her sister Sarah, and dined with us; and old Mr. Hawly, whose condition pities me, he being forced to turne under parish-clerke at St. Gyles's, I think at the other end of the towne. Thence I to the office, where busy all the afternoon, and in the evening with Sir W. Pen, walking with whom in the garden I am of late mighty great, and it is wisdom to continue myself so, for he is of all the men of the office at present most manifestly usefull and best thought of. He and I supped together upon the seat in the garden, and thence, he gone, my wife and Mercer come and walked and sang late, and then home to bed.

21st. Up and to the office, where all the morning sitting. At noon walked in the garden with Commissioner Pett (newly come to towne), who tells me how infinite the disorders are among the commanders and all officers of the fleete. No discipline: nothing but swearing and cursing, and every body doing what they please; and the Generalls, understanding no better, suffer it, to the reproaching of this Board, or whoever it will be. He himself hath been challenged twice to the field, or something as good, by Sir Edward Spragge and Captain Seymour. He tells me that captains carry, for all the late orders, what men they please; demand and consume what provisions they please. So that he fears, and I do no less, that God Almighty cannot bless us while we keep in this disorder that we are in: he observing to me too, that there is no man of counsel or advice in the fleete; and the truth is, the gentlemen captains will undo us, for they are not to be kept in order, their friends about the King and Duke, and their own house, is so free, that it is not for any person but the Duke himself to have any command over them. He gone I to dinner, and then to the office, where busy all the afternoon. At night walked in the garden with my wife, and so I home to supper and to bed. Sir W. Pen is gone down to Sheernesse to-day to see things made ready against the fleete shall come in again, which makes Pett mad, and calls him dissembling knave, and that himself takes all the pains and is blamed, while he do nothing but hinder business and takes all the honour of it to himself, and tells me plainly he will fling, up his commission rather than bear it.

22nd (Lord's day). Up, and to my chamber, and there till noon mighty busy, setting money matters and other things of mighty moment to rights to the great content of my mind, I finding that accounts but a little let go can never be put in order by strangers, for I cannot without much difficulty do it myself. After dinner to them again till about four o'clock and then walked to White Hall, where saw nobody almost but walked up and down with Hugh May, who is a very ingenious man. Among other things, discoursing of the present fashion of gardens to make them plain, that we have the best walks of gravell in the world, France having no nor Italy; and our green of our bowling allies is better than any they have. So our business here being ayre, this is the best way, only with a little mixture of statues, or pots, which may be handsome, and so filled with another pot of such and such a flower or greene as the season of the year will bear. And then for flowers, they are best seen in a little plat by themselves; besides, their borders spoil the walks of another garden: and then for fruit, the best way is to have walls built circularly one within another, to the South, on purpose for fruit, and leave the walking garden only for that use. Thence walked through the House, where most people mighty hush and, methinks, melancholy. I see not a smiling face through the whole Court; and, in my conscience, they are doubtfull of the conduct again of the Generalls, and I pray God they may not make their fears reasonable. Sir Richard Fanshaw is lately dead at Madrid. Guyland is lately overthrowne wholly in Barbary by the King of Tafiletta. The fleete cannot yet get clear of the River, but expect the first wind to be out, and then to be sure they fight. The Queene and Maids of Honour are at Tunbridge.

23rd. Up, and to my chamber doing several things there of moment, and then comes Sympson, the Joyner; and he and I with great pains contriving presses to put my books up in: they now growing numerous, and lying one upon another on my chairs, I lose the use to avoyde the trouble of removing them, when I would open a book. Thence out to the Excise office about business, and then homewards met Colvill, who tells me he hath L1000 ready for me upon a tally; which pleases me, and yet I know not now what to do with it, having already as much money as is fit for me to have in the house, but I will have it. I did also meet Alderman Backewell, who tells me of the hard usage he now finds from Mr. Fen, in not getting him a bill or two paid, now that he can be no more usefull to him; telling me that what by his being abroad and Shaw's death he hath lost the ball, but that he doubts not to come to give a kicke at it still, and then he shall be wiser and keepe it while he hath it. But he says he hath a good master, the King, who will not suffer him to be undone, as otherwise he must have been, and I believe him. So home and to dinner, where I confess, reflecting upon the ease and plenty that I live in, of money, goods, servants, honour, every thing, I could not but with hearty thanks to Almighty God ejaculate my thanks to Him while I was at dinner, to myself. After dinner to the office and there till five or six o'clock, and then by coach to St. James's and there with Sir W. Coventry and Sir G. Downing to take the gyre in the Parke. All full of expectation of the fleete's engagement, but it is not yet. Sir W. Coventry says they are eighty-nine men-of-warr, but one fifth-rate, and that, the Sweepstakes, which carries forty guns. They are most infinitely manned. He tells me the Loyall London, Sir J. Smith (which, by the way, he commends to be the-best ship in the world, large and small), hath above eight hundred men; and moreover takes notice, which is worth notice, that the fleete hath lane now near fourteen days without any demand for a farthingworth of any thing of any kind, but only to get men. He also observes, that with this excesse of men, nevertheless, they have thought fit to leave behind them sixteen ships, which they have robbed of their men, which certainly might have been manned, and they been serviceable in the fight, and yet the fleete well-manned, according to the excesse of supernumeraries, which we hear they have. At least two or three of them might have been left manned, and sent away with the Gottenburgh ships. They conclude this to be much the best fleete, for force of guns, greatnesse and number of ships and men, that ever England did see; being, as Sir W. Coventry reckons, besides those left behind, eighty-nine men of warr and twenty fire-ships, though we cannot hear that they have with them above eighteen. The French are not yet joined with the Dutch, which do dissatisfy the Hollanders, and if they should have a defeat, will undo De Witt; the people generally of Holland do hate this league with France. We cannot think of any business, but lie big with expectation of the issue of this fight, but do conclude that, this fight being over, we shall be able to see the whole issue of the warr, good or bad. So homeward, and walked over the Parke (St. James's) with Sir G. Downing, and at White Hall took a coach; and there to supper with much pleasure and to bed.

24th. Up, and to the office, where little business done, our heads being full of expectation of the fleete's being engaged, but no certain notice of it, only Sheppeard in the Duke's yacht left them yesterday morning within a league of the Dutch fleete, and making after them, they standing into the sea. At noon to dinner, and after dinner with Mercer (as of late my practice is) a song and so to the office, there to set up again my frames about my Platts, which I have got to be all gilded, and look very fine, and then to my business, and busy very late, till midnight, drawing up a representation of the state of my victualling business to the Duke, I having never appeared to him doing anything yet and therefore I now do it in writing, I now having the advantage of having had two fleetes dispatched in better condition than ever any fleetes were yet, I believe; at least, with least complaint, and by this means I shall with the better confidence get my bills out for my salary. So home to bed.

25th. Up betimes to write fair my last night's paper for the Duke, and so along with Sir W. Batten by hackney coach to St. James's, where the Duke is gone abroad with the King to the Parke, but anon come back to White Hall, and we, after an houre's waiting, walked thither (I having desired Sir W. Coventry in his chamber to read over my paper about the victualling, which he approves of, and I am glad I showed it him first, it makes it the less necessary to show it the Duke at all, if I find it best to let it alone). At White Hall we find [the Court] gone to Chappell, it being St. James's-day. And by and by, while they are at chappell, and we waiting chappell being done, come people out of the Parke, telling us that the guns are heard plain. And so every body to the Parke, and by and by the chappell done, and the King and Duke into the bowling-green, and upon the leads, whither I went, and there the guns were plain to be heard; though it was pretty to hear how confident some would be in the loudnesse of the guns, which it was as much as ever I could do to hear them. By and by the King to dinner, and I waited there his dining; but, Lord! how little I should be pleased, I think, to have so many people crowding about me; and among other things it astonished me to see my Lord Barkeshire waiting at table, and serving the King drink, in that dirty pickle as I never saw man in my life. Here I met Mr. Williams, who in serious discourse told me he did hope well of this fight because of the equality of force or rather our having the advantage in number, and also because we did not go about it with the presumption that we did heretofore, when, he told me, he did before the last fight look upon us by our pride fated to be overcome. He would have me to dine where he was invited to dine, at the Backe-stayres. So after the King's meat was taken away, we thither; but he could not stay, but left me there among two or three of the King's servants, where we dined with the meat that come from his table; which was most excellent, with most brave drink cooled in ice (which at this hot time was welcome), and I drinking no wine, had metheglin for the King's owne drinking, which did please me mightily. Thence, having dined mighty nobly, I away to Mrs. Martin's new lodgings, where I find her, and was with her close, but, Lord! how big she is already. She is, at least seems, in mighty trouble for her husband at sea, when I am sure she cares not for him, and I would not undeceive her, though I know his ship is one of those that is not gone, but left behind without men. Thence to White Hall again to hear news, but found none; so back toward Westminster, and there met Mrs. Burroughs, whom I had a mind to meet, but being undressed did appear a mighty ordinary woman. Thence by water home, and out again by coach to Lovett's to see my Crucifix, which is not done. So to White Hall again to have met Sir G. Carteret, but he is gone, abroad, so back homewards, and seeing Mr. Spong took him up, and he and I to Reeves, the glass maker's, and did set several glasses and had pretty discourse with him, and so away, and set down Mr. Spong in London, and so home and with my wife, late, twatling at my Lady Pen's, and so home to supper and to bed. I did this afternoon call at my woman that ruled my paper to bespeak a musique card, and there did kiss Nan. No news to-night from the fleete how matters go yet.

26th. Up, and to the office, where all the morning. At noon dined at home: Mr. Hunt and his wife, who is very gallant, and newly come from Cambridge, because of the sicknesse, with us. Very merry at table, and the people I do love mightily, but being in haste to go to White Hall I rose, and Mr. Hunt with me, and by coach thither, where I left him in the boarded gallery, and I by appointment to attend the Duke of Yorke at his closett, but being not come, Sir G. Carteret and I did talke together, and [he] advises me, that, if I could, I would get the papers of examination touching the business of the last year's prizes, which concern my Lord Sandwich, out of Warcupp's hands, who being now under disgrace and poor, he believes may be brought easily to part with them. My Lord Crew, it seems, is fearfull yet that maters may be enquired into. This I will endeavour to do, though I do not thinke it signifies much. By and by the Duke of Yorke comes and we had a meeting and, among other things, I did read my declaration of the proceedings of the Victualling hired this yeare, and desired his Royall Highnesse to give me the satisfaction of knowing whether his Royall Highnesse were pleased therewith. He told me he was, and that it was a good account, and that the business of the Victualling was much in a better condition than it was the last yeare; which did much joy me, being said in the company of my fellows, by which I shall be able with confidence to demand my salary and the rest of the subsurveyors. Thence away mightily satisfied to Mrs. Pierces, there to find my wife. Mrs. Pierce hath lain in of a boy about a month. The boy is dead this day. She lies in good state, and very pretty she is, but methinks do every day grow more and more great, and a little too much, unless they get more money than I fear they do. Thence with my wife and Mercer to my Lord Chancellor's new house, and there carried them up to the leads, where I find my Lord Chamberlain, Lauderdale, Sir Robert Murray, and others, and do find it the most delightfull place for prospect that ever was in the world, and even ravishing me, and that is all, in short, I can say of it. Thence to Islington to our old house and eat and drank, and so round by Kingsland home, and there to the office a little and Sir W. Batten's, but no newes at all from the fleete, and so home to bed.

27th. Up and to the office, where all the morning busy. At noon dined at home and then to the office again, and there walking in the garden with Captain Cocke till 5 o'clock. No newes yet of the fleete. His great bargaine of Hempe with us by his unknown proposition is disliked by the King, and so is quite off; of which he is glad, by this means being rid of his obligation to my Lord Bruncker, which he was tired with, and especially his mistresse, Mrs. Williams, and so will fall into another way about it, wherein he will advise only with myself, which do not displease me, and will be better for him and the King too. Much common talke of publique business, the want of money, the uneasinesse that Parliament will find in raising any, and the ill condition we shall be in if they do not, and his confidence that the Swede is true to us, but poor, but would be glad to do us all manner of service in the world. He gone, I away by water from the Old Swan to White Hall. The waterman tells me that newes is come that our ship Resolution is burnt, and that we had sunke four or five of the enemy's ships. When I come to White Hall I met with Creed, and he tells me the same news, and walking with him to the Park I to Sir W. Coventry's lodging, and there he showed me Captain Talbot's letter, wherein he says that the fight begun on the 25th; that our White squadron begun with one of the Dutch squadrons, and then the Red with another so hot that we put them both to giving way, and so they continued in pursuit all the day, and as long as he stayed with them: that the Blue fell to the Zealand squadron; and after a long dispute, he against two or three great ships, he received eight or nine dangerous shots, and so come away; and says, he saw the Resolution burned by one of their fire-ships, and four or five of the enemy's. But says that two or three of our great ships were in danger of being fired by our owne fire-ships, which Sir W. Coventry, nor I, cannot understand. But upon the whole, he and I walked two or three turns in the Parke under the great trees, and do doubt that this gallant is come away a little too soon, having lost never a mast nor sayle. And then we did begin to discourse of the young gentlemen captains, which he was very free with me in speaking his mind of the unruliness of them; and what a losse the King hath of his old men, and now of this Hannam, of the Resolution, if he be dead, and that there is but few old sober men in the fleete, and if these few of the Flags that are so should die, he fears some other gentlemen captains will get in, and then what a council we shall have, God knows. He told me how he is disturbed to hear the commanders at sea called cowards here on shore, and that he was yesterday concerned publiquely at a dinner to defend them, against somebody that said that not above twenty of them fought as they should do, and indeed it is derived from the Duke of Albemarle himself, who wrote so to the King and Duke, and that he told them how they fought four days, two of them with great disadvantage. The Count de Guiche, who was on board De Ruyter, writing his narrative home in French of the fight, do lay all the honour that may be upon the English courage above the Dutch, and that he himself [Sir W. Coventry] was sent down from the King and Duke of Yorke after the fight, to pray them to spare none that they thought had not done their parts, and that they had removed but four, whereof Du Tell is one, of whom he would say nothing; but, it seems, the Duke of Yorke hath been much displeased at his removal, and hath now taken him into his service, which is a plain affront to the Duke of Albemarle; and two of the others, Sir W. Coventry did speake very slenderly of their faults. Only the last, which was old Teddiman, he says, is in fault, and hath little to excuse himself with; and that, therefore, we should not be forward in condemning men of want of courage, when the Generalls, who are both men of metal, and hate cowards, and had the sense of our ill successe upon them (and by the way must either let the world thinke it was the miscarriage of the Captains or their owne conduct), have thought fit to remove no more of them, when desired by the King and Duke of Yorke to do it, without respect to any favour any of them can pretend to in either of them. At last we concluded that we never can hope to beat the Dutch with such advantage as now in number and force and a fleete in want of nothing, and he hath often repeated now and at other times industriously that many of the Captains have: declared that they want nothing, and again, that they did lie ten days together at the Nore without demanding of any thing in the world but men, and of them they afterward, when they went away, the generalls themselves acknowledge that they have permitted several ships to carry supernumeraries, but that if we do not speede well, we must then play small games and spoile their trade in small parties. And so we parted, and I, meeting Creed in the Parke again, did take him by coach and to Islington, thinking to have met my Lady Pen and wife, but they were gone, so we eat and drank and away back, setting him down in Cheapside and I home, and there after a little while making of my tune to "It is decreed," to bed.

28th. Up, and to the office, where no more newes of the fleete than was yesterday. Here we sat and at noon to dinner to the Pope's Head, where my Lord Bruncker and his mistresse dined and Commissioner Pett, Dr. Charleton, and myself, entertained with a venison pasty by Sir W. Warren. Here very pretty discourse of Dr. Charleton's, concerning Nature's fashioning every creature's teeth according to the food she intends them; and that men's, it is plain, was not for flesh, but for fruit, and that he can at any time tell the food of a beast unknown by the teeth. My Lord Bruncker made one or two objections to it that creatures find their food proper for their teeth rather than that the teeth were fitted for the food, but the Doctor, I think, did well observe that creatures do naturally and from the first, before they have had experience to try, do love such a food rather than another, and that all children love fruit, and none brought to flesh, but against their wills at first. Thence with my Lord Bruncker to White Hall, where no news. So to St. James's to Sir W. Coventry, and there hear only of the Bredah's being come in and gives the same small account that the other did yesterday, so that we know not what is done by the body of the fleete at all, but conceive great reason to hope well. Thence with my Lord to his coach-house, and there put in his six horses into his coach, and he and I alone to Highgate. All the way going and coming I learning of him the principles of Optickes, and what it is that makes an object seem less or bigger and how much distance do lessen an object, and that it is not the eye at all, or any rule in optiques, that can tell distance, but it is only an act of reason comparing of one mark with another, which did both please and inform me mightily. Being come thither we went to my Lord Lauderdale's house to speake with him, about getting a man at Leith to joyne with one we employ to buy some prize goods for the King; we find [him] and his lady and some Scotch people at supper. Pretty odd company; though my Lord Bruncker tells me, my Lord Lauderdale is a man of mighty good reason and judgement. But at supper there played one of their servants upon the viallin some Scotch tunes only; several, and the best of their country, as they seemed to esteem them, by their praising and admiring them: but, Lord! the strangest ayre that ever I heard in my life, and all of one cast. But strange to hear my Lord Lauderdale say himself that he had rather hear a cat mew, than the best musique in the world; and the better the musique, the more sicke it makes him; and that of all instruments, he hates the lute most, and next to that, the baggpipe. Thence back with my Lord to his house, all the way good discourse, informing of myself about optiques still, and there left him and by a hackney home, and after writing three or four letters, home to supper and to bed.

29th (Lord's day). Up and all the morning in my chamber making up my accounts in my book with my father and brother and stating them. Towards noon before sermon was done at church comes newes by a letter to Sir W. Batten, to my hand, of the late fight, which I sent to his house, he at church. But, Lord! with what impatience I staid till sermon was done, to know the issue of the fight, with a thousand hopes and fears and thoughts about the consequences of either. At last sermon is done and he come home, and the bells immediately rung soon as the church was done. But coming; to Sir W. Batten to know the newes, his letter said nothing of it; but all the towne is full of a victory. By and by a letter from Sir W. Coventry tells me that we have the victory. Beat them into the Weelings;

had taken two of their great ships; but by the orders of the Generalls they are burned. This being, methought, but a poor result after the fighting of two so great fleetes, and four days having no tidings of them, I was still impatient; but could know no more. So away home to dinner, where Mr. Spong and Reeves dined with me by invitation. And after dinner to our business of my microscope to be shown some of the observables of that, and then down to my office to looke in a darke room with my glasses and tube, and most excellently things appeared indeed beyond imagination. This was our worke all the afternoon trying the several glasses and several objects, among others, one of my plates, where the lines appeared so very plain that it is not possible to thinke how plain it was done. Thence satisfied exceedingly with all this we home and to discourse many pretty things, and so staid out the afternoon till it began to be dark, and then they away and I to Sir W. Batten, where the Lieutenant of the Tower was, and Sir John Minnes, and the newes I find is no more or less than what I had heard before; only that our Blue squadron, it seems, was pursued the most of the time, having more ships, a great many, than its number allotted to her share. Young Seamour is killed, the only captain slain. The Resolution burned; but, as they say, most of her [crew] and commander saved. This is all, only we keep the sea, which denotes a victory, or at least that we are not beaten; but no great matters to brag of, God knows. So home to supper and to bed.

30th. Up, and did some business in my chamber, then by and by comes my boy's Lute-Master, and I did direct him hereafter to begin to teach him to play his part on the Theorbo, which he will do, and that in a little time I believe. So to the office, and there with Sir W. Warren, with whom I have spent no time a good while. We set right our business of the Lighters, wherein I thinke I shall get L100. At noon home to dinner and there did practise with Mercer one of my new tunes that I have got Dr. Childe to set me a base to and it goes prettily. Thence abroad to pay several debts at the end of the month, and so to Sir W. Coventry, at St. James's, where I find him in his new closett, which is very fine, and well supplied with handsome books. I find him speak very slightly of the late victory: dislikes their staying with the fleete up their coast, believing that the Dutch will come out in fourteen days, and then we with our unready fleete, by reason of some of the ships being maymed, shall be in bad condition to fight them upon their owne coast: is much dissatisfied with the great number of men, and their fresh demands of twenty-four victualling ships, they going out but the other day as full as they could stow. I asked him whether he did never desire an account of the number of supernumeraries, as I have done several ways, without which we shall be in great errour about the victuals; he says he has done it again and again, and if any mistake should happen they must thanke themselves. He spoke slightly of the Duke of Albemarle, saying, when De Ruyter come to give him a broadside—"Now," says he, chewing of tobacco the while, "will this fellow come and give, me two broadsides, and then he will run;" but it seems he held him to it two hours, till the Duke himself was forced to retreat to refit, and was towed off, and De Ruyter staid for him till he come back again to fight. One in the ship saying to the Duke, "Sir, methinks De Ruyter hath given us more: than two broadsides;"—"Well," says the Duke, "but you shall find him run by and by," and so he did, says Sir W. Coventry; but after the Duke himself had been first made to fall off. The Resolution had all brass guns, being the same that Sir J. Lawson had in her in the Straights. It is observed that the two fleetes were even in number to one ship. Thence home; and to sing with my wife and Mercer in the garden; and coming in I find my wife plainly dissatisfied with me, that I can spend so much time with Mercer, teaching her to sing and could never take the pains with her. Which I acknowledge; but it is because that the girl do take musique mighty readily, and she do not, and musique is the thing of the world that I love most, and all the pleasure almost that I can now take. So to bed in some little discontent, but no words from me.

31st. Good friends in the morning and up to the office, where sitting all the morning, and while at table we were mightily joyed with newes brought by Sir J. Minnes and Sir W. Batten of the death of De Ruyter, but when Sir W. Coventry come, he told us there was no such thing, which quite dashed me again, though, God forgive me! I was a little sorry in my heart before lest it might give occasion of too much glory to the Duke of Albemarle. Great bandying this day between Sir W. Coventry and my Lord Bruncker about Captain Cocke, which I am well pleased with, while I keepe from any open relyance on either side, but rather on Sir W. Coventry's. At noon had a haunch of venison boiled and a very good dinner besides, there dining with me on a sudden invitation the two mayden sisters, Bateliers, and their elder brother, a pretty man, understanding and well discoursed, much pleased with his company. Having dined myself I rose to go to a Committee of Tangier, and did come thither time enough to meet Povy and Creed and none else. The Court being empty, the King being gone to Tunbridge, and the Duke of Yorke a-hunting. I had some discourse with Povy, who is mightily discontented, I find, about his disappointments at Court; and says, of all places, if there be hell, it is here. No faith, no truth, no love, nor any agreement between man and wife, nor friends. He would have spoke broader, but I put it off to another time; and so parted. Then with Creed and read over with him the narrative of the late [fight], which he makes a very poor thing of, as it is indeed, and speaks most slightingly of the whole matter. Povy discoursed with me about my Lord Peterborough's L50 which his man did give me from him, the last year's salary I paid him, which he would have Povy pay him again; but I have not taken it to myself yet, and therefore will most heartily return him, and mark him out for a coxcomb. Povy went down to Mr. Williamson's, and brought me up this extract out of the Flanders' letters to-day come: That Admiral Everson, and the Admiral and Vice-Admiral of Freezeland, with many captains and men, are slain; that De Ruyter is safe, but lost 250 men out of his own ship; but that he is in great disgrace, and Trump in better favour; that Bankert's ship is burned, himself hardly escaping with a few men on board De Haes; that fifteen captains are to be tried the seventh of August; and that the hangman was sent from Flushing to assist the Council of Warr. How much of this is true, time will shew. Thence to Westminster Hall and walked an hour with Creed talking of the late fight, and observing the ridiculous management thereof and success of the Duke of Albemarle. Thence parted and to Mrs. Martin's lodgings, and sat with her a while, and then by water home, all the way reading the Narrative of the late fight in order, it may be, to the making some marginal notes upon it. At the Old Swan found my Betty Michell at the doore, where I staid talking with her a pretty while, it being dusky, and kissed her and so away home and writ my letters, and then home to supper, where the brother and Mary Batelier are still and Mercer's two sisters. They have spent the time dancing this afternoon, and we were very merry, and then after supper into the garden and there walked, and then home with them and then back again, my wife and I and the girle, and sang in the garden and then to bed. Colville was with me this morning, and to my great joy I could now have all my money in, that I have in the world. But the times being open again, I thinke it is best to keepe some of it abroad. Mighty well, and end this month in content of mind and body. The publique matters looking more safe for the present than they did, and we having a victory over the Dutch just such as I could have wished, and as the kingdom was fit to bear, enough to give us the name of conquerors, and leave us masters of the sea, but without any such great matters done as should give the Duke of Albemarle any honour at all, or give him cause to rise to his former insolence.

AUGUST 1666

August 1st. Up betimes to the settling of my last month's accounts, and I bless God I find them very clear, and that I am worth L5700, the most that ever my book did yet make out. So prepared to attend the Duke of Yorke as usual, but Sir W. Pen, just as I was going out, comes home from Sheernesse, and held me in discourse about publique business, till I come by coach too late to St. James's, and there find that every thing stood still, and nothing done for want of me. Thence walked over the Parke with Sir W. Coventry, who I clearly see is not thoroughly pleased with the late management of the fight, nor with any thing that the Generalls do; only is glad to hear that De Ruyter is out of favour, and that this fight hath cost them 5,000 men, as they themselves do report. And it is a strange thing, as he observes, how now and then the slaughter runs on one hand; there being 5,000 killed on theirs, and not above 400 or 500 killed and wounded on ours, and as many flag-officers on theirs as ordinary captains in ours; there being Everson, and the Admiral and Vice-Admiral of Freezeland on theirs, and Seamour, Martin, and——, on ours. I left him going to Chappell, it being the common fast day, and the Duke of York at Chappell. And I to Mrs. Martin's, but she abroad, so I sauntered to or again to the Abbey, and then to the parish church, fearfull of being seen to do so, and so after the parish church was ended, I to the Swan and there dined upon a rabbit, and after dinner to Mrs. Martin's, and there find Mrs. Burroughs, and by and by comes a pretty widow, one Mrs. Eastwood, and one Mrs. Fenton, a maid; and here merry kissing and looking on their breasts, and all the innocent pleasure in the world. But, Lord! to see the dissembling of this widow, how upon the singing of a certain jigg by Doll, Mrs. Martin's sister, she seemed to be sick and fainted and God knows what, because the jigg, which her husband (who died this last sickness) loved. But by and by I made her as merry as is possible, and towzed and tumbled her as I pleased, and then carried her and her sober pretty kinswoman Mrs. Fenton home to their lodgings in the new market of my Lord Treasurer's, and there left them. Mightily pleased with this afternoon's mirth, but in great pain to ride in a coach with them, for fear of being seen. So home, and there much pleased with my wife's drawing today in her pictures, and so to supper and to bed very pleasant.

2nd. [Up] and to the office, where we sat, and in discourse at the table with Sir W. Batten, I was obliged to tell him it was an untruth, which did displease him mightily, and parted at noon very angry with me. At home find Lovett, who brought me some papers varnished, and showed me my crucifix, which will be very fine when done. He dined with me and Balty's wife, who is in great pain for her husband, not hearing of him since the fight; but I understand he was not in it, going hence too late, and I am glad of it. Thence to the office, and thither comes to me Creed, and he and I walked a good while, and then to the victualling office together, and there with Mr. Gawden I did much business, and so away with Creed again, and by coach to see my Lord Bruncker, who it seems was not well yesterday, but being come thither, I find his coach ready to carry him abroad, but Tom, his footman, whatever the matter was, was lothe to desire me to come in, but I walked a great while in the Piatza till I was going away, but by and by my Lord himself comes down and coldly received me. So I soon parted, having enough for my over officious folly in troubling myself to visit him, and I am apt to think that he was fearfull that my coming was out of design to see how he spent his time [rather] than to enquire after his health. So parted, and I with Creed down to the New Exchange Stairs, and there I took water, and he parted, so home, and then down to Woolwich, reading and making an end of the "Rival Ladys," and find it a very pretty play. At Woolwich, it being now night, I find my wife and Mercer, and Mr. Batelier and Mary there, and a supper getting ready. So I staid, in some pain, it being late, and post night. So supped and merrily home, but it was twelve at night first. However, sent away some letters, and home to bed.

3rd. Up and to the office, where Sir W. Batten and I sat to contract for some fire-ships. I there close all the morning. At noon home to dinner, and then abroad to Sir Philip Warwicke's at White Hall about Tangier one quarter tallys, and there had some serious discourse touching money, and the case of the Navy, wherein all I could get of him was that we had the full understanding of the treasure as much as my Lord Treasurer himself, and knew what he can do, and that whatever our case is, more money cannot be got till the Parliament. So talked of getting an account ready as soon as we could to give the Parliament, and so very melancholy parted. So I back again, calling my wife at her sister's, from whose husband we do now hear that he was safe this week, and going in a ship to the fleete from the buoy of the Nore, where he has been all this while, the fleete being gone before he got down. So home, and busy till night, and then to Sir W. Pen, with my wife, to sit and chat, and a small supper, and home to bed. The death of Everson, and the report of our success, beyond expectation, in the killing of so great a number of men, hath raised the estimation of the late victory considerably; but it is only among fools: for all that was but accidental. But this morning, getting Sir.W. Pen to read over the Narrative with me, he did sparingly, yet plainly, say that we might have intercepted their Zealand squadron coming home, if we had done our parts; and more, that we might have spooned before the wind as well as they, and have overtaken their ships in the pursuite, in all the while.

4th. Up, and to the office, where all the morning, and, at noon to dinner, and Mr. Cooke dined with us, who is lately come from Hinchingbroke, [Lord Hinchingbrooke] who is also come to town: The family all well. Then I to the office, where very busy to state to Mr. Coventry the account of the victuals of the fleete, and late at it, and then home to supper and to bed. This evening, Sir W. Pen come into the garden, and walked with me, and told me that he had certain notice that at Flushing they are in great distraction. De Ruyter dares not come on shore for fear of the people; nor any body open their houses or shops for fear of the tumult: which is a every good hearing.

5th. (Lord's day). Up, and down to the Old Swan, and there called Betty Michell and her husband, and had two or three a long salutes from her out of sight of 'su mari', which pleased me mightily, and so carried them by water to West minster, and I to St. James's, and there had a meeting before the Duke of Yorke, complaining of want of money, but nothing done to any purpose, for want we shall, so that now our advices to him signify nothing. Here Sir W. Coventry did acquaint the Duke of Yorke how the world do discourse of the ill method of our books, and that we would consider how to answer any enquiry which shall be made after our practice therein, which will I think concern the Controller most, but I shall make it a memento to myself. Thence walked to the Parish Church to have one look upon Betty Michell, and so away homeward by water, and landed to go to the church, where, I believe, Mrs. Horsely goes, by Merchant-tailors' Hall, and there I find in the pulpit Elborough, my old schoolfellow and a simple rogue, and yet I find him preaching a very good sermon, and in as right a parson-like manner, and in good manner too, as I have heard any body; and the church very full, which is a surprising consideration; but I did not see her. So home, and had a good dinner, and after dinner with my wife, and Mercer, and Jane by water, all the afternoon up as high as Morclaeke with great pleasure, and a fine day, reading over the second part of the "Siege of Rhodes," with great delight. We landed and walked at Barne-elmes, and then at the Neat Houses I landed and bought a millon,—[melon]—and we did also land and eat and drink at Wandsworth, and so to the Old Swan, and thence walked home. It being a mighty fine cool evening, and there being come, my wife and I spent an houre in the garden, talking of our living in the country, when I shall be turned out of the office, as I fear the Parliament may find faults enough with the office to remove us all, and I am joyed to think in how good a condition I am to retire thither, and have wherewith very well to subsist. Nan, at Sir W. Pen's, lately married to one Markeham, a kinsman of Sir W. Pen's, a pretty wench she is.

6th. Up, and to the office a while, and then by water to my Lady Montagu's, at Westminster, and there visited my Lard Hinchingbroke, newly come from Hinchingbroke, and find him a mighty sober gentleman, to my great content. Thence to Sir Ph. Warwicke and my Lord Treasurer's, but failed in my business; so home and in Fenchurch-streete met with Mr. Battersby; says he, "Do you see Dan Rawlinson's door shut up?" (which I did, and wondered). "Why," says he, "after all the sickness, and himself spending all the last year in the country, one of his men is now dead of the plague, and his wife and one of his mayds sicke, and himself shut up;" which troubles me mightily. So home; and there do hear also from Mrs. Sarah Daniel, that Greenwich is at this time much worse than ever it was, and Deptford too: and she told us that they believed all the towne would leave the towne and come to London; which is now the receptacle of all the people from all infected places. God preserve us! So by and by to dinner, and, after dinner in comes Mrs. Knipp, and I being at the office went home to her, and there I sat and talked with her, it being the first time of her being here since her being brought to bed. I very pleasant with her; but perceive my wife hath no great pleasure in her being here, she not being pleased with my kindnesse to her. However, we talked and sang, and were very pleasant. By and by comes Mr. Pierce and his wife, the first time she also hath been here since her lying-in, both having been brought to bed of boys, and both of them dead. And here we talked, and were pleasant, only my wife in a chagrin humour, she not being pleased with my kindnesse to either of them, and by and by she fell into some silly discourse wherein I checked her, which made her mighty pettish, and discoursed mighty offensively to Mrs. Pierce, which did displease me, but I would make no words, but put the discourse by as much as I could (it being about a report that my wife said was made of herself and meant by Mrs. Pierce, that she was grown a gallant, when she had but so few suits of clothes these two or three years, and a great deale of that silly discourse), and by and by

Mrs. Pierce did tell her that such discourses should not trouble her, for there went as bad on other people, and particularly of herself at this end of the towne, meaning my wife, that she was crooked, which was quite false, which my wife had the wit not to acknowledge herself to be the speaker of, though she has said it twenty times. But by this means we had little pleasure in their visit; however, Knipp and I sang, and then I offered them to carry them home, and to take my wife with me, but she would not go: so I with them, leaving my wife in a very ill humour, and very slighting to them, which vexed me. However, I would not be removed from my civility to them, but sent for a coach, and went with them; and, in our way, Knipp saying that she come out of doors without a dinner to us, I took them to Old Fish Streete, to the very house and woman where I kept my wedding dinner, where I never was since, and there I did give them a joie of salmon, and what else was to be had. And here we talked of the ill-humour of my wife, which I did excuse as much as I could, and they seemed to admit of it, but did both confess they wondered at it; but from thence to other discourse, and among others to that of my Lord Bruncker and Mrs. Williams, who it seems do speake mighty hardly of me for my not treating them, and not giving her something to her closett, and do speake worse of my wife, and dishonourably, but it is what she do of all the world, though she be a whore herself; so I value it not. But they told me how poorly my Lord carried himself the other day to his kinswoman, Mrs. Howard, and was displeased because she called him uncle to a little gentlewoman that is there with him, which he will not admit of; for no relation is to be challenged from others to a lord, and did treat her thereupon very rudely and ungenteely. Knipp tells me also that my Lord keeps another woman besides Mrs. Williams; and that, when I was there the other day, there was a great hubbub in the house, Mrs. Williams being fallen sicke, because my Lord was gone to his other mistresse, making her wait for him, till his return from the other mistresse; and a great deale of do there was about it; and Mrs. Williams swounded at it, at the very time when I was there and wondered at the reason of my being received so negligently. I set them both at home, Knipp at her house, her husband being at the doore; and glad she was to be found to have staid out so long with me and Mrs. Pierce, and none else; and Mrs. Pierce at her house, and am mightily pleased with the discretion of her during the simplicity and offensiveness of my wife's discourse this afternoon. I perceive by the new face at Mrs. Pierces door that our Mary is gone from her. So I home, calling on W. Joyce in my coach, and staid and talked a little with him, who is the same silly prating fellow that ever he was, and so home, and there find my wife mightily out of order, and reproaching of Mrs. Pierce and Knipp as wenches, and I know not what. But I did give her no words to offend her, and quietly let all pass, and so to bed without any good looke or words to or from my wife.

7th. Up, and to the office, where we sat all the morning, and home to dinner, and then to the office again, being pretty good friends with my wife again, no angry words passed; but she finding fault with Mercer, suspecting that it was she that must have told Mary, that must have told her mistresse of my wife's saying that she was crooked. But the truth is, she is jealous of my kindnesse to her. After dinner, to the office, and did a great deale of business. In the evening comes Mr. Reeves, with a twelve-foote glasse, so I left the office and home, where I met Mr.

Batelier with my wife, in order to our going to-morrow, by agreement, to Bow to see a dancing meeting. But, Lord! to see how soon I could conceive evil fears and thoughts concerning them; so Reeves and I and they up to the top of the house, and there we endeavoured to see the moon, and Saturne and Jupiter; but the heavens proved cloudy, and so we lost our labour, having taken pains to get things together, in order to the managing of our long glasse. So down to supper and then to bed, Reeves lying at my house, but good discourse I had from him: in his own trade, concerning glasses, and so all of us late to bed. I receive fresh intelligence that Deptford and Greenwich are now afresh exceedingly afflicted with the sickness more than ever.

8th. Up, and with Reeves walk as far as the Temple, doing some business in my way at my bookseller's and elsewhere, and there parted, and I took coach, having first discoursed with Mr. Hooke a little, whom we met in the streete, about the nature of sounds, and he did make me understand the nature of musicall sounds made by strings, mighty prettily; and told me that having come to a certain number of vibrations proper to make any tone, he is able to tell how many strokes a fly makes with her wings (those flies that hum in their flying) by the note that it answers to in musique during their flying. That, I suppose, is a little too much refined; but his discourse in general of sound was mighty fine. There I left them, and myself by coach to St. James's, where we attended with the rest of my fellows on the Duke, whom I found with two or three patches upon his nose and about his right eye, which come from his being struck with the bough of a tree the other day in his hunting; and it is a wonder it did not strike out his eye. After we had done our business with him, which is now but little, the want of money being such as leaves us little to do but to answer complaints of the want thereof, and nothing to offer to the Duke, the representing of our want of money being now become uselesse, I into the Park, and there I met with Mrs. Burroughs by appointment, and did agree (after discoursing of some business of her's) for her to meet me at New Exchange, while I by coach to my Lord Treasurer's, and then called at the New Exchange, and thence carried her by water to Parliament stayres, and I to the Exchequer about my Tangier quarter tallys, and that done I took coach and to the west door of the Abby, where she come to me, and I with her by coach to Lissen-greene where we were last, and staid an hour or two before dinner could be got for us, I in the meantime having much pleasure with her, but all honest. And by and by dinner come up, and then to my sport again, but still honest; and then took coach and up and down in the country toward Acton, and then toward Chelsy, and so to Westminster, and there set her down where I took her up, with mighty pleasure in her company, and so I by coach home, and thence to Bow, with all the haste I could, to my Lady Pooly's, where my wife was with Mr. Batelier and his sisters, and there I found a noble supper, and every thing exceeding pleasant, and their mother, Mrs. Batelier, a fine woman, but mighty passionate upon sudden news brought her of the loss of a dog borrowed of the Duke of Albemarle's son to line a bitch of hers that is very pretty, but the dog was by and by found, and so all well again, their company mighty innocent and pleasant, we having never been here before. About ten o'clock we rose from table, and sang a song, and so home in two coaches (Mr. Batelier and his sister Mary and my wife and I in one, and Mercer alone in the other); and after being examined at Allgate, whether we were husbands and wives, home, and being there come, and sent away Mr. Batelierand his sister, I find Reeves there, it being a mighty fine bright night, and so upon my leads, though very sleepy, till one in the morning, looking on the moon and Jupiter, with this twelve-foote glasse and another of six foote, that he hath brought with him to-night, and the sights mighty pleasant, and one of the glasses I will buy, it being very usefull. So to bed mighty sleepy, but with much pleasure. Reeves lying at my house again; and mighty proud I am (and ought to be thankfull to God Almighty) that I am able to have a spare bed for my friends.

9th. Up and to the office to prepare business for the Board, Reeves being gone and I having lent him upon one of the glasses. Here we sat, but to little purpose, nobody coming at us but to ask for money, not to offer us any goods. At noon home to dinner, and then to the office again, being mightily pleased with a Virgin's head that my wife is now doing of. In the evening to Lumbard-streete about money, to enable me to pay Sir G. Carteret's L3000, which he hath lodged in my hands, in behalf of his son and my Lady Jemimah, toward their portion, which, I thank God, I am able to do at a minute's warning. In my [way] I inquired, and find Mrs. Rawlinson is dead of the sickness, and her mayde continues mighty ill. He himself is got out of the house. I met also with Mr. Evelyn in the streete, who tells me the sad condition at this very day at Deptford for the plague, and more at Deale (within his precinct as one of the Commissioners for sick and wounded seamen), that the towne is almost quite depopulated. Thence back home again, and after some business at my office, late, home to supper and to bed, I being sleepy by my late want of rest, notwithstanding my endeavouring to get a nap of an hour this afternoon after dinner. So home and to bed.

10th. Up and to my chamber; there did some business and then to my office, and towards noon by water to the Exchequer about my Tangier order, and thence back again and to the Exchange, where little newes but what is in the book, and, among other things, of a man sent up for by the King and Council for saying that Sir W. Coventry did give intelligence to the Dutch of all our matters here. I met with Colvill, and he and I did agree about his lending me L1000 upon a tally of L1000 for Tangier. Thence to Sympson, the joyner, and I am mightily pleased with what I see of my presses for my books, which he is making for me. So homeward, and hear in Fanchurch-streete, that now the mayde also is dead at Mr. Rawlinson's; so that there are three dead in all, the wife, a man-servant, and mayde-servant. Home to dinner, where sister Balty dined with us, and met a letter come to me from him. He is well at Harwich, going to the fleete. After dinner to the office, and anon with my wife and sister abroad, left them in Paternoster Row, while Creed, who was with me at the office, and I to Westminster; and leaving him in the Strand, I to my Lord Chancellor's, and did very little business, and so away home by water, with more and more pleasure, I every time reading over my Lord Bacon's "Faber Fortunae." So home, and there did little business, and then walked an hour talking of sundry things in the garden, and find him a cunning knave, as I always observed him to be, and so home to supper, and to bed. Pleased that this day I find, if I please, I can have all my money in that I have out of my hands, but I am at a loss whether to take it in or no, and pleased also to hear of Mrs. Barbara Sheldon's good fortune, who is like to have Mr. Wood's son, the mast-maker, a very rich man, and to be married speedily, she being already mighty fine upon it.

11th. Up and to the office, where we sat all the morning. At noon home to dinner, where mighty pleased at my wife's beginnings of a little Virgin's head. To the office and did much business, and then to Mr. Colvill's, and with him did come to an agreement about my L2600 assignment on the Exchequer, which I had of Sir W. Warren; and, to my great joy, I think I shall get above L100 by it, but I must leave it to be finished on Monday. Thence to the office, and there did the remainder of my business, and so home to supper and to bed. This afternoon I hear as if we had landed some men upon the Dutch coasts, but I believe it is but a foolery either in the report or the attempt.

12th (Lord's day). Up and to my chamber, where busy all the morning, and my thoughts very much upon the manner of my removal of my closett things the next weeke into my present musique room, if I find I can spare or get money to furnish it. By and by comes Reeves, by appointment, but did not bring the glasses and things I expected for our discourse and my information to-day, but we have agreed on it for next Sunday. By and by, in comes Betty Michell and her husband, and so to dinner, I mightily pleased with their company. We passed the whole day talking with them, but without any pleasure, but only her being there. In the evening, all parted, and I and my wife up to her closett to consider how to order that the next summer, if we live to it; and then down to my chamber at night to examine her kitchen accounts, and there I took occasion to fall out with her for her buying a laced handkercher and pinner without my leave. Though the thing is not much, yet I would not permit her begin to do so, lest worse should follow. From this we began both to be angry, and so continued till bed, and did not sleep friends.

13th. Up, without being friends with my wife, nor great enemies, being both quiet and silent. So out to Colvill's, but he not being come to town yet, I to Paul's Church-yarde, to treat with a bookbinder, to come and gild the backs of all my books, to make them handsome, to stand in my new presses, when they come. So back again to Colvill's, and there did end our treaty, to my full content, about my Exchequer assignment of L2600 of Sir W. Warren's, for which I give him L170 to stand to the hazard of receiving it. So I shall get clear by it L230, which is a very good jobb. God be praised for it! Having done with him, then he and I took coach, and I carried him to Westminster, and there set him down, in our way speaking of several things. I find him a bold man to say any thing of any body, and finds fault with our great ministers of state that nobody looks after any thing; and I thought it dangerous to be free with him, for I do not think he can keep counsel, because he blabs to me what hath passed between other people and him. Thence I to St. James's, and there missed Sir W. Coventry; but taking up Mr. Robinson in my coach, I towards London, and there in the way met Sir W. Coventry, and followed him to White Hall, where a little discourse very kind, and so I away with Robinson, and set him down at the 'Change, and thence I to Stokes the goldsmith, and sent him to and again to get me L1000 in gold; and so home to dinner, my wife and I friends, without any words almost of last night. After dinner, I abroad to Stokes, and there did receive L1000 worth in gold, paying 18 1/2d. and 19d. for others exchange. Home with them, and there to my office to business, and anon home in the evening, there to settle some of my accounts, and then to supper and to bed.

14th. (Thanksgiving day.)

Up, and comes Mr. Foley and his man, with a box of a great variety of carpenter's and joyner's tooles, which I had bespoke, to me, which please me mightily; but I will have more. Then I abroad down to the Old Swan, and there I called and kissed Betty Michell, and would have got her to go with me to Westminster, but I find her a little colder than she used to be, methought, which did a little molest me. So I away not pleased, and to White Hall, where I find them at Chappell, and met with Povy, and he and I together, who tells me how mad my letter makes my Lord Peterborough, and what a furious letter he hath writ to me in answer, though it is not come yet. This did trouble me; for though there be no reason, yet to have a nobleman's mouth open against a man may do a man hurt; so I endeavoured to have found him out and spoke with him, but could not. So to the chappell, and heard a piece of the Dean of Westminster's sermon, and a special good anthemne before the king, after a sermon, and then home by coach with Captain Cocke, who is in pain about his hempe, of which he says he hath bought great quantities, and would gladly be upon good terms with us for it, wherein I promise to assist him. So we 'light at the 'Change, where, after a small turn or two, taking no pleasure now-a-days to be there, because of answering questions that would be asked there which I cannot answer; so home and dined, and after dinner, with my wife and Mercer to the Beare-garden,

where I have not been, I think, of many years, and saw some good sport of the bull's tossing of the dogs: one into the very boxes. But it is a very rude and nasty pleasure. We had a great many hectors in the same box with us (and one very fine went into the pit, and played his dog for a wager, which was a strange sport for a gentleman), where they drank wine, and drank Mercer's health first, which I pledged with my hat off; and who should be in the house but Mr. Pierce the surgeon, who saw us and spoke to us. Thence home, well enough satisfied, however, with the variety of this afternoon's exercise; and so I to my chamber, till in the evening our company come to supper. We had invited to a venison pasty Mr. Batelier and his sister Mary, Mrs. Mercer, her daughter Anne, Mr. Le Brun, and W. Hewer; and so we supped, and very merry. And then about nine o'clock to Mrs. Mercer's gate, where the fire and boys expected us, and her son had provided abundance of serpents and rockets; and there mighty merry (my Lady Pen and Pegg going thither with us, and Nan Wright), till about twelve at night, flinging our fireworks, and burning one another and the people over the way. And at last our businesses being most spent, we into Mrs. Mercer's, and there mighty merry, smutting one another with candle grease and soot, till most of us were like devils. And that being done, then we broke up, and to my house; and there I made them drink, and upstairs we went, and then fell into dancing (W. Batelier dancing well), and dressing, him and I and one Mr. Banister (who with his wife come over also with us) like women; and Mercer put on a suit of Tom's, like a boy, and mighty mirth we had, and Mercer danced a jigg; and Nan Wright and my wife and Pegg Pen put on perriwigs. Thus we spent till three or four in the morning, mighty merry; and then parted, and to bed.

15th. Mighty sleepy; slept till past eight of the clock, and was called up by a letter from Sir W. Coventry, which, among other things, tells me how we have burned one hundred and sixty ships of the enemy within the Fly.

I up, and with all possible haste, and in pain for fear of coming late, it being our day of attending the Duke of Yorke, to St. James's, where they are full of the particulars; how they are generally good merchant ships, some of them laden and supposed rich ships. We spent five fire-ships upon them. We landed on the Schelling (Sir Philip Howard with some men, and Holmes, I think; with others, about 1000 in all), and burned a town; and so come away. By and by the Duke of Yorke with his books showed us the very place and manner, and that it was not our design or expectation to have done this, but only to have landed on the Fly, and burned some of their store; but being come in, we spied those ships, and with our long boats, one by one, fired them, our ships running all aground, it being so shoal water. We were led to this by, it seems, a renegado captain of the Hollanders, who found himself ill used by De Ruyter for his good service, and so come over to us, and hath done us good service; so that now we trust him, and he himself did go on this expedition. The service is very great, and our joys as great for it. All this will make the Duke of Albemarle in repute again, I doubt, though there is nothing of his in this. But, Lord! to see what successe do, whether with or without reason, and making a man seem wise, notwithstanding never so late demonstration of the profoundest folly in the world. Thence walked over the Parke with Sir W. Coventry, in our way talking of the unhappy state of our office; and I took an opportunity to let him know, that though the backwardnesses of all our matters of the office may be well imputed to the known want of money, yet, perhaps, there might be personal and particular failings; and that I did, therefore, depend still upon his promise of telling me whenever he finds any ground to believe any defect or neglect on my part, which he promised me still to do; and that there was none he saw, nor, indeed, says he, is there room now-a-days to find fault with any particular man, while we are in this condition for money. This, methought, did not so well please me; but, however, I am glad I have said this, thereby giving myself good grounds to believe that at this time he did not want an occasion to have said what he pleased to me, if he had had anything in his mind, which by his late distance and silence I have feared. But then again I am to consider he is grown a very great man, much greater than he was, and so must keep more distance; and, next, that the condition of our office will not afford me occasion of shewing myself so active and deserving as heretofore; and, lastly, the muchness of his business cannot suffer him to mind it, or give him leisure to reflect on anything, or shew the freedom and kindnesse that he used to do. But I think I have done something considerable to my satisfaction in doing this; and that if I do but my duty remarkably from this time forward, and not neglect it, as I have of late done, and minded my pleasures, I may be as well as ever I was. Thence to the Exchequer, but did nothing, they being all gone from their offices; and so to the Old Exchange, where the towne full of the good newes, but I did not stay to tell or hear any, but home, my head akeing and drowsy, and to dinner, and then lay down upon the couch, thinking to get a little rest, but could not. So down the river, reading "The Adventures of Five Houres," which the more I read the more I admire. So down below Greenwich, but the wind and tide being against us, I back again to Deptford, and did a little business there, and thence walked to Redriffe; and so home, and to the office a while. In the evening comes W. Batelier and his sister, and my wife, and fair Mrs. Turner into the garden, and there we walked, and then with my Lady

Pen and Pegg in a-doors, and eat and were merry, and so pretty late broke up, and to bed. The guns of the Tower going off, and there being bonefires also in the street for this late good successe.

16th. Up, having slept well, and after entering my journal, to the office, where all the morning, but of late Sir W. Coventry hath not come to us, he being discouraged from the little we have to do but to answer the clamours of people for money. At noon home, and there dined with me my Lady Pen only and W. Hewer at a haunch of venison boiled, where pretty merry, only my wife vexed me a little about demanding money to go with my Lady Pen to the Exchange to lay out. I to the office, where all the afternoon and very busy and doing much business; but here I had a most eminent experience of the evil of being behindhand in business. I was the most backward to begin any thing, and would fain have framed to myself an occasion of going abroad, and should, I doubt, have done it, but some business coming in, one after another, kept me there, and I fell to the ridding away of a great deale of business, and when my hand was in it was so pleasing a sight to [see] my papers disposed of, and letters answered, which troubled my book and table, that I could have continued there with delight all night long, and did till called away by my Lady Pen and Pegg and my wife to their house to eat with them; and there I went, and exceeding merry, there being Nan Wright, now Mrs. Markham, and sits at table with my Lady. So mighty merry, home and to bed. This day Sir W. Batten did show us at the table a letter from Sir T. Allen, which says that we have taken ten or twelve' ships (since the late great expedition of burning their ships and towne), laden with hempe, flax, tarr, deales, &c. This was good newes; but by and by comes in Sir G. Carteret, and he asked us with full mouth what we would give for good newes. Says Sir W. Batten, "I have better than you, for a wager." They laid sixpence, and we that were by were to give sixpence to him that told the best newes. So Sir W. Batten told his of the ten or twelve ships Sir G. Carteret did then tell us that upon the newes of the burning of the ships and towne the common people a Amsterdam did besiege De Witt's house, and he was force to flee to the Prince of Orange, who is gone to Cleve to the marriage of his sister. This we concluded all the best newest and my Lord Bruncker and myself did give Sir G. Carteret our sixpence a-piece, which he did give Mr. Smith to give the poor. Thus we made ourselves mighty merry.

17th. Up and betimes with Captain Erwin down by water to Woolwich, I walking alone from Greenwich thither, making an end of the "Adventures of Five Hours," which when all is done is the best play that ever I read in my life. Being come thither I did some business there and at the Rope Yarde, and had a piece of bride-cake sent me by Mrs. Barbary into the boate after me, she being here at her uncle's, with her husband, Mr. Wood's son, the mast-maker, and mighty nobly married, they say, she was, very fine, and he very rich, a strange fortune for so odd a looked mayde, though her hands and body be good, and nature very good, I think. Back with Captain Erwin, discoursing about the East Indys, where he hath often been. And among other things he tells me how the King of Syam seldom goes out without thirty or forty thousand people with him, and not a word spoke, nor a hum or cough in the whole company to be heard. He tells me the punishment frequently there for malefactors is cutting off the crowne of their head, which they do very dexterously, leaving their brains bare, which kills them presently. He told me what I remember he hath once done heretofore: that every body is to lie flat down at the coming by of the King, and nobody to look upon him upon pain of death. And that he and his fellows, being strangers, were invited to see the sport of taking of a wild elephant, and they did only kneel, and look toward the King. Their druggerman did desire them to fall down, for otherwise he should suffer for their contempt of the King. The sport being ended, a messenger comes from the King, which the druggerman thought had been to have taken away his life; but it was to enquire how the strangers liked the sport. The druggerman answered that they did cry it up to be the best that ever they saw, and that they never heard of any Prince so great in every thing as this King. The messenger being gone back, Erwin and his company asked their druggerman what he had said, which he told them. "But why," say they, "would you say that without our leave, it being not true?"—"It is no matter for that," says he, "I must have said it, or have been hanged, for our King do not live by meat, nor drink, but by having great lyes told him." In our way back we come by a little vessel that come into the river this morning, and says he left the fleete in Sole Bay, and that he hath not heard (he belonging to Sir W. Jenings, in the fleete) of any such prizes taken as the ten or twelve I inquired about, and said by Sir W. Batten yesterday to be taken, so I fear it is not true. So to Westminster, and there, to my great content, did receive my L2000 of Mr. Spicer's telling, which I was to receive of Colvill, and brought it home with me [to] my house by water, and there I find one of my new presses for my books brought home, which pleases me mightily. As, also, do my wife's progresse upon her head that she is making. So to dinner, and thence abroad with my wife, leaving her at Unthanke's; I to White Hall, waiting at the Council door till it rose, and there spoke with Sir W. Coventry, who and I do much fear our Victuallers, they having missed the fleete in their going. But Sir W. Coventry says it is not our fault, but theirs, if they have not left ships to secure them. This he spoke in a chagrin sort of way, methought. After a little more discourse of several businesses, I away homeward, having in the gallery the good fortune to see Mrs. Stewart, who is grown a little too tall, but is a woman of most excellent features. The narrative of the late expedition in burning the ships is in print, and makes it a great thing, and I hope it is so. So took up my wife and home, there I to the office, and thence with Sympson the joyner home to put together the press he hath brought me for my books this day, which pleases me exceedingly. Then to Sir W. Batten's, where Sir Richard Ford did very understandingly, methought, give us an account of the originall of the Hollands Bank,

and the nature of it, and how they do never give any interest at all to any person that brings in their money, though what is brought in upon the public faith interest is given by the State for. The unsafe condition of a Bank under a Monarch, and the little safety to a Monarch to have any; or Corporation alone (as London in answer to Amsterdam) to have so great a wealth or credit, it is, that makes it hard to have a Bank here. And as to the former, he did tell us how it sticks in the memory of most merchants how the late King (when by the war between Holland and France and Spayne all the bullion of Spayne was brought hither, one-third of it to be coyned; and indeed it was found advantageous to the merchant to coyne most of it), was persuaded in a strait by my Lord Cottington to seize upon the money in the Tower, which, though in a few days the merchants concerned did prevail to get it released, yet the thing will never be forgot. So home to supper and to bed, understanding this evening, since I come home, that our Victuallers are all come in to the fleete, which is good newes. Sir John Minnes come home tonight not well, from Chatham, where he hath been at a pay, holding it at Upnor Castle, because of the plague so much in the towne of Chatham. He hath, they say, got an ague, being so much on the water.

18th. All the morning at my office; then to the Exchange (with my Lord Bruncker in his coach) at noon, but it was only to avoid Mr. Chr. Pett's being invited by me to dinner. So home, calling at my little mercer's in Lumbard Streete, who hath the pretty wench, like the old Queene, and there cheapened some stuffs to hang my roome, that I intend to turn into a closett. So home to dinner, and after dinner comes Creed to discourse with me about several things of Tangier concernments and accounts, among others starts the doubt, which I was formerly aware of, but did wink at it, whether or no Lanyon and his partners be not paid for more than they should be, which he presses, so that it did a little discompose me; but, however, I do think no harm will arise thereby. He gone, I to the office, and there very late, very busy, and so home to supper and to bed.

19th (Lord's day). Up and to my chamber, and there began to draw out fair and methodically my accounts of Tangier, in order to shew them to the Lords. But by and by comes by agreement Mr. Reeves, and after him Mr. Spong, and all day with them, both before and after dinner, till ten o'clock at night, upon opticke enquiries, he bringing me a frame he closes on, to see how the rays of light do cut one another, and in a darke room with smoake, which is very pretty. He did also bring a lanthorne with pictures in glasse, to make strange things appear on a wall, very pretty. We did also at night see Jupiter and his girdle and satellites, very fine, with my twelve-foote glasse, but could not Saturne, he being very dark. Spong and I had also several fine discourses upon the globes this afternoon, particularly why the fixed stars do not rise and set at the same houre all the yeare long, which he could not demonstrate, nor I neither, the reason of. So, it being late, after supper they away home. But it vexed me to understand no more from Reeves and his glasses touching the nature and reason of the several refractions of the several figured glasses, he understanding the acting part, but not one bit the theory, nor can make any body understand it, which is a strange dullness, methinks. I did not hear anything yesterday or at all to confirm either Sir Thos. Allen's news of the 10 or 12 ships taken, nor of the disorder at Amsterdam upon the news of the burning of the ships, that he [De Witt] should be fled to the Prince of Orange, it being generally believed that he was gone to France before.

20th. Waked this morning, about six o'clock, with a violent knocking at Sir J. Minnes's doore, to call up Mrs. Hammon, crying out that Sir J. Minnes is a-dying. He come home ill of an ague on Friday night. I saw him on Saturday, after his fit of the ague, and then was pretty lusty. Which troubles me mightily, for he is a very good, harmless, honest gentleman, though not fit for the business. But I much fear a worse may come, that may be more uneasy to me. Up, and to Deptford by water, reading "Othello, Moore of Venice," which I ever heretofore esteemed a mighty good play, but having so lately read "The Adventures of Five Houres," it seems a mean thing. Walked back, and so home, and then down to the Old Swan and drank at Betty Michell's, and so to Westminster to the Exchequer about my quarter tallies, and so to Lumbard Streete to choose stuff to hang my new intended closet, and have chosen purple. So home to dinner, and all the afternoon till almost midnight upon my Tangier accounts, getting Tom Wilson to help me in writing as I read, and at night W. Hewer, and find myself most happy in the keeping of all my accounts, for that after all the changings and turnings necessary in such an account, I find myself right to a farthing in an account of L127,000. This afternoon I visited Sir J. Minnes, who, poor man, is much impatient by these few days' sickness, and I fear indeed it will kill him.

21st. Up, and to the office, where much business and Sir W. Coventry there, who of late hath wholly left us, most of our business being about money, to which we can give no answer, which makes him weary of coming to us. He made an experiment to-day, by taking up a heape of petitions that lay upon the table. They proved seventeen in number, and found them thus: one for money for reparation for clothes, four desired to have tickets made out to them, and the other twelve were for money. Dined at home, and sister Balty with us. My wife snappish because I denied her money to lay out this afternoon; however, good friends again, and by coach set them down at the New Exchange, and I to the Exchequer, and there find my business of my tallys in good forwardness. I passed down into the Hall, and there hear that Mr. Bowles, the grocer, after 4 or 5 days' sickness, is dead, and this day buried. So away, and taking up my wife, went homewards. I 'light and with Harman to my mercer's in Lumbard Streete, and there agreed for, our purple serge for my closett, and so I away home. So home and late at the office, and then home, and there found Mr. Batelier and his sister Mary, and we sat chatting a great while, talking of witches and spirits, and he told me of his own knowledge, being with some others at Bourdeaux, making a bargain with another man at a taverne for some clarets, they did hire a fellow to thunder (which he had the art of doing upon a deale board) and to rain and hail, that is, make the noise of, so as did give them a pretence of undervaluing their merchants' wines, by saying this thunder would spoil and turne them. Which was so reasonable to the merchant, that he did abate two pistolls per ton for the wine in belief of that, whereas, going out, there was no such thing. This Batelier did see and was the cause of to his profit, as is above said. By and by broke up and to bed.

22nd. Up and by coach with L100 to the Exchequer to pay fees there. There left it, and I to St. James's, and there with; the Duke of Yorke. I had opportunity of much talk with Sir. W. Pen to-day (he being newly come from the fleete); and he, do much undervalue the honour that is given to the conduct of the late business of Holmes in burning the ships and town

saying it was a great thing indeed, and of great profit to us in being of great losse to the enemy, but that it was wholly a business of chance, and no conduct employed in it. I find Sir W. Pen do hold up his head at this time higher than ever he did in his life. I perceive he do look after Sir J. Minnes's place if he dies, and though I love him not nor do desire to have him in, yet I do think [he] is the first man in England for it. To the Exchequer, and there received my tallys, and paid my fees in good order, and so home, and there find Mrs. Knipp and my wife going to dinner. She tells me my song, of "Beauty Retire" is mightily cried up, which I am not a little proud of; and do think I have done "It is Decreed" better, but I have not finished it. My closett is doing by upholsters, which I am pleased with, but fear my purple will be too sad for that melancholy roome. After dinner and doing something at the office, I with my wife, Knipp, and Mercer, by coach to Moorefields, and there saw "Polichinello," which pleases me mightily, and here I saw our Mary, our last chamber-maid, who is gone from Mrs. Pierces it seems. Thence carried Knipp home, calling at the Cocke alehouse at the doore and drank, and so home, and there find Reeves, and so up to look upon the stars, and do like my glasse very well, and did even with him for it and a little perspective and the Lanthorne that shows tricks, altogether costing me L9 5s. 0d. So to bed, he lying at our house.

23rd. At the office all the morning, whither Sir W. Coventry sent me word that the Dutch fleete is certainly abroad; and so we are to hasten all we have to send to our fleete with all speed. But, Lord! to see how my Lord Bruncker undertakes the despatch of the fire-ships, when he is no more fit for it than a porter; and all the while Sir W. Pen, who is the most fit, is unwilling to displease him, and do not look after it; and so the King's work is like to be well done. At noon dined at home, Lovett with us; but he do not please me in his business, for he keeps things long in hand, and his paper do not hold so good as I expected—the varnish wiping off in a little time—a very sponge; and I doubt by his discourse he is an odde kind of fellow, and, in plain terms, a very rogue. He gone, I to the office (having seen and liked the upholsters' work in my roome—which they have almost done), and there late, and in the evening find Mr. Batelier and his sister there and then we talked and eat and were merry, and so parted late, and to bed.

24th. Up, and dispatched several businesses at home in the morning, and then comes Sympson to set up my other new presses

for my books, and so he and I fell in to the furnishing of my new closett, and taking out the things out of my old, and I kept him with me all day, and he dined with me, and so all the afternoon till it was quite darke hanging things, that is my maps and pictures and draughts, and setting up my books, and as much as we could do, to my most extraordinary satisfaction; so that I think it will be as noble a closett as any man hath, and light enough—though, indeed, it would be better to have had a little more light. He gone, my wife and I to talk, and sup, and then to setting right my Tangier accounts and enter my Journall, and then to bed with great content in my day's worke. This afternoon comes Mrs. Barbary Sheldon, now Mrs. Wood, to see my wife. I was so busy I would not see her. But she came, it seems, mighty rich in rings and fine clothes, and like a lady, and says she is matched mighty well, at which I am very glad, but wonder at her good fortune and the folly of her husband, and vexed at myself for not paying her the respect of seeing her, but I will come out of her debt another time.

25th. All the morning at the office. At noon dined at home, and after dinner up to my new closett, which pleases me mightily, and there I proceeded to put many things in order as far as I had time, and then set it in washing, and stood by myself a great while to see it washed; and then to the office, and then wrote my letters and other things, and then in mighty good humour home to supper and to bed.

26th (Lord's day). Up betimes, and to the finishing the setting things in order in my new closett out of my old, which I did thoroughly by the time sermon was done at church, to my exceeding joy, only I was a little disturbed with newes my Lord Bruncker brought me, that we are to attend the King at White Hall this afternoon, and that it is about a complaint from the Generalls against us. Sir W. Pen dined by invitation with me, his Lady and daughter being gone into the country. We very merry. After dinner we parted, and I to my office, whither I sent for Mr. Lewes and instructed myself fully in the business of the Victualling, to enable me to answer in the matter; and then Sir W. Pen and I by coach to White Hall, and there staid till the King and Cabinet were met in the Green Chamber, and then we were called in; and there the King begun with me, to hear how the victualls of the fleete stood. I did in a long discourse tell him and the rest (the Duke of Yorke, Lord Chancellor, Lord Treasurer, both the Secretarys, Sir G. Carteret, and Sir W. Coventry,) how it stood, wherein they seemed satisfied, but press mightily for more supplies; and the letter of the Generalls, which was read, did lay their not going or too soon returning from the Dutch coast, this next bout, to the want of victuals. They then proceeded to the enquiry after the fireships; and did all very superficially, and without any severity at all. But, however, I was in pain, after we come out, to know how I had done; and hear well enough. But, however, it shall be a caution to me to prepare myself against a day of inquisition. Being come out, I met with Mr. Moore, and he and I an houre together in the Gallery, telling me how far they are gone in getting my Lord [Sandwich's] pardon, so as the Chancellor is prepared in it; and Sir H. Bennet do promote it, and the warrant for the King's signing is drawn. The business between my Lord Hinchingbroke and Mrs. Mallett is quite broke off; he attending her at Tunbridge, and she declaring her affections to be settled; and he not being fully pleased with the vanity and liberty of her carriage. He told me how my Lord has drawn a bill of exchange from Spayne of L1200, and would have me supply him with L500 of it, but I avoyded it, being not willing to embarke myself in money there, where I see things going to ruine. Thence to discourse of the times; and he tells me he believes both my Lord Arlington and Sir W. Coventry, as well as my Lord Sandwich and Sir G. Carteret, have reason to fear, and are afeard of this Parliament now coming on. He tells me that Bristoll's faction is getting ground apace against my Lord Chancellor. He told me that my old Lord Coventry was a cunning, crafty man, and did make as many bad decrees in Chancery as any man; and that in one case, that occasioned many years' dispute, at last when the King come in, it was hoped by the party grieved, to get my Lord Chancellor to reverse a decree of his. Sir W. Coventry took the opportunity of the business between the Duke of Yorke and the Duchesse, and said to my Lord Chancellor, that he had rather be drawn up Holborne to be hanged, than live to see his father pissed upon (in these very terms) and any decree of his reversed. And so the Chancellor did not think fit to do it, but it still stands, to the undoing of one Norton, a printer, about his right to the printing of the Bible, and Grammar, &c. Thence Sir W. Pen and I to Islington and there drank at the Katherine Wheele, and so down the nearest way home, where there was no kind of pleasure at all. Being come home, hear that Sir J. Minnes has had a very bad fit all this day, and a hickup do take him, which is a very bad sign, which troubles me truly. So home to supper a little and then to bed.

27th. Up, and to my new closett, which pleases me mightily, and there did a little business. Then to break open a window, to the leads' side in my old closett, which will enlighten the room mightily, and make it mighty pleasant. So to the office, and then home about one thing or other, about my new closet, for my mind is full of nothing but that. So at noon to dinner, mightily pleased with my wife's picture that she is upon. Then to the office, and thither come and walked an hour with me Sir G. Carteret, who tells me what is done about my Lord's pardon, and is not for letting the Duke of Yorke know any thing of it beforehand, but to carry it as speedily and quietly as we can. He seems to be very apprehensive that the Parliament will be troublesome and inquisitive into faults, but seems not to value them as to himself. He gone, I to the Victualling Office, there with Lewes' and Willson setting the business of the state of the fleete's victualling even and plain, and that being done, and other good discourse about it over, Mr. Willson and I by water down the River for discourse only, about business of the office, and then back, and I home, and after a little at my office home to my new closet, and there did much business on my Tangier account and my Journall for three days. So to supper and to bed. We are not sure that the Dutch fleete is out. I have another memento from Sir W. Coventry of the want of provisions in the fleete, which troubles me, though there is no reason for it; but will have the good effect of making me more wary. So, full of thoughts, to bed.

28th. Up, and in my new closet a good while doing business. Then called on Mrs. Martin and Burroughs of Westminster about business of the former's husband. Which done, I to the office, where we sat all the morning. At noon I, with my wife and Mercer, to Philpott Lane, a great cook's shop, to the wedding of Mr. Longracke, our purveyor, a good, sober, civil man, and hath married a sober, serious mayde. Here I met much ordinary company, I going thither at his great request; but there was Mr. Madden and his lady, a fine, noble, pretty lady, and he, and a fine gentleman seems to be. We four were most together; but the whole company was very simple and innocent. A good-dinner, and, what was best, good musique. After dinner the young women went to dance; among others Mr. Christopher Pett his daughter, who is a very pretty, modest girle, I am mightily taken with her; and that being done about five o'clock, home, very well pleased with the afternoon's work. And so we broke up mightily civilly, the bride and bridegroom going to Greenwich (they keeping their dinner here only for my sake) to lie, and we home, where I to the office, and anon am on a sudden called to meet Sir W. Pen and Sir W. Coventry at the Victualling Office, which did put me out of order to be so surprised. But I went, and there Sir William Coventry did read me a letter from the Generalls to the King,

a most scurvy letter, reflecting most upon Sir W. Coventry, and then upon me for my accounts (not that they are not true, but that we do not consider the expence of the fleete), and then of the whole office, in neglecting them and the King's service, and this in very plain and sharp and menacing terms. I did give a good account of matters according to our computation of the expence of the fleete. I find Sir W. Coventry willing enough to accept of any thing to confront the Generalls. But a great supply must be made, and shall be in grace of God! But, however, our accounts here will be found the true ones. Having done here, and much work set me, I with greater content home than I thought I should have done, and so to the office a while, and then home, and a while in my new closet, which delights me every day more and more, and so late to bed.

29th. Up betimes, and there to fit some Tangier accounts, and then, by appointment, to my Lord Bellasses, but about Paul's thought of the chant paper I should carry with me, and so fain to come back again, and did, and then met with Sir W. Pen, and with him to my Lord Bellasses, he sitting in the coach the while, while I up to my Lord and there offered him my account of the bills of exchange I had received and paid for him, wherein we agree all but one L200 bill of Vernatty's drawing, wherein I doubt he hath endeavoured to cheate my Lord; but that will soon appear. Thence took leave, and found Sir W. Pen talking to Orange Moll, of the King's house, who, to our great comfort, told us that they begun to act on the 18th of this month. So on to St. James's, in the way Sir W. Pen telling me that Mr. Norton, that married Sir J. Lawson's daughter, is dead. She left L800 a year jointure, a son to inherit the whole estate. She freed from her father-in-law's tyranny, and is in condition to helpe her mother, who needs it; of which I am glad, the young lady being very pretty. To St. James's, and there Sir W. Coventry took Sir W. Pen and me apart, and read to us his answer to the Generalls' letter to the King that he read last night; wherein he is very plain, and states the matter in full defence of himself and of me with him, which he could not avoid; which is a good comfort to me, that I happen to be involved with him in the same cause. And then, speaking of the supplies which have been made to this fleete, more than ever in all kinds to any, even that wherein the Duke of Yorke himself was, "Well," says he, "if this will not do, I will say, as Sir J. Falstaffe did to the Prince, 'Tell your father, that if he do not like this let him kill the next Piercy himself,'"—["King Henry IV.," Part I, act v., sc. 4.]—and so we broke up, and to the Duke, and there did our usual business. So I to the Parke and there met Creed, and he and I walked to Westminster to the Exchequer, and thence to White Hall talking of Tangier matters and Vernatty's knavery, and so parted, and then I homeward and met Mr. Povy in Cheapside, and stopped and talked a good while upon the profits of the place which my Lord Bellasses hath made this last year, and what share we are to have of it, but of this all imperfect, and so parted, and I home, and there find Mrs. Mary Batelier, and she dined with us; and thence I took them to Islington, and there eat a custard; and so back to Moorfields, and shewed Batelier, with my wife, "Polichinello," which I like the more I see it; and so home with great content, she being a mighty good-natured, pretty woman, and thence I to the Victualling office, and there with Mr. Lewes and Willson upon our Victualling matters till ten at night, and so I home and there late writing a letter to Sir W. Coventry, and so home to supper and to bed. No newes where the Dutch are. We begin to think they will steale through the Channel to meet Beaufort. We think our fleete sayled yesterday, but we have no newes of it.

30th. Up and all the morning at the office, dined at home, and in the afternoon, and at night till two in the morning, framing my great letter to Mr. Hayes about the victualling of the fleete, about which there has been so much ado and exceptions taken by the Generalls.

31st. To bed at 2 or 3 in the morning and up again at 6 to go by appointment to my Lord Bellasses, but he out of town, which vexed me. So back and got Mr. Poynter to enter into, my book while I read from my last night's notes the letter, and that being done to writing it fair. At noon home to dinner, and then the boy and I to the office, and there he read while I writ it fair, which done I sent it to Sir W. Coventry to peruse and send to the fleete by the first opportunity;

and so pretty betimes to bed. Much pleased to-day with thoughts of gilding the backs of all my books alike in my new presses.

SEPTEMBER 1666

September 1st. Up and at the office all the morning, and then dined at home. Got my new closet made mighty clean against to-morrow. Sir W. Pen and my wife and Mercer and I to "Polichinelly," but were there horribly frighted to see Young Killigrew come in with a great many more young sparks; but we hid ourselves, so as we think they did not see us. By and by, they went away, and then we were at rest again; and so, the play being done, we to Islington, and there eat and drank and mighty merry; and so home singing, and, after a letter or two at the office, to bed.

2nd (Lord's day). Some of our mayds sitting up late last night to get things ready against our feast to-day, Jane called us up about three in the morning, to tell us of a great fire they saw in the City. So I rose and slipped on my nightgowne, and went to her window, and thought it to be on the backside of Marke-lane at the farthest; but, being unused to such fires as followed, I thought it far enough off; and so went to bed again and to sleep. About seven rose again to dress myself, and there looked out at the window, and saw the fire not so much as it was and further off. So to my closett to set things to rights after yesterday's cleaning. By and by Jane comes and tells me that she hears that above 300 houses have been burned down to-night by the fire we saw, and that it is now burning down all Fish-street, by London Bridge. So I made myself ready presently, and walked to the Tower, and there got up upon one of the high places, Sir J. Robinson's little son going up with me; and there I did see the houses at that end of the bridge all on fire, and an infinite great fire on this and the other side the end of the bridge; which, among other people, did trouble me for poor little Michell and our Sarah on the bridge. So down, with my heart full of trouble, to the Lieutenant of the Tower, who tells me that it begun this morning in the King's baker's' house in Pudding-lane, and that it hath burned St. Magnus's Church and most part of Fish-street already. So I down to the water-side, and there got a boat and through bridge, and there saw a lamentable fire. Poor Michell's house, as far as the Old Swan, already burned that way, and the fire running further, that in a very little time it got as far as the Steeleyard, while I was there. Everybody endeavouring to remove their goods, and flinging into the river or bringing them into lighters that layoff; poor people staying in their houses as long as till the very fire touched them, and then running into boats, or clambering from one pair of stairs by the water-side to another. And among other things, the poor pigeons, I perceive, were loth to leave their houses, but hovered about the windows and balconys till they were, some of them burned, their wings, and fell down. Having staid, and in an hour's time seen the fire: rage every way, and nobody, to my sight, endeavouring to quench it, but to remove their goods, and leave all to the fire, and having seen it get as far as the Steele-yard, and the wind mighty high and driving it into the City; and every thing, after so long a drought, proving combustible, even the very stones of churches, and among other things the poor steeple by which pretty Mrs.————lives, and whereof my old school-fellow Elborough is parson, taken fire in the very top, an there burned till it fell down: I to White Hall (with a gentleman with me who desired to go off from the Tower, to see the fire, in my boat); to White Hall, and there up to the Kings closett in the Chappell, where people come about me, and did give them an account dismayed them all, and word was carried in to the King. So I was called for, and did tell the King and Duke of Yorke what I saw, and that unless his Majesty did command houses to be pulled down nothing could stop the fire. They seemed much troubled, and the King commanded me to go to my Lord Mayor—[Sir Thomas Bludworth. See June 30th, 1666.]—from him, and command him to spare no houses, but to pull down before the fire every way. The Duke of York bid me tell him that if he would have any more soldiers he shall; and so did my Lord Arlington afterwards, as a great secret.

Here meeting, with Captain Cocke, I in his coach, which he lent me, and Creed with me to Paul's, and there walked along Watlingstreet, as well as I could, every creature coming away loaden with goods to save, and here and there sicke people carried away in beds. Extraordinary good goods carried in carts and on backs. At last met my Lord Mayor in Canningstreet, like a man spent, with a handkercher about his neck. To the King's message he cried, like a fainting woman, "Lord! what can I do? I am spent: people will not obey me. I have been pulling down houses; but the fire overtakes us faster than we can do it." That he needed no more soldiers; and that, for himself, he must go and refresh himself, having been up all night. So he left me, and I him, and walked home, seeing people all almost distracted, and no manner of means used to quench the fire. The houses, too, so very thick thereabouts, and full of matter for burning, as pitch and tarr, in Thames-street; and warehouses of oyle, and wines, and brandy, and other things. Here I saw Mr. Isaake Houblon, the handsome man, prettily dressed and dirty, at his door at Dowgate, receiving some of his brothers' things, whose houses were on fire; and, as he says, have been removed twice already; and he doubts (as it soon proved) that they must be in a little time removed from his house also, which was a sad consideration. And to see the churches all filling with goods by people who themselves should have been quietly there at this time. By this time it was about twelve o'clock; and so home, and there find my guests, which was Mr. Wood and his wife Barbary Sheldon, and also Mr. Moons: she mighty fine, and her husband; for aught I see, a likely man. But Mr. Moone's design and mine, which was to look over my closett and please him with the sight thereof, which he hath long desired, was wholly disappointed; for we were in great trouble and disturbance at this fire, not knowing what to think of it. However, we had an extraordinary good dinner, and as merry, as at this time we could be. While at dinner Mrs. Batelier come to enquire after Mr. Woolfe and Stanes (who, it seems, are related to them), whose houses in Fish-street are all burned; and they in a sad condition. She would not stay in the fright. Soon as dined, I and Moone away, and walked, through the City, the streets full of nothing but people and horses and carts loaden with goods, ready to run over one another, and, removing goods from one burned house to another. They now removing out of Canning-streets (which received goods in the morning) into Lumbard-streets, and further;

and among others I now saw my little goldsmith, Stokes, receiving some friend's goods, whose house itself was burned the day after. We parted at Paul's; he home, and I to Paul's Wharf, where I had appointed a boat to attend me, and took in Mr. Carcasse and his brother, whom I met in the streets and carried them below and above bridge to and again to see the fire, which was now got further, both below and above and no likelihood of stopping it. Met with the King and Duke of

York in their barge, and with them to Queenhith and there called Sir Richard Browne to them. Their order was only to pull down houses apace, and so below bridge the water-side; but little was or could be done, the fire coming upon them so fast. Good hopes there was of stopping it at the Three Cranes above, and at Buttolph's Wharf below bridge, if care be used; but the wind carries it into the City so as we know not by the water-side what it do there. River full of lighters and boats taking in goods, and good goods swimming in the water, and only I observed that hardly one lighter or boat in three that had the goods of a house in, but there was a pair of Virginalls

in it. Having seen as much as I could now, I away to White Hall by appointment, and there walked to St. James's Parks, and there met my wife and Creed and Wood and his wife, and walked to my boat; and there upon the water again, and to the fire up and down, it still encreasing, and the wind great. So near the fire as we could for smoke; and all over the Thames, with one's face in the wind, you were almost burned with a shower of firedrops. This is very true; so as houses were burned by these drops and flakes of fire, three or four, nay, five or six houses, one from another. When we could endure no more upon the water; we to a little ale-house on the Bankside, over against the 'Three Cranes, and there staid till it was dark almost, and saw the fire grow; and, as it grew darker, appeared more and more, and in corners and upon steeples, and between churches and houses, as far as we could see up the hill of the City, in a most horrid malicious bloody flame, not like the fine flame of an ordinary fire. Barbary and her husband away before us. We staid till, it being darkish, we saw the fire as only one entire arch of fire from this to the other side the bridge, and in a bow up the hill for an arch of above a mile long: it made me weep to see it. The churches, houses, and all on fire and flaming at once; and a horrid noise the flames made, and the cracking of houses at their ruins. So home with a sad heart, and there find every body discoursing and lamenting the fire; and poor Tom Hater come with some few of his goods saved out of his house, which is burned upon Fish-streets Hall. I invited him to lie at my house, and did receive his goods, but was deceived in his lying there, the newes coming every moment of the growth of the fire; so as we were forced to begin to pack up our owne goods; and prepare for their removal; and did by moonshine (it being brave dry, and moon: shine, and warm weather) carry much of my goods into the garden, and Mr. Hater and I did remove my money and iron chests into my cellar, as thinking that the safest place. And got my bags of gold into my office, ready to carry away, and my chief papers of accounts also there, and my tallys into a box by themselves. So great was our fear, as Sir W. Batten hath carts come out of the country to fetch away his goods this night. We did put Mr. Hater, poor man, to bed a little; but he got but very little rest, so much noise being in my house, taking down of goods.

3rd. About four o'clock in the morning, my Lady Batten sent me a cart to carry away all my money, and plate, and best things, to Sir W. Rider's at Bednall-greene. Which I did riding myself in my night-gowne in the cart; and, Lord! to see how the streets and the highways are crowded with people running and riding, and getting of carts at any rate to fetch away things. I find Sir W. Rider tired with being called up all night, and receiving things from several friends. His house full of goods, and much of Sir W. Batten's and Sir W. Pen's I am eased at my heart to have my treasure so well secured. Then home, with much ado to find a way, nor any sleep all this night to me nor my poor wife. But then and all this day she and I, and all my people labouring to get away the rest of our things, and did get Mr. Tooker to get me a lighter to take them in, and we did carry them (myself some) over Tower Hill, which was by this time full of people's goods, bringing their goods thither; and down to the lighter, which lay at next quay, above the Tower Docke. And here was my neighbour's wife, Mrs.————,with her pretty child, and some few of her things, which I did willingly give way to be saved with mine; but there was no passing with any thing through the postern, the crowd was so great. The Duke of Yorke of this day by the office, and spoke to us, and did ride with his guard up and down the City, to keep all quiet (he being now Generall, and having the care of all). This day, Mercer being not at home, but against her mistress's order gone to her mother's, and my wife going thither to speak with W. Hewer, met her there, and was angry; and her mother saying that she was not a 'prentice girl, to ask leave every time she goes abroad, my wife with good reason was angry, and, when she came home, bid her be gone again. And so she went away, which troubled me, but yet less than it would, because of the condition we are in, fear of coming into in a little time of being less able to keepe one in her quality. At night lay down a little upon a quilt of W. Hewer's in the office, all my owne things being packed up or gone; and after me my poor wife did the like, we having fed upon the remains of yesterday's dinner, having no fire nor dishes, nor any opportunity of dressing any thing.

4th. Up by break of day to get away the remainder of my things; which I did by a lighter at the Iron gate and my hands so few, that it was the afternoon before we could get them all away. Sir W. Pen and I to Tower-streete, and there met the fire burning three or four doors beyond Mr. Howell's, whose goods, poor man, his trayes, and dishes, shovells, &c., were flung all along Tower-street in the kennels, and people working therewith from one end to the other; the fire coming on in that narrow streete, on both sides, with infinite fury. Sir W. Batten not knowing how to remove his wine, did dig a pit in the garden, and laid it in there; and I took the opportunity of laying all the papers of my office that I could not otherwise dispose of. And in the evening Sir W. Pen and I did dig another, and put our wine in it; and I my Parmazan cheese, as well as my wine and some other things. The Duke of Yorke was at the office this day, at Sir W. Pen's; but I happened not to be within. This afternoon, sitting melancholy with Sir W. Pen in our garden, and thinking of the certain burning of this office, without extraordinary means, I did propose for the sending up of all our workmen from Woolwich and Deptford yards (none whereof yet appeared), and to write to Sir W. Coventry to have the Duke of Yorke's permission to pull down houses, rather than lose this office, which would, much hinder, the King's business. So Sir W. Pen he went down this night, in order to the sending them up to-morrow morning; and I wrote to Sir W. Coventry about the business, but received no answer. This night Mrs. Turner (who, poor woman, was removing her goods all this day, good goods into the garden, and knows not how to dispose of them), and her husband supped with my wife and I at night, in the office; upon a shoulder of mutton from the cook's, without any napkin or any thing, in a sad manner, but were merry. Only now and then walking into the garden, and saw how horridly the sky looks, all on a fire in the night, was enough to put us out of our wits; and, indeed, it was extremely dreadful, for it looks just as if it was at us; and the whole heaven on fire. I after supper walked in the darke down to Tower-streete, and there saw it all on fire, at the Trinity House on that side, and the Dolphin Taverne on this side, which was very near us; and the fire with extraordinary vehemence. Now begins the practice of blowing up of houses in Tower-streete, those next the Tower, which at first did frighten people more than anything, but it stopped the fire where it was done, it bringing down the

houses to the ground in the same places they stood, and then it was easy to quench what little fire was in it, though it kindled nothing almost. W. Newer this day went to see how his mother did, and comes late home, telling us how he hath been forced to remove her to Islington, her house in Pye-corner being burned; so that the fire is got so far that way, and all the Old Bayly, and was running down to Fleete-streete; and Paul's is burned, and all Cheapside. I wrote to my father this night, but the post-house being burned, the letter could not go.

5th. I lay down in the office again upon W. Hewer's, quilt, being mighty weary, and sore in my feet with going till I was hardly able to stand. About two in the morning my wife calls me up and tells me of new cryes of fire, it being come to Barkeing Church, which is the bottom of our lane. I up, and finding it so, resolved presently to take her away, and did, and took my gold, which was about L2350, W. Newer, and Jane, down by Proundy's boat to Woolwich; but, Lord! what sad sight it was by moone-light to see, the whole City almost on fire, that you might see it plain at Woolwich, as if you were by it. There, when I come, I find the gates shut, but no guard kept at all, which troubled me, because of discourse now begun, that there is plot in it, and that the French had done it. I got the gates open, and to Mr. Shelden's, where I locked up my gold, and charged, my wife and W. Newer never to leave the room without one of them in it, night, or day. So back again, by the way seeing my goods well in the lighters at Deptford, and watched well by people. Home; and whereas I expected to have seen our house on fire, it being now about seven o'clock, it was not. But to the fyre, and there find greater hopes than I expected; for my confidence of finding our Office on fire was such, that I durst not ask any body how it was with us, till I come and saw it not burned. But going to the fire, I find by the blowing up of houses, and the great helpe given by the workmen out of the King's yards, sent up by Sir W. Pen, there is a good stop given to it, as well as at Marke-lane end as ours; it having only burned the dyall of Barking Church, and part of the porch, and was there quenched. I up to the top of Barking steeple, and there saw the saddest sight of desolation that I ever saw; every where great fires, oyle-cellars, and brimstone, and other things burning. I became afeard to stay there long, and therefore down again as fast as I could, the fire being spread as far as I could see it; and to Sir W. Pen's, and there eat a piece of cold meat, having eaten nothing since Sunday, but the remains of Sunday's dinner. Here I met with Mr. Young and Whistler; and having removed all my things, and received good hopes that the fire at our end; is stopped, they and I walked into the town, and find Fanchurch-streete, Gracious-streete; and Lumbard-streete all in dust. The Exchange a sad sight, nothing standing there, of all the statues or pillars, but Sir Thomas Gresham's picture in the corner. Walked into Moorefields (our feet ready to burn, walking through the towne among the hot coles), and find that full of people, and poor wretches carrying their good there, and every body keeping his goods together by themselves (and a great blessing it is to them that it is fair weathe for them to keep abroad night and day); drank there, and paid two-pence for a plain penny loaf. Thence homeward, having passed through Cheapside and Newgate Market, all burned, and seen Anthony Joyce's House in fire. And took up (which I keep by me) a piece of glasse of Mercers' Chappell in the streete, where much more was, so melted and buckled with the heat of the fire like parchment. I also did see a poor cat taken out of a hole in the chimney, joyning to the wall of the Exchange; with, the hair all burned off the body, and yet alive. So home at night, and find there good hopes of saving our office; but great endeavours of watching all night, and having men ready; and so we lodged them in the office, and had drink and bread and cheese for them. And I lay down and slept a good night about midnight, though when I rose I heard that there had been a great alarme of French and Dutch being risen, which proved, nothing. But it is a strange thing to see how long this time did look since Sunday, having been always full of variety of actions, and little sleep, that it looked like a week or more, and I had forgot, almost the day of the week.

6th. Up about five o'clock, and where met Mr. Gawden at the gate of the office (I intending to go out, as I used, every now and then to-day, to see how the fire is) to call our men to Bishop's-gate, where no fire had yet been near, and there is now one broke out which did give great grounds to people, and to me too, to think that there is some kind of plot

in this (on which many by this time have been taken, and, it hath been dangerous for any stranger to walk in the streets), but I went with the men, and we did put it out in a little time; so that that was well again. It was pretty to see how hard the women did work in the cannells, sweeping of water; but then they would scold for drink, and be as drunk as devils. I saw good butts of sugar broke open in the street, and people go and take handsfull out, and put into beer, and drink it. And now all being pretty well, I took boat, and over to Southwarke, and took boat on the other side the bridge, and so to Westminster, thinking to shift myself, being all in dirt from top to bottom; but could not there find any place to buy a shirt or pair of gloves, Westminster Hall being full of people's goods, those in Westminster having removed all their goods, and the Exchequer money put into vessels to carry to Nonsuch; but to the Swan, and there was trimmed; and then to White Hall, but saw nobody; and so home. A sad sight to see how the River looks: no houses nor church near it, to the Temple, where it stopped. At home, did go with Sir W. Batten, and our neighbour, Knightly (who, with one more, was the only man of any fashion left in all the neighbourhood thereabouts, they all removing their goods and leaving their houses to the mercy of the fire), to Sir R. Ford's, and there dined in an earthen platter—a fried breast of mutton; a great many of us, but very merry, and indeed as good a meal, though as ugly a one, as ever I had in my life. Thence down to Deptford, and there with great satisfaction landed all my goods at Sir G. Carteret's safe, and nothing missed I could see, or hurt. This being done to my great content, I home, and to Sir W. Batten's, and there with Sir R. Ford, Mr. Knightly, and one Withers, a professed lying rogue, supped well, and mighty merry, and our fears over. From them to the office, and there slept with the office full of labourers, who talked, and slept, and walked all night long there. But strange it was to see Cloathworkers' Hall on fire these three days and nights in one body of flame, it being the cellar full of oyle.

7th. Up by five o'clock; and, blessed be God! find all well, and by water to Paul's Wharfe. Walked thence, and saw, all the towne burned, and a miserable sight of Paul's church; with all the roofs fallen, and the body of the quire fallen into St. Fayth's; Paul's school also, Ludgate, and Fleet-street, my father's house, and the church, and a good part of the Temple the like. So to Creed's lodging, near the New Exchange, and there find him laid down upon a bed; the house all unfurnished, there being fears of the fire's coming to them. There borrowed a shirt of him, and washed. To Sir W. Coventry, at St. James's, who lay without curtains, having removed all his goods; as the King at White Hall, and every body had done, and was doing. He hopes we shall have no publique distractions upon this fire, which is what every body fears, because of the talke of the French having a hand in it. And it is a proper time for discontents; but all men's minds are full of care to protect themselves, and save their goods: the militia is in armes every where. Our fleetes, he tells me, have been in sight one of another, and most unhappily by fowle weather were parted, to our great losse, as in reason they do conclude; the Dutch being come out only to make a shew, and please their people; but in very bad condition as to stores; victuals, and men. They are at Bullen; and our fleete come to St. Ellen's. We have got nothing, but have lost one ship, but he knows not what. Thence to the Swan, and there drank: and so home, and find all well. My Lord Bruncker, at Sir W. Batten's, and tells us the Generall is sent for up, to come to advise with the King about business at this juncture, and to keep all quiet; which is great honour to him, but I am sure is but a piece of dissimulation. So home, and did give orders for my house to be made clean; and then down to Woolwich, and there find all well: Dined, and Mrs. Markham come to see my wife. So I up again, and calling at Deptford for some things of W. Hewer's, he being with me, and then home and spent the evening with Sir R. Ford, Mr. Knightly, and Sir W. Pen at Sir W. Batten's: This day our Merchants first met at Gresham College, which, by proclamation, is to be their Exchange. Strange to hear what is bid for houses all up and down here; a friend of Sir W. Rider's: having L150 for what he used to let for L40 per annum. Much dispute where the Custome-house shall be thereby the growth of the City again to be foreseen. My Lord Treasurer, they say, and others; would have it at the other end of the towne. I home late to Sir W. Pen's, who did give me a bed; but without curtains or hangings, all being down. So here I went the first time into a naked bed, only my drawers on; and did sleep pretty well: but still hath sleeping and waking had a fear of fire in my heart, that I took little rest. People do all the world over cry out of the simplicity of my Lord Mayor in generall; and more particularly in this business of the fire, laying it all upon' him. A proclamation

is come out for markets to be kept at Leadenhall and Mileendgreene, and several other places about the towne; and Tower-hill, and all churches to be set open to receive poor people.

8th. Up and with Sir W. Batten and Sir W. Pen by water to White Hall and they to St. James's. I stopped with Sir G. Carteret to desire him to go with us, and to enquire after money. But the first he cannot do, and the other as little, or says, "when we can get any, or what shall we do for it?" He, it seems, is employed in the correspondence between the City and the King every day, in settling of things. I find him full of trouble, to think how things will go. I left him, and to St. James's, where we met first at Sir W. Coventry's chamber, and there did what business we can, without any books. Our discourse, as every thing else, was confused. The fleete is at Portsmouth, there staying a wind to carry them to the Downes, or towards Bullen, where they say the Dutch fleete is gone, and stays. We concluded upon private meetings for a while, not having any money to satisfy any people that may come to us. I bought two eeles upon the Thames, cost me six shillings. Thence with Sir W. Batten to the Cock-pit, whither the Duke of Albemarle is come. It seems the King holds him so necessary at this time, that he hath sent for him, and will keep him here. Indeed, his interest in the City, being acquainted, and his care in keeping things quiet, is reckoned that wherein he will be very serviceable. We to him; he is courted in appearance by every body. He very kind to us; I perceive he lays by all business of the fleete at present, and minds the City, and is now hastening to Gresham College, to discourse with the Aldermen. Sir W. Batten and I home (where met by my brother John, come to town to see how things are with us), and then presently he with me to Gresham College; where infinity of people, partly through novelty to see the new place, and partly to find out and hear what is become one man of another. I met with many people undone, and more that have extraordinary great losses. People speaking their thoughts variously about the beginning of the fire, and the rebuilding; of the City. Then to Sir W. Batten's, and took my brothet with me, and there dined with a great company of neighbours; and much good discourse; among others, of the low spirits of some rich men in the City, in sparing any encouragement to the poor people that wrought for the saving their houses. Among others, Alderman Starling, a very rich man, without; children, the fire at next door to him in our lane, after our men had saved his house, did give 2s. 6d. among thirty of them, and did quarrel with some that would remove the rubbish out of the way of the fire, saying that they come to steal. Sir W. Coventry told me of another this morning, in Holborne, which he shewed the King that when it was offered to stop the fire near his house for such a reward that came but to 2s. 6d. a man among the neighbours he would, give but 18d. Thence to Bednall Green by coach, my brother with me, and saw all well there, and fetched away my journall book to enter for five days past, and then back to the office where I find Bagwell's wife, and her husband come home. Agreed to come to their house to-morrow, I sending him away to his ship to-day. To the office and late writing letters, and then to Sir W. Pen's, my brother lying with me, and Sir W. Pen gone down to rest himself at Woolwich. But I was much frighted and kept awake in my bed, by some noise I heard a great while below stairs; and the boys not coming up to me when I knocked. It was by their discovery of people stealing of some neighbours' wine that lay in vessels in the streets. So to sleep; and all well all night.

9th (Sunday). Up and was trimmed, and sent my brother to Woolwich to my wife, to dine with her. I to church, where our parson made a melancholy but good sermon; and many and most in the church cried, specially the women. The church mighty full; but few of fashion, and most strangers. I walked to Bednall Green, and there dined well, but a bad venison pasty at Sir W. Rider's. Good people they are, and good discourse; and his daughter, Middleton, a fine woman, discreet. Thence home, and to church again, and there preached Dean Harding; but, methinks, a bad, poor sermon, though proper for the time; nor eloquent, in saying at this time that the City is reduced from a large folio to a decimotertio. So to my office, there to write down my journall, and take leave of my brother, whom I sent back this afternoon, though rainy; which it hath not done a good while before. But I had no room or convenience for him here till my house is fitted; but I was very kind to him, and do take very well of him his journey. I did give him 40s. for his pocket, and so, he being gone, and, it presently rayning, I was troubled for him, though it is good for the fyre. Anon to Sir W. Pen's to bed, and made my boy Tom to read me asleep.

10th. All the morning clearing our cellars, and breaking in pieces all my old lumber, to make room, and to prevent fire. And then to Sir W. Batten's, and dined; and there hear that Sir W. Rider says that the towne is full of the report of the wealth that is in his house, and would be glad that his friends would provide for the safety of their goods there. This made me get a cart; and thither, and there brought my money all away. Took a hackney-coach myself (the hackney-coaches now standing at Allgate). Much wealth indeed there is at his house. Blessed be God, I got all mine well thence, and lodged it in my office; but vexed to have all the world see it. And with Sir W. Batten, who would have taken away my hands before they were stowed. But by and by comes brother Balty from sea, which I was glad of; and so got him, and Mr. Tooker, and the boy, to watch with them all in the office all night, while I upon Jane's coming went down to my wife, calling at Deptford, intending to see Bagwell, but did not 'ouvrir la porte comme je' did expect. So down late to Woolwich, and there find my wife out of humour and indifferent, as she uses upon her having much liberty abroad.

11th. Lay there, and up betimes, and by water with my gold, and laid it with the rest in my office, where I find all well and safe. So with Sir W. Batten to the New Exchange by water and to my Lord Bruncker's house, where Sir W. Coventry and Sir G. Carteret met. Little business before us but want of money. Broke up, and I home by coach round the town. Dined at home, Balty and myself putting up my papers in m closet in the office. He away, I down to Deptford and there spoke with Bagwell and agreed upon to-morrow, and come home in the rain by water. In the evening at Sir W. Pen's; with my wife, at supper, he in a mad, ridiculous, drunken humour; and it seems there have been some late distances between his lady and him, as my [wife] tells me. After supper, I home, and with Mr. Hater, Gibson, and Tom alone, got all my chests and money into the further cellar with much pains, but great content to me when done. So very late and weary, to bed.

12th. Up, and with Sir W. Batten and Sir W. Pen to St. James's by water, and there did our usual business with the Duke of Yorke. Thence I to Westminster, and there, spoke with Michell and Howlett, who tell me how their poor young ones are going to Shadwell's. The latter told me of the unkindness of the young man to his wife, which is now over, and I have promised to appear a counsellor to him. I am glad she is like to be so near us again. Thence to Martin, and there did 'tout ce que je voudrais avec' her, and drank, and away by water home and to dinner, Balty and his wife there. After dinner I took him down with me to Deptford, and there by the Bezan loaded above half my goods and sent them away. So we back home, and then I found occasion to return in the dark and to Bagwell, and there... did do all that I desired, but though I did intend 'pour avoir demeurais con elle' to-day last night, yet when I had done 'ce que je voudrais I did hate both elle and la cose', and taking occasion from the occasion of 'su marido's return... did me lever', and so away home late to Sir W. Pen's (Batty and his wife lying at my house), and there in the same simple humour I found Sir W. Pen, and so late to bed.

13th. Up, and down to Tower Wharfe; and there, with Batty and labourers from Deptford, did get my goods housed well at home. So down to Deptford again to fetch the rest, and there eat a bit of dinner at the Globe, with the master of the Bezan with me, while the labourers went to dinner. Here I hear that this poor towne do bury still of the plague seven or eight in a day. So to Sir G. Carteret's to work, and there did to my content ship off into the Bezan all the rest of my goods, saving my pictures and fine things, that I will bring home in wherrys when the house is fit to receive them: and so home, and unload them by carts and hands before night, to my exceeding satisfaction: and so after supper to bed in my house, the first time I have lain there; and lay with my wife in my old closett upon the ground, and Batty and his wife in the best chamber, upon the ground also.

14th. Up, and to work, having carpenters come to helpe in setting up bedsteads and hangings; and at that trade my people and I all the morning, till pressed by publique business to leave them against my will in the afternoon: and yet I was troubled in being at home, to see all my goods lie up and down the house in a bad condition, and strange workmen going to and fro might take what they would almost. All the afternoon busy; and Sir W. Coventry come to me, and found me, as God would have it, in my office, and people about me setting my papers to rights; and there discoursed about getting an account ready against the Parliament, and thereby did create me infinite of business, and to be done on a sudden; which troubled me: but, however, he being gone, I about it late, and to good purpose. And so home, having this day also got my wine out of the ground again, and set in my cellar; but with great pain to keep the porters that carried it in from observing the money-chests there. So to bed as last night, only my wife and I upon a bedstead with curtains in that which was Mercer's chamber, and Balty and his wife (who are here and do us good service), where we lay last night. This day, poor Tom Pepys, the turner, was with me, and Kate, Joyce, to bespeake places; one for himself, the other for her husband. She tells me he hath lost L140 per annum, but have seven houses left.

15th. All the morning at the office, Harman being come to my great satisfaction to put up my beds and hangings, so I am at rest, and followed my business all day. Dined with Sir W. Batten, mighty busy about this account, and while my people were busy, wrote near thirty letters and orders with my owne hand. At it till eleven at night; and it is strange to see how clear my head was, being eased of all the matter of all these letters; whereas one would think that I should have been dazed. I never did observe so much of myself in my life. In the evening there comes to me Captain Cocke, and walked a good while in the garden. He says he hath computed that the rents of houses lost by this fire in the City comes to L600,000 per annum; that this will make the Parliament, more quiet than otherwise they would have been, and give the King a more ready supply; that the supply must be by excise, as it is in Holland; that the Parliament will see it necessary to carry on the warr; that the late storm hindered our beating the Dutch fleete, who were gone out only to satisfy the people, having no business to do but to avoid us; that the French, as late in the yeare as it is, are coming; that the Dutch are really in bad condition, but that this unhappinesse of ours do give them heart; that there was a late difference between my Lord Arlington and Sir W. Coventry about neglect in the last to send away an express of the other's in time; that it come before the King, and the Duke of Yorke concerned himself in it; but this fire hath stopped it. The Dutch fleete is not gone home, but rather to the North, and so dangerous to our Gottenburgh fleete. That the Parliament is likely to fall foul upon some persons; and, among others, on the Vice-chamberlaine, though we both believe with little ground. That certainly never so great a loss as this was borne so well by citizens in the world; he believing that not one merchant upon the 'Change will break upon it. That he do not apprehend there will be any disturbances in State upon it; for that all men are busy in looking after their owne business to save themselves. He gone, I to finish my letters, and home to bed; and find to my infinite joy many rooms clean; and myself and wife lie in our own chamber again. But much terrified in the nights now-a-days with dreams of fire, and falling down of houses.

16th (Lord's day). Lay with much pleasure in bed talking with my wife about Mr. Hater's lying here and W. Hewer also, if Mrs. Mercer leaves her house. To the office, whither also all my people about this account, and there busy all the morning. At noon, with my wife, against her will, all undressed and dirty, dined at Sir W. Pen's, where was all the company of our families in towne; but, Lord! so sorry a dinner: venison baked in pans, that the dinner I have had for his lady alone hath been worth four of it. Thence, after dinner, displeased with our entertainment, to my office again, and there till almost midnight and my people with me, and then home, my head mightily akeing about our accounts.

17th. Up betimes, and shaved myself after a week's growth, but, Lord! how ugly I was yesterday and how fine to-day! By water, seeing the City all the way, a sad sight indeed, much fire being still in. To Sir W. Coventry, and there read over my yesterday's work: being a collection of the particulars of the excess of charge created by a war, with good content. Sir W. Coventry was in great pain lest the French fleete should be passed by our fleete, who had notice of them on Saturday, and were preparing to go meet them; but their minds altered, and judged them merchant-men, when the same day the Success, Captain Ball, made their whole fleete, and come to Brighthelmstone, and thence at five o'clock afternoon, Saturday, wrote Sir W. Coventry newes thereof; so that we do much fear our missing them. Here come in and talked with him Sir Thomas Clifford, who appears a very fine gentleman, and much set by at Court for his activity in going to sea, and stoutness everywhere, and stirring up and down. Thence by coach over the ruines, down Fleete Streete and Cheapside to Broad Streete to Sir G. Carteret, where Sir W. Batten (and Sir J. Minnes, whom I had not seen a long time before, being his first coming abroad) and Lord Bruncker passing his accounts. Thence home a little to look after my people at work and back to Sir G. Carteret's to dinner; and thence, after some discourse; with him upon our publique accounts, I back home, and all the day with Harman and his people finishing the hangings and beds in my house, and the hangings will be as good as ever, and particularly in my new closet. They gone and I weary, my wife and I, and Balty and his wife, who come hither to-day to helpe us, to a barrel of oysters I sent from the river today, and so to bed.

18th. Strange with what freedom and quantity I pissed this night, which I know not what to impute to but my oysters, unless the coldness of the night should cause it, for it was a sad rainy and tempestuous night. Soon as up I begun to have some pain in my bladder and belly, as usual, which made me go to dinner betimes, to fill my belly, and that did ease me, so as I did my business in the afternoon, in forwarding the settling of my house, very well. Betimes to bed, my wife also being all this day ill in the same manner. Troubled at my wife's haire coming off so much. This day the Parliament met, and adjourned till Friday, when the King will be with them.

19th. Up, and with Sir W. Pen by coach to St. James's, and there did our usual business before the Duke of Yorke; which signified little, our business being only complaints of lack of money. Here I saw a bastard of the late King of Sweden's come to kiss his hands; a mighty modish French-like gentleman. Thence to White Hall, with Sir W. Batten and Sir W. Pen, to Wilkes's; and there did hear the many profane stories of Sir Henry Wood damning the parsons for so much spending the wine at the sacrament, cursing that ever they took the cup to themselves, and then another story that he valued not all the world's curses, for two pence he shall get at any time the prayers of some poor body that is worth a 1000 of all their curses; Lord Norwich drawing a tooth at a health. Another time, he and Pinchbacke and Dr. Goffe, now a religious man, Pinchbacke did begin a frolick to drink out of a glass with a toad in it that he had taken up going out to shit, he did it without harm. Goffe, who knew sacke would kill the toad, called for sacke; and when he saw it dead, says he, "I will have a quick toad, and will not drink from a dead toad."

By that means, no other being to be found, he escaped the health. Thence home, and dined, and to Deptford and got all my pictures put into wherries, and my other fine things, and landed them all very well, and brought them home, and got Sympson to set them all up to-night; and he gone, I and the boy to finish and set up my books, and everything else in my house, till two o'clock; in the morning, and then to bed; but mightily troubled, and even in my sleep, at my missing four or five of my biggest books. Speed's Chronicle and Maps, and the two parts of Waggoner, and a book of cards, which I suppose I have put up with too much care, that I have forgot where they are; for sure they are not stole. Two little pictures of sea and ships and a little gilt frame belonging to my plate of the River, I want; but my books do heartily trouble me. Most of my gilt frames are hurt, which also troubles me, but most my books. This day I put on two shirts, the first time this year, and do grow well upon it; so that my disease is nothing but wind.

20th. Up, much troubled about my books, but cannot, imagine where they should be. Up, to the setting my closet to rights, and Sir W. Coventry takes me at it, which did not displease me. He and I to discourse about our accounts, and the bringing them to the Parliament, and with much content to see him rely so well on my part. He and I together to Broad Streete to the Vice-Chamberlain, and there discoursed a while and parted. My Lady Carteret come to town, but I did not see her. He tells me how the fleete is come into the Downes. Nothing done, nor French fleete seen: we drove all from our anchors. But he says newes is come that De Ruyter is dead, or very near it, of a hurt in his mouth, upon the discharge of one of his own guns; which put him into a fever, and he likely to die, if not already dead. We parted, and I home to dinner, and after dinner to the setting things in order, and all my people busy about the same work. In the afternoon, out by coach, my wife with me, which we have not done several weeks now, through all the ruines, to shew her them, which frets her much, and is a sad sight indeed. Set her down at her brother's, and thence I to Westminster Hall, and there staid a little while, and called her home. She did give me an account of great differences between her mother and Balty's wife. The old woman charges her with going abroad and staying out late, and painting in the absence of her husband, and I know not what; and they grow proud, both he and she, and do not help their father and mother out of what I help them to, which I do not like, nor my wife. So home, and to the office, to even my journall, and then home, and very late up with Jane setting my books in perfect order in my closet, but am mightily troubled for my great books that I miss, and I am troubled the more for fear there should be more missing than what I find, though by the room they take on the shelves I do not find any reason to think it. So to bed.

21st. Up, and mightily pleased with the setting of my books the last night in order, and that which did please me most of all is that W. Hewer tells me that upon enquiry he do find that Sir W. Pen hath a hamper more than his own, which he took for a hamper of bottles of wine, and are books in it. I was impatient to see it, but they were carried into a wine-cellar, and the boy is abroad with him at the House, where the Parliament met to-day, and the King to be with them. At noon after dinner I sent for Harry, and he tells me it is so, and brought me by and by my hamper of books to my great joy, with the same books I missed, and three more great ones, and no more. I did give him 5s. for his pains, And so home with great joy, and to the setting of some off them right, but could not finish it, but away by coach to the other end of the town, leaving my wife at the 'Change, but neither come time enough to the Council to speak with the Duke of Yorke, nor with Sir G. Carteret, and so called my wife, and paid for some things she bought, and so home, and there after a little doing at the office about our accounts, which now draw near the time they should be ready, the House having ordered Sir G. Carteret, upon his offering them, to bring them in on Saturday next, I home, and there, with great pleasure, very late new setting all my books; and now I am in as good condition as I desire to be in all worldly respects. The Lord of Heaven make me thankfull, and continue me therein! So to bed. This day I had new stairs of main timber put t my cellar going into the yard.

22nd. To my closet, and had it new washed, and now my house is so clean as I never saw it, or any other house in my life, and every thing in as good condition as ever before the fire; but with, I believe, about L20 cost one way or other besides about L20 charge in removing my goods, and do not find that I have lost any thing but two little pictures of ship and sea, and a little gold frame for one of my sea-cards. My glazier, indeed, is so full of worke that I cannot get him to come to perfect my house. To the office, and there busy now for good and all about my accounts. My Lord Brunck come thither, thinking to find an office, but we have not yet met. He do now give me a watch, a plain one, in the roome of my former watch with many motions which I did give him. If it goes well, I care not for the difference in worth, though believe there is above L5. He and I to Sir G. Carteret to discourse about his account, but Mr. Waith not being there nothing could be done, and therefore I home again, and busy all day. In the afternoon comes Anthony

Joyce to see me, and with tears told me his losse, but yet that he had something left that he can live well upon, and I doubt it not. But he would buy some place that he could have and yet keepe his trade where he is settled in St. Jones's. He gone, I to the office again, and then to Sir G. Carteret, and there found Mr. Wayth, but, Lord! how fretfully Sir G. Carteret do discourse with Mr. Wayth about his accounts, like a man that understands them not one word. I held my tongue and let him go on like a passionate foole. In the afternoon I paid for the two lighters that carried my goods to Deptford, and they cost me L8. Till past midnight at our accounts, and have brought them to a good issue, so as to be ready to meet Sir G. Carteret and Sir W. Coventry to-morrow, but must work to-morrow, which Mr. T. Hater had no mind to, it being the Lord's day, but, being told the necessity, submitted, poor man! This night writ for brother John to come to towne. Among other reasons, my estate lying in money, I am afeard of any sudden miscarriage. So to bed mightily contented in dispatching so much business, and find my house in the best condition that ever I knew it. Home to bed.

23rd (Lord's day). Up, and after being trimmed, all the morning at the office with my people about me till about one o'clock, and then home, and my people with me, and Mr. Wayth and I eat a bit of victuals in my old closet, now my little dining-room, which makes a pretty room, and my house being so clean makes me mightily pleased, but only I do lacke Mercer or somebody in the house to sing with. Soon as eat a bit Mr. Wayth and I by water to White Hall, and there at Sir G. Carteret's lodgings Sir W. Coventry met, and we did debate the whole business of our accounts to the Parliament; where it appears to us that the charge of the war from September 1st, 1664, to this Michaelmas, will have been but L3,200,000, and we have paid in that time somewhat about L2,200,000; so that we owe above L900,000: but our method of accounting, though it cannot, I believe, be far wide from the mark, yet will not abide a strict examination if the Parliament should be troublesome. Here happened a pretty question of Sir W. Coventry, whether this account of ours will not put my Lord Treasurer to a difficulty to tell what is become of all the money the Parliament have 'give' in this time for the war, which hath amounted to about L4,000,000, which nobody there could answer; but I perceive they did doubt what his answer could be. Having done, and taken from Sir W. Coventry the minutes of a letter to my Lord Treasurer, Wayth and I back again to the office, and thence back down to the water with my wife and landed him in Southwarke, and my wife and I for pleasure to Fox-hall, and there eat and drank, and so back home, and I to the office till midnight drawing the letter we are to send with our accounts to my Lord Treasurer, and that being done to my mind, I home to bed.

24th. Up, and with Sir W. Batten and Sir W. Pen to St. James's, and there with Sir W. Coventry read and all approved of my letter, and then home, and after dinner, Mr. Hater and Gibson dining with me, to the office, and there very late new moulding my accounts and writing fair my letter, which I did against the evening, and then by coach left my wife at her brother's, and I to St. James's, and up and down to look [for] Sir W. Coventry; and at last found him and Sir G. Carteret with the Lord Treasurer at White Hall, consulting how to make up my Lord Treasurer's general account, as well as that of the Navy particularly. Here brought the letter, but found that Sir G. Carteret had altered his account since he did give me the abstract of it: so all my letter must be writ over again, to put in his last abstract. So to Sir G. Carteret's lodgings, to speak a little about the alteration; and there looking over the book that Sir G. Carteret intends to deliver to the Parliament of his payments since September 1st, 1664, and there I find my name the very second for flags, which I had bought for the Navy, of calico; once, about 500 and odd pounds, which vexed me mightily. At last, I concluded of scraping out my name and putting in Mr. Tooker's, which eased me; though the price was such as I should have had glory by. Here I saw my Lady Carteret lately come to towne, who, good lady! is mighty kind, and I must make much of her, for she is a most excellent woman. So took up my wife and away home, and there to bed, and

25th. Up betimes, with all my people to get the letter writ over, and other things done, which I did, and by coach to Lord Bruncker's, and got his hand to it; and then to the Parliament House and got it signed by the rest, and then delivered it at the House-door to Sir Philip Warwicke; Sir G. Carteret being gone into the House with his book of accounts under his arme, to present to the House. I had brought my wife to White Hall, and leaving her with Mrs. Michell, where she sat in her shop and had burnt wine sent for her, I walked in the Hall, and among others with Ned Picketing, who continues still a lying, bragging coxcombe, telling me that my Lord Sandwich may thank himself for all his misfortune; for not suffering him and two or three good honest fellows more to take them by the throats that spoke ill of him, and told me how basely Lionell Walden hath carried himself towards my Lord; by speaking slightly of him, which I shall remember. Thence took my wife home to dinner, and then to the office, where Mr. Hater all the day putting in order and entering in a book all the measures that this account of the Navy hath been made up by, and late at night to Mrs. Turner's, where she had got my wife and Lady Pen and Pegg, and supped, and after, supper and the rest of the company by design gone, Mrs. Turner and her husband did lay their case to me about their lodgings, Sir J. Minnes being now gone wholly to his owne, and now, they being empty, they doubt Sir T. Harvy or Lord Bruncker may look after the lodgings. I did give them the best advice, poor people, that I could, and would do them any kindnesse, though it is strange that now they should have ne'er a friend of Sir W. Batten or Sir W. Pen to trust to but me, that they have disobliged. So home to bed, and all night still mightily troubled in my sleepe, with fire and houses pulling down.

26th. Up, and with Sir J. Minnes to St. James's, where every body going to the House, I away by coach to White Hall, and after a few turns, and hearing that our accounts come into the House but to-day, being hindered yesterday by other business, I away by coach home, taking up my wife and calling at Bennet's, our late mercer, who is come into Covent Garden to a fine house looking down upon the Exchange; and I perceive many Londoners every day come; and Mr. Pierce hath let his wife's closett, and the little blind bed chamber, and a garret to a silke man for L50 fine, and L30 per annum, and L40 per annum more for dieting the master and two prentices. So home, not agreeing for silk for a petticoat for her which she desired, but home to dinner and then back to White Hall, leaving my wife by the way to buy her petticoat of Bennet, and I to White Hall waiting all day on the Duke of Yorke to move the King for getting Lanyon some money at Plymouth out of some oyle prizes brought in thither, but could get nothing done, but here Mr. Dugdale I hear the great loss of books in St. Paul's Church-yarde, and at their Hall also, which they value about L150,000; some booksellers being wholly undone, among others, they say, my poor Kirton. And Mr. Crumlu all his books and household stuff burned; they trusting St. Fayth's, and the roof of the church falling, broke the arch down into the lower church, and so all the goods burned. A very great loss. His father hath lost above L1000 in books; one book newly printed, a Discourse, it seems, of Courts. Here I had the hap to see my Lady Denham: and at night went into the dining-room and saw several fine ladies; among others, Castlemayne, but chiefly Denham again; and the Duke of Yorke taking her aside and talking to her in the sight of all the world, all alone; which was strange, and what also I did not like. Here I met with good Mr. Evelyn, who cries out against it, and calls it bitchering,—[This word was apparently of Evelyn's own making.]—for the Duke of Yorke talks a little to her, and then she goes away, and then he follows her again like a dog. He observes that none of the nobility come out of the country at all to help the King, or comfort him, or prevent commotions at this fire; but do as if the King were nobody; nor ne'er a priest comes to give the King and Court good council, or to comfort the poor people that suffer; but all is dead, nothing of good in any of their minds: he bemoans it, and says he fears more ruin hangs over our heads. Thence away by coach, and called away my wife at Unthanke's, where she tells me she hath bought a gowne of 15s. per yard; the same, before her face, my Lady Castlemayne this day bought also, which I seemed vexed for, though I do not grudge it her, but to incline her to have Mercer again, which I believe I shall do, but the girle, I hear, has no mind to come to us again, which vexes me. Being come home, I to Sir W. Batten, and there hear our business was tendered to the House to-day, and a Committee of the whole House chosen to examine our accounts, and a great many Hotspurs enquiring into it, and likely to give us much trouble and blame, and perhaps (which I am afeard of) will find faults enow to demand better officers. This I truly fear. Away with Sir W. Pen, who was there, and he and I walked in the garden by moonlight, and he proposes his and my looking out into Scotland about timber, and to use Pett there; for timber will be a good commodity this time of building the City; and I like the motion, and doubt not that we may do good in it. We did also discourse about our Privateer, and hope well of that also, without much hazard, as, if God blesses us, I hope we shall do pretty well toward getting a penny. I was mightily pleased with our discourse, and so parted, and to the office to finish my journall for three or four days, and so home to supper, and to bed. Our fleete abroad, and the Dutch too, for all we know; the weather very bad; and under the command of an unlucky man, I fear. God bless him, and the fleete under him!

27th. A very furious blowing night all the night; and my mind still mightily perplexed with dreams, and burning the rest of the town, and waking in much pain for the fleete. Up, and with my wife by coach as far as the Temple, and there she to the mercer's again, and I to look out Penny, my tailor, to speak for a cloak and cassock for my brother, who is coming to town; and I will have him in a canonical dress, that he may be the fitter to go abroad with me. I then to the Exchequer, and there, among other things, spoke to Mr. Falconbridge about his girle I heard sing at Nonsuch, and took him and some other 'Chequer men to the Sun Taverne, and there spent 2s. 6d. upon them, and he sent for the girle, and she hath a pretty way of singing, but hath almost forgot for want of practice. She is poor in clothes, and not bred to any carriage, but will be soon taught all, and if Mercer do not come again, I think we may have her upon better terms, and breed her to what we please. Thence to Sir W. Coventry's, and there dined with him and Sir W. Batten, the Lieutenant of the Tower, and Mr. Thin, a pretty gentleman, going to Gottenburgh. Having dined, Sir W. Coventry, Sir W. Batten, and I walked into his closet to consider of some things more to be done in a list to be given to the Parliament of all our ships, and time of entry and discharge. Sir W. Coventry seems to think they will soon be weary of the business, and fall quietly into the giving the King what is fit. This he hopes. Thence I by coach home to the office, and there intending a meeting, but nobody being there but myself and Sir J. Minnes, who is worse than nothing, I did not answer any body, but kept to my business in the office till night, and then Sir W. Batten and Sir W. Pen to me, and thence to Sir W. Batten's, and eat a barrel of oysters I did give them, and so home, and to bed. I have this evening discoursed with W. Hewer about Mercer, I having a mind to have her again; and I am vexed to hear him say that she hath no mind to come again, though her mother hath. No newes of the fleete yet, but that they went by Dover on the 25th towards the Gunfleete, but whether the Dutch be yet abroad, or no, we hear not. De Ruyter is not dead, but like to do well. Most think that the gross of the French fleete are gone home again.

28th. Lay long in bed, and am come to agreement with my wife to have Mercer again, on condition she may learn this winter two months to dance, and she promises me she will endeavour to learn to sing, and all this I am willing enough to. So up, and by and by the glazier comes to finish the windows of my house, which pleases me, and the bookbinder to gild the backs of my books. I got the glass of my book-presses to be done presently, which did mightily content me, and to setting my study in a little better order; and so to my office to my people, busy about our Parliament accounts; and so to dinner, and then at them again close. At night comes Sir W. Pen, and he and I a turn in the garden, and he broke to me a proposition of his and my joining in a design of fetching timber and deals from Scotland, by the help of Mr. Pett upon the place; which, while London is building, will yield good money. I approve it. We judged a third man, that is knowing, is necessary, and concluded on Sir W. Warren, and sent for him to come to us to-morrow morning. I full of this all night, and the project of our man of war; but he and, I both dissatisfied with Sir W. Batten's proposing his son to be Lieutenant, which we, neither of us, like. He gone, I discoursed with W. Hewer about Mercer, having a great mind she should come to us again, and instructed him what to say to her mother about it. And so home, to supper, and to bed.

29th. A little meeting at the office by Sir W. Batten, Sir W. Pen, and myself, being the first since the fire. We rose soon, and comes Sir W. Warren, by our desire, and with Sir W. Pen and I talked of our Scotch motion, which Sir W. Warren did seem to be stumbled at, and did give no ready answer, but proposed some thing previous to it, which he knows would find us work, or writing to Mr. Pett to be informed how matters go there as to cost and ways of providing sawyers or saw-mills. We were parted without coming to any good resolution in it, I discerning plainly that Sir W. Warren had no mind to it, but that he was surprised at our motion. He gone, I to some office business, and then home to dinner, and then to office again, and then got done by night the lists that are to be presented to the Parliament Committee of the ships, number of men, and time employed since the war, and then I with it (leaving my wife at Unthanke's) to St. James's, where Sir W. Coventry staid for me, and I perused our lists, and find to our great joy that wages, victuals, wear and tear, cast by the medium of the men, will come to above 3,000,000; and that the extraordinaries, which all the world will allow us, will arise to more than will justify the expence we have declared to have been at since the war, viz., L320,000, he and I being both mightily satisfied, he saying to me, that if God send us over this rub we must take another course for a better Comptroller. So parted, and I to my wife [at Unthanke's], who staid for the finishing her new best gowne (the best that ever I made her coloured tabby, flowered, and so took it and her home; and then I to my people, and having cut them out a little more work than they expected, viz., the writing over the lists in new method, I home to bed, being in good humour, and glad of the end we have brought this matter to.

30th (Lord's day). Up, and to church, where I have not been a good while: and there the church infinitely thronged with strangers since the fire come into our parish; but not one handsome face in all of them, as if, indeed, there was a curse, as Bishop Fuller heretofore said, upon our parish. Here I saw Mercer come into the church, which I had a mind to, but she avoided looking up, which vexed me. A pretty good sermon, and then home, and comes Balty and dined with us. A good dinner; and then to have my haire cut against winter close to my head, and then to church again. A sorry sermon, and away home. [Sir] W. Pen and I to walk to talk about several businesses, and then home; and my wife and I to read in Fuller's Church History, and so to supper and to bed. This month ends with my mind full of business and concernment how this office will speed with the Parliament, which begins to be mighty severe in the examining our accounts, and the expence of the Navy this war.

OCTOBER 1666

October 1st, 1666. Up, and all the morning at the office, getting the list of all the ships and vessels employed since the war, for the Committee of Parliament. At noon with it to Sir W. Coventry's chamber, and there dined with him and [Sir] W. Batten, and [Sir] W. Pen, and after dinner examined it and find it will do us much right in the number of men rising to near the expense we delivered to the Parliament. [Sir] W. Coventry and I (the others going before the Committee) to Lord Bruncker's for his hand, and find him simply mighty busy in a council of the Queen's. He come out and took in the papers to sign, and sent them mighty wisely out again. Sir W. Coventry away to the Committee, and I to the Mercer's, and there took a bill of what I owe of late, which comes to about L17. Thence to White Hall, and there did hear Betty Michell was at this end of the towne, and so without breach of vowe did stay to endeavour to meet with her and carry her home; but she did not come, so I lost my whole afternoon. But pretty! how I took another pretty woman for her, taking her a clap on the breech, thinking verily it had been her. Staid till [Sir] W. Batten and [Sir] W. Pen come out, and so away home by water with them, and to the office to do some business, and then home, and my wife do tell me that W. Hewer tells her that Mercer hath no mind to come. So I was angry at it, and resolved with her to have Falconbridge's girle, and I think it will be better for us, and will please me better with singing. With this resolution, to supper and to bed.

2nd. Up, and am sent for to Sir G. Carteret, and to him, and there he tells me how our lists are referred to a Sub-committee to consider and examine, and that I am ordered to be there this afternoon. So I away thence to my new bookbinder to see my books gilding in the backs, and then to White Hall to the House, and spoke to Sir W. Coventry, where he told me I must attend the Committee in the afternoon, and received some hints of more work to do. So I away to the 'Chequer, and thence to an alehouse, and found Mr. Falconbridge, and agreed for his kinswoman to come to me. He says she can dress my wife, and will do anything we would have her to do, and is of a good spirit and mighty cheerful. He is much pleased therewith, and so we shall be. So agreed for her coming the next week. So away home, and eat a short dinner, and then with Sir W. Pen to White Hall, and do give his boy my book of papers to hold while he went into the Committee Chamber in the Inner Court of Wards, and I walked without with Mr. Slingsby, of the Tower, who was there, and who did in walking inform me mightily in several things; among others, that the heightening or lowering of money is only a cheat, and do good to some particular men, which, if I can but remember how, I am now by him fully convinced of. Anon Sir W. Pen went away, telling me that Sir W. Coventry that was within had told him that the fleete is all come into the buoy of the Nore, and that he must hasten down to them, and so went away, and I into the Committee Chamber before the Committee sat, and there heard Birch discourse highly and understandingly about the Navy business and a proposal made heretofore to farm the Navy; but Sir W. Coventry did abundantly answer him, and is a most excellent person. By and by the Committee met, and I walked out, and anon they rose and called me in, and appointed me to attend a Committee of them to-morrow at the office to examine our lists. This put me into a mighty fear and trouble; they doing it in a very ill humour, methought. So I away and called on my Lord Bruncker to desire him to be there to-morrow, and so home, having taken up my wife at Unthanke's, full of trouble in mind to think what I shall be obliged to answer, that am neither fully fit, nor in any measure concerned to take the shame and trouble of this office upon me, but only from the inability and folly of the Comptroller that occasions it. When come home I to Sir W. Pen's, to his boy, for my book, and there find he hath it not, but delivered it to the doorekeeper of the Committee for me. This, added to my former disquiet, made me stark mad, considering all the nakedness of the office lay open in papers within those covers. I could not tell in the world what to do, but was mad on all sides, and that which made me worse Captain Cocke was there, and he did so swear and curse at the boy that told me. So Cocke, Griffin, and the boy with me, they to find the housekeeper of the Parliament, Hughes, while I to Sir W. Coventry, but could hear nothing of it there. But coming to our rendezvous at the Swan Taverne, in Ding Streete, I find they have found the housekeeper, and the book simply locked up in the Court. So I staid and drank, and rewarded the doore-keeper, and away home, my heart lighter by all this, but to bed very sad notwithstanding, in fear of what will happen to-morrow upon their coming.

3rd. Waked betimes, mightily troubled in mind, and in the most true trouble that I ever was in my life, saving in the business last year of the East India prizes. So up, and with Mr. Hater and W. Hewer and Griffin to consider of our business, and books and papers necessary for this examination; and by and by, by eight o'clock, comes Birch, the first, with the lists and books of accounts delivered in. He calls me to work, and there he and I begun, when, by and by, comes Garraway,

the first time I ever saw him, and Sir W. Thompson and Mr. Boscawen. They to it, and I did make shift to answer them better than I expected. Sir W. Batten, Lord Bruncker, [Sir] W. Pen, come in, but presently went out; and [Sir] J. Minnes come in, and said two or three words from the purpose, but to do hurt; and so away he went also, and left me all the morning with them alone to stand or fall. At noon Sir W. Batten comes to them to invite them (though fast day) to dinner, which they did, and good company they were, but especially Garraway. Here I have news brought me of my father's coming to town, and I presently to him, glad to see him, poor man, he being come to town unexpectedly to see us and the city. I could not stay with him, but after dinner to work again, only the Committee and I, till dark night, and by that time they cast up all the lists, and found out what the medium of men was borne all the war, of all sorts, and ended with good peace, and much seeming satisfaction; but I find them wise and reserved, and instructed to hit all our blots, as among others, that we reckon the ships full manned from the beginning. They gone, and my heart eased of a great deale of fear and pain, and reckoning myself to come off with victory, because not overcome in anything or much foiled, I away to Sir W. Coventry's chamber, but he not within, then to White Hall, and there among the ladies, and saw my Lady Castlemaine never looked so ill, nor Mrs. Stewart neither, as in this plain, natural dress. I was not pleased with either of them. Away, not finding [Sir] W. Coventry, and so home, and there find my father and my brother come to towne—my father without my expectation; but glad I am to see him. And so to supper with him, and to work again at the office; then home, to set up all my folio books, which are come home gilt on the backs, very handsome to the eye, and then at midnight to bed. This night [Sir] W. Pen told me [Sir] W. Batten swears he will have nothing to do with the Privateer if his son do not go Lieutenant, which angers me and him; but we will be even with him, one way or other.

4th. Up, and mighty betimes, to [Sir] W. Coventry, to give him an account of yesterday's work, which do give him good content. He did then tell me his speech lately to the House in his owne vindication about the report of his selling of places, he having a small occasion offered him by chance, which he did desire, and took, and did it to his content, and, he says, to the House's seeming to approve of it by their hum. He confessed how long he had done it, and how he desired to have something else; and, since then, he had taken nothing, and challenged all the world. I was glad of this also. Thence up to the Duke of York, by appointment, with fellow officers, to complaine, but to no purpose, of want of money, and so away. I to Sir G. Carteret, to his lodging, and here discoursed much of the want of money and our being designed for destruction. How the King hath lost his power, by submitting himself to this way of examining his accounts, and is become but as a private man. He says the King is troubled at it, but they talk an entry shall be made, that it is not to be brought into example; that the King must, if they do not agree presently, make them a courageous speech, which he says he may do, the City of London being now burned, and himself master of an army, better than any prince before him, and so I believe. Thence home, about noon, to dinner. After dinner the book binder come, and I sent by him some more books to gild. I to the office all day, and spent most of it with Sir W. Warren, whom I have had no discourse with a great while, and when all is done I do find him a mighty wise man as any I know, and his counsel as much to be followed. Late with Mr. Hater upon comparing the charge and husbandry of the last Dutch war with ours now, and do find good roome to think we have done little worse than they, whereof good use may and will be made. So home to supper, and to bed.

5th. Up, and with my father talking awhile, then to the office, and there troubled with a message from Lord Peterborough about money; but I did give as kind answer as I could, though I hate him. Then to Sir G. Carteret to discourse about paying of part of the great ships come in, and so home again to compare the comparison of the two Dutch wars' charges for [Sir] W. Coventry, and then by water (and saw old Mr. Michell digging like a painfull father for his son) to him, and find him at dinner. After dinner to look over my papers, and comparing them with some notes of his and brought me, the sight of some good Navy notes of his which I shall get. Then examined and liked well my notes, and away together to White Hall, in the way discoursing the inconvenience of the King's being thus subject to an account, but it will be remedied for the time to come, he thinks, if we can get this over, and I find he will have the Comptroller's business better done, swearing he will never be for a wit to be employed on business again. Thence I home, and back again to White Hall, and meeting Sir H. Cholmly to White Hall; there walked till night that the Committee come down, and there Sir W. Coventry tells me that the Subcommittee have made their report to the Grand Committee, and in pretty kind terms, and have agreed upon allowing us L4 per head, which I am sure will do the business, but he had endeavoured to have got more, but this do well, and he and I are both mighty glad it is come to this, and the heat of the present business seems almost over. But I have more worke cut out for me, to prepare a list of the extraordinaries, not to be included within the L4, against Monday. So I away from him, and met with the Vice-Chamberlain, and I told him when I had this evening in coming hither met with Captain Cocke, and he told me of a wild motion made in the House of Lords by the Duke of Buckingham for all men that had cheated the King to be declared traitors and felons, and that my Lord Sandwich was named. This put me into a great pain, so the Vice-Chamberlain, who had heard nothing of it, having been all day in the City, away with me to White Hall; and there come to me and told me that, upon Lord Ashly's asking their direction whether, being a peere, he should bring in his accounts to the Commons, which they did give way to, the Duke of Buckingham did move that, for the time to come, what I have written above might be declared by some fuller law than heretofore. Lord Ashly answered, that it was not the fault of the present laws, but want of proof; and so said the Lord Chancellor. He answered, that a better law, he thought, might be made so the House laughing, did refer it to him to bring in a Bill to that purpose, and this was all. So I away with joyful heart home, calling on Cocke and telling him the same. So I away home to the office to clear my Journall for five days, and so home to supper and to bed, my father who had staid out late and troubled me thereat being come home well and gone to bed, which pleases me also. This day, coming home, Mr. Kirton's kinsman, my bookseller, come in my way; and so I am told by him that Mr. Kirton is utterly undone, and made 2 or L3000 worse than nothing, from being worth 7 or L8,000. That the goods laid in the Churchyarde fired through the windows those in St. Fayth's church; and those coming to the warehouses' doors fired them, and burned all the books and the pillars of the church, so as the roof falling down, broke quite down, which it did not do in the other places of the church, which is alike pillared (which I knew not before); but being not burned, they stand still. He do believe there is above; L50,000 of books burned; all the great booksellers almost undone: not only these, but their warehouses at their Hall, and under Christchurch, and elsewhere being all burned. A great want thereof there will be of books, specially Latin books and foreign books; and, among others, the Polyglottes and new Bible, which he believes will be presently worth L40 a-piece.

6th. Up, and having seen my brother in his cassocke, which I am not the most satisfied in, being doubtfull at this time what course to have him profess too soon. To the office and there busy about a list of the extraordinaries of the charge of the fleete this war; and was led to go to the office of the ordnance to be satisfied in something, and find their accounts and books kept in mighty good order, but that they can give no light, nor will the nature of their affairs permit it to tell what the charge of the ordnance comes to a man a month. So home again and to dinner, there coming Creed to me; but what with business and my hatred to the man, I did not spend any time with him, but after dinner [my] wife and he and I took coach and to Westminster, but he 'light about Paul's, and set her at her tailor's, and myself to St. James's, but there missing [Sir] W. Coventry, returned and took up my wife, and calling at the Exchange home, whither Sir H. Cholmly come to visit me, but my business suffered me not to stay with him. So he gone I by water to Westminster Hall and thence to St. James's, and there found [Sir] W. Coventry waiting for me, and I did give him a good account to his mind of the business he expected about extraordinaries and then fell to other talke, among others, our sad condition contracted by want of a Comptroller;

and it was his words, that he believes, besides all the shame and trouble he hath brought on the office, the King had better have given L100,000 than ever have had him there. He did discourse about some of these discontented Parliament-men, and says that Birch is a false rogue, but that Garraway is a man that hath not been well used by the Court, though very stout to death, and hath suffered all that is possible for the King from the beginning. But discontented as he is, yet he never knew a Session of Parliament but he hath done some good deed for the King before it rose. I told him the passage Cocke told me of his having begged a brace of bucks of the Lord Arlington for him, and when it come to him, he sent it back again. Sir W. Coventry told me, it is much to be pitied that the King should lose the service of a man so able and faithfull; and that he ought to be brought over, but that it is always observed, that by bringing over one discontented man, you raise up three in his room; which is a State lesson I never knew before. But when others discover your fear, and that discontent procures favour, they will be discontented too, and impose on you. Thence to White Hall and got a coach and home, and there did business late, and so home and set up my little books of one of my presses come home gilt, which pleases me mightily, and then to bed. This morning my wife told me of a fine gentlewoman my Lady Pen tells her of, for L20 per annum, that sings, dances, plays on four or five instruments and many other fine things, which pleases me mightily: and she sent to have her see her, which she did this afternoon; but sings basely, and is a tawdry wench that would take L8, but [neither] my wife nor I think her fit to come.

7th (Lord's day). Up, and after visiting my father in his chamber, to church, and then home to dinner. Little Michell and his wife come to dine with us, which they did, and then presently after dinner I with Sir J. Minnes to White Hall, where met by Sir W. Batten and Lord Bruncker, to attend the King and Duke of York at the Cabinet; but nobody had determined what to speak of, but only in general to ask for money. So I was forced immediately to prepare in my mind a method of discoursing. And anon we were called in to the Green Room, where the King, Duke of York, Prince Rupert, Lord Chancellor, Lord Treasurer, Duke of Albemarle, [Sirs] G. Carteret, W. Coventry, Morrice. Nobody beginning, I did, and made a current, and I thought a good speech, laying open the ill state of the Navy: by the greatness of the debt; greatness of work to do against next yeare; the time and materials it would take; and our incapacity, through a total want of money. I had no sooner done, but Prince Rupert rose up and told the King in a heat, that whatever the gentleman had said, he had brought home his fleete in as good a condition as ever any fleete was brought home; that twenty boats would be as many as the fleete would want: and all the anchors and cables left in the storm might be taken up again. This arose from my saying, among other things we had to do, that the fleete was come in—the greatest fleete that ever his Majesty had yet together, and that in as bad condition as the enemy or weather could put it; and to use Sir W. Pen's words, who is upon the place taking a survey, he dreads the reports he is to receive from the Surveyors of its defects. I therefore did only answer, that I was sorry for his Highness's offence, but that what I said was but the report we received from those entrusted in the fleete to inform us. He muttered and repeated what he had said; and so, after a long silence on all hands, nobody, not so much as the Duke of Albemarle, seconding the Prince, nor taking notice of what he said, we withdrew. I was not a little troubled at this passage, and the more when speaking with Jacke Fenn about it, he told me that the Prince will be asking now who this Pepys is, and find him to be a creature of my Lord Sandwich's, and therefore this was done only to disparage him. Anon they broke, up, and Sir W. Coventry come out; so I asked his advice. He told me he had said something to salve it, which was, that his Highnesse had, he believed, rightly informed the King that the fleete is come in good condition to have staid out yet longer, and have fought the enemy, but yet that Mr. Pepys his meaning might be, that, though in so good condition, if they should come in and lie all the winter, we shall be very loth to send them to sea for another year's service with[out] great repairs. He said it would be no hurt if I went to him, and showed him the report himself brought up from the fleete, where every ship, by the Commander's report, do need more or less, and not to mention more of Sir W. Pen for doing him a mischief. So I said I would, but do not think that all this will redound to my hurt, because the truth of what I said will soon appear. Thence, having been informed that, after all this pains, the King hath found out how to supply us with 5 or L6000, when L100,000 were at this time but absolutely necessary, and we mentioned L50,000. This is every day a greater and greater omen of ruine. God fit us for it! Sir J. Minnes and I home (it raining) by coach, calling only on Sir G. Cartefet at his lodging (who is I find troubled at my Lord Treasurer and Sir Ph. Warwicke bungling in his accounts), and come home to supper with my father, and then all to bed. I made my brother in his cassocke to say grace this day, but I like his voice so ill that I begin to be sorry he hath taken this order upon him.

8th. Up and to my office, called up by Commissioner Middleton, newly come to town, but staid not with me; so I to my office busy all the morning. Towards noon, by water to Westminster Hall, and there by several hear that the Parliament do resolve to do something to retrench Sir G. Carteret's great salary; but cannot hear of any thing bad they can lay to his charge. The House did this day order to be engrossed the Bill against importing Irish cattle; a thing, it seems, carried on by the Western Parliament-men, wholly against the sense of most of the rest of the House; who think if you do this, you give the Irish again cause to rebel. Thus plenty on both sides makes us mad. The Committee of the Canary Company of both factions come to me for my Cozen Roger that is of the Committee. Thence with [Sir] W. Coventry when the House rose and [Sir] W. Batten to St. James's, and there agreed of and signed our paper of extraordinaries, and there left them, and I to Unthanke's, where Mr. Falconbridge's girle is, and by and by comes my wife, who likes her well, though I confess I cannot (though she be of my finding out and sings pretty well), because she will be raised from so mean a condition to so high all of a sudden; but she will be much to our profit, more than Mercer, less expense. Here we bespoke anew gowne for her, and to come to us on Friday. She being gone, my wife and I home by coach, and then I presently by water with Mr. Pierce to Westminster Hall, he in the way telling me how the Duke of York and Duke of Albemarle do not agree. The Duke of York is wholly given up to this bitch of Denham. The Duke of Albemarle and Prince Rupert do less agree. So that we are all in pieces, and nobody knows what will be done the next year. The King hath yesterday in Council declared his resolution of setting a fashion for clothes, which he will never alter.

It will be a vest, I know not well how; but it is to teach the nobility thrift, and will do good. By and by comes down from the Committee [Sir] W. Coventry, and I find him troubled at several things happened this afternoon, which vexes me also; our business looking worse and worse, and our worke growing on our hands. Time spending, and no money to set anything in hand with; the end thereof must be speedy ruine. The Dutch insult and have taken off Bruant's head,

which they have not dared to do (though found guilty of the fault he did die for, of something of the Prince of Orange's faction) till just now, which speaks more confidence in our being worse than before. Alderman Maynell, I hear, is dead. Thence returned in the darke by coach all alone, full of thoughts of the consequences of this ill complexion of affairs, and how to save myself and the little I have, which if I can do, I have cause to bless God that I am so well, and shall be well contented to retreat to Brampton, and spend the rest of my days there. So to my office, and did some business, and finished my Journall with resolutions, if God bless me, to apply myself soberly to settle all matters for myself, and expect the event of all with comfort. So home to supper and to bed.

9th. Up and to the office, where we sat the first day since the fire, I think. At noon home, and my uncle Thomas was there, and dined with my brother and I (my father and I were gone abroad), and then to the office again in the afternoon, and there close all day long, and did much business. At night to Sir W. Batten, where Sir R. Ford did occasion some discourse of sending a convoy to the Maderas; and this did put us upon some new thoughts of sending our privateer thither on merchants' accounts, which I have more mind to, the profit being certain and occasion honest withall. So home, and to supper with my father, and then to set my remainder of my books gilt in order with much pleasure, and so late to bed.

10th (Fast-day for the fire). Up with Sir W. Batten by water to White Hall, and anon had a meeting before the Duke of York, where pretty to see how Sir W. Batten, that carried the surveys of all the fleete with him, to shew their ill condition to the Duke of York, when he found the Prince there, did not speak one word, though the meeting was of his asking—for nothing else. And when I asked him, he told me he knew the Prince too well to anger him, so that he was afeard to do it. Thence with him to Westminster, to the parish church, where the Parliament-men, and Stillingfleete in the pulpit. So full, no standing there; so he and I to eat herrings at the Dog Taverne. And then to church again, and there was Mr. Frampton in the pulpit, they cry up so much, a young man, and of a mighty ready tongue. I heard a little of his sermon, and liked it; but the crowd so great, I could not stay. So to the Swan, and 'baise la fille', and drank, and then home by coach, and took father, wife, brother, and W. Hewer to Islington, where I find mine host dead. Here eat and drank, and merry; and so home, and to the office a while, and then to Sir W. Batten to talk a while, and with Captain Cocke into the office to hear his newes, who is mighty conversant with Garraway and those people, who tells me what they object as to the maladministration of things as to money. But that they mean well, and will do well; but their reckonings are very good, and show great faults, as I will insert here. They say the king hath had towards this war expressly thus much

He and I did bemoan our public condition. He tells me the Duke of Albemarle is under a cloud, and they have a mind at Court to lay him aside. This I know not; but all things are not right with him, and I am glad of it, but sorry for the time. So home to supper, and to bed, it being my wedding night,

but how many years I cannot tell; but my wife says ten.

11th. Up, and discoursed with my father of my sending some money for safety into the country, for I am in pain what to do with what I have. I did give him money, poor man, and he overjoyed. So left him, and to the office, where nothing but sad evidences of ruine coming on us for want of money. So home to dinner, which was a very good dinner, my father, brother, wife and I, and then to the office again, where I was all the afternoon till very late, busy, and then home to supper and to bed.

12th. Up, and after taking leave of my poor father, who is setting out this day for Brampton by the Cambridge coach, he having taken a journey to see the city burned, and to bring my brother to towne, I out by water; and so coach to St. James's, the weather being foul; and there, from Sir W. Coventry, do hear how the House have cut us off L150,000 of our wear and tear, for that which was saved by the King while the fleete lay in harbour in winter. However, he seems pleased, and so am I, that they have abated no more, and do intend to allow of 28,000 men for the next year; and this day have appointed to declare the sum they will give the King,

and to propose the way of raising it; so that this is likely to be the great day. This done in his chamber, I with him to Westminster Hall, and there took a few turns, the Hall mighty full of people, and the House likely to be very full to-day about the money business. Here I met with several people, and do find that people have a mighty mind to have a fling at the Vice-Chamberlain, if they could lay hold of anything, his place being, indeed, too much for such, they think, or any single subject of no greater parts and quality than he, to enjoy. But I hope he may weather all, though it will not be by any dexterity of his, I dare say, if he do stand, but by his fate only, and people's being taken off by other things. Thence home by coach, mighty dirty weather, and then to the Treasurer's office and got a ticket paid for my little Michell, and so again by coach to Westminster, and come presently after the House rose. So to the Swan, and there sent for a piece of meat and dined alone and played with Sarah, and so to the Hall a while, and thence to Mrs. Martin's lodging and did what I would with her. She is very big, and resolves I must be godfather. Thence away by water with Cropp to Deptford. It was almost night before I got thither. So I did only give directions concerning a press that I have making there to hold my turning and joyner's tooles that were lately given me, which will be very handsome, and so away back again, it being now dark, and so home, and there find my wife come home, and hath brought her new girle I have helped her to, of Mr. Falconbridge's. She is wretched poor; and but ordinary favoured; and we fain to lay out seven or eight pounds worth of clothes upon her back, which, methinks, do go against my heart; and I do not think I can ever esteem her as I could have done another that had come fine and handsome; and which is more, her voice, for want of use, is so furred, that it do not at present please me; but her manner of singing is such, that I shall, I think, take great pleasure in it. Well, she is come, and I wish us good fortune in her. Here I met with notice of a meeting of the Commissioners for Tangier tomorrow, and so I must have my accounts ready for them, which caused me to confine myself to my chamber presently and set to the making up my accounts, which I find very clear, but with much difficulty by reason of my not doing them sooner, things being out of my mind.

13th. It cost me till four o'clock in the morning, and, which was pretty to think, I was above an hour, after I had made all right, in casting up of about twenty sums, being dozed with much work, and had for forty times together forgot to carry the 60 which I had in my mind, in one denomination which exceeded 60; and this did confound me for above an hour together. At last all even and done, and so to bed. Up at seven, and so to the office, after looking over my last night's work. We sat all the morning. At noon by coach with my Lord Bruncker and 'light at the Temple, and so alone I to dinner at a cooke's, and thence to my Lord Bellasses, whom I find kind; but he had drawn some new proposal to deliver to the Lords Commissioners to-day, wherein one was, that the garrison would not be well paid without some goldsmith's undertaking the paying of the bills of exchange for Tallys. He professing so much kindness to me, and saying that he would not be concerned in the garrison without me; and that if he continued in the employment, no man should have to do with the money but myself. I did ask his Lordship's meaning of the proposition in his paper. He told me he had not much considered it, but that he meant no harm to me. I told him I thought it would render me useless; whereupon he did very frankly, after my seeming denials for a good while, cause it to be writ over again, and that clause left out, which did satisfy me abundantly. It being done, he and I together to White Hall, and there the Duke of York (who is gone over to all his pleasures again, and leaves off care of business, what with his woman, my Lady Denham, and his hunting three times a week) was just come in from hunting. So I stood and saw him dress himself, and try on his vest, which is the King's new fashion, and will be in it for good and all on Monday next, and the whole Court: it is a fashion, the King says; he will never change. He being ready, he and my Lord Chancellor, and Duke of Albemarle, and Prince Rupert, Lord Bellasses, Sir H. Cholmly, Povy, and myself, met at a Committee for Tangier. My Lord Bellasses's propositions were read and discoursed of, about reducing the garrison to less charge; and indeed I am mad in love with my Lord Chancellor, for he do comprehend and speak out well, and with the greatest easinesse and authority that ever I saw man in my life. I did never observe how much easier a man do speak when he knows all the company to be below him, than in him; for though he spoke, indeed, excellent welt, yet his manner and freedom of doing it, as if he played with it, and was informing only all the rest of the company, was mighty pretty. He did call again and again upon Mr. Povy for his accounts. I did think fit to make the solemn tender of my accounts that I intended. I said something that was liked, touching the want of money, and the bad credit of our tallys. My Lord Chancellor moved, that without any trouble to any of the rest of the Lords, I might alone attend the King, when he was with his private Council; and open the state of the garrison's want of credit; and all that could be done, should. Most things moved were referred to Committees, and so we broke up. And at the end Sir W. Coventry come; so I away with him, and he discoursed with me something of the Parliament's business. They have voted giving the [King] for next year L1,800,000; which, were it not for his debts, were a great sum. He says, he thinks the House may say no more to us for the present, but that we must mend our manners against the next tryall, and mend them we will. But he thinks it not a fit time to be found making of trouble among ourselves, meaning about Sir J. Minnes, who most certainly must be removed, or made a Commissioner, and somebody else Comptroller. But he tells me that the House has a great envy at Sir G. Carteret, and that had he ever thought fit in all his discourse to have touched upon the point of our want of money and badness of payment, it would have been laid hold on to Sir G. Carteret's hurt; but he hath avoided it, though without much reason for it, most studiously, and in short did end thus, that he has never shewn so much of the pigeon in all his life as in his innocence to Sir G. Carteret at this time; which I believe, and will desire Sir G. Carteret to thank him for it. So we broke up and I by coach home, calling for a new pair of shoes, and so, little being to do at the office, did go home, and after spending a little in righting some of my books, which stood out of order, I to bed.

14th (Lord's day). Lay long in bed, among other things, talking of my wife's renewing her acquaintance with Mrs. Pierce, which, by my wife's ill using her when she was here last, hath been interrupted. Herein we were a little angry together, but presently friends again; and so up, and I to church, which was mighty full, and my beauties, Mrs. Lethulier and fair Batelier, both there. A very foul morning, and rained; and sent for my cloake to go out of the church with. So dined, and after dinner (a good discourse thereat to my brother) he and I by water to White Hall, and he to Westminster Abbey. Here I met with Sir Stephen Fox, who told me how much right I had done myself, and how well it is represented by the Committee to the House, my readinesse to give them satisfaction in everything when they were at the office. I was glad of this. He did further discourse of Sir W. Coventry's, great abilities, and how necessary it were that I were of the House to assist him. I did not owne it, but do myself think it were not unnecessary if either he should die, or be removed to the Lords, or any thing to hinder his doing the like service the next trial, which makes me think that it were not a thing very unfit; but I will not move in it. He and I parted, I to Mrs. Martin's, thinking to have met Mrs. Burrows, but she was not there, so away and took my brother out of the Abbey and home, and there to set some accounts right, and to the office to even my Journall, and so home to supper and to bed.

15th. Called up, though a very rainy morning, by Sir H. Cholmley, and he and I most of the morning together evening of accounts, which I was very glad of. Then he and I out to Sir Robt. Viner's, at the African house (where I had not been since he come thither); but he was not there; but I did some business with his people, and then to Colvill's, who, I find, lives now in Lyme Streete, and with the same credit as ever, this fire having not done them any wrong that I hear of at all. Thence he and I together to Westminster Hall, in our way talking of matters and passages of state, the viciousness of the Court; the contempt the King brings himself into thereby; his minding nothing, but doing all things just as his people about him will have it; the Duke of York becoming a slave to this whore Denham, and wholly minds her; that there really was amours between the Duchesse and Sidney; a that there is reason to fear that, as soon as the Parliament have raised this money, the King will see that he hath got all that he can get, and then make up a peace. He tells me, what I wonder at, but that I find it confirmed by Mr. Pierce, whom I met by-and-by in the Hall, that Sir W. Coventry is of the caball with the Duke of York, and Bruncker, with this Denham; which is a shame, and I am sorry for it, and that Sir W. Coventry do make her visits; but yet I hope it is not so. Pierce tells me, that as little agreement as there is between the Prince—[Rupert]—and Duke of Albemarle, yet they are likely to go to sea again; for the first will not be trusted alone, and nobody will go with him but this Duke of Albemarle. He tells me much how all the commanders of the fleete and officers that are sober men do cry out upon their bad discipline, and the ruine that must follow it if it continue. But that which I wonder most at, it seems their secretaries have been the most exorbitant in their fees to all sorts of the people, that it is not to be believed that they durst do it, so as it is believed they have got L800 apiece by the very vacancies in the fleete. He tells me that Lady Castlemayne is concluded to be with child again; and that all the people about the King do make no scruple of saying that the King do lie with Mrs. Stewart, who, he says, is a most excellent-natured lady. This day the King begins to put on his vest, and I did see several persons of the House of Lords and Commons too, great courtiers, who are in it; being a long cassocke close to the body, of black cloth, and pinked with white silke under it, and a coat over it, and the legs ruffled with black riband like a pigeon's leg; and, upon the whole, I wish the King may keep it, for it is a very fine and handsome garment.

Walking with Pierce in the Court of Wards out comes Sir W. Coventry, and he and I talked of business. Among others I proposed the making Sir J. Minnes a Commissioner, and make somebody else Comptroller. He tells me it is the thing he hath been thinking of, and hath spoke to the Duke of York of it. He believes it will be done; but that which I fear is that Pen will be Comptroller, which I shall grudge a little. The Duke of Buckingham called him aside and spoke a good while with him. I did presently fear it might be to discourse something of his design to blemish my Lord of Sandwich, in pursuance of the wild motion he made the other day in the House. Sir W. Coventry, when he come to me again, told me that he had wrought a miracle, which was, the convincing the Duke of Buckingham that something—he did not name what— that he had intended to do was not fit to be done, and that the Duke is gone away of that opinion. This makes me verily believe it was something like what I feared. By and by the House rose, and then we parted, and I with Sir G. Carteret, and walked in the Exchequer Court, discoursing of businesses. Among others, I observing to him how friendly Sir W. Coventry had carried himself to him in these late inquiries, when, if he had borne him any spleen, he could have had what occasion he pleased offered him, he did confess he found the same thing, and would thanke him for it. I did give him some other advices, and so away with him to his lodgings at White Hall to dinner, where my Lady Carteret is, and mighty kind, both of them, to me. Their son and my Lady Jemimah will be here very speedily. She tells me the ladies are to go into a new fashion shortly, and that is, to wear short coats, above their ancles; which she and I do not like, but conclude this long trayne to be mighty graceful. But she cries out of the vices of the Court, and how they are going to set up plays already; and how, the next day after the late great fast, the Duchesse of York did give the King and Queene a play. Nay, she told me that they have heretofore had plays at Court the very nights before the fast for the death of the late King: She do much cry out upon these things, and that which she believes will undo the whole nation; and I fear so too. After dinner away home, Mr. Brisband along with me as far as the Temple, and there looked upon a new booke, set out by one Rycault, secretary to my Lord Winchelsea, of the policy and customs of the Turks, which is, it seems, much cried up. But I could not stay, but home, where I find Balty come back, and with him some muster-books, which I am glad of, and hope he will do me credit in his employment. By and by took coach again and carried him home, and my wife to her tailor's, while I to White Hall to have found out Povy, but miss him and so call in my wife and home again, where at Sir W. Batten's I met Sir W. Pen, lately come from the fleete at the Nore; and here were many good fellows, among others Sir R. Holmes, who is exceeding kind to me, more than usual, which makes me afeard of him, though I do much wish his friendship. Thereupon, after a little stay, I withdrew, and to the office and awhile, and then home to supper and to my chamber to settle a few papers, and then to bed. This day the great debate was in Parliament, the manner of raising the L1,800,000 they voted [the King] on Friday; and at last, after many proposals, one moved that the Chimney-money might be taken from the King, and an equal revenue of something else might be found for the King, and people be enjoyned to buy off this tax of Chimney-money for ever at eight years' purchase, which will raise present money, as they think, L1,600,000, and the State be eased of an ill burthen and the King be supplied of something as food or better for his use. The House seems to like this, and put off the debate to to-morrow.

16th. Up, and to the office, where sat to do little business but hear clamours for money. At noon home to dinner, and to the office again, after hearing my brother play a little upon the Lyra viall, which he do so as to show that he hath a love to musique and a spirit for it, which I am well pleased with. All the afternoon at the office, and at night with Sir W. Batten, Sir W. Pen, [and Sir] J. Minnes, at [Sir] W. Pen's lodgings, advising about business and orders fit presently to make about discharging of ships come into the river, and which to pay first, and many things in order thereto. But it vexed me that, it being now past seven o'clock, and the businesses of great weight, and I had done them by eight o'clock, and sending them to be signed, they were all gone to bed, and Sir W. Pen, though awake, would not, being in bed, have them brought to him to sign; this made me quite angry. Late at work at the office, and then home to supper and to bed. Not come to any resolution at the Parliament to-day about the manner of raising this L1,800,000.

17th. Up, and busy about public and private business all the morning at the office. At noon home to dinner, alone with my brother, with whom I had now the first private talke I have had, and find he hath preached but twice in his life. I did give him some advice to study pronunciation; but I do fear he will never make a good speaker, nor, I fear, any general good scholar, for I do not see that he minds optickes or mathematiques of any sort, nor anything else that I can find. I know not what he may be at divinity and ordinary school-learning. However, he seems sober, and that pleases me. After dinner took him and my wife and Barker (for so is our new woman called, and is yet but a sorry girle), and set them down at Unthanke's, and so to White Hall, and there find some of my brethren with the Duke of York, but so few I put off the meeting. So staid and heard the Duke discourse, which he did mighty scurrilously, of the French, and with reason, that they should give Beaufort orders when he was to bring, and did bring, his fleete hither, that his rendezvous for his fleete, and for all sluggs to come to, should be between Calais and Dover; which did prove the taking of La Roche[lle], who, among other sluggs behind, did, by their instructions, make for that place, to rendezvous with the fleete; and Beaufort, seeing them as he was returning, took them for the English fleete, and wrote word to the King of France that he had passed by the English fleete, and the English fleete durst not meddle with him. The Court is all full of vests, only my Lord St. Albans not pinked but plain black; and they say the King says the pinking upon white makes them look too much like magpyes, and therefore hath bespoke one of plain velvet. Thence to St. James's by coach, and spoke, at four o'clock or five, with Sir W. Coventry, newly come from the House, where they have sat all this day and not come to an end of the debate how the money shall be raised. He tells me that what I proposed to him the other day was what he had himself thought on and determined, and that he believes it will speedily be done—the making Sir J. Minnes a Commissioner, and bringing somebody else to be Comptroller, and that (which do not please me, I confess, for my own particulars, so well as Sir J. Minnes) will, I fear, be Sir W. Pen, for he is the only fit man for it. Away from him and took up my wife, and left her at Temple Bar to buy some lace for a petticoat, and I took coach and away to Sir R. Viner's about a little business, and then home, and by and by to my chamber, and there late upon making up an account for the Board to pass to-morrow, if I can get them, for the clearing all my imprest bills, which if I can do, will be to my very good satisfaction. Having done this, then to supper and to bed.

18th. Up, and to the office, where we sat all the morning. The waters so high in the roads, by the late rains, that our letters come not in till to-day, and now I understand that my father is got well home, but had a painful journey of it. At noon with Lord Bruncker to St. Ellen's, where the master of the late Pope's Head Taverne is now set up again, and there dined at Sir W. Warren's cost, a very good dinner. Here my Lord Bruncker proffered to carry me and my wife into a play at Court to-night, and to lend me his coach home, which tempted me much; but I shall not do it. Thence rose from table before dinner ended, and homewards met my wife, and so away by coach towards Lovett's (in the way wondering at what a good pretty wench our Barker makes, being now put into good clothes, and fashionable, at my charge; but it becomes her, so that I do not now think much of it, and is an example of the power of good clothes and dress), where I stood godfather. But it was pretty, that, being a Protestant, a man stood by and was my Proxy to answer for me. A priest christened it, and the boy's name is Samuel. The ceremonies many, and some foolish. The priest in a gentleman's dress, more than my owne; but is a Capuchin, one of the Queene-mother's priests. He did give my proxy and the woman proxy (my Lady Bills, absent, had a proxy also) good advice to bring up the child, and, at the end, that he ought never to marry the child nor the godmother, nor the godmother the child or the godfather: but, which is strange, they say that the mother of the child and the godfather may marry. By and by the Lady Bills come in, a well-bred but crooked woman. The poor people of the house had good wine, and a good cake; and she a pretty woman in her lying-in dress. It cost me near 40s. the whole christening: to midwife 20s., nurse 10s., mayde 2s. 6d., and the coach 5s. I was very well satisfied with what I have done, and so home and to the office, and thence to Sir W. Batten's, and there hear how the business of buying off the Chimney-money is passed in the House; and so the King to be satisfied some other way, and the King supplied with the money raised by this purchasing off of the chimnies. So home, mightily pleased in mind that I have got my bills of imprest cleared by bills signed this day, to my good satisfaction. To supper, and to bed.

19th. Up, and by coach to my Lord Ashly's, and thence (he being gone out), to the Exchequer chamber, and there find him and my Lord Bellasses about my Lord Bellasses' accounts, which was the business I went upon. This was soon ended, and then I with Creed back home to my house, and there he and I did even accounts for salary, and by that time dinner was ready, and merry at dinner, and then abroad to Povy's, who continues as much confounded in all his business as ever he was; and would have had me paid money, as like a fool as himself, which I troubled him in refusing; but I did persist in it. After a little more discourse, I left them, and to White Hall, where I met with Sir Robert Viner, who told me a little of what, in going home, I had seen; also a little of the disorder and mutiny among the seamen at the Treasurer's office, which did trouble me then and all day since, considering how many more seamen will come to towne every day, and no money for them. A Parliament sitting, and the Exchange close by, and an enemy to hear of, and laugh at it.

Viner too, and Backewell, were sent for this afternoon; and was before the King and his Cabinet about money; they declaring they would advance no more, it being discoursed of in the House of Parliament for the King to issue out his privy-seals to them to command them to trust him, which gives them reason to decline trusting. But more money they are persuaded to lend, but so little that (with horrour I speake it), coming after the Council was up, with Sir G. Carteret, Sir W. Coventry, Lord Bruncker, and myself, I did lay the state of our condition before the Duke of York, that the fleete could not go out without several things it wanted, and we could not have without money, particularly rum and bread, which we have promised the man Swan to helpe him to L200 of his debt, and a few other small sums of L200 a piece to some others, and that I do foresee the Duke of York would call us to an account why the fleete is not abroad, and we cannot answer otherwise than our want of money; and that indeed we do not do the King any service now, but do rather abuse and betray his service by being there, and seeming to do something, while we do not. Sir G. Carteret asked me (just in these words, for in this and all the rest I set down the very words for memory sake, if there should be occasion) whether L50 or L60 would do us any good; and when I told him the very rum man must have L200, he held up his eyes as if we had asked a million. Sir W. Coventry told the Duke of York plainly he did rather desire to have his commission called in than serve in so ill a place, where he cannot do the King service, and I did concur in saying the same. This was all very plain, and the Duke of York did confess that he did not see how we could do anything without a present supply of L20,000, and that he would speak to the King next Council day, and I promised to wait on him to put him in mind of it. This I set down for my future justification, if need be, and so we broke up, and all parted, Sir W. Coventry being not very well, but I believe made much worse by this night's sad discourse. So I home by coach, considering what the consequence of all this must be in a little time. Nothing but distraction and confusion; which makes me wish with all my heart that I were well and quietly settled with what little I have got at Brampton, where I might live peaceably, and study, and pray for the good of the King and my country. Home, and to Sir W. Batten's, where I saw my Lady, who is now come down stairs after a great sickness. Sir W. Batten was at the pay to-day, and tells me how rude the men were, but did go away quietly, being promised pay on Wednesday next. God send us money for it! So to the office, and then to supper and to bed. Among other things proposed in the House to-day, to give the King in lieu of chimneys, there was the bringing up of sealed paper, such as Sir J. Minnes shewed me to-night, at Sir W. Batten's, is used in Spayne, and brings the King a great revenue; but it shows what shifts we are put to too much.

20th. Up, and all the morning at the office, where none met but myself. So I walked a good while with Mr. Gawden in the garden, who is lately come from the fleete at the buoy of the Nore, and he do tell me how all the sober commanders, and even Sir Thomas Allen himself, do complain of the ill government of the fleete. How Holmes and Jennings have commanded all the fleete this yeare, that nothing is done upon deliberation, but if a sober man give his opinion otherwise than the Prince would have it the Prince would cry, "Damn him, do you follow your orders, and that is enough for you." He tells me he hears of nothing but of swearing and drinking and whoring, and all manner of profaneness, quite through the whole fleete. He being gone, there comes to me Commissioner Middleton, whom I took on purpose to walk in the garden with me, and to learn what he observed when the fleete was at Portsmouth. He says that the fleete was in such a condition, as to discipline, as if the Devil had commanded it; so much wickedness of all sorts. Enquiring how it come to pass that so many ships miscarried this year, he tells me that he enquired; and the pilots do say, that they dare not do nor go but as the Captains will have them; and if they offer to do otherwise, the Captains swear they will run them through. He says that he heard Captain Digby (my Lord of Bristoll's son, a young fellow that never was but one year, if that, in the fleete) say that he did hope he should not see a tarpaulin have the command of a ship within this twelve months. He observed while he was on board the Admirall, when the fleete was at Portsmouth, that there was a faction there. Holmes commanded all on the Prince's side, and Sir Jeremy Smith on the Duke's, and every body that come did apply themselves to one side or other; and when the Duke of Albemarle was gone away to come hither, then Sir Jeremy Smith did hang his head, and walked in the Generall's ship but like a private commander. He says he was on board The Prince, when the newes come of the burning of London; and all the Prince said was, that now Shipton's prophecy was out; and he heard a young commander presently swear, that now a citizen's wife that would not take under half a piece before, would be occupied for half-a-crowne: and made mighty sport of it. He says that Hubberd that commanded this year the Admiral's ship is a proud conceited fellow (though I thought otherwise of him), and fit to command a single ship but not a fleete, and he do wonder that there hath not been more mischief this year than there hath. He says the fleete come to anchor between the Horse and the Island, so that when they came to weigh many of the ships could not turn, but run foul of the Horse, and there stuck, but that the weather was good. He says that nothing can do the King more disservice, nor please the standing officers of the ship better than these silly commanders that now we have, for they sign to anything that their officers desire of them, nor have judgment to contradict them if they would. He told me other good things, which made me bless God that we have received no greater disasters this year than we have, though they have been the greatest that ever was known in England before, put all their losses of the King's ships by want of skill and seamanship together from the beginning. He being gone, comes Sir G. Carteret, and he and I walked together awhile, discoursing upon the sad condition of the times, what need we have, and how impossible it is to get money. He told me my Lord Chancellor the other day did ask him how it come to pass that his friend Pepys do so much magnify all things to worst, as I did on Sunday last, in the bad condition of the fleete. Sir G. Carteret tells me that he answered him, that I was but the mouth of the rest, and spoke what they have dictated to me; which did, as he says, presently take off his displeasure. So that I am well at present with him, but I must have a care not to be over busy in the office again, and burn my fingers. He tells me he wishes he had sold his place at some good rate to somebody or other at the beginning of the warr, and that he would do it now, but no body will deale with him for it. He tells me the Duke of Albemarle is very much discontented, and the Duke of York do not, it seems, please him. He tells me that our case as to money is not to be made good at present, and therefore wishes a good and speedy peace before it be too late, and from his discourse methinks I find that there is something moving towards it. Many people at the office, but having no more of the office I did put it off till the next meeting. Thence, with Sir G. Carteret, home to dinner, with him, my Lady and Mr. Ashburnham, the Cofferer. Here they talk that the Queene hath a great mind to alter her fashion, and to have the feet seen, which she loves mightily; and they do believe that it [will] come into it in a little time. Here I met with the King's declaration about his proceedings with the King of Denmarke, and particularly the business of Bergen; but it is so well writ, that, if it be true, the King of Denmarke is one of the most absolute wickednesse in the world for a person of his quality. After dinner home, and there met Mr. Povy by appointment, and there he and I all the afternoon, till late at night, evening of all accounts between us, which we did to both our satisfaction; but that which troubles me most is, that I am to refund to the ignoble Lord Peterborough what he had given us six months ago, because we did not supply him with money; but it is no great matter. He gone I to the office, and there did some business; and so home, my mind in good ease by having done with Povy in order to the adjusting of all my accounts in a few days. So home to supper and to bed.

21st (Lord's day). Up, and with my wife to church, and her new woman Barker with her the first time. The girle will, I think, do very well. Here a lazy sermon, and so home to dinner, and took in my Lady Pen and Peg (Sir William being below with the fleete), and mighty merry we were, and then after dinner presently (it being a mighty cool day) I by coach to White Hall, and there attended the Cabinet, and was called in before the King and them to give an account of our want of money for Tangier, which troubles me that it should be my place so often and so soon after one another to come to speak there of their wants—the thing of the world that they love least to hear of, and that which is no welcome thing to be the solicitor for—and to see how like an image the King sat and could not speak one word when I had delivered myself was very strange; only my Lord Chancellor did ask me, whether I thought it was in nature at this time to help us to anything. So I was referred to another meeting of the Lords Commissioners for Tangier and my Lord Treasurer, and so went away, and by coach home, where I spent the evening in reading Stillingfleet's defence of the Archbishopp, the part about Purgatory, a point I had never considered before, what was said for it or against it, and though I do believe we are in the right, yet I do not see any great matter in this book. So to supper; and my people being gone, most of them, to bed, my boy and Jane and I did get two of my iron chests out of the cellar into my closett, and the money to my great satisfaction to see it there again, and the rather because the damp cellar spoils all my chests. This being done, and I weary, to bed. This afternoon walking with Sir H. Cholmly long in the gallery, he told me, among many other things, how Harry Killigrew is banished the Court lately, for saying that my Lady Castlemayne was a little lecherous girle when she was young.... This she complained to the King of, and he sent to the Duke of York, whose servant he is, to turn him away. The Duke of York hath done it, but takes it ill of my Lady that he was not complained to first. She attended him to excute it, but ill blood is made by it. He told me how Mr. Williamson stood in a little place to have come into the House of Commons, and they would not choose him; they said, "No courtier." And which is worse, Bab May went down in great state to Winchelsea with the Duke of York's letters, not doubting to be chosen; and there the people chose a private gentleman in spite of him, and cried out they would have no Court pimp to be their burgesse; which are things that bode very ill. This afternoon I went to see and sat a good while with Mrs. Martin, and there was her sister Doll, with whom, contrary to all expectation, I did what I would, and might have done anything else.

22nd. Up, and by coach to Westminster Hall, there thinking to have met Betty Michell, who I heard yesterday staid all night at her father's, but she was gone. So I staid a little and then down to the bridge by water, and there overtook her and her father. So saluted her and walked over London Bridge with them and there parted, the weather being very foul, and so to the Tower by water, and so heme, where I find Mr. Caesar playing the treble to my boy upon the Theorbo, the first time I heard him, which pleases me mightily. After dinner I carried him and my wife towards Westminster, by coach, myself 'lighting at the Temple, and there, being a little too soon, walked in the Temple Church, looking with pleasure on the monuments and epitaphs, and then to my Lord Belasses, where Creed and Povy by appointment met to discourse of some of their Tangier accounts between my Lord and Vernatty, who will prove a very knave. That being done I away with Povy to White Hall, and thence I to Unthanke's, and there take up my wife, and so home, it being very foule and darke. Being there come, I to the settling of some of my money matters in my chests, and evening some accounts, which I was at late, to my extraordinary content, and especially to see all things hit so even and right and with an apparent profit and advantage since my last accounting, but how much I cannot particularly yet come to adjudge.

23rd. Up, and to the office all the morning. At noon Sir W. Batten told me Sir Richard Ford would accept of one-third of my profit of our private man-of-war, and bear one-third of the charge, and be bound in the Admiralty, so I shall be excused being bound, which I like mightily of, and did draw up a writing, as well as I could, to that purpose and signed and sealed it, and so he and Sir R. Ford are to go to enter into bond this afternoon. Home to dinner, and after dinner, it being late, I down by water to Shadwell, to see Betty Michell, the first time I was ever at their new dwelling since the fire, and there find her in the house all alone. I find her mighty modest. But had her lips as much as I would, and indeed she is mighty pretty, that I love her exceedingly. I paid her L10 1s. that I received upon a ticket for her husband, which is a great kindness I have done them, and having kissed her as much as I would, I away, poor wretch, and down to Deptford to see Sir J. Minnes ordering of the pay of some ships there, which he do most miserably, and so home. Bagwell's wife, seeing me come the fields way, did get over her pales to come after and talk with me, which she did for a good way, and so parted, and I home, and to the office, very busy, and so to supper and to bed.

24th. Up, and down to the Old Swan, and there find little Michell come to his new shop that he hath built there in the room of his house that was burned. I hope he will do good here. I drank and bade him joy, for I love him and his wife well, him for his care, and her for her person, and so to White Hall, where we attended the Duke; and to all our complaints for want of money, which now we are tired out with making, the Duke only tells us that he is sorry for it, and hath spoke to the King of it, and money we shall have as soon as it can be found; and though all the issue of the war lies upon it, yet that is all the answer we can get, and that is as bad or worse than nothing. Thence to Westminster Hall, where the term is begun, and I did take a turn or two, and so away by coach to Sir R. Viner's, and there received some money, and then home and to dinner. After dinner to little business, and then abroad with my wife, she to see her brother, who is sick, and she believes is from some discontent his wife hath given him by her loose carriage, which he is told, and he hath found has been very suspicious in his absence, which I am sorry for. I to the Hall and there walked long, among others talking with Mr. Hayes, Prince Rupert's Secretary, a very ingenious man, and one, I think, fit to contract some friendship with. Here I staid late, walking to and again, hearing how the Parliament proceeds, which is mighty slowly in the settling of the money business, and great factions growing every day among them. I am told also how Holmes did last Sunday deliver in his articles to the King and Cabinet against [Sir Jeremy] Smith, and that Smith hath given in his answer, and lays his not accompanying the fleete to his pilot, who would not undertake to carry the ship further; which the pilot acknowledges. The thing is not accommodated, but only taken up, and both sides commanded to be quiet; but no peace like to be. The Duke of Albemarle is Smith's friend, and hath publiquely swore that he would never go to sea again unless Holmes's commission were taken from him.

I find by Hayes that they did expect great glory in coming home in so good condition as they did with the fleete, and therefore I the less wonder that the Prince was distasted with my discourse the other day about the bad state of the fleete. But it pleases me to hear that he did expect great thanks, and lays the fault of the want of it upon the fire, which deadened everything, and the glory of his services. About seven at night home, and called my wife, and, it being moonshine, took her into the garden, and there layed open our condition as to our estate, and the danger of my having it [his money] all in the house at once, in case of any disorder or troubles in the State, and therefore resolved to remove part of it to Brampton, and part some whither else, and part in my owne house, which is very necessary, and will tend to our safety, though I shall not think it safe out of my owne sight. So to the office, and then to supper and to bed.

25th. Up betimes and by water to White Hall, and there with Sir G. Carteret to Sir W. Coventry, who is come to his winter lodgings at White Hall, and there agreed upon a method of paying of tickets; and so I back again home and to the office, where we sate all the morning, but to little purpose but to receive clamours for money. At noon home to dinner, where the two Mrs. Daniels come to see us, and dined with us. After dinner I out with my wife to Mrs. Pierces, where she hath not been a great while, from some little unkindness of my wife's to her when she was last here, but she received us with mighty respect and discretion, and was making herself mighty fine to go to a great ball to-night at Court, being the Queene's birthday; so the ladies for this one day do wear laces, but to put them off again to-morrow. Thence I to my Lord Bruncker's, and with him to Mrs. Williams's where we met Knipp. I was glad to see the jade. Made her sing; and she told us they begin at both houses to act on Monday next. But I fear, after all this sorrow, their gains will be but little. Mrs. Williams says, the Duke's house will now be much the better of the two, because of their women; which I am glad to hear. Thence with Lord Bruncker to White Hall and there spoke with Sir W. Coventry about some office business, and then I away to Mrs. Pierces, and there saw her new closet, which is mighty rich and fine. Her daughter Betty grows mighty pretty. Thence with my wife home and to do business at the office. Then to Sir W. Batten's, who tells me that the House of Parliament makes mighty little haste in settling the money, and that he knows not when it will be done; but they fall into faction, and libells have been found in the House. Among others, one yesterday, wherein they reckon up divers great sums to be given away by the King, among others, L10,000 to Sir W. Coventry, for weare and teare (the point he stood upon to advance that sum by, for them to give the King); Sir G. Carteret L50,000 for something else, I think supernumerarys; and so to Matt. Wren L5000 for passing the Canary Company's patent; and so a great many other sums to other persons. So home to supper and to bed.

26th. Up, and all the morning and most of the afternoon within doors, beginning to set my accounts in order from before this fire, I being behindhand with them ever since; and this day I got most of my tradesmen to bring in their bills and paid them. Dined at home, and busy again after dinner, and then abroad by water to Westminster Hall, where I walked till the evening, and then out, the first time I ever was abroad with Doll Lane, to the Dog tavern, and there drank with her, a bad face, but good bodied girle. Did nothing but salute and play with her and talk, and thence away by coach, home, and so to do a little more in my accounts, and then to supper and to bed. Nothing done in the House yet as to the finishing of the bill for money, which is a mighty sad thing, all lying at stake for it.

27th. Up, and there comes to see me my Lord Belasses, which was a great honour. He tells me great newes, yet but what I suspected, that Vernatty is fled, and so hath cheated him and twenty more, but most of all, I doubt, Mr. Povy. Thence to talk about publique business; he tells me how the two Houses begin to be troublesome; the Lords to have quarrels one with another. My Lord Duke of Buckingham having said to the Lord Chancellor (who is against the passing of the Bill for prohibiting the bringing over of Irish cattle), that whoever was against the Bill, was there led to it by an Irish interest, or an Irish understanding, which is as much as to say he is a Poole; this bred heat from my Lord Chancellor, and something he [Buckingham] said did offend my Lord of Ossory (my Lord Duke' of Ormond's son), and they two had hard words, upon which the latter sends a challenge to the former; of which the former complains to the House, and so the business is to be heard on Monday next. Then as to the Commons; some ugly knives, like poignards, to stab people with, about two or three hundred of them were brought in yesterday to the House, found in one of the house's rubbish that was burned, and said to be the house of a Catholique. This and several letters out of the country, saying how high the Catholiques are everywhere and bold in the owning their religion, have made the Commons mad, and they presently voted that the King be desired to put all Catholiques out of employment, and other high things; while the business of money hangs in the hedge. So that upon the whole, God knows we are in a sad condition like to be, there being the very beginnings of the late troubles. He gone, I at the office all the morning. At noon home to dinner, where Mrs. Pierce and her boy and Knipp, who sings as well, and is the best company in the world, dined with us, and infinite merry. The playhouses begin to play next week. Towards evening I took them out to the New Exchange, and there my wife bought things, and I did give each of them a pair of Jesimy

plain gloves, and another of white. Here Knipp and I walked up and down to see handsome faces, and did see several. Then carried each of them home, and with great pleasure and content, home myself, where, having writ several letters, I home, and there, upon some serious discourse between my wife and I upon the business, I called to us my brother, and there broke to him our design to send him into the country with some part of our money, and so did seriously discourse the whole thing, and then away to supper and to bed. I pray God give a blessing to our resolution, for I do much fear we shall meet with speedy distractions for want of money.

28th (Lord's day). Up, and to church with my wife, and then home, and there is come little Michell and his wife, I sent for them, and also tomes Captain Guy to dine with me, and he and I much talk together. He cries out of the discipline of the fleete, and confesses really that the true English valour we talk of is almost spent and worn out; few of the commanders doing what they should do, and he much fears we shall therefore be beaten the next year. He assures me we were beaten home the last June fight, and that the whole fleete was ashamed to hear of our bonefires. He commends Smith, and cries out of Holmes for an idle, proud, conceited, though stout fellow. He tells me we are to owe the losse of so many ships on the sands, not to any fault of the pilots, but to the weather; but in this I have good authority to fear there was something more. He says the Dutch do fight in very good order, and we in none at all. He says that in the July fight, both the Prince and Holmes had their belly-fulls, and were fain to go aside; though, if the wind had continued, we had utterly beaten them. He do confess the whole to be governed by a company of fools, and fears our ruine. After dinner he gone, I with my brother to White Hall and he to

Westminster Abbey. I presently to Mrs. Martin's, and there met widow Burroughes and Doll, and did tumble them all the afternoon as I pleased, and having given them a bottle of wine I parted and home by boat (my brother going by land), and thence with my wife to sit and sup with my uncle and aunt Wight, and see Woolly's wife, who is a pretty woman, and after supper, being very merry, in abusing my aunt with Dr. Venner, we home, and I to do something in my accounts, and so to bed. The Revenge having her forecastle blown up with powder to the killing of some men in the River, and the Dyamond's being overset in the careening at Sheernesse, are further marks of the method all the King's work is now done in. The Foresight also and another come to disasters in the same place this week in the cleaning; which is strange.

29th. Up, and to the office to do business, and thither comes to me Sir Thomas Teddiman, and he and I walked a good while in the garden together, discoursing of the disorder and discipline of the fleete, wherein he told me how bad every thing is; but was very wary in speaking any thing to the dishonour of the Prince or Duke of Albemarle, but do magnify my Lord Sandwich much before them both, for ability to serve the King, and do heartily wish for him here. For he fears that we shall be undone the next year, but that he will, however, see an end of it. To prevent the necessity of his dining with me I was forced to pretend occasion of going to Westminster, so away I went, and Mr. Barber, the clerk, having a request to make to me to get him into employment, did walk along with me, and by water to Westminster with me, he professing great love to me, and an able clerk he is. When I come thither I find the new Lord Mayor Bolton a-swearing at the Exchequer, with some of the Aldermen and Livery; but, Lord! to see how meanely they now look, who upon this day used to be all little lords, is a sad sight and worthy consideration. And every body did reflect with pity upon the poor City, to which they are now coming to choose and swear their Lord Mayor, compared with what it heretofore was. Thence by coach (having in the Hall bought me a velvet riding cap, cost me 20s.) to my taylor's, and there bespoke a plain vest, and so to my goldsmith to bid him look out for some gold for me; and he tells me that ginnys, which I bought 2,000 of not long ago, and cost me but 18 1/2d. change, will now cost me 22d.; and but very few to be had at any price. However, some more I will have, for they are very convenient, and of easy disposal. So home to dinner and to discourse with my brother upon his translation of my Lord Bacon's "Faber Fortunae," which I gave him to do and he has done it, but meanely; I am not pleased with it at all, having done it only literally, but without any life at all. About five o'clock I took my wife (who is mighty fine, and with a new fair pair of locks, which vex me, though like a foole I helped her the other night to buy them), and to Mrs. Pierces, and there staying a little I away before to White Hall, and into the new playhouse there, the first time I ever was there, and the first play I have seen since before the great plague. By and by Mr. Pierce comes, bringing my wife and his, and Knipp. By and by the King and Queene, Duke and Duchesse, and all the great ladies of the Court; which, indeed, was a fine sight. But the play being "Love in a Tub," a silly play, and though done by the Duke's people, yet having neither Betterton nor his wife, and the whole thing done ill, and being ill also, I had no manner of pleasure in the play. Besides, the House, though very fine, yet bad for the voice, for hearing. The sight of the ladies, indeed, was exceeding noble; and above all, my Lady Castlemayne. The play done by ten o'clock. I carried them all home, and then home myself, and well satisfied with the sight, but not the play, we with great content to bed.

30th. Up, and to the office, where sat all the morning, and at noon home to dinner, and then to the office again, where late, very busy, and dispatching much business. Mr. Hater staying most of the afternoon abroad, he come to me, poor man, to make excuse, and it was that he had been looking out for a little house for his family. His wife being much frightened in the country with the discourses of troubles and disorders like to be, and therefore durst not be from him, and therefore he is forced to bring her to towne that they may be together. This is now the general apprehension of all people; particulars I do not know, but my owne fears are also great, and I do think it time to look out to save something, if a storm should come. At night home to supper, and singing with my wife, who hath lately begun to learn, and I think will come to do something, though her eare is not good, nor I, I confess, have patience enough to teach her, or hear her sing now and then a note out of tune, and am to blame that I cannot bear with that in her which is fit I should do with her as a learner, and one that I desire much could sing, and so should encourage her. This I was troubled at, for I do find that I do put her out of heart, and make her fearfull to sing before me. So after supper to bed.

31st. Out with Sir W. Batten toward White Hall, being in pain in my cods by being squeezed the other night in a little coach when I carried Pierce and his wife and my people. But I hope I shall be soon well again. This day is a great day at the House, so little to do with the Duke of York, but soon parted. Coming out of the Court I met Colonell Atkins, who tells me the whole city rings to-day of Sir Jeremy Smith's killing of Holmes in a duell, at which I was not much displeased, for I fear every day more and more mischief from the man, if he lives; but the thing is not true, for in my coach I did by and by meet Sir Jer. Smith going to Court. So I by coach to my goldsmith, there to see what gold I can get, which is but little, and not under 22d. So away home to dinner, and after dinner to my closett, where I spent the whole afternoon till late at evening of all my accounts publique and private, and to my great satisfaction I do find that I do bring my accounts to a very near balance, notwithstanding all the hurries and troubles I have been put to by the late fire, that I have not been able to even my accounts since July last before; and I bless God I do find that I am worth more than ever I yet was, which is L6,200, for which the Holy Name of God be praised! and my other accounts of Tangier in a very plain and clear condition, that I am not liable to any trouble from them; but in fear great I am, and I perceive the whole city is, of some distractions and disorders among us, which God of his goodness prevent! Late to supper with my wife and brother, and then to bed. And thus ends the month with an ill aspect, the business of the Navy standing wholly still. No credit, no goods sold us, nobody will trust. All we have to do at the office is to hear complaints for want of money. The Duke of York himself for now three weeks seems to rest satisfied that we can do nothing without money, and that all must stand still till the King gets money, which the Parliament have been a great while about; but are so dissatisfied with the King's management, and his giving himself up to pleasures, and not minding the calling to account any of his officers, and they observe so much the expense of the war, and yet that after we have made it the most we can, it do not amount to what they have given the King for the warn that they are backward of giving any more. However, L1,800,000 they have voted, but the way of gathering it has taken up more time than is fit to be now lost: The seamen grow very rude, and every thing out of order; commanders having no power over their seamen, but the seamen do what they please. Few stay on board, but all coming running up hither to towne, and nobody can with justice blame them, we owing them so much money; and their familys must starve if we do not give them money, or they procure upon their tickets from some people that will trust them. A great folly is observed by all people in the King's giving leave to so many merchantmen to go abroad this winter, and some upon voyages where it is impossible they should be back again by the spring, and the rest will be doubtfull, but yet we let them go; what the reason of State is nobody can tell, but all condemn it. The Prince and Duke of Albemarle have got no great credit by this year's service. Our losses both of reputation and ships having been greater than is thought have ever been suffered in all ages put together before; being beat home, and fleeing home the first fight, and then losing so many ships then and since upon the sands, and some falling into the enemy's hands, and not one taken this yeare, but the Ruby, French prize, now at the end of the yeare, by the Frenchmen's mistake in running upon us. Great folly in both Houses of Parliament, several persons falling together by the eares, among others in the House of Lords, the Duke of Buckingham and my Lord Ossory. Such is our case, that every body fears an invasion the next yeare; and for my part, I do methinks foresee great unhappiness coming upon us, and do provide for it by laying by something against a rainy day, dividing what I have, and laying it in several places, but with all faithfulness to the King in all respects; my grief only being that the King do not look after his business himself, and thereby will be undone both himself and his nation, it being not yet, I believe, too late if he would apply himself to it, to save all, and conquer the Dutch; but while he and the Duke of York mind their pleasure, as they do and nothing else, we must be beaten. So late with my mind in good condition of quiet after the settling all my accounts, and to bed.

NOVEMBER 1666

November 1st. Up, and was presented by Burton, one of our smith's wives, with a very noble cake, which I presently resolved to have my wife go with to-day, and some wine, and house-warme my Betty Michell, which she readily resolved to do. So I to the office and sat all the morning, where little to do but answer people about want of money; so that there is little service done the King by us, and great disquiet to ourselves; I am sure there is to me very much, for I do not enjoy myself as I would and should do in my employment if my pains could do the King better service, and with the peace that we used to do it. At noon to dinner, and from dinner my wife and my brother, and W. Hewer and Barker away to Betty Michell's, to Shadwell, and I to my office, where I took in Mrs. Bagwell and did what I would with her, and so she went away, and I all the afternoon till almost night there, and then, my wife being come back, I took her and set her at her brother's, who is very sicke, and I to White Hall, and there all alone a pretty while with Sir W. Coventry at his chamber. I find him very melancholy under the same considerations of the King's service that I am. He confesses with me he expects all will be undone, and all ruined; he complains and sees perfectly what I with grief do, and said it first himself to me that all discipline is lost in the fleete, no order nor no command, and concurs with me that it is necessary we do again and again represent all things more and more plainly to the Duke of York, for a guard to ourselves hereafter when things shall come to be worse. He says the House goes on slowly in finding of money, and that the discontented party do say they have not done with us, for they will have a further bout with us as to our accounts, and they are exceedingly well instructed where to hit us. I left him with a thousand sad reflections upon the times, and the state of the King's matters, and so away, and took up my wife and home, where a little at the office, and then home to supper, and talk with my wife (with whom I have much comfort) and my brother, and so to bed.

2nd. Up betimes, and with Sir W. Batten to Woolwich, where first we went on board the Ruby, French prize, the only ship of war we have taken from any of our enemies this year. It seems a very good ship, but with galleries quite round the sterne to walk in as a balcone, which will be taken down. She had also about forty good brass guns, but will make little amends to our loss in The Prince. Thence to the Ropeyarde and the other yards to do several businesses, he and I also did buy some apples and pork; by the same token the butcher commended it as the best in England for cloath and colour. And for his beef, says he, "Look how fat it is; the lean appears only here and there a speck, like beauty-spots." Having done at Woolwich, we to Deptford (it being very cold upon the water), and there did also a little more business, and so home, I reading all the why to make end of the "Bondman" (which the oftener I read the more I like), and begun "The Duchesse of Malfy;" which seems a good play. At home to dinner, and there come Mr. Pierce, surgeon, to see me, and after I had eat something, he and I and my wife by coach to Westminster, she set us down at White Hall, and she to her brother's. I up into the House, and among other things walked a good while with the Serjeant Trumpet, who tells me, as I wished, that the King's Italian here is about setting three parts for trumpets, and shall teach some to sound them, and believes they will be admirable musique. I also walked with Sir Stephen Fox an houre, and good discourse of publique business with him, who seems very much satisfied with my discourse, and desired more of my acquaintance. Then comes out the King and Duke of York from the Council, and so I spoke awhile to Sir W. Coventry about some office business, and so called my wife (her brother being now a little better than he was), and so home, and I to my chamber to do some business, and then to supper and to bed.

3rd. This morning comes Mr. Lovett, and brings me my print of the Passion, varnished by him, and the frame black, which indeed is very fine, though not so fine as I expected; however, pleases me exceedingly. This, and the sheets of paper he prepared for me, come to L3, which I did give him, and though it be more than is fit to lay out on pleasure, yet, it being ingenious, I did not think much of it. He gone, I to the office, where all the morning to little purpose, nothing being before us but clamours for money: So at noon home to dinner, and after dinner to hang up my new varnished picture and set my chamber in order to be made clean, and then to; the office again, and there all the afternoon till late at night, and so to supper and to bed.

4th (Lord's day). Comes my taylor's man in the morning, and brings my vest home, and coate to wear with it, and belt, and silver-hilted sword. So I rose and dressed myself, and I like myself mightily in it, and so do my wife. Then, being dressed, to church; and after church pulled my Lady Pen and Mrs. Markham into my house to dinner, and Sir J. Minnes he got Mrs. Pegg along with him. I had a good dinner for them, and very merry; and after dinner to the waterside, and so, it being very cold, to White Hall, and was mighty fearfull of an ague, my vest being new and thin, and the coat cut not to meet before upon my breast. Here I waited in the gallery till the Council was up, and among others did speak with Mr. Cooling, my Lord Chamberlain's secretary, who tells me my Lord Generall is become mighty low in all people's opinion, and that he hath received several slurs from the King and Duke of York. The people at Court do see the difference between his and the Prince's management, and my Lord Sandwich's. That this business which he is put upon of crying out against the Catholiques and turning them out of all employment, will undo him, when he comes to turn-out the officers out of the Army, and this is a thing of his own seeking. That he is grown a drunken sot, and drinks with nobody but Troutbecke, whom nobody else will keep company with. Of whom he told me this story: That once the Duke of Albemarle in his drink taking notice as of a wonder that Nan Hide should ever come to be Duchesse of York, "Nay," says Troutbecke, "ne'er wonder at that; for if you will give me another bottle of wine, I will tell you as great, if not greater, a miracle." And what was that, but that our dirty Besse (meaning his Duchesse) should come to be Duchesse of Albemarle? Here we parted, and so by and by the Council rose, and out comes Sir G. Carteret and Sir W. Coventry, and they and my Lord Bruncker and I went to Sir G. Carteret's lodgings, there to discourse about some money demanded by Sir W. Warren, and having done that broke up. And Sir G. Carteret and I alone together a while, where he shows a long letter, all in cipher, from my Lord Sandwich to him. The contents he hath not yet found out, but he tells me that my Lord is not sent for home, as several people have enquired after of me. He spoke something reflecting upon me in the business of pursers, that their present bad behaviour is what he did foresee, and had convinced me of, and yet when it come last year to be argued before the Duke of York I turned and said as the rest did. I answered nothing to it, but let it go, and so to other discourse of the ill state of things, of which all people are full of sorrow and observation, and so parted, and then by water, landing in Southwarke, home to the Tower, and so home, and there began to read "Potter's Discourse upon 1666," which pleases me mightily, and then broke off and to supper and to bed.

5th (A holyday). Lay long; then up, and to the office, where vexed to meet with people come from the fleete at the Nore, where so many ships are laid up and few going abroad, and yet Sir Thomas Allen hath sent up some Lieutenants with warrants to presse men for a few ships to go out this winter, while every day thousands appear here, to our great trouble and affright, before our office and the ticket office, and no Captains able to command one-man aboard. Thence by water to Westminster, and there at the Swan find Sarah is married to a shoemaker yesterday, so I could not see her, but I believe I shall hereafter at good leisure. Thence by coach to my Lady Peterborough, and there spoke with my Lady, who had sent to speak with me. She makes mighty moan of the badness of the times, and her family as to money. My Lord's passionateness for want thereof, and his want of coming in of rents, and no wages from the Duke of York. No money to be had there for wages nor disbursements, and therefore prays my assistance about his pension. I was moved with her story, which she largely and handsomely told me, and promised I would try what I could do in a few days, and so took leave, being willing to keep her Lord fair with me, both for his respect to my Lord Sandwich and for my owne sake hereafter, when I come to pass my accounts. Thence to my Lord Crew's, and there dined, and mightily made of, having not, to my shame, been there in 8 months before. Here my Lord and Sir Thomas Crew, Mr. John, and Dr. Crew, and two strangers. The best family in the world for goodness and sobriety. Here beyond my expectation I met my Lord Hinchingbroke, who is come to towne two days since from Hinchingbroke, and brought his sister and brother Carteret with him, who are at Sir G. Carteret's. After dinner I and Sir Thomas Crew went aside to discourse of public matters, and do find by him that all the country gentlemen are publickly jealous of the courtiers in the Parliament, and that they do doubt every thing that they propose; and that the true reason why the country gentlemen are for a land-tax and against a general excise, is, because they are fearful that if the latter be granted they shall never get it down again; whereas the land-tax will be but for so much; and when the war ceases, there will be no ground got by the Court to keep it up. He do much cry out upon our accounts, and that all that they have had from the King hath been but estimates both from my Lord Treasurer and us, and from all people else, so that the Parliament is weary of it. He says the House would be very glad to get something against Sir G. Carteret, and will not let their inquiries die till they have got something. He do, from what he hath heard at the Committee for examining the burning of the City, conclude it as a thing certain that it was done by plots; it being proved by many witnesses that endeavours were made in several places to encrease the fire, and that both in City and country it was bragged by several Papists that upon such a day or in such a time we should find the hottest weather that ever was in England, and words of plainer sense. But my Lord Crew was discoursing at table how the judges have determined in the case whether the landlords or the tenants (who are, in their leases, all of them generally tied to maintain and uphold their houses) shall bear the losse of the fire; and they say that tenants should against all casualties of fire beginning either in their owne or in their neighbour's; but, where it is done by an enemy, they are not to do it. And this was by an enemy, there having been one convicted and hanged upon this very score. This is an excellent salvo for the tenants, and for which I am glad, because of my father's house. After dinner and this discourse I took coach, and at the same time find my Lord Hinchingbroke and Mr. John Crew and the Doctor going out to see the ruins of the City; so I took the Doctor into my hackney coach (and he is a very fine sober gentleman), and so through the City. But, Lord! what pretty and sober observations he made of the City and its desolation; till anon we come to my house, and there I took them upon Tower Hill to shew them what houses were pulled down there since the fire; and then to my house, where I treated them with good wine of several sorts, and they took it mighty respectfully, and a fine company of gentlemen they are; but above all I was glad to see my Lord Hinchingbroke drink no wine at all. Here I got them to appoint Wednesday come se'nnight to dine here at my house, and so we broke up and all took coach again, and I carried the Doctor to Chancery Lane, and thence I to White Hall, where I staid walking up and down till night, and then got almost into the play house, having much mind to go and see the play at Court this night; but fearing how I should get home, because of the bonefires and the lateness of the night to get a coach, I did not stay; but having this evening seen my Lady Jemimah, who is come to towne, and looks very well and fat, and heard how Mr. John Pickering is to be married this week, and to a fortune with L5000, and seen a rich necklace of pearle and two pendants of dyamonds, which Sir G. Carteret hath presented her with since her coming to towne, I home by coach, but met not one bonefire through the whole town in going round by the wall, which is strange, and speaks the melancholy disposition of the City at present, while never more was said of, and feared of, and done against the Papists than just at this time. Home, and there find my wife and her people at cards, and I to my chamber, and there late, and so to supper and to bed.

6th. Up, and to the office, where all the morning sitting. At noon home to dinner, and after dinner down alone by water to Deptford, reading "Duchesse of Malfy," the play, which is pretty good, and there did some business, and so up again, and all the evening at the office. At night home, and there find Mr. Batelier, who supped with us, and good company he is, and so after supper to bed.

7th. Up, and with Sir W. Batten to White Hall, where we attended as usual the Duke of York and there was by the folly of Sir W. Batten prevented in obtaining a bargain for Captain Cocke, which would, I think have [been] at this time (during our great want of hempe), both profitable to the King and of good convenience to me; but I matter it not, it being done only by the folly, not any design, of Sir W. Batten's. Thence to Westminster Hall, and, it being fast day, there was no shops open, but meeting with Doll Lane, did go with her to the Rose taverne, and there drank and played with her a good while. She went away, and I staid a good while after, and was seen going out by one of our neighbours near the office and two of the Hall people that I had no mind to have been seen by, but there was no hurt in it nor can be alledged from it. Therefore I am not solicitous in it, but took coach and called at Faythorne's, to buy some prints for my wife to draw by this winter, and here did see my Lady Castlemayne's picture, done by him from Lilly's, in red chalke and other colours, by which he hath cut it in copper to be printed. The picture in chalke is the finest thing I ever saw in my life, I think; and did desire to buy it; but he says he must keep it awhile to correct his copper-plate by, and when that is done he will sell it me. Thence home and find my wife gone out with my brother to see her brother. I to dinner and thence to my chamber to read, and so to the office (it being a fast day and so a holiday), and then to Mrs. Turner's, at her request to speake and advise about Sir Thomas Harvy's coming to lodge there, which I think must be submitted to, and better now than hereafter, when he gets more ground, for I perceive he intends to stay by it, and begins to crow mightily upon his late being at the payment of tickets; but a coxcombe he is and will never be better in the business of the Navy. Thence home, and there find Mr. Batelier come to bring my wife a very fine puppy of his mother's spaniel, a very fine one indeed, which my wife is mighty proud of. He staid and supped with us, and they to cards. I to my chamber to do some business, and then out to them to play and were a little merry, and then to bed. By the Duke of York his discourse to-day in his chamber, they have it at Court, as well as we here, that a fatal day is to be expected shortly, of some great mischiefe to the remainder of this day; whether by the Papists, or what, they are not certain. But the day is disputed; some say next Friday, others a day sooner, others later, and I hope all will prove a foolery. But it is observable how every body's fears are busy at this time.

8th. Up, and before I went to the office I spoke with Mr. Martin for his advice about my proceeding in the business of the private man-of-war, he having heretofore served in one of them, and now I have it in my thoughts to send him purser in ours. After this discourse I to the office, where I sat all the morning, Sir W. Coventry with us, where he hath not been a great while, Sir W. Pen also, newly come from the Nore, where he hath been some time fitting of the ships out. At noon home to dinner and then to the office awhile, and so home for my sword, and there find Mercer come to see her mistresse. I was glad to see her there, and my wife mighty kind also, and for my part, much vexed that the jade is not with us still. Left them together, designing to go abroad to-morrow night to Mrs. Pierces to dance; and so I to Westminster Hall, and there met Mr. Grey, who tells me the House is sitting still (and now it was six o'clock), and likely to sit till midnight; and have proceeded fair to give the King his supply presently; and herein have done more to-day than was hoped for. So to White Hall to Sir W. Coventry, and there would fain have carried Captain Cocke's business for his bargain of hemp, but am defeated and disappointed, and know hardly how to carry myself in it between my interest and desire not to offend Sir W. Coventry. Sir W. Coventry did this night tell me how the business is about Sir J. Minnes; that he is to be a Commissioner, and my Lord Bruncker and Sir W. Pen are to be Controller joyntly, which I am very glad of, and better than if they were either of them alone; and do hope truly that the King's business will be better done thereby, and infinitely better than now it is. Thence by coach home, full of thoughts of the consequence of this alteration in our office, and I think no evil to me. So at my office late, and then home to supper and to bed. Mr. Grey did assure me this night, that he was told this day, by one of the greater Ministers of State in

England, and one of the King's Cabinet, that we had little left to agree on between the Dutch and us towards a peace, but only the place of treaty; which do astonish me to hear, but I am glad of it, for I fear the consequence of the war. But he says that the King, having all the money he is like to have, we shall be sure of a peace in a little time.

9th. Up and to the office, where did a good deale of business, and then at noon to the Exchange and to my little goldsmith's, whose wife is very pretty and modest, that ever I saw any. Upon the 'Change, where I seldom have of late been, I find all people mightily at a losse what to expect, but confusion and fears in every man's head and heart. Whether war or peace, all fear the event will be bad. Thence home and with my brother to dinner, my wife being dressing herself against night; after dinner I to my closett all the afternoon, till the porter brought my vest back from the taylor's, and then to dress myself very fine, about 4 or 5 o'clock, and by that time comes Mr. Batelier and Mercer, and away by coach to Mrs. Pierces, by appointment, where we find good company: a fair lady, my Lady Prettyman, Mrs. Corbet, Knipp; and for men, Captain Downing, Mr. Lloyd, Sir W. Coventry's clerk, and one Mr. Tripp, who dances well. After some trifling discourse, we to dancing, and very good sport, and mightily pleased I was with the company. After our first bout of dancing, Knipp and I to sing, and Mercer and Captain Downing (who loves and understands musique) would by all means have my song of "Beauty, retire." which Knipp had spread abroad; and he extols it above any thing he ever heard, and, without flattery, I know it is good in its kind. This being done and going to dance again, comes news that White Hall was on fire; and presently more particulars, that the Horse-guard was on fire;

and so we run up to the garret, and find it so; a horrid great fire; and by and by we saw and heard part of it blown up with powder. The ladies begun presently to be afeard: one fell into fits. The whole town in an alarme. Drums beat and trumpets, and the guards every where spread, running up and down in the street. And I begun to have mighty apprehensions how things might be at home, and so was in mighty pain to get home, and that that encreased all is that we are in expectation, from common fame, this night, or to-morrow, to have a massacre, by the having so many fires one after another, as that in the City, and at same time begun in Westminster, by the Palace, but put out; and since in Southwarke, to the burning down some houses; and now this do make all people conclude there is something extraordinary in it; but nobody knows what. By and by comes news that the fire has slackened; so then we were a little cheered up again, and to supper, and pretty merry. But, above all, there comes in the dumb boy that I knew in Oliver's time, who is mightily acquainted here, and with Downing; and he made strange signs of the fire, and how the King was abroad, and many things they understood, but I could not, which I wondering at, and discoursing with Downing about it, "Why," says he, "it is only a little use, and you will understand him, and make him understand you with as much ease as may be." So I prayed him to tell him that I was afeard that my coach would be gone, and that he should go down and steal one of the seats out of the coach and keep it, and that would make the coachman to stay. He did this, so that the dumb boy did go down, and, like a cunning rogue, went into the coach, pretending to sleep; and, by and by, fell to his work, but finds the seats nailed to the coach. So he did all he could, but could not do it; however, stayed there, and stayed the coach till the coachman's patience was quite spent, and beat the dumb boy by force, and so went away. So the dumb boy come up and told him all the story, which they below did see all that passed, and knew it to be true. After supper, another dance or two, and then newes that the fire is as great as ever, which put us all to our wit's-end; and I mightily [anxious] to go home, but the coach being gone, and it being about ten at night, and rainy dirty weather, I knew not what to do; but to walk out with Mr. Batelier, myself resolving to go home on foot, and leave the women there. And so did; but at the Savoy got a coach, and come back and took up the women; and so, having, by people come from the fire, understood that the fire was overcome, and all well, we merrily parted, and home. Stopped by several guards and constables quite through the town, round the wall, as we went, all being in armes. We got well home .... Being come home, we to cards, till two in the morning, and drinking lamb's-wool.

So to bed.

10th. Up and to the office, where Sir W. Coventry come to tell us that the Parliament did fall foul of our accounts again yesterday; and we must arme to have them examined, which I am sorry for: it will bring great trouble to me, and shame upon the office. My head full this morning how to carry on Captain Cocke's bargain of hemp, which I think I shall by my dexterity do, and to the King's advantage as well as my own. At noon with my Lord Bruncker and Sir Thomas Harvy, to Cocke's house, and there Mrs. Williams and other company, and an excellent dinner. Mr. Temple's wife; after dinner, fell to play on the harpsicon, till she tired everybody, that I left the house without taking leave, and no creature left standing by her to hear her. Thence I home and to the office, where late doing of business, and then home. Read an hour, to make an end of Potter's Discourse of the Number 666, which I like all along, but his close is most excellent; and, whether it be right or wrong, is mighty ingenious. Then to supper and to bed. This is the fatal day that every body hath discoursed for a long time to be the day that the Papists, or I know not who, had designed to commit a massacre upon; but, however, I trust in God we shall rise to-morrow morning as well as ever. This afternoon Creed comes to me, and by him, as, also my Lady Pen, I hear that my Lady Denham is exceeding sick, even to death, and that she says, and every body else discourses, that she is poysoned; and Creed tells me, that it is said that there hath been a design to poison the King. What the meaning of all these sad signs is, the Lord knows; but every day things look worse and worse. God fit us for the worst!

11th (Lord's day). Up, and to church, myself and wife, where the old dunce Meriton, brother to the known Meriton; of St. Martin's, Westminster, did make a very good sermon, beyond my expectation. Home to dinner, and we carried in Pegg Pen, and there also come to us little Michell and his wife, and dined very pleasantly. Anon to church, my wife and I and Betty Michell, her husband being gone to Westminster.... Alter church home, and I to my chamber, and there did finish the putting time to my song of "It is decreed," and do please myself at last and think it will be thought a good song. By and by little Michell comes and takes away his wife home, and my wife and brother and I to my uncle Wight's, where my aunt is grown so ugly and their entertainment so bad that I am in pain to be there; nor will go thither again a good while, if sent for, for we were sent for to-night, we had not gone else. Wooly's wife, a silly woman, and not very handsome, but no spirit in her at all; and their discourse mean, and the fear of the troubles of the times hath made them not to bring their plate to town, since it was carried out upon the business of the fire, so that they drink in earth and a wooden can, which I do not like. So home, and my people to bed. I late to finish my song, and then to bed also, and the business of the firing of the city, and the fears we have of new troubles and violences, and the fear of fire among ourselves, did keep me awake a good while, considering the sad condition I and my family should be in. So at last to sleep.

12th. Lay long in bed, and then up, and Mr. Carcasse brought me near 500 tickets to sign, which I did, and by discourse find him a cunning, confident, shrewd man, but one that I do doubt hath by his discourse of the ill will he hath got with my Lord Marquess of Dorchester (with whom he lived), he hath had cunning practices in his time, and would not now spare to use the same to his profit. That done I to the office; whither by and by comes Creed to me, and he and I walked in the garden a little, talking of the present ill condition of things, which is the common subject of all men's discourse and fears now-a-days, and particularly of my Lady Denham, whom everybody says is poisoned, and he tells me she hath said it to the Duke of York; but is upon the mending hand, though the town says she is dead this morning. He and I to the 'Change. There I had several little errands, and going to Sir R. Viner's, I did get such a splash and spots of dirt upon my new vest, that I was out of countenance to be seen in the street. This day I received 450 pieces of gold more of Mr. Stokes, but cost me 22 1/2d. change; but I am well contented with it,—I having now near L2800 in gold, and will not rest till I get full L3000, and then will venture my fortune for the saving that and the rest. Home to dinner, though Sir R. Viner would have staid us to dine with him, he being sheriffe; but, poor man, was so out of countenance that he had no wine ready to drink to us, his butler being out of the way, though we know him to be a very liberal man. And after dinner I took my wife out, intending to have gone and have seen my Lady Jemimah, at White Hall, but so great a stop there was at the New Exchange, that we could not pass in half an houre, and therefore 'light and bought a little matter at the Exchange, and then home, and then at the office awhile, and then home to my chamber, and after my wife and all the mayds abed but Jane, whom I put confidence in—she and I, and my brother, and Tom, and W. Hewer, did bring up all the remainder of my money, and my plate-chest, out of the cellar, and placed the money in my study, with the rest, and the plate in my dressing-room; but indeed I am in great pain to think how to dispose of my money, it being wholly unsafe to keep it all in coin in one place. 'But now I have it all at my hand, I shall remember it better to think of disposing of it. This done, by one in the morning to bed. This afternoon going towards Westminster, Creed and I did stop, the Duke of York being just going away from seeing of it, at Paul's, and in the Convocation House Yard did there see the body of Robert Braybrooke, Bishop of London, that died 1404: He fell down in his tomb out of the great church into St. Fayth's this late fire, and is here seen his skeleton with the flesh on; but all tough and dry like a spongy dry leather, or touchwood all upon his bones. His head turned aside. A great man in his time, and Lord Chancellor; and his skeletons now exposed to be handled and derided by some, though admired for its duration by others. Many flocking to see it.

13th. At the office all the morning, at noon home to dinner, and out to Bishopsgate Street, and there bought some drinking-glasses, a case of knives, and other things, against tomorrow, in expectation of my Lord Hinchingbroke's coming to dine with me. So home, and having set some things in the way of doing, also against to-morrow, I to my office, there to dispatch business, and do here receive notice from my Lord Hinchingbroke that he is not well, and so not in condition to come to dine with me to-morrow, which I am not in much trouble for, because of the disorder my house is in, by the bricklayers coming to mend the chimney in my dining-room for smoking, which they were upon almost till midnight, and have now made it very pretty, and do carry smoke exceeding well. This evening come all the Houblons to me, to invite me to sup with them to-morrow night. I did take them home, and there we sat and talked a good while, and a glass of wine, and then parted till to-morrow night. So at night, well satisfied in the alteration of my chimney, to bed.

14th. Up, and by water to White Hall, and thence to Westminster, where I bought several things, as a hone, ribbon, gloves, books, and then took coach and to Knipp's lodging, whom I find not ready to go home with me. So I away to do a little business, among others to call upon Mr. Osborne for my Tangier warrant for the last quarter, and so to the Exchange for some things for my wife, and then to Knipp's again, and there staid reading of Waller's verses, while she finished dressing, her husband being by. I had no other pastime. Her lodging very mean, and the condition she lives in; yet makes a shew without doors, God bless us! I carried him along with us into the City, and set him down in Bishopsgate Street, and then home with her. She tells me how Smith, of the Duke's house, hath killed a man upon a quarrel in play; which makes every body sorry, he being a good actor, and, they say, a good man, however this happens. The ladies of the Court do much bemoan him, she says. Here she and we alone at dinner to some good victuals, that we could not put off, that was intended for the great dinner of my Lord Hinchingbroke's, if he had come. After dinner I to teach her my new recitative of "It is decreed," of which she learnt a good part, and I do well like it and believe shall be well pleased when she hath it all, and that it will be found an agreeable thing. Then carried her home, and my wife and I intended to have seen my Lady Jemimah at White Hall, but the Exchange Streete was so full of coaches, every body, as they say, going thither to make themselves fine against tomorrow night, that, after half an hour's stay, we could not do any [thing], only my wife to see her brother, and I to go speak one word with Sir G. Carteret about office business, and talk of the general complexion of matters, which he looks upon, as I do, with horrour, and gives us all for an undone people. That there is no such thing as a peace in hand, nor possibility of any without our begging it, they being as high, or higher, in their terms than ever, and tells me that, just now, my Lord Hollis had been with him, and wept to think in what a condition we are fallen. He shewed me my Lord Sandwich's letter to him, complaining of the lack of money, which Sir G. Carteret is at a loss how in the world to get the King to supply him with, and wishes him, for that reason, here; for that he fears he will be brought to disgrace there, for want of supplies. He says the House is yet in a bad humour; and desiring to know whence it is that the King stirs not, he says he minds it not, nor will be brought to it, and that his servants of the House do, instead of making the

Parliament better, rather play the rogue one with another, and will put all in fire. So that, upon the whole, we are in a wretched condition, and I went from him in full apprehensions of it. So took up my wife, her brother being yet very bad, and doubtful whether he will recover or no, and so to St. Ellen's [St. Helen's], and there sent my wife home, and myself to the Pope's Head, where all the Houblons were, and Dr. Croone,

and by and by to an exceeding pretty supper, excellent discourse of all sorts, and indeed [they] are a set of the finest gentlemen that ever I met withal in my life. Here Dr. Croone told me, that, at the meeting at Gresham College to-night, which, it seems, they now have every Wednesday again, there was a pretty experiment of the blood of one dogg let out, till he died, into the body of another on one side, while all his own run out on the other side.

The first died upon the place, and the other very well, and likely to do well. This did give occasion to many pretty wishes, as of the blood of a Quaker to be let into an Archbishop, and such like; but, as Dr. Croone says, may, if it takes, be of mighty use to man's health, for the amending of bad blood by borrowing from a better body. After supper, James Houblon and another brother took me aside and to talk of some businesses of their owne, where I am to serve them, and will, and then to talk of publique matters, and I do find that they and all merchants else do give over trade and the nation for lost, nothing being done with care or foresight, no convoys granted, nor any thing done to satisfaction; but do think that the Dutch and French will master us the next yeare, do what we can: and so do I, unless necessity makes the King to mind his business, which might yet save all. Here we sat talking till past one in the morning, and then home, where my people sat up for me, my wife and all, and so to bed.

15th. This [morning] come Mr. Shepley (newly out of the country) to see me; after a little discourse with him, I to the office, where we sat all the morning, and at noon home, and there dined, Shepley with me, and after dinner I did pay him L70, which he had paid my father for my use in the country. He being gone, I took coach and to Mrs. Pierce's, where I find her as fine as possible, and himself going to the ball at night at Court, it being the Queen's birth-day, and so I carried them in my coach, and having set them into the house, and gotten Mr. Pierce to undertake the carrying in my wife, I to Unthanke's, where she appointed to be, and there told her, and back again about business to White Hall, while Pierce went and fetched her and carried her in. I, after I had met with Sir W. Coventry and given him some account of matters, I also to the ball, and with much ado got up to the loft, where with much trouble I could see very well. Anon the house grew full, and the candles light, and the King and Queen and all the ladies set: and it was, indeed, a glorious sight to see Mrs. Stewart in black and white lace, and her head and shoulders dressed with dyamonds, and the like a great many great ladies more, only the Queen none; and the King in his rich vest of some rich silke and silver trimming, as the Duke of York and all the dancers were, some of cloth of silver, and others of other sorts, exceeding rich. Presently after the King was come in, he took the Queene, and about fourteen more couple there was, and began the Bransles. As many of the men as I can remember presently, were, the King, Duke of York, Prince Rupert, Duke of Monmouth, Duke of Buckingham, Lord Douglas,' Mr. [George] Hamilton, Colonell Russell, Mr. Griffith, Lord Ossory, Lord Rochester; and of the ladies, the

Queene, Duchess of York, Mrs. Stewart, Duchess of Monmouth, Lady Essex Howard, Mrs. Temples Swedes Embassadress, Lady Arlington; Lord George Barkeley's daughter, and many others I remember not; but all most excellently dressed in rich petticoats and gowns, and dyamonds, and pearls. After the Bransles, then to a Corant, and now and then a French dance; but that so rare that the Corants grew tiresome, that I wished it done. Only Mrs. Stewart danced mighty finely, and many French dances, specially one the King called the New Dance, which was very pretty; but upon the whole matter, the business of the dancing of itself was not extraordinary pleasing. But the clothes and sight of the persons was indeed very pleasing, and worth my coming, being never likely to see more gallantry while I live, if I should come twenty times. About twelve at night it broke up, and I to hire a coach with much difficulty, but Pierce had hired a chair for my wife, and so she being gone to his house, he and I, taking up Barker at Unthanke's, to his house, whither his wife was come home a good while ago and gone to bed. So away home with my wife, between displeased with the dull dancing, and satisfied at the clothes and persons. My Lady Castlemayne, without whom all is nothing, being there, very rich, though not dancing. And so after supper, it being very cold, to bed.

16th. Up again betimes to attend the examination of Mr. Gawden's, accounts, where we all met, but I did little but fit myself for the drawing my great letter to the Duke of York of the state of the Navy for want of money. At noon to the 'Change, and thence back to the new taverne come by us; the Three Tuns, where D. Gawden did feast us all with a chine of beef and other good things, and an infinite dish of fowl, but all spoiled in the dressing. This noon I met with Mr. Hooke, and he tells me the dog which was filled with another dog's blood, at the College the other day, is very well, and like to be so as ever, and doubts not its being found of great use to men; and so do Dr. Whistler, who dined with us at the taverne. Thence home in the evening, and I to my preparing my letter, and did go a pretty way in it, staying late upon it, and then home to supper and to bed, the weather being on a sudden set in to be very cold.

17th. Up, and to the office, where all the morning. At noon home to dinner, and in the afternoon shut myself in my chamber, and there till twelve at night finishing my great letter to the Duke of York, which do lay the ill condition of the Navy so open to him, that it is impossible if the King and he minds any thing of their business, but it will operate upon them to set all matters right, and get money to carry on the war, before it be too late, or else lay out for a peace upon any termes. It was a great convenience to-night that what I had writ foule in short hand, I could read to W. Hewer, and he take it fair in short hand, so as I can read it to-morrow to Sir W. Coventry, and then come home, and Hewer read it to me while I take it in long-hand to present, which saves me much time. So to bed.

18th (Lord's day). Up by candle-light and on foote to White Hall, where by appointment I met Lord Bruncker at Sir W. Coventry's chamber, and there I read over my great letter, and they approved it: and as I do do our business in defence of the Board, so I think it is as good a letter in the manner, and believe it is the worst in the matter of it, as ever come from any office to a Prince. Back home in my Lord Bruncker's coach, and there W. Hewer and I to write it over fair; dined at noon, and Mercer with us, and mighty merry, and then to finish my letter; and it being three o'clock ere we had done, when I come to Sir W. Batten; he was in a huffe, which I made light of, but he signed the letter, though he would not go, and liked the letter well. Sir W. Pen, it seems, he would not stay for it: so, making slight of Sir W. Pen's putting so much weight upon his hand to Sir W. Batten, I down to the Tower Wharf, and there got a sculler, and to White Hall, and there met Lord Bruncker, and he signed it, and so I delivered it to Mr. Cheving,

and he to Sir W. Coventry, in the cabinet, the King and councill being sitting, where I leave it to its fortune, and I by water home again, and to my chamber, to even my Journall; and then comes Captain Cocke to me, and he and I a great deal of melancholy discourse of the times, giving all over for gone, though now the Parliament will soon finish the Bill for money. But we fear, if we had it, as matters are now managed, we shall never make the best of it, but consume it all to no purpose or a bad one. He being gone, I again to my Journall and finished it, and so to supper and to bed.

19th. Lay pretty long in bed talking with pleasure with my wife, and then up and all the morning at my own chamber fitting some Tangier matters against the afternoon for a meeting. This morning also came Mr. Caesar, and I heard him on the lute very finely, and my boy begins to play well. After dinner I carried and set my wife down at her brother's, and then to Barkeshire-house, where my Lord Chancellor hath been ever since the fire, but he is not come home yet, so I to Westminster Hall, where the Lords newly up and the Commons still sitting. Here I met with Mr. Robinson, who did give me a printed paper wherein he states his pretence to the post office, and intends to petition the Parliament in it. Thence I to the Bull-head tavern, where I have not been since Mr. Chetwind and the time of our club, and here had six bottles of claret filled, and I sent them to Mrs. Martin, whom I had promised some of my owne, and, having none of my owne, sent her this. Thence to my Lord Chancellor's, and there Mr. Creed and Gawden, Cholmley, and Sir G. Carteret walking in the Park over against the house. I walked with Sir G. Carteret, who I find displeased with the letter I have drawn and sent in yesterday, finding fault with the account we give of the ill state of the Navy, but I said little, only will justify the truth of it. Here we walked to and again till one dropped away after another, and so I took coach to White Hall, and there visited my Lady Jemimah, at Sir G. Carteret's lodgings. Here was Sir Thomas Crew, and he told me how hot words grew again to-day in the House of Lords between my Lord Ossory and Ashly, the former saying that something said by the other was said like one of Oliver's Council. Ashly said that he must give him reparation, or he would take it his owne way. The House therefore did bring my Lord Ossory to confess his fault, and ask pardon for it, as he was also to my Lord Buckingham, for saying that something was not truth that my Lord Buckingham had said. This will render my Lord Ossory very little in a little time. By and by away, and calling my wife went home, and then a little at Sir W. Batten's to hear news, but nothing, and then home to supper, whither Captain Cocke, half foxed, come and sat with us, and so away, and then we to bed.

20th. Called up by Mr. Sheply, who is going into the country to-day to Hinchingbroke, I sent my service to my Lady, and in general for newes: that the world do think well of my Lord, and do wish he were here again, but that the publique matters of the State as to the war are in the worst condition that is possible. By and by Sir W. Warren, and with him half an hour discoursing of several businesses, and some I hope will bring me a little profit. He gone, and Sheply, I to the office a little, and then to church, it being thanksgiving-day for the cessation of the plague; but, Lord! how the towne do say that it is hastened before the plague is quite over, there dying some people still,

but only to get ground for plays to be publickly acted, which the Bishops would not suffer till the plague was over; and one would thinke so, by the suddenness of the notice given of the day, which was last Sunday, and the little ceremony. The sermon being dull of Mr. Minnes, and people with great indifferency come to hear him. After church home, where I met Mr. Gregory, who I did then agree with to come to teach my wife to play on the Viall, and he being an able and sober man, I am mightily glad of it. He had dined, therefore went away, and I to dinner, and after dinner by coach to Barkeshire-house, and there did get a very great meeting; the Duke of York being there, and much business done, though not in proportion to the greatness of the business, and my Lord Chancellor sleeping and snoring the greater part of the time. Among other things I declared the state of our credit as to tallys to raise money by, and there was an order for payment of L5000 to Mr. Gawden, out of which I hope to get something against Christmas. Here we sat late, and here I did hear that there are some troubles like to be in Scotland, there being a discontented party already risen, that have seized on the Governor of Dumfreeze and imprisoned him,

but the story is yet very uncertain, and therefore I set no great weight on it. I home by Mr. Gawden in his coach, and so with great pleasure to spend the evening at home upon my Lyra Viall, and then to supper and to bed. With mighty peace of mind and a hearty desire that I had but what I have quietly in the country, but, I fear, I do at this day see the best that either I or the rest of our nation will ever see.

21st. Up, with Sir W. Batten to Charing Cross, and thence I to wait on Sir Philip Howard, whom I find dressing himself in his night-gown and turban like a Turke, but one of the finest persons that ever I saw in my life. He had several gentlemen of his owne waiting on him, and one playing finely on the gittar: he discourses as well as ever I heard man, in few words and handsome. He expressed all kindness to Balty, when I told him how sick he is: he says that, before he comes to be mustered again, he must bring a certificate of his swearing the oaths of Allegiance and Supremacy, and having taken the Sacrament according to the rites of the Church of England. This, I perceive, is imposed on all, and he will be ready to do. I pray God he may have his health again to be able to do it. Being mightily satisfied with his civility, I away to Westminster Hall, and there walked with several people, and all the discourse is about some trouble in Scotland I heard of yesterday, but nobody can tell the truth of it. Here was Betty Michell with her mother. I would have carried her home, but her father intends to go with her, so I lost my hopes. And thence I to the Excise Office about some tallies, and then to the Exchange, where I did much business, and so home to dinner, and then to the office, where busy all the afternoon till night, and then home to supper, and after supper an hour reading to my wife and brother something in Chaucer with great pleasure, and so to bed.

22nd. Up, and to the office, where we sat all the morning, and my Lord Bruncker did show me Hollar's new print of the City, with a pretty representation of that part which is burnt, very fine indeed; and tells me that he was yesterday sworn the King's servant, and that the King hath commanded him to go on with his great map of the City, which he was upon before the City was burned, like Gombout of Paris, which I am glad of. At noon home to dinner, where my wife and I fell out, I being displeased with her cutting away a lace handkercher sewed about the neck down to her breasts almost, out of a belief, but without reason, that it is the fashion. Here we did give one another the lie too much, but were presently friends, and then I to my office, where very late and did much business, and then home, and there find Mr. Batelier, and did sup and play at cards awhile. But he tells me the newes how the King of France hath, in defiance to the King of England, caused all his footmen to be put into vests, and that the noblemen of France will do the like; which, if true, is the greatest indignity ever done by one Prince to another, and would incite a stone to be revenged; and I hope our King will, if it be so, as he tells me it is:

being told by one that come over from Paris with my Lady Fanshaw, who is come over with the dead body of her husband, and that saw it before he come away. This makes me mighty merry, it being an ingenious kind of affront; but yet it makes me angry, to see that the King of England is become so little as to have the affront offered him. So I left my people at cards, and so to my chamber to read, and then to bed. Batelier did bring us some oysters to-night, and some bottles of new French wine of this year, mighty good, but I drank but little. This noon Bagwell's wife was with me at the office, and I did what I would, and at night comes Mrs. Burroughs, and appointed to meet upon the next holyday and go abroad together.

23rd. Up, and with Sir J. Minnes to White Hall, where we and the rest attended the Duke of York, where, among other things, we had a complaint of Sir William Jennings against his lieutenant, Le Neve, one that had been long the Duke's page, and for whom the Duke of York hath great kindness. It was a drunken quarrel, where one was as blameable as the other. It was referred to further examination, but the Duke of York declared, that as he would not favour disobedience, so neither drunkenness, and therein he said very well. Thence with Sir W. Coventry to Westminster Hall, and there parted, he having told me how Sir J. Minnes do disagree from the proposition of resigning his place, and that so the whole matter is again at a stand, at which I am sorry for the King's sake, but glad that Sir W. Pen is again defeated, for I would not have him come to be Comptroller if I could help it, he will be so cruel proud. Here I spoke with Sir G. Downing about our prisoners in Holland, and their being released; which he is concerned in, and most of them are. Then, discoursing of matters of the House of Parliament, he tells me that it is not the fault of the House, but the King's own party, that have hindered the passing of the Bill for money, by their popping in of new projects for raising it: which is a strange thing; and mighty confident he is, that what money is raised, will be raised and put into the same form that the last was, to come into the Exchequer; and, for aught I see, I must confess I think it is the best way. Thence down to the Hall, and there walked awhile, and all the talk is about Scotland, what news thence; but there is nothing come since the first report, and so all is given over for nothing. Thence home, and after dinner to my chamber with Creed, who come and dined with me, and he and I to reckon for his salary, and by and by comes in Colonel Atkins, and I did the like with him, and it was Creed's design to bring him only for his own ends, to seem to do him a courtesy, and it is no great matter. The fellow I hate, and so I think all the world else do. Then to talk of my report I am to make of the state of our wants of money to the Lord Treasurer, but our discourse come to little. However, in the evening, to be rid of him, I took coach and saw him to the Temple and there 'light, and he being gone, with all the haste back again and to my chamber late to enter all this day's matters of account, and to draw up my report to my Lord Treasurer, and so to bed. At the Temple I called at Playford's, and there find that his new impression of his ketches

are not yet out, the fire having hindered it, but his man tells me that it will be a very fine piece, many things new being added to it.

24th. Up, and to the office, where we sat all the morning. At noon rose and to my closet, and finished my report to my Lord Treasurer of our Tangier wants, and then with Sir J. Minnes by coach to Stepney to the Trinity House, where it is kept again now since the burning of their other house in London. And here a great many met at Sir Thomas Allen's feast, of his being made an Elder Brother; but he is sick, and so could not be there. Here was much good company, and very merry; but the discourse of Scotland, it seems, is confirmed, and that they are 4000 of them in armes, and do declare for King and Covenant, which is very ill news. I pray God deliver us from the ill consequences we may justly fear from it. Here was a good venison pasty or two and other good victuals; but towards the latter end of the dinner I rose, and without taking leave went away from the table, and got Sir J. Minnes' coach and away home, and thence with my report to my Lord Treasurer's, where I did deliver it to Sir Philip Warwicke for my Lord, who was busy, my report for him to consider against to-morrow's council. Sir Philip Warwicke, I find, is full of trouble in his mind to see how things go, and what our wants are; and so I have no delight to trouble him with discourse, though I honour the man with all my heart, and I think him to be a very able and right honest man. So away home again, and there to my office to write my letters very late, and then home to supper, and then to read the late printed discourse of witches by a member of Gresham College, and then to bed; the discourse being well writ, in good stile, but methinks not very convincing. This day Mr. Martin is come to tell me his wife is brought to bed of a girle, and I promised to christen it next Sunday.

25th (Lord's day). Up, and with Sir J. Minnes by coach to White Hall, and there coming late, I to rights to the chapel, where in my usual place I heard one of the King's chaplains, one Mr. Floyd, preach. He was out two or three times in his prayer, and as many in his sermon, but yet he made a most excellent good sermon, of our duty to imitate the lives and practice of Christ and the saints departed, and did it very handsomely and excellent stile; but was a little overlarge in magnifying the graces of the nobility and prelates, that we have seen in our memorys in the world, whom God hath taken from us. At the end of the sermon an excellent anthem; but it was a pleasant thing, an idle companion in our pew, a prating, bold counsellor that hath been heretofore at the Navy Office, and noted for a great eater and drinker, not for quantity, but of the best, his name Tom Bales, said, "I know a fitter anthem for this sermon," speaking only of our duty of

following the saints, and I know not what. "Cooke should have sung, 'Come, follow, follow me.'"
I After sermon up into the gallery, and then to Sir G. Carteret's to dinner; where much company. Among others, Mr. Carteret and my Lady Jemimah, and here was also Mr. [John] Ashburnham, the great man, who is a pleasant man, and that hath seen much of the world, and more of the Court. After dinner Sir G. Carteret and I to another room, and he tells me more and more of our want of money and in how ill condition we are likely to be soon in, and that he believes we shall not have a fleete at sea the next year. So do I believe; but he seems to speak it as a thing expected by the King and as if their matters were laid accordingly. Thence into the Court and there delivered copies of my report to my Lord Treasurer, to the Duke of York, Sir W. Coventry, and others, and attended there till the Council met, and then was called in, and I read my letter. My Lord Treasurer declared that the King had nothing to give till the Parliament did give him some money. So the King did of himself bid me to declare to all that would take our tallys for payment, that he should, soon as the Parliament's money do come in, take back their tallys, and give them money: which I giving him occasion to repeat to me, it coming from him against the 'gre'

I perceive, of my Lord Treasurer, I was content therewith, and went out, and glad that I have got so much. Here staid till the Council rose, walking in the gallery. All the talke being of Scotland, where the highest report, I perceive, runs but upon three or four hundred in armes; but they believe that it will grow more, and do seem to apprehend it much, as if the King of France had a hand in it. My Lord Lauderdale do make nothing of it, it seems, and people do censure him for it, he from the beginning saying that there was nothing in it, whereas it do appear to be a pure rebellion; but no persons of quality being in it, all do hope that it cannot amount to much. Here I saw Mrs. Stewart this afternoon, methought the beautifullest creature that ever I saw in my life, more than ever I thought her so, often as I have seen her; and I begin to think do exceed my Lady Castlemayne, at least now. This being St. Catherine's day, the Queene was at masse by seven o'clock this morning; and. Mr. Ashburnham do say that he never saw any one have so much zeale in his life as she hath: and, the question being asked by my Lady Carteret, much beyond the bigotry that ever the old Queen-mother had. I spoke with Mr. Maya who tells me that the design of building the City do go on apace, and by his description it will be mighty handsome, and to the satisfaction of the people; but I pray God it come not out too late. The Council up, after speaking with Sir W. Coventry a little, away home with Captain Cocke in his coach, discourse about the forming of his contract he made with us lately for hempe, and so home, where we parted, and I find my uncle Wight and Mrs. Wight and Woolly, who staid and supped, and mighty merry together, and then I to my chamber to even my journal, and then to bed. I will remember that Mr. Ashburnham to-day at dinner told how the rich fortune Mrs. Mallett reports of her servants; that my Lord Herbert would have had her; my Lord Hinchingbroke was indifferent to have her;

my Lord John Butler might not have her; my Lord of Rochester would have forced her; and Sir————Popham, who nevertheless is likely to have her, would kiss her breach to have her.

26th. Up, and to my chamber to do some business. Then to speak with several people, among others with Mrs. Burroughs, whom I appointed to meet me at the New Exchange in the afternoon. I by water to Westminster, and there to enquire after my tallies, which I shall get this week. Thence to the Swan, having sent for some burnt claret, and there by and by comes Doll Lane, and she and I sat and drank and talked a great while, among other things about her sister's being brought to bed, and I to be godfather to the girle. I did tumble Doll, and do almost what I would with her, and so parted, and I took coach, and to the New Exchange, buying a neat's tongue by the way, thinking to eat it out of town, but there I find Burroughs in company of an old woman, an aunt of hers, whom she could not leave for half an hour. So after buying a few baubles to while away time, I down to Westminster, and there into the House of Parliament, where, at a great Committee, I did hear, as long as I would, the great case against my Lord Mordaunt, for some arbitrary proceedings of his against one Taylor, whom he imprisoned, and did all the violence to imaginable, only to get him to give way to his abusing his daughter. Here was Mr. Sawyer, my old chamber-fellow, a counsel against my Lord; and I am glad to see him in so good play. Here I met, before the committee sat, with my cozen Roger Pepys, the first time I have spoke with him this parliament. He hath promised to come, and bring Madam Turner with him, who is come to towne to see the City, but hath lost all her goods of all kinds in Salisbury Court, Sir William Turner having not endeavoured, in her absence, to save one penny, to dine with me on Friday next, of which I am glad. Roger bids me to help him to some good rich widow; for he is resolved to go, and retire wholly, into the country; for, he says, he is confident we shall be all ruined very speedily, by what he sees in the State, and I am much in his mind. Having staid as long as I thought fit for meeting of Burroughs, I away and to the 'Change again, but there I do not find her now, I having staid too long at the House, and therefore very hungry, having eat nothing to-day. Home, and there to eat presently, and then to the office a little, and to Sir W. Batten, where Sir J. Minnes and Captain Cocke was; but no newes from the North at all to-day; and the newes-book makes the business nothing, but that they are all dispersed. I pray God it may prove so. So home, and, after a little, to my chamber to bed.

27th. Up, and to the office, where we sat all the morning, and here I had a letter from Mr. Brisband on another occasion, which, by the by, intimates my Lord Hinchingbroke's intention to come and dine with me to-morrow. This put me into a great surprise, and therefore endeavoured all I could to hasten over our business at the office, and so home at noon and to dinner, and then away by coach, it being a very foul day, to White Hall, and there at Sir G. Carteret's find my Lord Hinchingbroke, who promises to dine with me to-morrow, and bring Mr. Carteret along with him. Here I staid a little while talking with him and the ladies, and then away to my Lord Crew's, and then did by the by make a visit to my Lord Crew, and had some good discourse with him, he doubting that all will break in pieces in the kingdom; and that the taxes now coming out, which will tax the same man in three or four several capacities, as for lands, office, profession, and money at interest, will be the hardest that ever come out; and do think that we owe it, and the lateness of its being given, wholly to the unpreparedness of the King's own party, to make their demand and choice; for they have obstructed the giving it by land-tax, which had been done long since. Having ended my visit, I spoke to Sir Thomas Crew, to invite him and his brother John to dinner tomorrow, at my house, to meet Lord Hinchingbroke; and so homewards, calling at the cook's, who is to dress it, to bespeak him, and then home, and there set things in order for a very fine dinner, and then to the office, where late very busy and to good purpose as to dispatch of business, and then home. To bed, my people sitting up to get things in order against to-morrow. This evening was brought me what Griffin had, as he says, taken this evening off of the table in the office, a letter sealed and directed to the Principal Officers and Commissioners of the Navy. It is a serious and just libel against our disorder in paying of our money, making ten times more people wait than we have money for, and complaining by name of Sir W. Batten for paying away great sums to particular people, which is true. I was sorry to see this way of reproach taken against us, but more sorry that there is true ground for it.

28th. Up, and with Sir W. Pen to White Hall (setting his lady and daughter down by the way at a mercer's in the Strand, where they are going to lay out some money), where, though it blows hard and rains hard, yet the Duke of York is gone a-hunting. We therefore lost our labour, and so back again, and by hackney coach to secure places to get things ready against dinner, and then home, and did the like there, and to my great satisfaction: and at noon comes my Lord Hinchingbroke, Sir Thomas Crew, Mr. John Crew, Mr. Carteret, and Brisband. I had six noble dishes for them, dressed by a man-cook, and commended, as indeed they deserved, for exceeding well done. We eat with great pleasure, and I enjoyed myself in it with reflections upon the pleasures which I at best can expect, yet not to exceed this; eating in silver plates, and all things mighty rich and handsome about me. A great deal of fine discourse, sitting almost till dark at dinner, and then broke up with great pleasure, especially to myself; and they away, only Mr. Carteret and I to Gresham College, where they meet now weekly again, and here they had good discourse how this late experiment of the dog, which is in perfect good health, may be improved for good uses to men, and other pretty things, and then broke up. Here was Mr. Henry Howard, that will hereafter be Duke of Norfolke, who is admitted this day into the Society, and being a very proud man, and one that values himself upon his family, writes his name, as he do every where, Henry Howard of Norfolke. Thence home and there comes my Lady Pen, Pegg, and Mrs. Turner, and played at cards and supped with us, and were pretty merry, and Pegg with me in my closet a good while, and did suffer me 'a la baiser mouche et toucher ses cosas' upon her breast, wherein I had great pleasure, and so spent the evening and then broke up, and I to bed, my mind mightily pleased with the day's entertainment.

29th. Up, and to the office, where busy all the morning. At noon home to dinner, where I find Balty come out to see us, but looks like death, and I do fear he is in a consumption; he has not been abroad many weeks before, and hath now a well day, and a fit day of the headake in extraordinary torture. After dinner left him and his wife, they having their mother hard by and my wife, and I a wet afternoon to White Hall to have seen my Lady Carteret and Jemimah, but as God would have it they were abroad, and I was well contented at it. So my wife and I to Westminster Hall, where I left her a little, and to the Exchequer, and then presently home again, calling at our man-cooke's for his help to-morrow, but he could not come. So I home to the office, my people all busy to get a good dinner to-morrow again. I late at the office, and all the newes I hear I put into a letter this night to my Lord Bruncker at Chatham, thus:—

Having writ my letter, I home to supper and to bed, the world being mightily troubled at the ill news from Barbadoes, and the consequence of the Scotch business, as little as we do make of it. And to shew how mad we are at home, here, and unfit for any troubles: my Lord St. John did, a day or two since, openly pull a gentleman in Westminster Hall by the nose, one Sir Andrew Henly, while the judges were upon their benches, and the other gentleman did give him a rap over the pate with his cane, of which fray the judges, they say, will make a great matter: men are only sorry the gentle man did proceed to return a blow; for, otherwise, my Lord would have been soundly fined for the affront, and may be yet for his affront to the judges.

30th. Up, and with Sir W. Batten to White Hall, and there we did attend the Duke of York, and had much business with him; and pretty to see, it being St. Andrew's day, how some few did wear St. Andrew's crosse; but most did make a mockery at it, and the House of Parliament, contrary to practice, did sit also: people having no mind to observe the Scotch saints' days till they hear better newes from Scotland. Thence to Westminster Hall and the Abbey, thinking as I had appointed to have met Mrs. Burroughs there, but not meeting her I home, and just overtook my cozen Roger Pepys, Mrs. Turner, Dicke, and Joyce Norton, coming by invitation to dine with me. These ladies I have not seen since before the plague. Mrs. Turner is come to towne to look after her things in her house, but all is lost. She is quite weary of the country, but cannot get her husband to let her live here any more, which troubles her mightily. She was mighty angry with me, that in all this time I never writ to her, which I do think and take to myself as a fault, and which I have promised to mend. Here I had a noble and costly dinner for them, dressed by a man-cooke, as that the other day was, and pretty merry we were, as I could be with this company and so great a charge. We sat long, and after much talk of the plenty of her country in fish, but in nothing also that is pleasing, we broke up with great kindness, and when it begun to be dark we parted, they in one coach home, and I in another to Westminster Hall, where by appointment Mrs. Burroughs and I were to meet, but did not after I had spent the whole evening there. Only I did go drink at the Swan, and there did meet with Sarah, who is now newly married, and there I did lay the beginnings of a future 'amour con elle'..... Thence it being late away called at Mrs. Burroughs' mother's door, and she come out to me, and I did hazer whatever I would.... and then parted, and home, and after some playing at cards with my wife, we to supper and to bed.

DECEMBER 1666

December 1st. Up, and to the office, where we sat all the morning. At home to dinner, and then abroad walking to the Old Swan, and in my way I did see a cellar in Tower Streete in a very fresh fire, the late great winds having blown it up.

It seemed to be only of log-wood, that Hath kept the fire all this while in it. Going further, I met my late Lord Mayor Bludworth, under whom the City was burned, and went with him by water to White Hall. But, Lord! the silly talk that this fellow had, only how ready he would be to part with all his estate in these difficult times to advance the King's service, and complaining that now, as every body did lately in the fire, every body endeavours to save himself, and let the whole perish: but a very weak man he seems to be. I left him at White Hall, he giving 6d. towards the boat, and I to Westminster Hall, where I was again defeated in my expectation of Burroughs. However, I was not much sorry for it, but by coach home, in the evening, calling at Faythorne's, buying three of my Lady Castlemayne's heads, printed this day, which indeed is, as to the head, I think, a very fine picture, and like her. I did this afternoon get Mrs. Michell to let me only have a sight of a pamphlet lately printed, but suppressed and much called after, called "The Catholique's Apology;" lamenting the severity of the Parliament against them, and comparing it with the lenity of other princes to Protestants; giving old and late instances of their loyalty to their princes, whatever is objected against them; and excusing their disquiets in Queen Elizabeth's time, for that it was impossible for them to think her a lawfull Queen, if Queen Mary, who had been owned as such, were so; one being the daughter of the true, and the other of a false wife: and that of the Gunpowder Treason, by saying that it was only the practice of some of us, if not the King, to trepan some of their religion into it, it never being defended by the generality of their Church, nor indeed known by them; and ends with a large Catalogue, in red letters, of the Catholiques which have lost their lives in the quarrel of the late King and this. The thing is very well writ indeed. So home to my letters, and then to my supper and to bed.

2nd (Lord's day). Up, and to church, and after church home to dinner, where I met Betty Michell and her husband, very merry at dinner, and after dinner, having borrowed Sir W. Pen's coach, we to Westminster, they two and my wife and I to Mr. Martin's, where find the company almost all come to the christening of Mrs. Martin's child, a girl. A great deal of good plain company. After sitting long, till the church was done, the Parson comes, and then we to christen the child. I was Godfather, and Mrs. Holder (her husband, a good man, I know well), and a pretty lady, that waits, it seems, on my Lady Bath, at White Hall, her name, Mrs. Noble, were Godmothers. After the christening comes in the wine and the sweetmeats, and then to prate and tattle, and then very good company they were, and I among them. Here was old Mrs. Michell and Howlett, and several married women of the Hall, whom I knew mayds. Here was also Mrs. Burroughs and Mrs. Bales, the young widow, whom I led home, and having staid till the moon was up, I took my pretty gossip to White Hall with us, and I saw her in her lodging, and then my owne company again took coach, and no sooner in the coach but something broke, that we were fain there to stay till a smith could be fetched, which was above an hour, and then it costing me

6s. to mend. Away round by the wall and Cow Lane,

for fear it should break again; and in pain about the coach all the way. But to ease myself therein Betty Michell did sit at the same end with me. ... Being very much pleased with this, we at last come home, and so to supper, and then sent them by boat home, and we to bed. When I come home I went to Sir W. Batten's, and there I hear more ill newes still: that all our New England fleete, which went out lately, are put back a third time by foul weather, and dispersed, some to one port and some to another; and their convoys also to Plymouth; and whether any of them be lost or not, we do not know. This, added to all the rest, do lay us flat in our hopes and courages, every body prophesying destruction to the nation.

3rd. Up, and, among a great many people that come to speak with me, one was my Lord Peterborough's gentleman, who comes to me to dun me to get some money advanced for my Lord; and I demanding what newes, he tells me that at Court they begin to fear the business of Scotland more and more; and that the Duke of York intends to go to the North to raise an army, and that the King would have some of the Nobility and others to go and assist; but they were so served the last year, among others his Lord, in raising forces at their own charge, for fear of the French invading us, that they will not be got out now, without money advanced to them by the King, and this is like to be the King's case for certain, if ever he comes to have need of any army. He and others gone, I by water to Westminster, and there to the Exchequer, and put my tallys in a way of doing for the last quarter. But my not following it the last week has occasioned the clerks some trouble, which I am sorry for, and they are mad at. Thence at noon home, and there find Kate Joyce, who dined with me: Her husband and she are weary of their new life of being an Innkeeper, and will leave it, and would fain get some office; but I know none the foole is fit for, but would be glad to help them, if I could, though they have enough to live on, God be thanked! though their loss hath been to the value of L3000 W. Joyce now has all the trade, she says, the trade being come to that end of the towne. She dined with me, my wife being ill of her months in bed. I left her with my wife, and away myself to Westminster Hall by appointment and there found out Burroughs, and I took her by coach as far as the Lord Treasurer's and called at the cake house by Hales's, and there in the coach eat and drank and then carried her home.... So having set her down in the palace I to the Swan, and there did the first time 'baiser' the little sister of Sarah that is come into her place, and so away by coach home, where to my vyall and supper and then to bed, being weary of the following of my pleasure and sorry for my omitting (though with a true salvo to my vowes) the stating my last month's accounts in time, as I should, but resolve to settle, and clear all my business before me this month, that I may begin afresh the next yeare, and enjoy some little pleasure freely at Christmasse. So to bed, and with more cheerfulness than I have done a good while, to hear that for certain the Scott rebells are all routed; they having been so bold as to come within three miles of Edinburgh, and there given two or three repulses to the King's forces, but at last were mastered. Three or four hundred killed or taken, among which their leader, one Wallis, and seven ministers, they having all taken the Covenant a few days before, and sworn to live and die in it, as they did; and so all is likely to be there quiet again. There is also the very good newes come of four New-England ships come home safe to Falmouth with masts for the King; which is a blessing mighty unexpected, and without which, if for nothing else, we must have failed the next year. But God be praised for thus much good fortune, and send us the continuance of his favour in other things! So to bed.

4th. Up, and to the office, where we sat all the morning. At noon dined at home. After dinner presently to my office, and there late and then home to even my Journall and accounts, and then to supper much eased in mind, and last night's good news, which is more and more confirmed with particulars to very good purpose, and so to bed.

5th. Up, and by water to White Hall, where we did much business before the Duke of York, which being done, I away home by water again, and there to my office till noon busy. At noon home, and Goodgroome dined with us, who teaches my wife to sing. After dinner I did give him my song, "Beauty retire," which he has often desired of me, and without flattery I think is a very good song. He gone, I to the office, and there late, very busy doing much business, and then home to supper and talk, and then scold with my wife for not reckoning well the times that her musique master hath been with her, but setting down more than I am sure, and did convince her, they had been with her, and in an ill humour of anger with her to bed.

6th. Up, but very good friends with her before I rose, and so to the office, where we sat all the forenoon, and then home to dinner, where Harman dined with us, and great sport to hear him tell how Will Joyce grows rich by the custom of the City coming to his end of the towne, and how he rants over his brother and sister for their keeping an Inne, and goes thither and tears like a prince, calling him hosteller and his sister hostess. Then after dinner, my wife and brother, in another habit; go out to see a play; but I am not to take notice that I know of my brother's going. So I to the office, where very busy till late at night, and then home. My wife not pleased with the play, but thinks that it is because she is grown more critical than she used to be, but my brother she says is mighty taken with it. So to supper and to bed. This day, in the Gazette, is the whole story of defeating the Scotch rebells, and of the creation of the Duke of Cambridge, Knight of the Garter.

7th. Up, and by water to the Exchequer, where I got my tallys finished for the last quarter for Tangier, and having paid all my fees I to the Swan, whither I sent for some oysters, and thither comes Mr. Falconbridge and Spicer and many more clerks; and there we eat and drank, and a great deal of their sorry discourse, and so parted, and I by coach home, meeting Balty in the streete about Charing Crosse walking, which I am glad to see and spoke to him about his mustering business, I being now to give an account how the several muster-masters have behaved themselves, and so home to dinner, where finding the cloth laid and much crumpled but clean, I grew angry and flung the trenchers about the room, and in a mighty heat I was: so a clean cloth was laid, and my poor wife very patient, and so to dinner, and in comes Mrs. Barbara Sheldon, now Mrs. Wood, and dined with us, she mighty fine, and lives, I perceive, mighty happily, which I am glad [of] for her sake, but hate her husband for a block-head in his choice. So away after dinner, leaving my wife and her, and by water to the Strand, and so to the King's playhouse, where two acts were almost done when I come in; and there I sat with my cloak about my face, and saw the remainder of "The Mayd's Tragedy;" a good play, and well acted, especially by the younger Marshall, who is become a pretty good actor, and is the first play I have seen in either of the houses since before the great plague, they having acted now about fourteen days publickly. But I was in mighty pain lest I should be seen by any body to be at a play. Soon as done I home, and then to my office awhile, and then home and spent the night evening my Tangier accounts, much to my satisfaction, and then to supper, and mighty good friends with my poor wife, and so to bed.

8th. Up, and to the office, where we sat all the morning, and at noon home to dinner, and there find Mr. Pierce and his wife and Betty, a pretty girle, who in discourse at table told me the great Proviso passed the House of Parliament yesterday; which makes the King and Court mad, the King having given order to my Lord Chamberlain to send to the playhouses and bawdy houses, to bid all the Parliament-men that were there to go to the Parliament presently. This is true, it seems; but it was carried against the Court by thirty or forty voices. It is a Proviso to the Poll Bill, that there shall be a Committee of nine persons that shall have the inspection upon oath, and power of giving others, of all the accounts of the money given and spent for this warr. This hath a most sad face, and will breed very ill blood. He tells me, brought in by Sir Robert Howard, who is one of the King's servants, at least hath a great office, and hath got, they say, L20,000 since the King come in. Mr. Pierce did also tell me as a great truth, as being told it by Mr. Cowly, who was by, and heard it, that Tom Killigrew should publiquely tell the King that his matters were coming into a very ill state; but that yet there was a way to help all, which is, says he, "There is a good, honest, able man, that I could name, that if your Majesty would employ, and command to see all things well executed, all things would soon be mended; and this is one Charles Stuart, who now spends his time in employing his lips.... about the Court, and hath no other employment; but if you would give him this employment, he were the fittest man in the world to perform it." This, he says, is most true; but the King do not profit by any of this, but lays all aside, and remembers nothing, but to his pleasures again; which is a sorrowful consideration. Very good company we were at dinner, and merry, and after dinner, he being gone about business, my wife and I and Mrs. Pierce and Betty and Balty, who come to see us to-day very sick, and went home not well, together out, and our coach broke the wheel off upon Ludgate Hill. So we were fain to part ourselves and get room in other people's coaches, and Mrs. Pierce and I in one, and I carried her home and set her down, and myself to the King's playhouse, which troubles me since, and hath cost me a forfeit of 10s., which I have paid, and there did see a good part of "The English Monsieur," which is a mighty pretty play, very witty and pleasant. And the women do very well; but, above all, little Nelly; that I am mightily pleased with the play, and much with the House, more than ever I expected, the women doing better than ever I expected, and very fine women. Here I was in pain to be seen, and hid myself; but, as God would have it, Sir John Chichly come, and sat just by me. Thence to Mrs. Pierce's, and there took up my wife and away home, and to the office and Sir W. Batten's, of whom I hear that this Proviso in Parliament is mightily ill taken by all the Court party as a mortal blow, and that, that strikes deep into the King's prerogative, which troubles me mightily. Home, and set some papers right in my chamber, and then to supper and to bed, we being in much fear of ill news of our colliers. A fleete of two hundred sail, and fourteen Dutch men-of-war between them and us and they coming home with small convoy; and the City in great want, coals being at L3 3s. per chaldron, as I am told. I saw smoke in the ruines this very day.

9th (Lord's day). Up, not to church, but to my chamber, and there begun to enter into this book my journall of September, which in the fire-time I could not enter here, but in loose papers. At noon dined, and then to my chamber all the afternoon and night, looking over and tearing and burning all the unnecessary letters, which I have had upon my file for four or five years backward, which I intend to do quite through all my papers, that I may have nothing by me but what is worth keeping, and fit to be seen, if I should miscarry. At this work till midnight, and then to supper and to bed.

10th. Up, and at my office all the morning, and several people with me, Sir W. Warren, who I do every day more and more admire for a miracle of cunning and forecast in his business, and then Captain Cocke, with whom I walked in the garden, and he tells me how angry the Court is at the late Proviso brought in by the House. How still my Lord Chancellor is, not daring to do or say any thing to displease the Parliament; that the Parliament is in a very ill humour, and grows every day more and more so; and that the unskilfulness of the Court, and their difference among one another, is the occasion of all not agreeing in what they would have, and so they give leisure and occasion to the other part to run away with what the Court would not have. Then comes Mr. Gawden, and he and I in my chamber discoursing about his business, and to pay him some Tangier orders which he delayed to receive till I had money instead of tallies, but do promise me consideration for my victualling business for this year, and also as Treasurer for Tangier, which I am glad of, but would have been gladder to have just now received it. He gone, I alone to dinner at home, my wife and her people being gone down the river to-day for pleasure, though a cold day and dark night to come up. In the afternoon I to the Excise Office to enter my tallies, which I did, and come presently back again, and then to the office and did much business, and then home to supper, my wife and people being come well and hungry home from Erith. Then I to begin the setting of a Base to "It is Decreed," and so to bed.

11th. Up, and to the office, where we sat, and at noon home to dinner, a small dinner because of a good supper. After dinner my wife and I by coach to St. Clement's Church, to Mrs. Turner's lodgings, hard by, to take our leaves of her. She is returning into the North to her children, where, I perceive, her husband hath clearly got the mastery of her, and she is likely to spend her days there, which for her sake I am a little sorry for, though for his it is but fit she should live where he hath a mind. Here were several people come to see and take leave of her, she going to-morrow: among others, my Lady Mordant, which was Betty Turner, a most homely widow, but young, and pretty rich, and good natured. Thence, having promised to write every month to her, we home, and I to my office, while my wife to get things together for supper. Dispatching my business at the office. Anon come our guests, old Mr. Batelier, and his son and daughter, Mercer, which was all our company. We had a good venison pasty and other good cheer, and as merry as in so good, innocent, and understanding company I could be. He is much troubled that wines, laden by him in France before the late proclamation was out, cannot now be brought into

England, which is so much to his and other merchants' loss. We sat long at supper and then to talk, and so late parted and so to bed. This day the Poll Bill was to be passed, and great endeavours used to take away the Proviso.

12th. Up, and to the office, where some accounts of Mr. Gawden's were examined, but I home most of the morning to even some accounts with Sir H. Cholmly, Mr. Moone, and others one after another. Sir H. Cholmly did with grief tell me how the Parliament hath been told plainly that the King hath been heard to say, that he would dissolve them rather than pass this Bill with the Proviso; but tells me, that the Proviso is removed, and now carried that it shall be done by a Bill by itself. He tells me how the King hath lately paid about L30,000

to clear debts of my Lady Castlemayne's; and that she and her husband are parted for ever, upon good terms, never to trouble one another more. He says that he hears L400,000 hath gone into the Privypurse since this warr; and that that hath consumed so much of our money, and makes the King and Court so mad to be brought to discover it. He gone, and after him the rest, I to the office, and at noon to the 'Change, where the very good newes is just come of our four ships from Smyrna, come safe without convoy even into the Downes, without seeing any enemy; which is the best, and indeed only considerable good newes to our Exchange, since the burning of the City; and it is strange to see how it do cheer up men's hearts. Here I saw shops now come to be in this Exchange, and met little Batelier, who sits here but at L3 per annum, whereas he sat at the other at L100, which he says he believes will prove of as good account to him now as the other did at that rent. From the 'Change to Captain Cocke's, and there, by agreement, dined, and there was Charles Porter, Temple, Fern, Debasty, whose bad English and pleasant discourses was exceeding good entertainment, Matt. Wren, Major Cooper, and myself, mighty merry and pretty discourse. They talked for certain, that now the King do follow Mrs. Stewart wholly, and my Lady Castlemayne not above once a week; that the Duke of York do not haunt my Lady Denham so much; that she troubles him with matters of State, being of my Lord Bristoll's faction, and that he avoids; that she is ill still. After dinner I away to the office, where we sat late upon Mr. Gawden's accounts, Sir J. Minnes being gone home sick. I late at the office, and then home to supper and to bed, being mightily troubled with a pain in the small of my back, through cold, or (which I think most true) my straining last night to get open my plate chest, in such pain all night I could not turn myself in my bed. Newes this day from Brampton, of Mr. Ensum, my sister's sweetheart, being dead: a clowne.

13th. Up, and to the office, where we sat. At noon to the 'Change and there met Captain Cocke, and had a second time his direction to bespeak L100 of plate, which I did at Sir R. Viner's, being twelve plates more, and something else I have to choose. Thence home to dinner, and there W. Hewer dined with me, and showed me a Gazette, in April last, which I wonder should never be remembered by any body, which tells how several persons were then tried for their lives, and were found guilty of a design of killing the King and destroying the Government; and as a means to it, to burn the City; and that the day intended for the plot was the 3rd of last September.

And the fire did indeed break out on the 2nd of September, which is very strange, methinks, and I shall remember it. At the office all the afternoon late, and then home to even my accounts in my Tangier book, which I did to great content in all respects, and joy to my heart, and so to bed. This afternoon Sir W. Warren and Mr. Moore, one after another, walked with me in the garden, and they both tell me that my Lord Sandwich is called home, and that he do grow more and more in esteem everywhere, and is better spoken of, which I am mighty glad of, though I know well enough his deserving the same before, and did foresee that it will come to it. In mighty great pain in my back still, but I perceive it changes its place, and do not trouble me at all in making of water, and that is my joy, so that I believe it is nothing but a strain, and for these three or four days I perceive my overworking of my eyes by candlelight do hurt them as it did the last winter, that by day I am well and do get them right, but then after candlelight they begin to be sore and run, so that I intend to get some green spectacles.

14th. Up, and very well again of my pain in my back, it having been nothing but cold. By coach to White Hall, seeing many smokes of the fire by the way yet, and took up into the coach with me a country gentleman, who asked me room to go with me, it being dirty—one come out of the North to see his son, after the burning his house: a merchant. Here endeavoured to wait on the Duke of York, but he would not stay from the Parliament. So I to Westminster Hall, and there met my good friend Mr. Evelyn, and walked with him a good while, lamenting our condition for want of good council, and the King's minding of his business and servants. I out to the Bell Taverne, and thither comes Doll to me...., and after an hour's stay, away and staid in Westminster Hall till the rising of the house, having told Mr. Evelyn, and he several others, of my Gazette which I had about me that mentioned in April last a plot for which several were condemned of treason at the Old Bayly for many things, and among others for a design of burning the city on the 3rd of September. The house sat till three o'clock, and then up: and I home with Sir Stephen Fox to his house to dinner, and the Cofferer with us. There I find Sir S. Fox's lady, a fine woman, and seven the prettiest children of theirs that ever I knew almost. A very genteel dinner, and in great state and fashion, and excellent discourse; and nothing like an old experienced man and a courtier, and such is the Cofferer Ashburnham. The House have been mighty hot to-day against the Paper Bill, showing all manner of averseness to give the King money; which these courtiers do take mighty notice of, and look upon the others as bad rebells as ever the last were. But the courtiers did carry it against those men upon a division of the House, a great many, that it should be committed; and so it was: which they reckon good news. After dinner we three to the Excise Office, and there had long discourse about our monies, but nothing to satisfaction, that is, to shew any way of shortening the time which our tallies take up before they become payable, which is now full two years, which is 20 per, cent. for all the King's money for interest, and the great disservice of his Majesty otherwise. Thence in the evening round by coach home, where I find Foundes his present, of a fair pair of candlesticks, and half a dozen of plates come, which cost him full L50, and is a very good present; and here I met with, sealed up, from Sir H. Cholmly, the lampoone, or the Mocke-Advice to a Paynter,

abusing the Duke of York and my Lord Sandwich, Pen, and every body, and the King himself, in all the matters of the navy and warr. I am sorry for my Lord Sandwich's having so great a part in it. Then to supper and musique, and to bed.

15th. Up and to the office, where my Lord Bruncker newly come to town, from his being at Chatham and Harwich to spy enormities: and at noon I with him and his lady Williams, to Captain Cocke's, where a good dinner, and very merry. Good news to-day upon the Exchange, that our Hamburgh fleete is got in; and good hopes that we may soon have the like of our Gottenburgh, and then we shall be well for this winter. Very merry at dinner. And by and by comes in Matt. Wren from the Parliament-house; and tells us that he and all his party of the House, which is the Court party, are fools, and have been made so this day by the wise men of the other side; for, after the Court party had carried it yesterday so powerfully for the Paper-Bill,

yet now it is laid aside wholly, and to be supplied by a land-tax; which it is true will do well, and will be the sooner finished, which was the great argument for the doing of it. But then it shews them fools, that they would not permit this to have been done six weeks ago, which they might have had. And next, they have parted with the Paper Bill, which, when once begun, might have proved a very good flower in the Crowne, as any there. So do really say that they are truly outwitted by the other side. Thence away to Sir R. Viner's, and there chose some plate besides twelve plates which I purpose to have with Captain Cocke's gift of L100, and so home and there busy late, and then home and to bed.

16th (Lord's day). Lay long talking with my wife in bed, then up with great content and to my chamber to set right a picture or two, Lovett having sent me yesterday Sancta Clara's head varnished, which is very fine, and now my closet is so full stored, and so fine, as I would never desire to have it better. Dined without any strangers with me, which I do not like on Sundays. Then after dinner by water to Westminster to see Mrs. Martin, whom I found up in her chamber and ready to go abroad. I sat there with her and her husband and others a pretty while, and then away to White Hall, and there walked up and down to the Queen's side, and there saw my dear Lady Castlemayne, who continues admirable, methinks, and I do not hear but that the King is the same to her still as ever. Anon to chapel, by the King's closet, and heard a very good anthemne. Then with Lord Bruncker to Sir W. Coventry's chamber; and there we sat with him and talked. He is weary of anything to do, he says, in the Navy. He tells us this Committee of Accounts will enquire sharply into our office. And, speaking of Sir J. Minnes, he says he will not bear any body's faults but his own. He discoursed as bad of Sir W. Batten almost, and cries out upon the discipline of the fleete, which is lost, and that there is not in any of the fourth rates and under scarce left one Sea Commander, but all young gentlemen; and what troubles him, he hears that the gentlemen give out that in two or three years a Tarpaulin shall not dare to look after being better than a Boatswain. Which he is troubled at, and with good reason, and at this day Sir Robert Holmes is mighty troubled that his brother do not command in chief, but is commanded by Captain Hannum, who, Sir W. Coventry says, he believes to be at least of as good blood, is a longer bred seaman, an elder officer, and an elder commander, but such is Sir R. Holmes's pride as never to be stopt, he being greatly troubled at my Lord Bruncker's late discharging all his men and officers but the standing officers at Chatham, and so are all other Commanders, and a very great cry hath been to the King from them all in my Lord's absence. But Sir W. Coventry do undertake to defend it, and my Lord Bruncker got ground I believe by it, who is angry at Sir W.

Batten's and Sir W. Pen's bad words concerning it, and I have made it worse by telling him that they refuse to sign to a paper which he and I signed on Saturday to declare the reason of his actions, which Sir W. Coventry likes and would have it sent him and he will sign it, which pleases me well. So we parted, and I with Lord Bruncker to Sir P. Neale's chamber, and there sat and talked awhile, Sir Edward Walker being there, and telling us how he hath lost many fine rowles of antiquity in heraldry by the late fire, but hath saved the most of his papers. Here was also Dr. Wallis, the famous scholar and mathematician; but he promises little. Left them, and in the dark and cold home by water, and so to supper and to read and so to bed, my eyes being better to-day, and I cannot impute it to anything but by my being much in the dark to-night, for I plainly find that it is only excess of light that makes my eyes sore. This after noon I walked with Lord Bruncker into the Park and there talked of the times, and he do think that the King sees that he cannot never have much more money or good from this Parliament, and that therefore he may hereafter dissolve them, that as soon as he has the money settled he believes a peace will be clapped up, and that there are overtures of a peace, which if such as the Lord Chancellor can excuse he will take. For it is the Chancellor's interest, he says, to bring peace again, for in peace he can do all and command all, but in war he cannot, because he understands not the nature of the war as to the management thereof. He tells me he do not believe the Duke of York will go to sea again, though there are a great many about the King that would be glad of any occasion to take him out of the world, he standing in their ways; and seemed to mean the Duke of Monmouth, who spends his time the most viciously and idly of any man, nor will be fit for any thing; yet bespeaks as if it were not impossible but the King would own him for his son, and that there was a marriage between his mother and him; which God forbid should be if it be not true, nor will the Duke of York easily be gulled in it. But this put to our other distractions makes things appear very sad, and likely to be the occasion of much confusion in a little time, and my Lord Bruncker seems to say that nothing can help us but the King's making a peace soon as he hath this money; and thereby putting himself out of debt, and so becoming a good husband, and then he will neither need this nor any other Parliament, till he can have one to his mind: for no Parliament can, as he says, be kept long good, but they will spoil one another, and that therefore it hath been the practice of kings to tell Parliaments what he hath for them to do, and give them so long time to do it in, and no longer. Harry Kembe, one of our messengers, is lately dead.

17th. Up, and several people to speak with me, and then comes Mr. Caesar, and then Goodgroome, and, what with one and the other, nothing but musique with me this morning, to my great content; and the more, to see that God Almighty hath put me into condition to bear the charge of all this. So out to the 'Change, and did a little business, and then home, where they two musicians and Mr. Cooke come to see me, and Mercer to go along with my wife this afternoon to a play. To dinner, and then our company all broke up, and to my chamber to do several things. Among other things, to write a letter to my Lord Sandwich, it being one of the burdens upon my mind that I have not writ to him since he went into Spain, but now I do intend to give him a brief account of our whole year's actions since he went, which will make amends. My wife well home in the evening from the play; which I was glad of, it being cold and dark, and she having her necklace of pearl on, and none but Mercer with her. Spent the evening in fitting my books, to have the number set upon each, in order to my having an alphabet of my whole, which will be of great ease to me. This day Captain Batters come from sea in his fireship and come to see me, poor man, as his patron, and a poor painful wretch he is as can be. After supper to bed.

18th. Up, and to the office, where I hear the ill news that poor Batters, that had been born and bred a seaman, and brought up his ship from sea but yesterday, was, going down from me to his ship, drowned in the Thames, which is a sad fortune, and do make me afeard, and will do, more than ever I was. At noon dined at home, and then by coach to my Lord Bellasses, but not at home. So to Westminster Hall, where the Lords are sitting still, I to see Mrs. Martin, who is very well, and intends to go abroad to-morrow after her childbed. She do tell me that this child did come is 'meme jour that it ought to hazer after my avoir ete con elle before her marid did venir home.... Thence to the Swan, and there I sent for Sarah, and mighty merry we were.... So to Sir Robert Viner's about my plate, and carried home another dozen of plates, which makes my stock of plates up 2 1/2 dozen, and at home find Mr. Thomas Andrews, with whom I staid and talked a little and invited him to dine with me at Christmas, and then I to the office, and there late doing business, and so home and to bed. Sorry for poor Batters.

19th. Up, and by water down to White Hall, and there with the Duke of York did our usual business, but nothing but complaints of want of money [without] success, and Sir W. Coventry's complaint of the defects of our office (indeed Sir J. Minnes's) without any amendment, and he tells us so plainly of the Committee of Parliament's resolution to enquire home into all our managements that it makes me resolve to be wary, and to do all things betimes to be ready for them. Thence going away met Mr. Hingston the organist (my old acquaintance) in the Court, and I took him to the Dog Taverne and got him to set me a bass to my "It is decreed," which I think will go well, but he commends the song not knowing the words, but says the ayre is good, and believes the words are plainly expressed. He is of my mind against having of 8ths unnecessarily in composition. This did all please me mightily. Then to talk of the King's family. He says many of the musique are ready to starve, they being five years behindhand for their wages; nay, Evens, the famous man upon the Harp having not his equal in the world, did the other day die for mere want, and was fain to be buried at the almes of the parish, and carried to his grave in the dark at night without one linke, but that Mr. Hingston met it by chance, and did give 12d. to buy two or three links. He says all must come to ruin at this rate, and I believe him. Thence I up to the Lords' House to enquire for Lord Bellasses; and there hear how at a conference this morning between the two Houses about the business of the Canary Company, my Lord Buckingham leaning rudely over my Lord Marquis Dorchester, my Lord Dorchester removed his elbow. Duke of Buckingham asked him whether he was uneasy; Dorchester replied, yes, and that he durst not do this were he any where else: Buckingham replied, yes he would, and that he was a better man than himself; Dorchester answered that he lyed. With this Buckingham struck off his hat, and took him by his periwigg, and pulled it aside, and held him. My Lord Chamberlain and others interposed, and, upon coming into the House, the Lords did order them both to the Tower, whither they are to go this afternoon. I down into the Hall, and there the Lieutenant of the Tower took me with him, and would have me to the Tower to dinner; where I dined at the head of his table, next his lady,' who is comely and seeming sober and stately, but very proud and very cunning, or I am mistaken, and wanton, too. This day's work will bring the Lieutenant of the Tower L350. But a strange, conceited, vain man he is that ever I met withal, in his own praise, as I have heretofore observed of him. Thence home, and upon Tower Hill saw about 3 or 400 seamen get together; and one, standing upon a pile of bricks, made his sign, with his handkercher, upon his stick, and called all the rest to him, and several shouts they gave. This made me afeard; so I got home as fast as I could. And hearing of no present hurt did go to Sir Robert Viner's about my plate again, and coming home do hear of 1000 seamen said in the streets to be in armes. So in great fear home, expecting to find a tumult about my house, and was doubtful of my riches there. But I thank God I found all well. But by and by Sir W. Batten and Sir R. Ford do tell me, that the seamen have been at some prisons, to release some seamen, and the Duke of Albemarle is in armes, and all the Guards at the other end of the town; and the Duke of Albemarle is gone with some forces to Wapping, to quell the seamen; which is a thing of infinite disgrace to us. I sat long talking with them; and, among other things, Sir R. Ford did make me understand how the House of Commons is a beast not to be understood, it being impossible to know beforehand the success almost of any small plain thing, there being so many to think and speak to any business, and they of so uncertain minds and interests and passions. He did tell me, and so did Sir W. Batten, how Sir Allen Brodericke and Sir Allen Apsly did come drunk the other day into the House, and did both speak for half an hour together, and could not be either laughed, or pulled, or bid to sit down and hold their peace, to the great contempt of the King's servants and cause; which I am grieved at with all my heart. We were full in discourse of the sad state of our times, and the horrid shame brought on the King's service by the just clamours of the poor seamen, and that we must be undone in a little time. Home full of trouble on these considerations, and, among other things, I to my chamber, and there to ticket a good part of my books, in order to the numbering of them for my easy finding them to read as I have occasion. So to supper and to bed, with my heart full of trouble.

20th. Up, and to the office, where we sat all the morning, and here among other things come Captain Cocke, and I did get him to sign me a note for the L100 to pay for the plate he do present me with, which I am very glad of. At noon home to dinner, where was Balty come, who is well again, and the most recovered in his countenance that ever I did see. Here dined with me also Mrs. Batters, poor woman! now left a sad widow by the drowning of her husband the other day. I pity her, and will do her what kindness I can; yet I observe something of ill-nature in myself more than should be, that I am colder towards her in my charity than I should be to one so painful as he and she have been and full of kindness to their power to my wife and I. After dinner out with Balty, setting him down at the Maypole in the Strand, and then I to my Lord Bellasses, and there spoke with Mr. Moone about some business, and so away home to my business at the office, and then home to supper and to bed, after having finished the putting of little papers upon my books to be numbered hereafter.

21st. Lay long, and when up find Mrs. Clerk of Greenwich and her daughter Daniel, their business among other things was a request her daughter was to make, so I took her into my chamber, and there it was to help her husband to the command of a little new pleasure boat building, which I promised to assist in. And here I had opportunity 'para baiser elle, and toucher ses mamailles'.... Then to the office, and there did a little business, and then to the 'Change and did the like. So home to dinner, and spent all the afternoon in putting some things, pictures especially, in order, and pasting my Lady Castlemayne's print on a frame, which I have made handsome, and is a fine piece. So to the office in the evening to marshall my papers of accounts presented to the Parliament, against any future occasion to recur to them, which I did do to my great content. So home and did some Tangier work, and so to bed.

22nd. At the office all the morning, and there come news from Hogg that our shipp hath brought in a Lubecker to Portsmouth, likely to prove prize, of deals, which joys us. At noon home to dinner, and then Sir W. Pen, Sir R. Ford, and I met at Sir W. Batten's to examine our papers, and have great hopes to prove her prize, and Sir R. Ford I find a mighty yare—[Quick or ready, a naval term frequently used by Shakespeare.]—man in this business, making exceeding good observations from the papers on our behalf. Hereupon concluded what to write to Hogg and Middleton, which I did, and also with Mr. Oviatt (Sir R. Ford's son, who is to be our solicitor), to fee some counsel in the Admiralty, but none in town. So home again, and after writing letters by the post, I with all my clerks and Carcasse and Whitfield to the ticket-office, there to be informed in the method and disorder of the office, which I find infinite great, of infinite concernment to be mended, and did spend till 12 at night to my great satisfaction, it being a point of our office I was wholly unacquainted in. So with great content home and to bed.

23rd (Lord's day). Up and alone to church, and meeting Nan Wright at the gate had opportunity to take two or three 'baisers', and so to church, where a vain fellow with a periwigg preached, Chaplain, as by his prayer appeared, to the Earl of Carlisle? Home, and there dined with us Betty Michell and her husband. After dinner to White Hall by coach, and took them with me. And in the way I would have taken 'su main' as I did the last time, but she did in a manner withhold it. So set them down at White Hall, and I to the Chapel to find Dr. Gibbons, and from him to the Harp and Ball to transcribe the treble which I would have him to set a bass to. But this took me so much time, and it growing night, I was fearful of missing a coach, and therefore took a coach and to rights to call Michell and his wife at their father Howlett's, and so home, it being cold, and the ground all snow.... They gone I to my chamber, and with my brother and wife did number all my books in my closet, and took a list of their names, which pleases me mightily, and is a jobb I wanted much to have done. Then to supper and to bed.

24th. Up, and to the office, where Lord Bruncker, [Sir] J. Mimics, [Sir] W. Yen, and myself met, and there I did use my notes I took on Saturday night about tickets, and did come to a good settlement in the business of that office, if it be kept to, this morning being a meeting on purpose. At noon to prevent my Lord Bruncker's dining here I walked as if upon business with him, it being frost and dry, as far as Paul's, and so back again through the City by Guildhall, observing the ruines thereabouts, till I did truly lose myself, and so home to dinner. I do truly find that I have overwrought my eyes, so that now they are become weak and apt to be tired, and all excess of light makes them sore, so that now to the candlelight I am forced to sit by, adding, the snow upon the ground all day, my eyes are very bad, and will be worse if not helped, so my Lord Bruncker do advise as a certain cure to use greene spectacles, which I will do. So to dinner, where Mercer with us, and very merry. After dinner she goes and fetches a little son of Mr. Backeworth's, the wittiest child and of the most spirit that ever I saw in my life for discourse of all kind, and so ready and to the purpose, not above four years old. Thence to Sir Robert Viner's, and there paid for the plate I have bought to the value of L94, with the L100 Captain Cocke did give me to that purpose, and received the rest in money. I this evening did buy me a pair of green spectacles, to see whether they will help my eyes or no. So to the 'Change, and went to the Upper 'Change, which is almost as good as the old one; only shops are but on one side. Then home to the office, and did business till my eyes began to be bad, and so home to supper. My people busy making mince pies, and so to bed. No newes yet of our Gottenburgh fleete; which makes [us] have some fears, it being of mighty concernment to have our supply of masts safe. I met with Mr. Cade to-night, my stationer; and he tells me that he hears for certain that the Queene-Mother is about and hath near finished a peace with France, which, as a Presbyterian, he do not like, but seems to fear it will be a means to introduce Popery.

25th (Christmas day). Lay pretty long in bed, and then rose, leaving my wife desirous to sleep, having sat up till four this morning seeing her mayds make mince-pies. I to church, where our parson Mills made a good sermon. Then home, and dined well on some good ribbs of beef roasted and mince pies; only my wife, brother, and Barker, and plenty of good wine of my owne, and my heart full of true joy; and thanks to God Almighty for the goodness of my condition at this day. After dinner, I begun to teach my wife and Barker my song, "It is decreed," which pleases me mightily as now I have Mr. Hinxton's base. Then out and walked alone on foot to the Temple, it being a fine frost, thinking to have seen a play all alone; but there, missing of any bills, concluded there was none, and so back home; and there with my brother reducing the names of all my books to an alphabet, which kept us till 7 or 8 at night, and then to supper, W. Hewer with us, and pretty merry, and then to my chamber to enter this day's journal only, and then to bed. My head a little thoughtfull how to behave myself in the business of the victualling, which I think will be prudence to offer my service in doing something in passing the pursers' accounts, thereby to serve the King, get honour to myself, and confirm me in my place in the victualling, which at present yields not work enough to deserve my wages.

26th. Up, and walked all the way (it being a most fine frost), to White Hall, to Sir W. Coventry's chamber, and thence with him up to the Duke of York, where among other things at our meeting I did offer my assistance to Sir J. Minnes to do the business of his office, relating to the Pursers' accounts, which was well accepted by the Duke of York, and I think I have and shall do myself good in it, if it be taken, for it will confirm me in the business of the victualling office, which I do now very little for. Thence home, carrying a barrel of oysters with me. Anon comes Mr. John Andrews and his wife by invitation from Bow to dine with me, and young Batelier and his wife with her great belly, which has spoiled her looks mightily already. Here was also Mercer and Creed, whom I met coming home, who tells me of a most bitter lampoone now out against the Court and the management of State from head to foot, mighty witty and mighty severe. By and by to dinner, a very good one, and merry. After dinner I put the women into a coach, and they to the Duke's house, to a play which was acted, "The————." It was indifferently done, but was not pleased with the song, Gosnell not singing, but a new wench, that sings naughtily. Thence home, all by coach, and there Mr. Andrews to the vyall, who plays most excellently on it, which I did not know before. Then to dance, here being Pembleton come, by my wife's direction, and a fiddler; and we got, also, the elder Batelier to-night, and Nan Wright, and mighty merry we were, and I danced; and so till twelve at night, and to supper, and then to cross purposes, mighty merry, and then to bed, my eyes being sore. Creed lay here in Barker's bed.

27th. Up; and called up by the King's trumpets, which cost me 10s. So to the office, where we sat all the morning. At noon, by invitation, my wife, who had not been there these to months, I think, and I, to meet all our families at Sir W. Batten's at dinner, whither neither a great dinner for so much company nor anything good or handsome. In the middle of dinner I rose, and my wife, and by coach to the King's playhouse, and meeting Creed took him up, and there saw "The Scornfull Lady" well acted; Doll Common doing Abigail most excellently, and Knipp the widow very well, and will be an excellent actor, I think. In other parts the play not so well done as used to be, by the old actors. Anon to White Hall by coach, thinking to have seen a play there to-night, but found it a mistake, so back again, and missed our coach[man], who was gone, thinking to come time enough three hours hence, and we could not blame him. So forced to get another coach, and all three home to my house, and there to Sir W. Batten's, and eat a bit of cold chine of beef, and then staid and talked, and then home and sat and talked a little by the fireside with my wife and Creed, and so to bed, my left eye being very sore. No business publick or private minded all these two days. This day a house or two was blown up with powder in the Minorys, and several people spoiled, and many dug out from under the rubbish.

28th. Up, and Creed and I walked (a very fine walk in the frost) to my Lord Bellasses, but missing him did find him at White Hall, and there spoke with him about some Tangier business. That done, we to Creed's lodgings, which are very pretty, but he is going from them. So we to Lincoln's Inne Fields, he to Ned Pickering's, who it seems lives there, keeping a good house, and I to my Lord Crew's, where I dined, and hear the newes how my Lord's brother, Mr. Nathaniel Crew, hath an estate of 6 or L700 per annum, left him by the death of an old acquaintance of his, but not akin to him at all. And this man is dead without will, but had, above ten years since, made over his estate to this Mr. Crew, to him and his heirs for ever, and given Mr. Crew the keeping of the deeds in his own hand all this time; by which, if he would, he might have taken present possession of the estate, for he knew what they were. This is as great an act of confident friendship as this latter age, I believe, can shew. From hence to the Duke's house, and there saw "Macbeth" most excellently acted, and a most excellent play for variety. I had sent for my wife to meet me there, who did come, and after the play was done, I out so soon to meet her at the other door that I left my cloake in the playhouse, and while I returned to get it, she was gone out and missed me, and with W. Hewer away home. I not sorry for it much did go to White Hall, and got my Lord Bellasses to get me into the playhouse; and there, after all staying above an hour for the players, the King and all waiting, which was absurd, saw "Henry the Fifth" well done by the Duke's people, and in most excellent habits, all new vests, being put on but this night. But I sat so high and far off, that I missed most of the words, and sat with a wind coming into my back and neck, which did much trouble me. The play continued till twelve at night; and then up, and a most horrid cold night it was, and frosty, and moonshine. But the worst was, I had left my cloak at Sir G. Carteret's, and they being abed I was forced to go home without it. So by chance got a coach and to the Golden Lion Taverne in the Strand, and there drank some mulled sack, and so home, where find my poor wife staying for me, and then to bed mighty cold.

29th. Up, called up with newes from Sir W. Batten that Hogg hath brought in two prizes more: and so I thither, and hear the particulars, which are good; one of them, if prize, being worth L4,000: for which God be thanked! Then to the office, and have the newes brought us of Captain Robinson's coming with his fleete from Gottenburgh: dispersed, though, by foul weather. But he hath light of five Dutch men-of-war, and taken three, whereof one is sunk; which is very good newes to close up the year with, and most of our merchantmen already heard of to be safely come home, though after long lookings-for, and now to several ports, as they could make them. At noon home to dinner, where Balty is and now well recovered. Then to the office to do business, and at night, it being very cold, home to my chamber, and there late writing, but my left eye still very sore. I write by spectacles all this night, then to supper and to bed. This day's good news making me very lively, only the arrears of much business on my hands and my accounts to be settled for the whole year past do lie as a weight on my mind.

30th (Lord's day). Lay long, however up and to church, where Mills made a good sermon. Here was a collection for the sexton; but it come into my head why we should be more bold in making the collection while the psalm is singing, than in the sermon or prayer. Home, and, without any strangers, to dinner, and then all the afternoon and evening in my chamber preparing all my accounts in good condition against to-morrow, to state them for the whole year past, to which God give me a good issue when I come to close them! So to supper and to bed.

31st. Rising this day with a full design to mind nothing else but to make up my accounts for the year past, I did take money, and walk forth to several places in the towne as far as the New Exchange, to pay all my debts, it being still a very great frost and good walking. I staid at the Fleece Tavern in Covent Garden while my boy Tom went to W. Joyce's to pay what I owed for candles there. Thence to the New Exchange to clear my wife's score, and so going back again I met Doll Lane (Mrs. Martin's sister), with another young woman of the Hall, one Scott, and took them to the Half Moon Taverne and there drank some burnt wine with them, without more pleasure, and so away home by coach, and there to dinner, and then to my accounts, wherein, at last, I find them clear and right; but, to my great discontent, do find that my gettings this year have been L573 less than my last: it being this year in all but L2,986; whereas, the last, I got L3,560. And then again my spendings this year have exceeded my spendings the last by L644: my whole spendings last year being but L509; whereas this year, it appears, I have spent L1154, which is a sum not fit to be said that ever I should spend in one year, before I am master of a better estate than I am. Yet, blessed be God! and I pray God make me thankful for it, I do find myself worth in money, all good, above L6,200; which is above L1800 more than I was the last year. This, I trust in God, will make me thankfull for what I have, and carefull to make up by care next year what by my negligence and prodigality I have lost and spent this year. The doing of this, and entering of it fair, with the sorting of all my expenses, to see how and in what points I have exceeded, did make it late work, till my eyes become very sore and ill, and then did give over, and supper, and to bed. Thus ends this year of publick wonder and mischief to this nation, and, therefore, generally wished by all people to have an end. Myself and family well, having four mayds and one clerk, Tom, in my house, and my brother, now with me, to spend time in order to his preferment. Our healths all well, only my eyes with overworking them are sore as candlelight comes to them, and not else; publick matters in a most sad condition; seamen discouraged for want of pay, and are become not to be governed: nor, as matters are now, can any fleete go out next year. Our enemies, French and Dutch, great, and grow more by our poverty. The Parliament backward in raising, because jealous of the spending of the money; the City less and less likely to be built again, every body settling elsewhere, and nobody encouraged to trade. A sad, vicious, negligent Court, and all sober men there fearful of the ruin of the whole kingdom this next year; from which, good God deliver us! One thing I reckon remarkable in my owne condition is, that I am come to abound in good plate, so as at all entertainments to be served wholly with silver plates, having two dozen and a half.

Printed in Great Britain
by Amazon